INSIDE THE JIHAD
My Life with Al Qaeda

A Spy's Story

OMAR NASIRI

BASIC
BOOKS

A Member of the Perseus Books Group
New York

Published by Basic Books,
A Member of the Perseus Books Group

Books published by Basic Books are available at special discounts
for bulk purchases in the United States by corporations, institutions, and
other organizations. For more information, please contact
the Special Markets Department at the Perseus Books Group,
11 Cambridge Center, Cambridge MA 02142, or call (617) 252-5298
or (800) 255-1514, or e-mail special.markets@perseusbooks.com.

Interior design by Cynthia Young

In the course of this book, the names of several characters have been changed along
with identifying details. A very small number of non-essential facts have also been
altered. We have restricted these changes to only those cases in which their revelation
would jeopardize the safety of the author, members of his family, secret service
officers, as well as the secrecy of ongoing intelligence operations.

A CIP catalog record for this book is available from the Library of Congress.
10 ISBN 0-465-02388-6
13 ISBN 978-0-465-02388-2

06 07 / 10 9 8 7 6 5 4 3 2 1

Contents

CONTENTS

Introduction

The attacks of September 11, 2001, did not come out of the blue. During the 1990s an array of violent Islamist movements began to coalesce, raising their sights from local conflicts to the "far enemy" of the United States and the West. The emerging organization would become known as Al Qaeda. Omar Nasiri's account provides a unique insight into this crucial period, which remains poorly understood. His story is unique not least because he provides the unusual perspective of someone who infiltrated these terrorist networks. The often repeated notion that defeating terrorism requires good intelligence masks the reality that gathering intelligence requires individuals willing to risk their lives by becoming spies. Their stories are rarely told.

Nasiri offers a vantage point rarely glimpsed: a portrait of the growing strength of Islamic terrorist groups in the 1990s, of what it takes to infiltrate these groups, and how inadequately authorities understood the emerging threat. Family circumstances brought Nasiri into contact with a terrorist network, and his unusual upbringing, divided between North Africa and Belgium, provided him with the means to lead a double life.

Having spent over seven years working for the French, British, and German intelligence services, Nasiri provides us with an insider's look at how these agencies functioned. His account of meetings, conversations, and the "tradecraft" of the various services is unusually detailed. Nasiri is also unusual in having been run jointly by the French and British while based in the UK, shedding light on how the two countries cooperated despite differing attitudes towards the threat from terrorism. And he reveals the complexity of his own motivations and the ethical compromises made both by spies and those who handle them. The morally ambiguous decisions made by Nasiri and his handlers puts paid to the simplistic notions of what counterterrorism espionage is really about. Nasiri's own apparent confusion over where his loyalties lay at various points underlines the difficulties in leading a double life as spy and jihadist as well as those faced by intelligence services in working with such individuals.

While it may be impossible to confirm every detail of Nasiri's story, there is no doubt about the veracity of his unusual career path: becoming involved with an important Algerian terrorist network in Europe, working for the French secret service, traveling to the training camps in Afghanistan, and then infiltrating radical Islamist circles in London. Any personal memoir such as this is bound to reflect the viewpoint of the narrator and provide a highly personal and sometimes incomplete picture of events. But what is clear from this account is that the emerging network was far better organized and far more determined than has been previously understood. The Afghan training camps were the breeding ground for the current terrorist threat, and Nasiri provides the most detailed picture yet of life inside those camps—A picture far richer and more worrying than any previously seen.

Although he is of Moroccan background, Algerians form a central part of Nasiri's account, since they comprised the core of Europe's Islamist terrorist network before 9/11. Algeria had been plunged into a bloody civil war after the army cancelled elections in January 1992 to prevent the Islamic Salvation Front (FIS) from taking power. Violence erupted and a number of insurgent groups emerged. The most violent of these was the Armed Islamic Group (GIA). As many as three thousand Algerians are thought to have fought against the Soviets in Afghanistan in the 1980s, and Algeria was the first country to feel the impact of the returning veterans of the Afghan war. The GIA was led by hundreds of battle-hardened men who came back radicalized and willing to use increasingly brutal tactics. It drew on support networks within Europe's immigrant communities. Initially these support networks dealt primarily in propaganda, but soon they began to provide funds, logistical support like false passports, and eventually weapons for the GIA.

When he returned to Belgium in 1994, Nasiri found that his mother's house had become an important hub for GIA operations. Because Belgium had few antiterrorist laws, groups faced less surveillance and disturbance from the police and security services than in neighboring France. According to his account, Nasiri did not become involved with the GIA for ideological reasons, but initially out of the desire to make money by supplying weapons. However, he soon found himself deeply embroiled in their activities.

A confrontation with the GIA members caused by the theft of some money, led Nasiri to a fateful choice. Like many others who have taken this path, he was drawn into becoming a spy by expediency rather than moral choice, offering himself to the French overseas intelligence service, the DGSE, in order to extract himself from a difficult situation. France began working closely with Belgium during this time, conducting a number of lengthy joint surveillance operations, particularly after the French realized the scale of the networks and the threat they posed.

A veritable who's who of Algerian militants and activists passed through Nasiri's house. Not only that, but the key GIA publication—the *Al Ansar* newsletter—was also put together and distributed there. The evolution of *Al Ansar* was itself indicative of the transformation Islamist networks were undergoing throughout the 1990s. It emerged as the official publication of the GIA, although over time articles from other sources started to appear in it, including other Islamist organizations like the Libyan Islamic Fighting Group, Moroccan groups, and Egyptian groups linked to Alman al-Zawahiri. Its content also became increasingly violent, justifying the murder of any civilians who did not support GIA activity. *Al Ansar* was a pioneer in uniting national Islamist militant networks into a global movement, and its contents were a warning to the authorities of what was to come.

It did not take long for the bloody conflict in Algeria to begin to bleed over into Europe. France, Algeria's former colonial master, was perceived by jihadists as having supported the coup and so became a target. The first dramatic illustration of the threat came when a group of GIA operatives took over an Air France jet on the tarmac at the Algiers airport on December 24, 1994. The GIA may also have intended to fly the plane into the Eiffel Tower, one of the first examples of the possible use of planes as weapons. In the end the plane was flown to Marseille, where a French antiterrorist force stormed it, killing all four hijackers.

In March 1995, the Belgian authorities conducted a series of raids that Nasiri describes. They were one of the first major police operations against the Algerian networks in Europe. Nasiri's family home was raided, and weapons, munitions, and false papers were discovered in other houses, garages, and cars. Also found during a vehicle search was a parcel containing an eight-thousand-page terrorist training manual, the frontispiece of which was dedicated to Osama bin Laden and Abdullah Azzam, bin Laden's mentor. According to Alain Grignard, a Belgian antiterrorist detective involved in the raids, the manual proved to be a treasure trove of information and one of the first indications of both the scale of the network and bin Laden's role in it.

The raids underlined growing concerns that the network was considering initiating campaigns within Europe itself. This was confirmed only a few months later, in the summer of 1995, when a wave of bomb attacks struck France, including the Paris metro. Some of those involved in that bombing campaign were in turn linked to the network uncovered in the March raids. That bombing campaign transformed France's attitude towards terrorist networks, making it one of the first Western nations to appreciate the potential dangers involved, although France primarily saw the problem as spillover from its involvement in the Algerian conflict rather than as part of a broader international *jihad*.

One of the people who spent time in Nasiri's house but evaded arrest in the March 1995 raids was a senior GIA organizer named Ali Touchent. Touchent exemplifies the murkiness of terrorism and counterterrorism during this period and the depth of confusion over the loyalties of individuals. One school of thought holds that the GIA was riddled from the start with spies from the Algerian secret service. And further, that these included agent provocateurs who by 1995 were deliberately shifting the campaign of violence into France, to try and draw Paris into the conflict in opposition to the Islamists and in support for the Algerian state. Much suspicion centers on Ali Touchent, who some have argued may have been working for the Algerian state all along and who managed to evade arrest on a number of occasions. This suspicion is given some weight by French officials who say they kept pursuing Touchent until they found evidence he had returned to Algeria—and that he was actually the son of a commissar of police.

When the French told the Algerians they believed Touchent had returned to Algeria, they replied that they had forgotten to mention he had been killed in a gun battle in Algiers in May 1997. "We don't know if he's dead or alive, an agent or not," says one former French intelligence officer. Nasiri also believes he saw Touchent in London, although Touchent was not arrested despite being identified, again raising questions. There are few answers about who he really was and for whom he was working.

Following the Belgian raids, Nasiri embarked on a new mission: infiltrating the Afghan training camps. French officials appear to have known that a number of French residents were disappearing and then returning months later. According to one former intelligence officer, around one to two hundred French residents traveled to Afghanistan for training during the 1990s. Some went to sign up with an international *jihad*; others simply wanted to be able to return home and boast that they knew how to fire an AK-47.

√ Nasiri proved adept in carrying out his mission. His account of his travels provides a personal but highly revealing picture of how he entered *jihadist* circles and made his way into the heart of Al Qaeda. Traveling through Turkey and then Pakistan, he moved within radical Islamist groups. He spent time at a complex run by the Jama'at al-Tabligh, a proselytising group that rejects violence—although critics argue that its centers have recently become a recruiting ground for those involved in violent *jihad*. Through a contact there Nasiri found his way to the gateway from Pakistan into Afghanistan, the bustling city of Peshawar, a city of spies, militants, and secrets. It was also the base for many of the Arab Afghans who fought in the *jihad* of the 1980s and remained in the region.

Here Nasiri met the Palestinian Abu Zubayda, coordinator and gatekeeper of a number of Afghan training camps. "He was a man who got things done in the administrative sense," explains Mike Scheuer, head of the CIA's bin Laden unit from 1996 until 1999. "Abu Zubayda's name was always very prominent in the mechanics of getting people into the camps, getting people out of the camps, getting people fed, documented, armed and trained." Abu Zubayda was eventually captured in March 2002 (a capture that led to a vigorous debate within Washington over how harshly to treat him). As with many figures later described as senior Al Qaeda leaders, Abu Zubayda's exact relationship to Al Qaeda and bin Laden appears more complex because he was working at the camps as a recruiter and organizer before bin Laden arrived, and it is not clear when or if he formally swore an oath of loyalty to bin Laden.

Nasiri then traveled over the border into Afghanistan for training. Around two dozen training camps were established in the country, most of them holdovers from the fight against the Soviet Union. The camps played a pivotal role in the transition of the Afghan-based formative *jihad* of the 1980s into the multiple-nation *jihad* of the 1990s, and the emergence by the late 1990s of a global *jihad* under Al Qaeda. They were the melting pot in which different groups began to work together, forging a common identity.

No single source of funding or control for the camps existed. Afghanistan was in chaos in the mid-1990s. The Soviets had been driven out in 1989, but what little unity there had been in fighting them soon dissipated. A client government led by Mohammad Najibullah lasted until 1992, when it was finally overwhelmed by the *mujahidin* factions that began to battle among themselves for power, with local warlords maintaining control in pockets of the country.

The environment of a failed state was perfect for maintaining international training camps. Some were run by local warlords like Gulbuddin Hekmatyar and Abd al-Rabb al-Rasul Sayyaf, and often funded by supporters of *jihad* in the Persian Gulf. Although bin Laden left Afghanistan after the end of the battle against the Soviets (partly out of frustration at factional infighting) and was resident in Sudan during the early 1990s, he continued to finance guesthouses and training facilities within Afghanistan, including, according to Nasiri, paying for food at the camp he attended.

Pakistan's Inter-Services Intelligence Agency (ISI) was also involved in supporting some Afghan camps. In 1993, the United States began to pressure Pakistan about training camps because of rising concerns over jihadist activity in Kashmir. Washington went as far as to threaten to put Pakistan on its list of state sponsors of terrorism. Many of these camps were in Pakistani-controlled Kashmir but appear to have been shut down following the U.S. complaints. Training facilities were moved to Afghanistan after 1993. Soon after, the ISI began backing the Taliban as a proxy force to stabilize Afghanistan and support Pakistan's security interests.

Nasiri's time at the camp, between 1995 and 1996, coincided with the Taliban's rapid rise. As he recalls it, relations were extremely tense between the Arabs who ran the camp and Afghans in general, and particularly the Taliban. The Taliban were suspected of wanting to shut down the camps and seize their weapons. They were also viewed as dangerous religious innovators. The alliance of convenience between the two sides would only come later.

Khaldan was the entry-level camp that Nasiri first attended. According to his account, even in the mid-1990s the range of nationalities represented and the discipline of the training was remarkable, and far greater than was previously suspected. Groups from Algeria, Chechnya, Kashmir, Kyrgyzstan, the Philippines, Tajikistan, and Uzbekistan were provided with military training, which they would apply when they returned to fight in their homelands. Large numbers of Arabs, especially from Saudi Arabia, Egypt, Jordan, and Yemen, also passed through, as well as individuals from Europe, North Africa, and elsewhere looking to take part in *jihad*. The Bosnian conflict, in which many had fought during the early 1990s, was winding down, but Chechnya remained a popular cause. These two key conflicts of the 1990s provided a focus for radicalization, combat training, and networking among militants that was not fully appreciated at the time. Just like the Afghan conflict of the 1980s, they provided the means by which different groups and individuals met and formed connections.

The training Nasiri received at Khaldan was highly organized and extensive. Discipline in the camps was strict, but a sense of camaraderie also developed among those who attended. Recruits learned how to use a wide variety of weapons and explosives as well as carry out specific operations such as assassinations, bombings, kidnappings, and urban guerrilla warfare—much of it based on U.S. training manuals obtained during the fight against the Soviets.

Attendees at the camp also spent nearly as much time on religious training as they did on combat. Spiritual preparation was considered a central aspect of *jihad*, more important than the physical training. The camps were crucial to developing and disseminating a broad, theologically grounded justification for the use of extreme violence, even against civilians. The theological precepts developed not just in Afghanistan but also in Europe during the 1990s were crucial in influencing tens of thousands of individuals. These guiding ideas served to underpin the post-9/11 jihadist ideology that has not merely survived but grown since the targeting of Al Qaeda's leadership.

Nasiri's first stop, the Khaldan camp, was originally established by bin Laden's mentor Abdullah Azzam in the 1980s. Among those who passed through Khaldan were individuals involved in both the 1993 and 2001 attacks on the World Trade Center (including Muhammad Atta, ringleader of the 9/11 attacks); individuals involved in the 1998 U.S. embassy bombings; Ahmed Ressam, the failed Millenium bomber; both of the British "shoe-bombers," Richard Reid and Sajid Badat; and Zacarias Moussaoui, sentenced to life imprisonment in 2006 for involvement in the 9/11 plot. But the mid-1990s Khaldan's leader was a man called Ibn al-Sheikh al-Libi, with whom Nasiri spent considerable time. Al-Libi had fought in Afghanistan in the 1980s; like others, he was not necessarily part of Al Qaeda in the 1990s, but rather an independent operator whose work and camp would eventually come under the Al Qaeda banner.

Al-Libi later became a crucial figure in the debate surrounding prewar intelligence on Iraq. Caught in November 2001, the Libyan trainer was the first high-ranking member of Al Qaeda to be captured by the United States after the attacks. Following a tussle between the FBI and CIA, the CIA won control and handed him over to Egypt, where he may have been subjected to mistreatment or torture. Intelligence gleaned from his interrogation was used by senior U.S. officials to assert a link between Iraq and Al Qaeda, based on al-Libi's claim that Iraq had offered training to Al Qaeda beginning in December 2000. This was cited by Vice President Cheney, by Secretary of State Colin Powell in his pivotal speech before the UN in February 2003, and by President George W. Bush in Cincinnati in October 2002, when he said, "We've learned that Iraq has trained Al Qaeda members in bomb making and poisons and gases."

The problem was that al-Libi was lying. As early as February 2002, a Defence Intelligence Agency report argued that it was likely he was "intentionally misleading the debriefers" because he couldn't provide specific details of the training that had supposedly taken place. In January 2004 al-Libi recanted his claims about Iraq, forcing the CIA to recall intelligence reports based on his statements.

There has been speculation that he may have been deliberately providing false information in order to draw the United States into attacking Iraq. Nasiri's account tends to substantiate this viewpoint, since he says al-Libi expressed his dislike of Saddam Hussein's secular regime in Iraq and was also highly skilled in withstanding interrogation. Documents and training manuals found in Afghanistan after 2001 also showed that members of Al Qaeda were taught to think of *jihad* not only as something that took place in the battlefield but also as a battle that could be fought when captured by providing false information. In the spring of 2006 al-Libi was reportedly handed over to the Libyan authorities.

At Khaldan, Nasiri's background appears to have made him stand out from other recruits. Just as the intelligence agencies found that his unusual upbringing would make him a good spy, the leaders of the camp also believed he could be useful, partly because he could move through Western populations more easily and partly because of his independence of mind, a contrast to most of those at the camp. As a result he was one of the few selected to attend the more advanced Darunta camp.

Where Khaldan focused on combat training, often for groups, Derunta provided more individualized training in explosives and terrorism for those who had graduated from the initial phase. In Khaldan recruits learned how to detonate explosives; in Darunta they learned how to make explosives and detonators from scratch. Those who attended Darunta were less likely to be members of a group preparing for military combat in their homeland and more likely to be lone individuals preparing to act as classic terrorist sleepers, thus requiring a different set of skills.

The Darunta complex was built around a former Soviet military base west of Jalalabad. It included a number of buildings and camps for different militant groups. Among those who graduated from Darunta before its destruction by U.S. air strikes in late October 2001 was Ahmed Ressam, later convicted of involvement in the Millennium bombing plot against Los Angeles International Airport.

It was here that Al Qaeda engaged in chemical weapons experiments, led by Abu Khabab al-Masri, whom Nasiri also says he met. U.S. intelligence began to learn of al-Masri's dabbling in chemical weapons around 1998–1999 and this was confirmed after the fall of the Talbian in 2001, when reporters found a lab containing chemical compounds and documents with instructions on how to make the nerve gas Sarin. Chained to metal poles outside the lab were the remains of dead animals used for experimentation. Nasiri's account points to chemical weapons experiments conducted as far back as the mid-1990s, earlier than reported.

How much did the United States know about the camps and the nature of the training going on within them? Although U.S. policymakers had turned their back on Afghanistan following the withdrawal of Soviet troops in 1989, American intelligence and counterterrorism experts were becoming increasingly aware of the role of the camps and the danger they posed. When investigators looked into the 1993 World Trade Center bombing as well as other related activity, they found a common thread for these early operations: Afghanistan.

Ramzi Yousef, who planned the 1993 attack, had trained at Khaldan and met his co-conspirator there. A still-classified National Intelligence Estimate published in 1995 entitled "The Foreign Terrorist Threat to the United States" argued that the most likely foreign terrorist threat to the United States was radical Islamists with ties to Afghanistan.

But intelligence remained fragmentary and partial. Some human intelligence was available from the camps near the Pakistan border, but other camps, like Darunta, were far harder to penetrate. The United States largely relied on satellite imagery until the CIA established Alec Station in 1996, a unit tasked with tracking Osama bin Laden's activities. Some estimates claim that between 1996 and the 9/11 attacks, ten to twenty thousand individuals went through the camps for training. Others believe the figure could be much higher, even up to a hundred thousand. No one traced where these people went or who they, in turn, went on to train.

Just as Nasiri departed Afghanistan in the spring of 1996, bin Laden returned. He arrived from Sudan on May 19, 1996, on board a twelve-seater chartered plane, having been cleared to land at Jalalabad by Pakistan's ISI. The pressure on his former hosts in Sudan had become too intense, and the message had gotten through that he would no longer enjoy the protection he had been afforded in previous years.

Bin Laden was arriving at a crucial point as the Taliban were rising to power. He had initially kept his distance, but by the summer of 1996 clearly the Taliban were on the rise. In a meeting possibly brokered by the ISI, bin Laden met with Mullah Omar and senior Taliban leaders to offer his support, including funding and fighters to help secure victory in the bitter factional battles among the *mujahidin.*

By September, the Taliban had taken Jalalabad. The Taliban would provide bin Laden and Al Qaeda with a safe haven in which to begin planning more dramatic operations. The Taliban had little interest in the training camps, especially the ones that brought in Arabs and outsiders, but bin Laden most likely persuaded them that he should take over their operation.

After his return from Afghanistan and a long period out of contact, Nasiri was reunited with the DGSE and offered a new mission. Following the raids in March 1995 and the bombing campaign that summer, the support structure for the GIA—including the editing and publishing of *Al Ansar*—had made the short journey from France and Belgium over to the UK. As France and Belgium cracked down, it was to London's more tolerant environment that many of the jihadists began to move. "London was the focal point," explains Alain Grignard, a Belgian antiterrorist officer who believes it provided the "stepping stone" from the era of national Islamic extremists to the global network founded in the Afghan melting pot.

The mid- to late 1990s were the years when Britain's capital earned the sobriquet of "Londonistan," a title provided by French officials infuriated at the growing presence of Islamist radicals in London and the failure of British authorities to do anything about it. London historically had always been a home for dissidents, and from the 1980s had increasingly also become a shelter for Islamic extremists given asylum by officials who had little understanding of their activity.

As Nasiri's account reveals, relations between French and British intelligence agencies were cordial, but the French were beginning to voice their frustration. Raids in France and Belgium had produced phone and fax numbers linked to the UK, and names of suspects were passed on. Some French officials believe that if more had been done by Britain at the time, the network behind the summer of 1995 bombings might have been broken up and the attacks prevented.

Soon after arriving, Nasiri was again brought into contact with *Al Ansar*, now being printed in London. Among those who had become involved with *Al Ansar* in London before Nasiri's arrival was Rachid Ramda, previously seen in France and Belgium moving within GIA circles. When French counterterrorist judge Jean-Louis Bruguière asked Britain to pick up Ramda, who was wanted in connection with financing the Paris metro bombings, the initial British reaction was to say that it wasn't possible to pick him up since he had done nothing wrong in the UK, a problem frequently cited by British officials. Ramda was arrested but fought being extradited for ten years, to the increasing annoyance of the French. His case became emblematic of the tensions between the two countries in fighting terrorism. It was only in December 2005 that Britain finally transferred him to French custody. He was convicted in Paris in March 2006 in relation to the bombings of the mid-1990s.

In London, Nasiri was run jointly by the French and British intelligence services and given the task of infiltrating its radical community. It did not take long for Nasiri to arrive at the Finsbury Park mosque, situated in North London, at a pivotal moment in its history. A new preacher, a man on the rise named Abu Hamza, had just arrived. He was missing an eye and both hands— one hand was replaced by a hook. An Egyptian who had spent time in the Afghan camps, he managed to hide his extremist views from the trustees who appointed him at the mosque. But very quickly strains emerged between Abu Hamza's largely North African supporters and the old guard of the mosque, largely drawn from the Pakistani and Bengali communities. The tension soon spilled over into intimidation, and it became clear that a new, younger, more radical group was taking over.

Abu Hamza and his supporters turned the Finsbury Park mosque into not just Britain's but Europe's premier sanctuary and networking home for those committed to international *jihad*. Up to two hundred people at a time slept in its basement. Among those who passed through its doors were Zacarias Moussaoui, and also former footballer Nizar Trabelsi and French convert Jerome Courtailler, both convicted of planning to attack U.S. targets in Europe. One recent account estimates that as many as fifty men from the mosque died in terrorist operations and insurgent attacks in a dozen or more conflicts abroad.

Abu Hamza initially portrayed himself as spiritual adviser to the GIA and editor of *Al Ansar*. But by around 1997, the GIA had become increasingly controversial, even within Islamic circles, because of its extreme violence. Massacres of civilians were causing even jihadists to question whether it was out of control, and the group began to splinter. Nasiri was a close witness to the debates among European Islamists over whether to stay with the GIA or break from it. Abu Hamza distanced himself from GIA activities in October 1997, just as others did over time.

Abu Hamza preached sermons of hate and violence that affected countless young men. He boosted his credibility with rumors of how he might have lost his eye and hands fighting the *jihad*. Nasiri knew the real story was that his injuries were the result of an accident during experiments in a training camp. When he told Abu Hamza this, the cleric asked him to keep his secret in order to avoid undermining his reputation.

The mosque functioned as a recruitment center for groups allied to Al Qaeda. Individuals were sent to Afghanistan with plane tickets, money, and letters of introduction from Abu Hamza. Jerome Courtailler claimed that Abu Hamza was his reference to get into Khaldan and that he was given two thousand dollars for expenses. U.S. investigators are thought to have information that Abu Hamza also directly bankrolled the training camps in Afghanistan, including Darunta and the work of al-Masri. Some of Europe's top *jihadist* recruiters operated out of the mosque, talent-spotting for potential *jihadists*. Among the most important was an Algerian named Djamel Beghal. He moved from Paris to London in 1997. He was eventually picked up in Dubai, triggering a wave of arrests across Europe and the foiling of an alleged plot against the U.S. embassy in Paris. At one stage Beghal admitted being recruited by Abu Zubayda but later retracted his confession. He is currently awaiting trial in France.

The British Security Service (commonly known as MI5) and police were meeting secretly with Hamza soon after he took over the mosque in 1997, but they appear to have underestimated him. The authorities clearly knew—not least from Nasiri's intelligence and likely that of other spies—that Abu Hamza was at the very least a troublemaker. But they believed he was avoiding targeting Britain and therefore could not be touched. Critics of the UK argue that this was effectively a deal with the militants: do what you like overseas as long as you don't target the UK and you will be left alone. British officials argue that this was never a formal deal but was simply the result of the legal framework under which they operated; they could not prosecute anyone for activities overseas and were instead warning individuals not to plan anything against the UK.

The tolerance of the British, along with their traditions of free speech, multiculturalism, and the granting of asylum, were abused. British authorities, not wanting to interfere with free speech, failed to appreciate the kind of inflammatory rhetoric coming out of the Finsbury Park mosque as well as its activities.

Many countries other than France complained about the Finsbury Park mosque, but nothing was done. It was not until January 2003 that British authorities took firm action. Intelligence about a possible plot to develop the poison Ricin led to an early-morning raid on the mosque, and a number of incriminating items were found.

But Abu Hamza remained at large, preaching on the street in front of the mosque (speeches attended by some of those who carried out the July 7, 2005, bombings in London). It was only when the United States issued an extradition warrant—based on allegations of plans to set up a training camp in Oregon—

that British authorities acted, partly out of embarrassment by the American pressure. In October 2004, Abu Hamza was charged and eventually convicted of solicitation to murder and other offenses.

Another key figure whom Nasiri spied on was Abu Qatada, a Palestinian-Jordanian. He had arrived in the UK in 1993 on a forged United Arab Emirates passport. Jordan sought his extradition after he was sentenced in absentia for terrorism offenses, but Britain refused and offered him refugee status in 1994. Unlike Abu Hamza, Qatada was as serious scholar. He was not a leader of any particular group or an organizer, but something far more significant—an ideologue and spiritual mentor.

For Islamic militants, the need for religious rulings is highly significant. Many militants went to Abu Qatada for guidance and religious justification for their actions. The names of those believed to have received religious training from him make up a who's who of European-based Islamic militants, among them Zacarias Moussaoui, Nizar Trabelsi, and Kamal Daoudi. Djamel Beghal initially went to London specifically to study under Abu Qatada. Tapes of Abu Qatada's sermons were also found in the Hamburg flat used by Muhammad Atta, tied to the 9/11 attacks. Spain's chief antiterrorist investigator once described Abu Qatada as the "spiritual leader" of Islamic militants in Europe.

Abu Qatada's base of operations was in the Four Feathers Club, a youth club near London's Baker Street. Nasiri's recollection is that Abu Qatada's sermons were far more dangerous than Abu Hamza's precisely because they were more disciplined, and focused on spiritual preparation for action rather than rhetoric. Nasiri also believes that Abu Qatada's teachings were almost identical to those he received in the Afghan training camps as part of the process of indoctrination and the instillment of discipline among jihadists. Yet Nasiri says British officials told him to leave Abu Qatada alone and instead focus his spying on Hamza. It is not clear why. As with Abu Hamza, Qatada is thought to have been in touch with MI5, but who was manipulating whom is not necessarily clear.

In February 2001, Abu Qatada was questioned by the police, who found £170,000 in cash in his house, part of it in an envelope marked "For the Mujahidin of Chechnya." He was supposed to be living off state benefits, but he was not charged. Much to the embarrassment of the authorities, in December 2001, shortly before new antiterrorism laws were due to come into effect, Abu Qatada suddenly fled from his house in West London and, remarkably, managed to remain at large for nearly a year until he was captured in London. Since then a series of legal battles have ensued as the government seeks to extradite him to Jordan.

Well aware of Abu Qatada and Abu Hamza, the French were concerned about their influence on young people in French suburbs. But when they pressed British counterparts, French intelligence officials say they got the usual answer that Britain was a country that tolerated free speech. Even when they presented evidence of the danger, French officials say they had little traction until after 9/11. They feel Britain's decision not to act was political, based on a reluctance to harass Islamic preachers and alienate the large Muslim community. The French are also thought to have considered kidnapping Hamza—a French version of the current U.S. practice of "extraordinary rendition." According to a former intelligence officer, the DGSE placed a team in London to look into the possibility and believed the British security services might have turned a blind eye, although the police might have been less accepting.

British officials claim they did work closely with the French to try and deal with GIA support and fund-raising networks within the UK, trying to track the sources of money. They cite the legislative framework as a problem. In the mid-1990s conspiring within Britain to commit terrorist acts abroad was not an offense. So groups like Hamas and the Tamil Tigers as well as the GIA began using the UK as a hub. The police investigated a problem only if there was evidence that an offense had been committed and laws broken. Police and security services did not prioritize gaining intelligence on these groups. "Did we have good coverage? It wasn't a priority," argues one British official involved in gathering intelligence during the mid-1990s. "Why would you want to know what the boy scouts are doing?" he asks, giving some sense of how the threat was viewed.

British counterterrorism experts remained focused on the threat from Irish Republican terrorism rather than Islamic terrorism. And the former threat appeared much more real. In February 1996, a huge half-ton bomb exploded in the London docklands area, signaling a new phase of activity after a cease-fire. MI5 and the police were also engaged in a bureaucratic tussle over who would run counterterrorist policy in Northern Ireland—that MI5 would eventually win—which also channeled resources and energy in that direction.

It was only in early 1998 that British authorities began to hear more about Al Qaeda. At that time concern was not focussed on Abu Qatada, Abu Hamza, or any of the North African networks. It centered on groups of Arabs who had arrived around 1998, largely from Egypt, as well as other Arabs with links to bin Laden, including Khalid al-Fawwaz. Al-Fawwaz was believed to have been managing bin Laden's London media office, organizing interviews for Western journalists and publishing statements on his behalf.

A few months before the African embassy bombings, FBI chief of counter-terrorism John O'Neill, who would die in the World Trade Center on 9/11, went to London to look for evidence against bin Laden. An investigation had been opened by the FBI following the publication of a 1996 fatwa (religious ruling) by bin Laden in a London-based Arabic newspaper. The embassy bombings of August 1998 created an even clearer evidence trail leading to London. Raids were made on addresses where a fax had been sent that claimed responsibility for the attack. The original fax's header and footer were alleged to have been found intact, proving it came into an office linked to Khalid al-Fawwaz and two other men before the attacks had taken place. Fawwaz is currently in British custody awaiting extradition to the United States.

While the relationship between the United States' and Britain's intelligence services remained strong, a much poorer relationship obtained on the law enforcement side, especially regarding counterterrorism. O'Neill and his FBI colleagues also had a difficult time with their British counterparts because the British believed the IRA was using the United States as a safe haven for its activities, much in the same way the French believed Britain provided a safe haven for Algerian terrorism. As a result, both sides felt requests for action were often not followed up on.

Although British authorities did begin to appreciate the notion of Al Qaeda's threat from the start of 1998, it was perceived as distinct from figures such as Abu Qatada, Abu Hamza, and the Algerians operating in the UK. Abu Hamza and Abu Qatada were on the radar of British authorities but very low down, along with veterans of the Afghan war who were being granted asylum in the UK, according to officials who served at the time. Simply put, the British had other priorities. International terrorism, and particularly Islamist-linked terrorism, was not seen as something that threatened to hurt it directly. France might be a primary target because of its involvement in Algeria, but not the UK.

Britain is now feeling the long-term impact of its policy to tolerate these radical elements in the 1990s. The radicalization that has spread in some British communities did not establish itself overnight. It is the result of a long process in which individuals and groups methodically targeted young people.

In the meantime, these different strands of jihadist activity were being brought together. In 1998, a new set of raids in Belgium led to more evidence of the international nature of the jihadist networks and the threat they posed. Those detained were from Algeria, Morocco, Syria, and Tunisia, and had links to a number of different Islamic groups as well as to Abu Zubayda, Afghanistan, Bosnia, and Pakistan. The raids uncovered detonators and materials for making explosives, and there were suspicions (never fully confirmed) that the World Cup, to be held in France that summer, was a target. A wave of arrests across Europe followed. The French believed London was the center of organization. The outlines of more complex terrorist networks were emerging.

Europe has always been a central base of operations for Al Qaeda, a place in which different Islamic radical groups have forged their alliances. The warning signs were there, but only a few understood them. Too many in Europe and elsewhere focused their energies on other issues and are now paying the price. Five years after the September 11 attack, it is Europe—and the UK particularly—not the United States, that faces the biggest challenge from terrorism.

It was Osama bin Laden's achievement to globalize the notion of *jihad*. To take groups that had previously focused solely on their own local conflicts—in Algeria, Central Asia, Chechnya, and elsewhere—and convince them they were part of a broader struggle. A struggle against the "far enemy" of the United States, which supported the governments they opposed. A struggle that was to be fought under the banner of Al Qaeda. In February 1998, bin Laden issued a statement declaring the formation of the World Islamic Front for Jihad against Jews and Crusaders. He announced a fatwa that "to kill the Americans and their allies—civilians and military—is an individual duty for every Muslim who can do it in any country in which it is possible to do it." Soon after, in August 1998, came Al Qaeda's first successful large-scale operation against the United States, striking its embassies in Tanzania and Kenya.

Nasiri's story ends when he moves to Germany. There his relationship with the German security services breaks down. As he sees it, they abandoned him, never providing the protection and new identity the French originally promised him. He attempted to reconnect with officials after the September 11 attacks but was rebuffed. Nearly four years later, as he watched the bombings in London on July 7, 2005, he decided he wanted to tell his story. That led him to approach the BBC and also to write down his own account of his seven years spent infiltrating the burgeoning jihadist movement as a spy.

Gordon Corera
London, September 2006

Prologue

I heard about the 9/11 attacks on the radio. I was in my car, driving to pick up my wife from work. The reporters had thought an airplane had hit the first tower accidentally. My wife got in the car. She, too, believed the collision had been an accident.

But I knew it was no accident. Even before the second plane hit, I knew. And I knew who had done it. When we got home I turned on CNN. Both towers were burning now, and people were screaming in the streets.

I did the only thing I could: I picked up the phone to call my contact at the German intelligence service. I hadn't spoken to him in a year and a half at this point, and I hated him. But thousands of people were dying and I had no choice.

He answered on the first ring. When I told him who it was he sounded surprised. "I'm calling to offer my help," I said.

"Do you know who did this? Do you know any of the hijackers?"

"No," I replied. "But I know who's behind this. I know why they did it. I know who these people are, and I know how they think."

I knew these things because I knew Al Qaeda. In Belgium I had lived with members of Al Qaeda for years, although they didn't call themselves that yet. I bought guns for them, which they shipped all over the world. I transported their explosives into Africa, where they were used in Algeria's civil war. I distributed their newsletters. I knew their top leaders in Europe. One of them organized the lethal metro bombings in Paris in 1995. Others were connected to a deadly hijacking. These men lived in my house.

Later, I went to Afghanistan, where I ate and slept and prayed with Al Qaeda in the training camps. I got as close to them as anyone could. I shared their rage and their pain; I shared my guns and my sweat with them. I offered up my blood for them, and more than once I offered up my life. They were my brothers, and I would happily have given them anything I had.

With them I became a *mujahid*, mastering almost every kind of weapon on the planet, from Kalashnikovs to antiaircraft missiles. I learned how to drive a tank, and how to blow one up. I learned how to lay a minefield, and how to throw a grenade to inflict maximum damage. I learned how to fight in cities, how to stage assassinations and kidnappings, how to resist torture. I learned how to make deadly bombs out of even the simplest ingredients—coffee, Vaseline. I learned how to kill a man with my hands.

I learned about guns and the Ku'ran and world politics from Ibn Al-Sheikh Al-Libi, who ran Osama bin Laden's training camps, and who would later lie to the CIA about bin Laden's links with Saddam Hussein. I met Abu Khabab al-Masri, bin Laden's top explosives expert, who tried to recruit me to bomb an embassy. I met Abu Zubayda, the top recruiter for Al Qaeda, who sent me back to Europe to work as a sleeper, to provide explosives expertise for attacks.

But none of these men knew the truth: that I had turned against them and their killing of innocents. I was a spy. I infiltrated the camps as an agent for the DGSE, the French counterespionage service. I was still working for the DGSE, and then MI5 as well, when I returned to Europe from Afghanistan, though Abu Zubayda continued to think I was working for him. For the services, I infiltrated the radical London mosques of Abu Qatada and Abu Hamza. For Abu Zubayda, I transmitted messages and even sent cash back to Pakistan to support the *jihad*—cash given to me by British intelligence officers.

Over the course of my journey, I met hundreds of men just like the 9/11 hijackers. Men who had no home. Men reviled in the West because they were not white and Christian, and reviled at home because they no longer dressed and spoke like Muslims. Their shared rage was their only anchor, the only thing that connected them to their faith, to their family, to the earth.

I understood all this because I was one of these men.

"Do you know who did this? Do you know any of the hijackers?"

"No. But I know who's behind this. I know why they did it. I know who these people are, and I know how they think." I paused. "I want to help."

There was a short silence on the other end of the line, and then a single sentence: "We'll call you back if we need you." Then a click. I never heard from him again.

BRUSSELS

Cast of Characters

Hakim   Omar's oldest brother

Rochdi   Omar's younger brother

Édouard   Omar's foster father in Belgium

Adil   Omar's youngest brother

Nabil   Omar's younger brother;
          lives in Brussels with Omar's mother and Hakim

Amin   Friend of Hakim and frequent guest
          at Omar's home in Brussels

Yasin   Friend of Hakim; also a frequent guest

Tarek   Friend of Hakim, Yasin, and Amin;
          editor of *Al Ansar*

Kamal   Tarek's translator for *Al Ansar*

Laurent   Omar's arms dealer

Gilles   DGSE officer; Omar's handler

Jamal   Drives with Omar to Spain

Thierry   Gilles's contact in the Belgian secret service

Timeline

December 24, 1979: U.S.S.R. deploys troops into Afghanistan, beginning the Soviet-Afghan War.

February 15, 1989: U.S.S.R. announces that all Soviet troops have withdrawn from Afghanistan.

January 1992: Civil war begins in Algeria after the government cancels democratic elections.

Spring 1992: The war in Bosnia and Herzegovina begins (exact date contested).

December 11, 1994: Russian troops enter Chechnya to prevent its secession from the Russian Federation.

December 24, 1994: Air France Flight 8969 hijacked in Algiers.

December 26, 1994: Hijacking ends when commandos from the French *gendarmerie's* elite counter-terrorism unit storm the plane on the tarmac in Marseilles.

January 30, 1995: Car bomb explodes outside a police station in Algiers, killing 42 people and injuring 286.

March 2, 1995: Belgian police carry out a series of raids across the country aimed at breaking up a European GIA network.

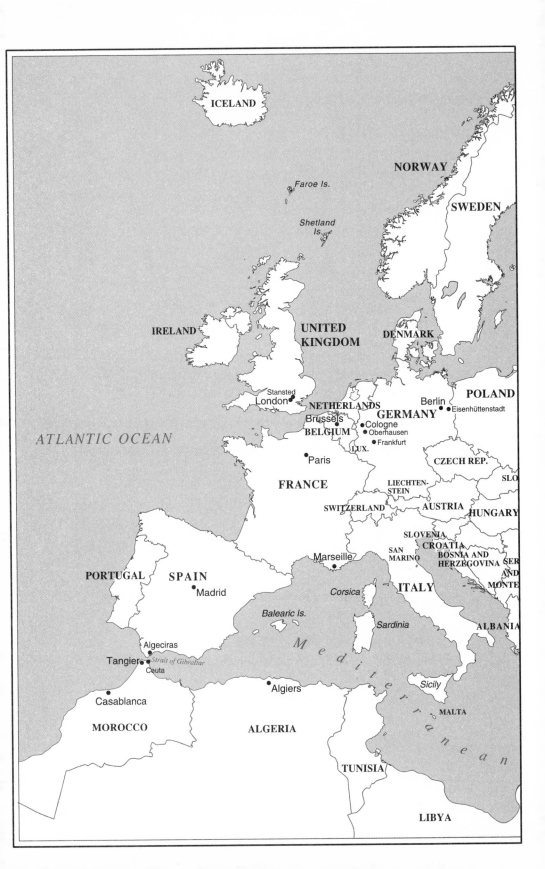

| 0 | 250 | 500 | 750 | 1000 km |

| 0 | | 250 | | 500 mi |

FINLAND

ESTONIA

RUSSIAN
FEDERATION

LATVIA

LITHUANIA

RUSS.
FED.

KAZAKHSTAN

BELARUS

UKRAINE

UZBEKISTAN

VAKIA

REP. OF
MOLDOVA

TURKMENISTAN

Crimea

ROMANIA

Black Sea

GEORGIA

BIA

AZERBAIJAN

NEGRO

BULGARIA

ARMENIA

Bosporus

Istanbul

TURKEY

IRAN

GREECE

SYRIA

Crete

IRAQ

CYPRUS

LEBANON

Sea

ISRAEL JORDAN

SAUDI
ARABIA

EGYPT

Omar

My name is Omar Nasiri. I am Moroccan. I was born in 1967. I am a Muslim.

I am very sorry. Almost none of this is true.

My name is not Omar Nasiri, or at least that is not the name my parents gave me. It is the name I am using to write this book, but it's only one of a long list of names I have used over the course of my life. Or perhaps I should say my *lives*—as a son, a brother, a student, a gunrunner, a *mujahid*, a secret agent, a civilian, a husband, and now an author.

I was not born in 1967. I have to protect my identity because members of my family still live in Morocco, and their lives would be in danger if my name were known. But anyway, what I'm saying is close enough. I was born in the 1960s.

I am Moroccan, but that is complicated also. My parents are Moroccan, of course, and I spent many years of my life there. I love the landscape and the people and the children's broad white smiles, and the smells of the food. I love the women in the bright silks of pink and green. Morocco is in my heart. Although I've traveled all over the world, Morocco is still the most beautiful country in the world to me. I miss her desperately, but know I can never return.

But if my heart lies in Morocco, my head is in Europe, where I was educated, where I grew up, where I've spent most of my life. I read *Le Monde*, books from America and England. My mind has been shaped by the West, by its patterns of thought, by its agitated, arrogant, thrilling individualism.

Because I'm part Arab, part European, my home is nowhere. When I went back to Morocco as a teenager, my Arabic was weak and other kids mocked me as a European and a foreigner. When last I visited, over a decade ago, I traveled as an outsider, a visitor from abroad. I drank whiskey on the deck of the ferry and smoked cigarettes and checked out girls. But I have no home in Europe either. I've lived in Germany for six years now with my wife, and I've worked in many jobs, but I'm not a citizen. I'm classified a refugee and I'm treated like any other Arab "guest worker."

So perhaps only one thing is completely true: I am a Muslim.

Buck Danny

My life ended when I was eight years old. I was in the bedroom, sitting at the desk building a model airplane. My oldest brother, Hakim, was wrestling on the bunk bed with Rochdi, one of my younger brothers. I was annoyed because I couldn't concentrate, so I took a break and went to the bathroom to get a Q-tip. When I returned to the room they were still wrestling, and I sat on the floor and started to clean my ears. Seconds later, my brothers tumbled off the bed and fell on top of me.

I felt the stick ram into my eardrum, and a searing pain shot through my body. I nearly passed out, but I could still hear myself screaming. When my brothers pulled themselves off of me, I saw that I was covered with blood. There was blood all around me.

It could have been just a tiny accident, boys roughhousing as they do. But it was much more than that. It changed my life forever, and deprived me of the one thing that mattered most to me. I have never really recovered.

But let me start at the very beginning. I was born into a large family—six boys, three girls. I am the second-oldest son.

I was full of energy as a child, too much energy sometimes. I talked back to my parents, and like all boys, I would fight with my brothers. Mostly, I fought with Hakim, who was older and bigger. He tried to put me in my place, but I always fought back.

I was mischievous and got into everything. I'd steal butter from the refrigerator—I loved the taste of butter—and climb up into a tree and eat it. One day, I ate so much that I ended up in the hospital, and my mother made me promise that I would never do it again. But of course I did do it again, and when my mother found out she was so angry that she punished me by burning my hand with a scalding spoon. Even that didn't stop me for long.

When I was three, my father moved to Belgium. He got a job in Brussels and left all of us behind in Morocco with our mother. Two years later, we followed him. Shortly after we arrived, our mother took us all to the doctor for a checkup. Medical care in Morocco was very expensive, so we saw a doctor only when there was an emergency. But in Belgium medical care was free, and so we all went at once. That's when my parents learned that I had tuberculosis.

Because of the tuberculosis, I couldn't live in the city with my family. Instead, I was installed in a sanitarium in the country, about seventy kilometers outside of Brussels. Overnight, I, a North African raised in the tradition of the Ku'ran, found myself in a Catholic school staffed by nuns. At any given time there were about two hundred other children there, all of them white Europeans. I was the only Arab.

It was obvious to me and to everyone else that I was different. No one was cruel to me in any way; the other children played with me and I with them. They'd taunt me a little bit sometimes, as children do, but I would just taunt them back. It wasn't a big deal.

But on Sundays it was different. We would all go to church together, and the services seemed incredibly strange to me. The prayers, the communion, the incense; it was so unlike the mosques I attended over the summer or when I went home on holiday. And there was music, a man who played guitar. In Islam, there is no music in the house of God; I had grown up considering it a great sacrilege. Mostly it just seemed funny to me, and at times I laughed openly. I think this made some of the other children nervous.

I didn't see my family very much during these years. Over the summers we all went home to Morocco, and once in a while I'd go back to Brussels to see them for a long weekend or a holiday. Sometimes—rarely, maybe two or three times a year—my parents would visit me and stay for a couple of hours. But my real life was at the sanitarium.

It was during this time that I fell in love with airplanes. My father had a friend who worked in the airline industry, and sometimes he'd teach me about airplanes and give me model planes to build. When I visited my family in Brussels I would go again and again to the Museum of the Army in Cinquantenaire Park. There was a huge hall filled with airplanes from World War II, and I would spend hours devouring every detail. I was incredibly curious; when we flew between Morocco and Belgium I would always run up to the cockpit and ask the pilots to show me the equipment.

Mostly, though, I learned about airplanes from Buck Danny. Buck Danny was the hero of a Belgian comic strip, and I read every book in the Buck Danny series from cover to cover. Big, athletic, handsome, and blond, Buck was a brave pilot who fought for America and flew on all sorts of dangerous missions with his friends Jerry Tumbler and Sonny Tuckson. The comics were very realistic; I learned the names of all the planes and lots of information about how to fly them. I read and reread all of the books, and at night I'd dream of becoming a fighter pilot like Buck Danny. I wanted it more than anything.

And then my eardrum was destroyed. The doctors in Belgium tried to fix it—I had three different surgeries—but there was nothing they could do. I'm still almost totally deaf in my left ear. I knew that I could never be in the army, that I would never fly a plane. I had nothing to live for. I had lost everything that mattered.

Every boy has a dream—to be a fireman or an astronaut or a president, to be something fantastic. Of course, most boys will never fulfill their childhood dream, but that's not the point. As a boy grows up and becomes a man, he gradually lets the dream go, although it may still linger in the form of nostalgia. But if his dream is destroyed at a very young age, the boy will either be destroyed totally along with it, or he will become strong. He will become strong because he no longer has anything to lose. He will give up on the future.

A boy without a dream is dangerous.

Édouard

"Hi, my name is Sonny Tuckson. I'm a friend of Buck Danny's."

It was late spring, and I was moving out of my dormitory at the sanitarium. I was ten years old, and it was time for me to go to a new school. I'd be living in the same town, but now with foster parents.

I knew this, but still nothing had prepared me for my meeting with Édouard. I was standing in front of the dormitory when he drove up in a yellow Volvo. He jumped out of the car and came towards me. He was a big man, tall and athletic. He had a sharp nose, very Gallic, and black hair that was turning gray. He took my bag and put it in the trunk of his car, and introduced himself as Sonny Tuckson. I will never forget that moment. Now, of course, I realize that he had read my files and knew that I loved Buck Danny and airplanes. But at the time it seemed like magic: a grownup who was part of my world. I was entranced.

I stayed with Édouard for five years in a castle in the countryside. He was about forty years old and lived on a rambling old estate with his parents and brother. They were Swiss. Eventually, I learned that Édouard had been in the civil service for many years, but that he had left that job and now took money from the state to raise foster children and help them through school. There were about twenty-five of us staying at the house at any given time.

Édouard was very intense, and felt things very deeply. He wanted all of us to succeed, and when we failed he felt it far more than we did. He was always very honest, and taught us to be honest, too.

As I grew older, I spent more and more time alone. By the time I moved in with Édouard I didn't play much at all with other children. I liked to do things on my own. I learned how to play the piano, and spent lots of time swimming in the pool behind the castle. I loved swimming—I felt so free in the water. My body was light and I could do anything with it. I could flip and dive and move in any direction. There was nothing to stop me.

I also spent a lot of time watching television. There was a TV in the parlor, and often after lessons I would sit there alone for hours. I watched many, many movies. Hundreds of films about World War II: *Tora! Tora! Tora!*, *The Battle of Midway*, *Thirty Seconds Over Tokyo*. I was transfixed by these films. Despite the fact that I knew I could never be a pilot—or maybe *because* I knew that—these films were incredibly intense for me. I imagined myself as an American fighter pilot over the Pacific; my imagination was so strong that I felt in my body that I was one of them, flying over the waves.

I hated the Germans and the Japanese because they were my enemies. I saw hundreds of films and documentaries about the concentration camps. They were horrible and frightening to me. Hitler, the emaciated bodies, the piles and piles of corpses—it was pure evil.

The Japanese were different. I was fascinated by the kamikazes, by the images of them crashing into American aircraft carriers and exploding in flames. They were the enemy, of course, but I also admired and understood them. In the face of a much stronger power, they did the only thing possible to save their country and their honor.

I also liked science fiction. I loved *The War of the Worlds* and I was addicted to *Star Trek*. We didn't have a television at home in Brussels, so when I was there over the holidays I'd go out at night and watch *Star Trek* on the televisions in the windows of electronics shops.

Early on, I even imagined myself as an extraterrestrial. Sometimes, I would hear a ringing in my ear and imagine that it was a message from outer space. Often, when the other boys were playing soccer, I'd walk to one of the empty playing fields. There, I would hold my arms high up in the air and close my eyes and imagine a great force sucking me up into space.

Édouard singled me out, maybe because I stood out. He was very kind to me, and would often come and sit by me when he saw that I was alone. I was fascinated by all sorts of scientific subjects, and he spent hours talking to me about stars and energy and nuclear power. I was so taken by him; he was the first man who ever took an interest in me, who tried to teach me things. And I wanted to learn because I knew it would please him.

But most of all I wanted to learn about guns. From the day I arrived, I knew there were guns in the castle. I could hear them firing at night—there was a shooting gallery in the basement that wasn't soundproof.

One afternoon, Édouard found me by myself and asked me to follow him. He took me to the basement. It was amazing—he owned every kind of gun imaginable. Pistols, rifles, everything. He walked me around and taught me the name of each one, explaining what it was for: a .44 Magnum, a .45 Smith & Wesson, a .22 rifle, a .44 Marlin, and on and on. I fell in love on the spot.

Over the next months and eventually years, Édouard would teach me how to use each and every one of these guns. He taught other children as well, but I was more interested than they were. And so it became something special that Édouard and I did together. He would take me down to the basement or out into a field and we would shoot at targets. Sometimes, the guns were so big that I'd be knocked off my feet by the kickback, and he would laugh. I loved the discipline of working with guns. I loved that I was getting better all the time. And I loved it when Édouard praised me.

I also learned how to make bullets during my time with him. Ammunition is very expensive, and we used a lot. So we would collect the casings after every target practice and keep them to reuse. We would scavenge bits of lead from anything we could find—hubcaps, pipes from old houses. Édouard taught me how to melt down the lead to make tips for new bullets, and how to fill the casings with gunpowder. It's not easy to make a bullet; it's a very precise art. If you use too much powder in the casing, the bullet can explode inside the gun and blow up in your face. I learned to be very careful.

Eventually, I realized that Édouard was using the guns to teach me discipline. I was a stubborn child, very independent. And I didn't care about school. But Édouard wouldn't let me use the guns unless I'd finished my homework, and so I started doing my homework most nights. I was becoming a better student, and Édouard praised me for that, too.

But I was no angel. When I was older, fifteen, I got into a terrible fight with Édouard. I wanted to spend the evening with him, firing the guns and making new bullets. He asked me if I had finished my homework and I told him I had. I spent the whole night downstairs with the guns. But I had lied about my home-work, and the next day Édouard found out. He was furious with me.

"Why did you lie to me?" he yelled. "You think you can get away with any-thing, don't you?"

His face was getting red. I had never seen him like this before. He was shout-ing at me, and there was a look of pure disgust on his face.

"You have everything—you are smart, you can do anything you want in this world. But instead you lie to me. You have no conscience."

And then, before he turned away, he said something I have never forgotten: "I don't think you will ever amount to anything."

I stayed in the foster home for a few more months after the fight, but that was the last real conversation I had with Édouard. After that there was a break be-tween us, a coldness.

"I don't think you will ever amount to anything."

For years afterward I would hear Édouard's words—half insult, half chal-lenge—ricochet in my head. At first, I decided he was right. Later, I would try desperately to prove him wrong.

Morocco

When I was fifteen, I returned to Tangier with my family. My health problems had cleared up, and my father was no longer working in Brussels. At first, I thought it would be a wonderful homecoming. I had never felt at home in Bel-gium, and so I longed for my real home in Morocco.

The longer I was away from Morocco, the more splendid it became. It had come to define me. As I grew older, the things that made me feel different in Belgium became the things that made me proud. I was an Arab, a Muslim. I was better than these white Europeans.

But when I finally returned to Morocco, I quickly realized that it was no longer any sort of home to me. I felt as foreign there as I had in Belgium. I'd been speaking French almost exclusively since I was five years old, and my ac-cent and my vocabulary were much more refined than those of the Moroccan boys. They made fun of me for that, and because I knew very little Arabic. In fact, they made fun of everything: the clothes I wore, even how I smelled. My mother had started using fabric softener in Belgium, which was unheard of in Morocco. The boys told me I smelled like a *gaouri,* a Christian.

I felt myself hardening. The country I loved no longer loved me back, and so in return I loved her less and less. Soon, Belgium seemed like the far better place, and Morocco came to look so weak, so backward in comparison. I missed the freedom of Europe, the way people could talk to each other openly, the way a man and a woman could be together without fear. The way people argued so loudly about everything.

Morocco, by contrast, was corrupt and repressive. Bribes were everything—a bit to this guy, a bit to another. There was no other way to get anything done. The government was rotten with bribery, with kickbacks and favors, and as a result the country was a disaster. No social welfare programs to speak of. The roads were ripped to shreds, when there were roads at all. The trains, the buses—a total catastrophe. The police were everywhere, and everyone lived in fear. The walls were always listening: neighbors spied on neighbors, and as a consequence no one talked about anything important. And everything was about class, who had what, how much. Anyone without money was treated like dirt. I hated it.

I had grown apart from my family as well. It had fallen apart in my absence. I'd had hints of this when we spent our summers together in Morocco. A typical Moroccan man, my father was a real patriarch and he treated my mother very badly. He took many other lovers, but he became furious with her at the slightest sign of independence. Sometimes he beat her, often brutally. My brothers and sisters all knew about this, but it was something we never discussed.

My mother was an angel. Once, when I was about ten, she and I were looking through a photo album. They were all pictures of her family, and as she pointed at each person she would tell me their name. There were lots of pretty girls in the album (I had only recently begun to pay attention to girls). I asked my mother to tell me about each one, and as she did so I would ask if I could marry her when I grew up. My mother laughed each time and explained that family members cannot marry one another.

When we came to the end of the album, there was a picture of a particularly beautiful young girl, but my mother closed the album before I could study it.

"*Maman,* you forgot to tell me about the last one!" I complained. I took the album from her hands and opened it again to the last page. I pointed at the picture, a girl of thirteen or fourteen with long black hair.

My mother smiled. "You don't need to know about her. She's not related to you."

I was ecstatic. "Then I can marry her!"

"Maybe, if you do well in school." My mother laughed, but she still wouldn't tell me the girl's name.

The picture stayed in my mind, and a few years later I asked my mother about the girl again. She looked surprised.

"You don't recognize her?"

"No," I said.

"That's a picture of me as a child! It's me, your *Maman*!" Then she laughed again; her eyes were bright and I recognized the girl in the picture.

A few months after I returned from Belgium, my father got a job in Sidi Kacem, in the center of Morocco. He wanted us all to move there with them, but none of us wanted to go. Tangier was a busy, cosmopolitan city, more like Europe than anything else in Morocco. But Sidi Kacem was a backwater in an undeveloped part of the country.

My mother and father fought about this all the time.

One day, my father came home still angry after a fight the night before. I was in the house with my mother and my older brother Hakim when he walked in. He immediately started yelling at my mother, and she yelled back. We had grown used to the yelling. But then my father began to kick her, and she fell to the floor.

I looked over at my brother to see if we should do something. I was used to Hakim telling me what to do; he was my older brother and he never let me forget it. He was a bully, but I was proud to have him as a brother because he was protective of me and my brothers and sisters. When he had money he would often take us to the cinema or give us a few francs to spend on our own.

But now Hakim would not even catch my eye; he just looked down at the floor. He was right, of course. As Muslims, we knew never to challenge the total authority of our father. But my mother was crying and screaming, and I could see that she was scared. I couldn't bear it.

By this time I was bigger than my father and he didn't frighten me. I walked over and pulled him off my mother. I picked him up and carried him out of the house, then set him down on the ground. I stared into his eyes and I could see that he was furious with me, but also scared. But I no longer cared what he thought.

"Never do that again," I told him. Then I walked back in the house and closed the door behind me. My mother was silent. I could see that she was still frightened, but also shocked at what I'd done. I looked over at Hakim, but he didn't look up. He just stared at the floor.

Of course, my father did do that again—many times. But I wasn't around to witness it. A few months after the fight, I took a job as a part of a sailboat crew and sailed around the world. I was happy to be away—from Morocco, from my family, from everything.

When I came back my mother was gone. She had finally divorced my father and moved back to Belgium along with some of my brothers and sisters. But I had grown so alienated from my family that this didn't bother me.

For the next ten years, I lived in Morocco by myself, sometimes on the streets, sometimes in hotels, depending on whether or not I had money. I drank hard and smoked hash every day and listened to reggae music and slept with lots of girls. I never thought about the future. If I had money, I spent it. If I didn't have it, I didn't really care.

At first I worked as a guide, and I hustled tourists for the carpet sellers. I was good at it. I'd spent so much time alone as a child watching other people that I had learned how to read them. I could understand a whole personality from just a few details: the arch of an eyebrow, a hand gesture, a way of walking. I knew instinctively how to pick out the most vulnerable foreigners, the ones who could be easily pressured. In just a few seconds I could tell if I could make money off someone or not.

More tourists came to Morocco for hash than for carpets, though, and soon I was also acting as a middleman between the producers in the mountains and the tourists in the cities. Before long I was setting up deals for hundreds of kilos of hash, not just for tourists anymore, but for clients overseas as well. It paid very well and that was all that mattered.

The streets of Tangier teemed with police. They were there primarily to protect the tourists from hustlers like me. There were many undercover cops, and I soon learned how to pick them out in a crowd. I watched them arrest the guys in the market who would lay out their smuggled goods—cheap perfume, electronics, toiletries from Europe—on blankets in the square. I studied the police when they snuck up on them from behind to arrest them. I'd study how they moved. I learned how to identify the police by the expressions on their faces—intense, so serious. I could recognize them instinctively after a while, so I knew how to avoid them.

I was a good fixer, and soon my name got around. People began coming to me for difficult jobs. Two journalists from *El País* sought me out when they wanted to write a story about immigrant trafficking on the coast between Tangier and Ceuta. It was a dangerous trade in Morocco, and it was hidden well underground. But I found them their story, and they took hundreds of photos. Later, another journalist asked me to take him to the university in Fez during some riots. The university was heavily guarded by police during the day; the riots had become very violent, so no one was getting inside. But at night I was able to sneak the journalist in. I persuaded some of the students to talk to him, and I stayed up with them all night translating.

But some things were too dangerous, even for me. One day, two Germans to whom I had been selling hash came to me with an offer. They wanted to buy hash in exchange for weapons. They came to me with a list of everything they had to sell. It was incredible: Kalashnikovs, tanks, rocket launchers, missiles, combat aircrafts. This was in the late 1980s, as the Soviet empire was collapsing. The Soviet generals were selling off everything they had for cash before it was all taken away from them. Weapons were pouring into Europe, available to anyone who wanted them.

"Are you crazy?" I asked the Germans after I looked at the list. "You're lucky you came to me. Anyone else would sell you out to the police, and you'd spend the rest of your lives here in prison." No one deals weapons like that in a Muslim country, and certainly not in Morocco. The Germans would have been thrown in jail if they were caught. They would have been tortured there, and they never would have gotten out. I quickly burned the paper and we never spoke of it again.

Hakim

I was twenty-six when my youngest brother, Adil, was killed. He was shot at his school in Belgium. It was an accident: a friend of his brought a pistol to school and the two of them were playing with it when it went off. The bullet went straight through my brother's heart, and he was dead in three minutes. He was fourteen years old.

I was in Tangier when it happened. I learned of it from a family friend, Jawad, who worked at a pharmacy in town. I went by his shop every few weeks because sometimes my mother would wire me money through him, and I'd go there to pick up the cash. That day, when I went in, one of the employees pulled me aside. He looked serious. He walked me up to Jawad's office. When I walked in the door, Jawad told me he had some news, and asked me to sit down.

"Your brother Adil died two days ago," he said, and gave me the details.

I wasn't surprised or even upset. Death had never upset me. I had always believed that God does everything for a reason. Who am I to challenge His will? If someone is suffering in front of me, I feel it very deeply. It tears me apart. But when a person dies, it's over. There is no suffering anymore.

A few years earlier my grandfather had died. He'd been very ill and many family members were gathered around him when he left the world. Everyone was wailing and crying, but I felt nothing. I loved my grandfather, but he was never mine. He belonged to God, and God had taken him back.

A few weeks later I ran into my oldest brother Hakim on the street. I hadn't expected to see him, but he told me he'd come back to Tangier to bury our brother, and that he was staying on for a while. I was completely shocked by the way he looked. I hadn't seen him for more than seven years, and I remembered him as a good-looking man, very sharp and flashy. He smoked, drank, went to parties, and always had women around him.

Now everything was different. He had a long beard and was wearing a *djellaba*. In my whole life I had never seen him wear one. And he had a *siwak* between his teeth. The *siwak* is a kind of twig from the Middle East which the Prophet Muhammad told his followers to use to make breath sweet before praying. Only the most pious Muslims do this.

Hakim was still a bully, though; that hadn't changed. We walked to the home of one of my sisters, and when we got there he told me to make my ablutions.

"Why?" I asked.

"So we can go to mosque and pray," he told me.

"I'm not going to pray," I said. I hadn't been to mosque for many years and the idea seemed ridiculous to me.

"Your brother has died," Hakim replied. "We must make our *salat*."

In the end I went along with it. Not because of Adil, but because I was beginning to realize that maybe I could get something for myself out of it. By now I was so sick of Morocco, sick of the life I was leading. I wanted to go back to Belgium. I realized that Hakim could help me get started there, help me find a job. And so I made my ablutions and went with him to the mosque to pray.

We stayed at our sister's house that night, and the next morning Hakim told me we were going to Casablanca. I didn't want to go to Casablanca. I had other things to do and I told him I wouldn't go.

"You must come with me," he said. "You have to change your life. I want to help you."

And so I let myself be persuaded and drove with Hakim to Casablanca. On the way I asked him what we were going to do when we got there.

"There is a group of brothers in Casablanca that I want you to meet," he told me. "I want you to spend a few weeks with them. I want you to learn from them because you must come back to God.

"Now you are *taghut*," he said. Impure. "You must come back to God."

I had no idea what he was talking about, who these brothers were. But I was focused on getting out of Morocco at this point, so I pretended to be interested and thanked him.

In Casablanca, we met up with the brothers at a mosque. After praying, we all traveled back to Tangier together. Hakim would leave me there for a month; he said he had other things to do while he was in Morocco.

During that month Hakim's friends watched over me to make sure I was leading a devout life. I performed the *salat* five times a day; it was easy to fall back into the pattern I had learned as a child. It had never left me. But I also had to stop smoking and drinking and that was much harder. I was willing to put up with it, though, because I saw this whole charade as a means to an end.

After Hakim returned we lived for six weeks with my sister. During this time we spoke constantly about Islam. Hakim taught me how to behave like a true Muslim: the way to walk, the way to pray, the way to dress. I learned to walk with my eyes down, always at the same angle. To never make eye contact with anyone on the street, never look at a woman above her chin. I learned how to dress. No cloth should ever hang below the ankle—that is a sign of arrogance. The head must be covered all the time to ward off the devil.

I learned the correct manner of prayer, also. I learned to stand with my feet close together, with my shoulder pressed up against the brother next to me. I learned not to look at my feet when I kneeled down. To train my eyes in front of me instead, and focus on the spot where I would place my forehead when I lay my head down before God.

Hakim taught me all of this. He also talked to me about *jihad*, the battle all devout Muslims constantly fight within themselves to show their devotion to God. He told me that I must give everything to God, and trust him completely, and to keep nothing for myself. But even if I give everything to God it is still not enough; I must give more still. It is not enough to perform the *salat* five times a day. I must pray constantly, repent at every moment for everything in me that is impure.

I began to notice that Hakim's lips were always moving just slightly. It was barely noticeable until I learned what I was seeing.

Hakim and I spent a lot of time talking about politics, about the injustices inflicted on Muslims all over the world. It was the end of 1993 and the war in Bosnia had been going on for almost two years already, as had the war in Algeria. I had been aware of all this long before Hakim returned to Morocco. Every Muslim was.

But it was the war in Afghanistan I knew most about. Like every young man in Morocco and throughout the Muslim world, I had watched the Red Army invade Afghanistan in 1979. And like everyone else, I hated the Russians. We would have hated them anyway—they had invaded Muslim land—but this was the end of the Cold War, and Morocco was allied with the United States. The television, the newspapers—they were all controlled by America through Morocco's puppet regime and filled with anti-Soviet propaganda. They riled us all up. I, like every young man, dreamed of fighting side by side with *mujahidin* in Afghanistan.

But I learned much more about the war in the early 1990s, after the Russians retreated. One summer, I traveled in Europe for a couple of months with a girl I had met in Morocco. I broke up with her soon enough. Before returning home, I went to Paris by myself. It was summer, and I spent a lot of time just walking around the city. One day, I walked by the Pompidou Center. I'd never heard anything about it and didn't know what was inside, but I saw a big line of people waiting to get in, and out of curiosity I joined it.

I ended up spending three months in Paris, mostly at the Pompidou Center. It had an astonishing library, and I devoured everything in sight: history, religion, science. But I spent the most time with the materials on the Soviet invasion of Afghanistan. They had an extraordinary collection of films and documentaries about both the Soviets and the *mujahidin*.

These men were amazing, like nothing I had ever seen before. I watched one film over and over again, of a man with a long beard standing up in a tank. Later, I learned that he had been killed in a battle in Kabul, but in the film he looked glorious. In his face I could see the intensity of his commitment, of his faith. "*Takbir! Allahu akbar!*" he shouted. "*Allahu akbar!*"

And the land was beautiful as well. I had never seen anything like those extraordinary dark mountains. As I watched more and more films I came to feel it in my body, the need to defend this beautiful land.

In one film the *mujahidin* sat high above a valley while a convoy of Soviets snaked through the valley below. Suddenly—an explosion. Then another. And another. The Soviet tanks blew up one by one, spitting smoke and fire into the air. The film must have been shot by one of the *mujahidin* or someone with them, because I saw the whole thing through his eyes. From high on the hill I could see soldiers stumbling out of the tanks and falling to the ground. Then we were racing down the hill towards them. Soon we were right on top of the Russians. A gun fired—a soldier fell to the ground. And another. Bam. Bam. Bam.

But a few of the soldiers were still alive. I watched as a *mujahid* lifted the head of one of the Soviets to expose the neck while another held a sword high above him. Then the film went black, just for a second. When it came back on I could see the soldier's lifeless body, and a black spot inserted by the censors where the head should have been.

I also learned a lot about politics within Afghanistan. I watched many, many interviews with Russian soldiers returning from the front lines, and it was from them that I learned about Ahmed Shah Massoud and Gulbuddin Hekmatyar, who both fought fiercely against the Soviets in the 1980s. In the films, the Soviets returning from the front spoke of how much they despised Hekmatyar; they thought he was a madman. He killed indiscriminately, rival Muslim factions as well as Soviets. But they admired Massoud, the Lion of Panjshir. They respected his bravery and fierce intelligence.

And so by the time Hakim came to Morocco in 1993, I already knew a great deal about Afghanistan. By that time all hell had broken loose there. The Russians had retreated. Warlords were fighting warlords for control of the country, and Muslims were killing Muslims. Hekmatyar was trying to consolidate his power, laying siege to Kabul and causing thousands and thousands of casualties.

Hakim tried to convince me that Hekmatyar was a pious Muslim fighting a true *jihad*. I disagreed completely. To me, he was a disgrace. The *mujahidin* I had seen killed invaders and infidels, not other Muslims. Hakim and I fought about this many times.

We clashed a great deal during these weeks in Tangier, as we always had. But we each wanted something from the other: Hakim wanted me to join him in his fundamentalist faith, and I wanted him to take me to Belgium and find me a job. And so we pretended to get along.

One day he turned to me: "What do you want to do with your life, Omar?"

"I want to go to Bosnia, to join the *jihad*." I knew this was what Hakim wanted to hear, but it was also completely true. Ever since I had watched those films in Paris, I wanted to be a *mujahidin*. I wanted to do something real with my life, and Bosnia seemed like the place to do it. I'd read about the Bosniaks, and seen pictures of them. I identified with them strongly, perhaps because they looked so European. In my mind, I was still a European Muslim in many ways.

"It is not that easy," Hakim replied. "You will have to go through many levels before you are ready for *jihad*. First you will need to prove yourself to God, prove that you have really returned to him. There are brothers in Europe who can help you with this, but it will take a long time."

I had only one question: "When do we leave?"

A month later we left. Hakim came to me one day, showed me the tickets, and told me we were leaving the next day. Before we left, he threw away all the traces of my old life, so I could be reborn into Islam. He burned my notebook with the names of all the people I'd known in Morocco, the people I sold drugs to. He didn't tell me until everything was already gone. I was absolutely furious, but there was nothing I could say. The most important thing was to get out of Morocco.

Sitting on the plane, I stared out the window as Morocco drifted farther and farther away. In my heart, I believed I would never go back. I was ecstatic.

Belgium

When I got off the plane in Brussels, my younger brother Nabil was waiting for me. I could tell from his face that something was wrong. "We don't know when the police are going to let Hakim go," he said.

I was totally confused—Hakim was on the plane with me. But when I looked back towards the gate, I didn't see him. We hadn't sat together on the flight because we were fighting, but I'd seen him board the plane. Now Nabil was telling me that he'd been taken off the plane in Casablanca by the Moroccan secret police and that he was being held for questioning. I remembered how loud my brother had been about his beliefs, his conviction that the entire government of Morocco was *taghut*. I wasn't particularly surprised that someone

had overheard him and reported him to the authorities. The Moroccan authorities arrested people all the time, sometimes just to get them off the streets, but
always when they saw the slightest sign of extremism.

Nabil drove me to my mother's house on the outskirts of Brussels, and when
we got there she opened the door. I was so happy to see her. Although we'd
talked on the phone and she'd sent me money in Morocco, I had not seen her in
person for over a decade. She looked older, but she was still very beautiful.

That night the three of us had dinner together. I was very happy to be back
in Europe.

Hakim was quickly released; a family friend who worked for the government
pulled some strings. When he arrived in Brussels three days after me, Hakim
told me the authorities had pressed him to become a spy for the government.
They had told him that it was his duty. "This is your country. You should help
your country. Your king needs you." They'd offered to pay him. Of course,
Hakim would never accept this kind of bargain.

Two days later, I met Amin and Yasin for the first time. I had been in the city all
day, and when I came home my brother was in the living room with five other
men. My mother had prepared wonderful food for everyone, and they were eating. The men were sharply dressed in expensive-looking, well-fitted clothes.
And their faces were all closely shaved. Hakim looked so strange sitting with
them, with his long beard and his *djellaba*.

Hakim called me over and introduced me. The men were Algerian, and
spoke in French. They were all very young, some still teenagers and others
in their early twenties. It was clear that one man, Amin, was in charge. He
had lighter skin than most Arabs, and huge eyes that seemed to bulge out of
his head.

Amin was extremely confident, and I could see that the other men looked up
to him. He smiled a lot, and was very friendly to me. He was constantly interrupted by incoming calls on his two mobile phones. It was very rare to see anyone with a mobile phone in 1993, so I immediately knew that he had money.

Yasin was a few centimeters shorter than Amin, and very athletic looking.
Yasin was clearly closer to Amin than the other men; they sat together much of
the time and spoke quietly to each other so that no one else could hear. At one
point, I saw Yasin hand money to Amin.

Two things struck me about both men: they both had very dark circles
under their eyes, and the way they walked was very odd. They were both so

graceful, like dancers, or cats. I had never seen anyone walk this way, and it seemed strange to me. Much later I would understand.

I didn't say much that evening. I knew these men were doing something secretive and probably illegal, though that first night I wasn't sure what it was exactly. I knew, of course, that it had something to do with the civil war in Algeria. This was the end of 1993. Two years earlier, the military government had cancelled elections when it realized the Islamist FIS (*Front Islamique du Salut*) was going to win. The GIA (*Groupe Islamique Armé*) had soon emerged to fight not only the military dictatorship, but even the FIS. The GIA did not want new elections; they wanted a theocracy.

Amin and Yasin spoke the same language of religious fanaticism as my brother. But their voices were always calm, soothing almost, even as they talked about *jihad* and the destruction of the infidels. Mostly, however, they spoke about logistics: cars going from France to Germany, and from Germany back to France. Which cars had engine trouble, things of that sort.

None of it was very interesting to me, so I got up and went to bed.

Amin and Yasin came again the following week. This time they brought boxes filled with copies of a newsletter and envelopes. Hakim and I sat down with them and started stuffing the envelopes. The envelopes were addressed to people all over the world: in Canada, the United States, England, Pakistan, Russia, China, France, Spain, Holland, Sweden, Denmark, Saudi Arabia. I glanced briefly at the newsletter and I could see that it was all about Algeria. Parts of it were in French, parts in Arabic.

When we were done, we drove around and unloaded the envelopes in mailboxes all over the city. A few in one, a few more in another. There must have been over a thousand envelopes.

The week after that Amin and Yasin came again, this time in the morning. I was downstairs eating breakfast when I heard them talking with Hakim in the living room. When they mentioned Kalashnikovs my ears pricked up; I began to listen very carefully. They were talking about ammunition. They needed bullets for Kalashnikovs. "We can't get them in Belgium," Amin said. "There are a lot in Germany, but they cost too much."

I went into the living room and continued listening. I already knew something about the arms trade from the Germans who'd tried to buy hash from me in exchange for guns. I knew that Germany was saturated with weapons from the former Soviet Union. I also understood that every time a runner crossed a border, there was a chance that he would get caught. And every risk carried a price. In this case the price was too high: they were paying thirteen francs for each bullet.

Sensing an opportunity to make money, I inserted myself into the conversation. "Maybe I can get you the bullets," I said. "How much are you willing to pay?"

All three of them smiled and laughed. "You just got here," said Hakim. "You've been away for ten years. You don't know anything about how all of this works."

Of course, I knew how it worked. I had been selling hash on the streets of Morocco. I knew how to find buyers and how to find sellers. I knew a lot about guns and bullets, too, from my years with Édouard. I knew what they looked like, how much all the components should cost. And I certainly knew how to make money. If I could get the bullets for much less than they could, I could take a cut for myself.

I looked at them without smiling. "I'm serious. I think I can get the bullets. What do you want?" They stopped laughing, but clearly they were still suspicious.

Yasin broke the silence. "AK-47, 7.62x39," he said. "We want to pay ten fifty."

It was a big discount they were hoping for, and I was worried that at that price there would be nothing left for me. "Why ten fifty?" I asked. "If I find them for eleven, then you're still saving two francs."

"We don't want to pay that much. We can't afford them."

"All right," I said. "I'll see what I can do."

They didn't believe me, of course. They just smiled.

<hr/>

Laurent

I had no idea how to find bullets for a Kalashnikov. As I went to bed that night, I thought about Hakim and how in Morocco he had burned my list of contacts. If only I had the names of those two Germans, I could have gotten everything Amin and Yasin wanted, and more! But life is like that.

The next evening I went into the city, to Schaerbeek, a very crowded part of Brussels inhabited mostly by Turks and North Africans. It's where men in Brussels go to find prostitutes and drugs.

I sat down in a café on a busy street and ordered a drink. I stayed there for an hour at least, watching passersby as I had in Morocco. But in Morocco I was always looking for buyers. Here I was looking for a seller. And soon enough I spotted one, a young Arab standing across the street from me. He was very flashy, wearing a brand new Nike tracksuit and constantly taking calls on his mobile. I watched him for a long time. Sometimes a car would slow down in front of him; then he'd drive off on his giant Kawasaki and the car would follow him. But he would always come back.

I had seen this sort of guy before, and I felt in my gut that he was the one who was going to find me my bullets. But I also knew this wasn't his regular business, and that if I asked him flat out to find them for me he would say no. Obviously, this kid was making a lot of money selling drugs, and he wasn't going to put his business at risk for nothing. So I was careful.

I walked across the street and approached him. "*Assalamu'alaykum.*"

"*Alaykum assalam,*" he replied. "What do you want?"

I signaled that he should walk with me. As we moved down the street together, we trained our eyes forward. "I want to ask you a question," I said, "but I don't want you to answer me right now. Just hear me out, but don't say anything." After a pause, I went on. "I'm looking for bullets. Bullets for Kalashnikovs."

He stopped and turned towards me, flustered. "You want—"

I cut him off and looked him straight in the eye. "I'm serious," I said. "I don't want you to answer me now. Just listen to what I say and think about it. I'll come back another time, and if you don't want to do it then that's OK. But for now just listen to me."

He nodded. "I'm looking for Kalashnikov bullets," I continued. "I know you don't sell this stuff, but maybe you know someone who does. I need a lot of bullets. I'm not going to use them to rob a bank or anything. They're going to move out of Europe very fast, I promise you." Then I leaned in even closer to him. I spoke in my lowest, most conspiratorial voice. "They are for the Muslim *umma*, for the *jihad.*"

His eyes flickered for a moment, and I knew I had him. There are guys like this all over the world: they drink, they smoke, they snort coke, they are complete infidels in the eyes of real Muslims. But at the first mention of the words *umma* or *jihad* they suddenly reconnect with Islam. I think this is particularly true in Europe, where young men are so far from everything, from the Muslim land. *Jihad* is nothing to them, nothing real. But it is also everything.

"Just think about it," I said. "I'll come back tomorrow."

I went back the next day. The dealer was standing in exactly the same spot, and when he saw me he smiled and waved. "I think I know someone who can help you," he said. "He's a friend of mine, I sell him coke. He knows weapons. Can you come back tonight at ten?"

When I returned that night he wasn't there. I waited, and after a few minutes he drove up on his motorcycle. "My guy is nervous," he said. "I can't promise you anything. But in a few minutes a friend of his is going to pass by here. He's going to check you out, and if you're OK he's going to put you in touch with my friend."

Half an hour later I saw a car coming towards us, a blue Renault. It stopped in front of us and the driver rolled down the window. The dealer went over to the car and spoke to the driver in a low voice.

Inside the car was an overweight, middle-aged man with his shirt unbuttoned. I could see the hair on his chest and a gold cross hanging from a chain around his neck. I didn't have much time to look at him, though, because the dealer jumped in the car and they drove off together.

A few minutes later the car came back. The dealer got out and the car drove off. "Sorry about that," he said. "I needed to give him something." Then he paused and looked at me intently. "Actually, that was the friend I was telling you about. He wants to meet you."

"When?" I asked. "Where?"

"Here. Meet us here. Tomorrow night."

When I went back the next night, the dealer was waiting for me. Soon the car drove up as well. This time the driver signaled me to get in. I got in the back seat and the dealer sat up front.

The driver looked back at me and introduced himself. "I'm Laurent." He asked what I wanted and I told him Kalashnikov bullets, lots of them. He nodded.

I studied the man. He looked like a typical French bourgeois. I don't think he was more than forty-five years old, but his face looked older. It was covered with wrinkles and there were strong lines in his forehead. His eyes were moving constantly.

As we drove off I continued to study him. There was something very strange about him, something I had not seen before. His body was completely wound up, intense. In all my life I had never seen a man so precise in his movements, so attentive to every detail. He checked his rearview mirror continuously, and I could see his eyes darting about.

We drove for about twenty minutes. Laurent spoke to the dealer while I remained silent in the back. Before I got anywhere near the ammunition, I needed to check these guys out. Maybe Laurent was a cop, or an informant. But my gut was telling me they were for real.

We slowed down in an industrial area in a part of Brussels I'd never been to. Laurent drove into a parking garage, several stories up to the top. All three of us got out, and the dealer and I stood by while Laurent opened the trunk. There was a sleeping bag inside. Laurent pulled it away, uncovering five CZ automatic pistols. I said nothing.

"I was supposed to deliver these to someone," Laurent explained, "but he never showed up. I have no idea where he is."

I looked over at the dealer, who seemed transfixed by the guns. He leaned down and picked one up, turning it over several times in his hands. I stood back and said nothing.

I knew they were testing me. They both wanted to know if I was serious about *jihad* or if I was just a petty criminal looking to shoot up a bank. And Laurent wanted to know that I was a pro, which is why I didn't pick up the gun like the dealer had. Only a kid would pick up a gun that way and leave his fingerprints everywhere. The whole thing was a performance, a test. The last three days had been nothing but tests. By asking me to come back again and again, the dealer was trying to figure me out. Maybe I was a cop, maybe I was a maniac. They needed to know that I wasn't fucking around.

Laurent looked down at the guns and then back up at me. "Are you interested?"

"No," I said. "I told you what I want. I want bullets. I want Kalashnikov bullets. Nothing else."

He nodded and we all got back in the car and drove out of the garage, back towards the city center. I had passed the test.

Bullets

Laurent drove us back to the city, and we dropped off the dealer. Then he and I drove around for about an hour. At first, it was hard to make conversation, so we talked mostly about the dealer; he was the only thing we had in common. Laurent went on about him for several minutes, complaining that he was unreliable; sometimes his coke was very good, but not always. None of it was very interesting. We were just trying to get to know each other, establish some trust.

After a little while we started talking about the bullets. I told him what I wanted: Kalashnikov bullets, probably several thousand. He didn't seem at all surprised by this. He said he thought he could get me the bullets for twelve francs each.

"I can't pay that much," I said. "I can pay ten francs fifty, no more."

He scoffed. "That's impossible. That's less than the bullet costs to make."

I knew he was lying. I knew how much it cost to make bullets. And he hadn't flinched when I told him how many I wanted, so I knew he had a lot of them to sell.

I kept pushing. "Ten fifty. That's it. If you can't do it, I'll find someone else." I was confident. Belgium produces more weapons and ammunition than almost any other country in the world. I knew the bullets were out there and that I'd be able to find them. It had only taken me three days to hook up with Laurent, and I was sure I could do it again.

"Maybe I can get them for a little bit less," Laurent conceded. "I'll have to talk to my friend. Maybe he'll let me go to eleven eighty."

Now I knew that he was hungry, that he wanted to close the deal. He needed a new client. I could tell that he was a fairly small fish; no major arms dealer would drive a Renault. And if I was buying this many bullets in our first transaction, he knew I'd be coming back for much more.

I wanted to close the deal, too, even if it meant I wouldn't make as much money. If I became the link between Yasin and Laurent, I could eventually work it to my advantage.

Eventually, we landed on eleven twenty-five as the price. I told Laurent that I would have to confirm it with my boss. I was planning to offer the bullets to Yasin for eleven fifty, and I knew he would agree to it. He would save one and one half francs on every bullet he bought, with none of the risk of carrying them across a border. And I would take the extra twenty-five cents for myself.

Laurent dropped me off at a bus station that night. Before I got out of the car, he wrote down the number of his mobile phone and told me to call him in two days.

When I came downstairs the next morning, Yasin and Amin were already in the house. They were coming by more and more often, almost every day now.

I walked into the living room and addressed Yasin. "I found someone," I said. "I can get the bullets for eleven fifty."

Yasin's eyebrows rose slightly as he looked at me. He turned to Amin and they said a few words to each other under their breath. Then Amin nodded.

"All right," Yasin said slowly, as he faced me again. "We'll give it a try. Tell your guy that we want five thousand. But tell him we need to see a sample before we hand over any money." Of course Amin and Yasin were cautious; they had no idea who I was dealing with, nor did I offer to tell them. Neither had any reason to trust me; I had been in Belgium for less than a month and neither of them knew anything about me.

The next day I called Laurent and told him that we were ready to deal at eleven twenty-five, and that we needed to talk about the quantity. I said we would need to see some samples before we went any further. He named a spot near the Grand-Place and told me to meet him there that night at nine o'clock.

As soon as he showed up I got in the car next to him. "For eleven twenty-five, we want five thousand," I told him.

"I can have them in two days," he said. Then he handed me an envelope. I opened it up—there were five bullets inside. I had never touched military-grade ammunition before. Although these bullets were different from anything I'd come across with Édouard, I knew enough to tell these were the real thing.

He asked me where we should meet to make the transaction. I proposed a place a kilometer or so from our house, and we drove there so I could show him the exact spot. It was about a hundred meters from a bus station, on a dark street; the area was normally deserted in the evenings. Laurent checked it out and agreed, and told me to call him in two days. Once he was sure he had the bullets, he would meet me there at midnight. I got out of the car and walked home.

Yasin was waiting for me when I got back to the house. I handed him the envelope and he opened it up. He just glanced at one of the bullets, or so it seemed to me. "Yes, this is what we want." He spoke with complete certainty.

I was impressed. Almost anyone who picked up a bullet would immediately look at the number on the casing to make sure it was the right kind. Yasin knew without looking. It suddenly dawned on me that Yasin was a pro.

I had learned how to distinguish between the pros and the bit players while I was selling hash in Morocco. There are at least a hundred different kinds of hash, but the real experts knew exactly what they were looking at without even touching it. They knew instinctively what grade it was, whether it was top quality or not. The amateurs, before they said anything, would pick it up and roll it in their hands, rip it open, smell it.

I learned something in that moment, something that maybe I had sensed before but hadn't really thought much about. I realized that Amin and Yasin were serious players, and that this was a serious business. They weren't like the young guys I knew in Morocco, who would try to prove what big men they were by talking about guns and *jihad* and pledging to join the fighting in Bosnia. Amin and Yasin were the real thing.

It was just a flash, and then it was gone.

Two days later I called Laurent and we arranged to meet that night. Yasin had prepared an envelope stuffed with francs. I didn't even look inside and try to count the money; I knew it was the full amount. I told him where the handover would take place, and then I left the house and walked towards the meeting point. I stood there for a few minutes in almost total darkness.

When Laurent arrived I got into his car, and we drove around for a couple of blocks and stopped in a deserted area. I took my cut from the envelope, handed him the rest of the money, and he counted it. Once he was satisfied he told me to look under my seat. There was a duffel bag there, and I pulled it out and opened it.

I had never seen anything like what I saw that night. When I was with Édouard we usually had just a handful of bullets, since we kept using the components over and over again. In front of me now were thousands of bullets, much bigger than any I had ever used with Édouard. There was only a meager light on in the car, but still the copper gleamed. It was thrilling.

I didn't need to count the bullets. I trusted Laurent, not because I thought he was a good guy, but because I knew that he wouldn't try to screw me. He knew that I could bring him valuable business in the future.

Laurent dropped me off at the bus stop and then quickly drove away. I began to walk back towards the house. The bag was incredibly heavy. Suddenly, a car pulled up in front of me. It was Yasin in his Volkswagen van. I hadn't expected to see him there, but I wasn't surprised either. I jumped in the van and showed him the bag. He opened it and looked inside. He smiled—a long, broad smile.

"*Masha'allah*," he said. "*Masha'allah*."

When we pulled up in front of the house, Yasin took the bag and immediately dashed inside. I was behind him, and as I walked towards the door I heard a sound. I turned around and saw another car driving up behind me. There were two men in the front seat; I had never seen either one of them before. But when they saw me they slowed down and stared at me for just an instant before driving off again. I realized then that Yasin had had me followed the entire time.

Uzis

The next morning Amin and Yasin were in the living room when I came down for breakfast. They were both smiling. Yasin stood up to greet me. "*Masha'allah,* brother." They had counted the bullets overnight and there were exactly five thousand. I could tell they were impressed.

I smiled back. "Where's my cut?" I asked.

Their faces went dark. I could see they were angry.

"Brother, you're not doing this for money," said Amin. His voice was low and slightly threatening. "You're doing this *fi sabil Allah,*" he said. In the path of God. "This is for the *umma.* Don't forget that."

I sneered at him. "Well then I'm not doing it anymore."

They were both surprised by my tone, and pulled back slightly. "I hope you'll reconsider that," Yasin said.

"I don't need to reconsider it," I replied. "Anyway, I can't get them for you at this price anymore. The dealer gave us that price just for the first time. From here on out they will cost eleven eighty."

I was lying, of course, and they knew it. But there was nothing they could do. Even at eleven eighty, the bullets were still more than a franc cheaper than the ones they were getting from Germany. And I wasn't losing anything by lying to them; they never quite trusted me as it was. I was nothing like Hakim: quiet, devout, pliable. Of course, I played along with them as much as I could. I performed the morning *salat* with them and was very careful to make sure I never had alcohol on my breath when I came home. I didn't go to mosque with them, but I told them it was because it would be dangerous for us to be seen together and that I attended a different mosque in the city center. But still, they knew I was different. I didn't talk about *jihad,* and sometimes when we talked about politics I'd challenge them. I don't think they knew what to make of me.

Over the next six weeks or so I would bring them three more deliveries from Laurent. At first, they just wanted more bullets: five thousand each time. Laurent and I always arranged it the same way. I'd call him on his mobile and tell him I needed to meet; we never discussed the orders over the phone. He would name a spot and I'd meet him there and tell him what I needed. A few days later I'd call him again and he would tell me when and where to meet him: a bus stop, a park, a forest. Yasin would drop me off somewhere nearby. Once Laurent and I made the exchange, he'd pick me up and drive me back to the house.

Each time I met with Laurent he'd tell me about other things he could get for me. He seemed to have everything. He was always offering me a new kind of sniper rifle or pistol, things I had never seen. I always said no, that all I wanted was the bullets. But I told Yasin about the other things and one day he pulled me aside. "Ask him if he can get us Uzis."

A few days later I met with Laurent and asked him. He smiled. "That's easy. How many do you want?"

"I don't know," I told him. "How much do they cost?"

They cost eleven thousand francs each. When I told Yasin, he said that was too high, that they needed ten Uzis but couldn't pay that much. I was taken aback; this wasn't what I had expected to hear. There was certainly no shortage of cash in the house. In fact, there was more and more of it as the weeks went by. Some of it was coming into the house, some of it was going out. Amin and Yasin would often count it in the living room in front of me. I had never seen so much money in my life.

Yasin was stubborn, though. He wasn't going to pay eleven thousand francs per Uzi. "Forget about the Uzis for now," he said. "Ask him if he has portable night scopes."

The next time I met Laurent I asked about the night scopes. He was surprised. "What about the Uzis?"

"Forget those," I said. "They're too expensive. We just want the scopes."

I could see it in Laurent's face: he was disappointed. And then I realized what Yasin's game was. Although he had never even met Laurent, Yasin was reeling him in and out like a fish on a line. "I can get you a good price on the scopes," he reassured me. "And maybe I can take the price down a bit on the Uzis as well."

We played the same game at every meeting. I would ask Laurent for something, Yasin would tell me it was too expensive, and then I would ask for something else instead. A few weeks later the price came down. I was able to buy all sorts of matériel this way: the night scopes, Uzis, Kalashnikovs, Dragunovs. I always marked them up a bit when I gave Yasin the price, but either he didn't notice or he didn't care. Laurent's price was always lower than anything Yasin could get across the border in Germany. Later, I would learn why: Laurent had a source in one of the largest Belgian arms manufacturers, someone who could get him anything he wanted. He had sources in other countries as well, but he didn't have to pay nearly as many runners as everyone else.

For months Laurent never asked me a thing. I'd bought tens of thousands of bullets from him and scores of guns without any questions at all. But one day, when we were sitting in his car making arrangements, he turned to me.

"What are you doing with all of this stuff?" he asked me calmly. Then he smiled just slightly, and raised his eyebrow. "Are you planning to start your own war?" There was no edge to the question; he spoke like a businessman. And that is what he was. He had no moral objections; I am quite sure of that. He just didn't want to get in trouble.

"You don't have to worry," I said. "We're not using any of this stuff in Belgium, or even in Europe. Everything leaves the country very quickly."

He nodded. "I understand. I do a lot of work with the FLNC, you know."

Laurent was referring to the Corsican National Liberation Front, a group of militants who wanted to throw off French control of the island. For years, they had been staging attacks on symbols of French colonial power—banks, police stations, military garrisons.

I could tell Laurent was trying to impress me by mentioning the FLNC, but I was also pretty sure that he was telling the truth.

I knew what I was doing, and it didn't bother me. For me this was a business. I was making good money, and the work was exciting. Of course, I knew where all these weapons were going. Most of them went to Algeria, some to other places as well. The operation was very simple. As the weeks went by, there were more and more people passing through the house. Young men, all of them. Men coming and going with cars—dropping cars off, picking them up. Sometimes, they would stay with us for a couple of nights and then I would never see them again.

As time went on, more and more of the men coming through the house were heading out for Chechnya. I envied them. I had started reading the newspaper a lot because we didn't have a television in our house. I spent hours on end at the Fnac, a giant news shop at the Place Rogier in downtown Brussels. I could sit on the floor and read for as long as I wanted. There I read the reports about the civil war in Chechnya.

I knew something about the war already; I had heard a bit about it during my last few months in Morocco. I knew in particular about Dzhokar Dudayev, who was leading the Chechen rebels against the Soviet Union. He was a hero to me; he had been a great fighter pilot earlier in his life. Russia was trying to push him out, even kill him. They wanted to crush the Chechen Muslims, just like they'd tried to crush the Muslims in Afghanistan.

Amin and Yasin talked a lot about Chechnya, and about other *jihad* around the world. Of course, they talked the most about Algeria. They wanted to overthrow the military regime, of course. But they wanted to see the FIS annihilated, because the FIS sought a political solution to Algeria's problems. For Amin and Yasin, politics were *taghut*. Islam was the only true law.

They talked about Bosnia also. I was eager to hear about Bosnia because I'd read so much about it and fantasized about going there. So I was very disturbed that Amin and Yasin seemed to disapprove of the Bosniaks, even though men were still coming through our house to fight alongside them. At times I wondered if Amin and Yasin had been there themselves, because they spoke so directly about what was happening there. They talked all the time about how the Bosniaks were not real Muslims. They said the women didn't wear headscarves and the men didn't go to mosque. That they drank alcohol and ate pigs. And that some of the Bosniaks had tried to kill the Arab brothers who had come to help them fight their *jihad* against the Serbs.

I didn't know what to make of all of this. I had always thought of Bosnia as something pure and holy. Now I wasn't so sure.

Amin and Yasin spoke about Afghanistan, too. Again they surprised me. I quickly learned that Hekmatyar was a great hero to them, just as he was to Hakim. But they hated the Taliban. I knew a bit about the Taliban because I'd seen reports about them on television, and I'd been reading about them at the Fnac. They were extremely devout, and I assumed that Amin and Yasin would approve of them just as they approved of Hekmatyar. But no, the Taliban were innovators, they said. Extremists. Not true Muslims. They were too zealous in the way they punished people, and did not follow the real law of Islam.

Amin and Yasin knew a great deal about Afghanistan because they had been in the training camps there. They almost never spoke about it, and I learned it almost by accident when they were joking one night at dinner. We had all eaten a huge meal, and when we were done Yasin leaned back in his chair with his hands on his belly.

"God forgive us," he said to Amin. "We're both getting fat."

Amin smiled and laughed. "Yes, we were both so thin in the camp," he said wistfully. Then he leaned back as well and put his hands on his small belly to show how fat he had become since, and Yasin and Hakim laughed, too.

When the laughter died down, Amin went on. "It's not easy to stay on the path of God when you live amongst infidels. We eat too much, we don't train. We grow weak."

The conversation seemed strange to me at the time. Both Amin and Yasin were exceptionally fit. They performed the *salat* and the *salat al-sunna* every day. To me they seemed incredibly disciplined. I was nothing like them. But I remembered what my brother had said in Morocco, that I had to go through many levels before I would be ready for *jihad*.

I knew that Hakim wanted this, too, but he was doing it in the wrong way. Compared to Amin and Yasin he seemed small somehow, a bit silly with his *siwak* and *djellaba*. I was beginning to realize that Amin and Yasin thought this, too. They were always nice to him, and happy to have him around. But I could tell they didn't really respect him. Of course, I never spoke to Hakim about any of this. In fact, I barely spoke to him at all.

No, I wasn't like Amin and Yasin. I didn't perform the *salat* five times a day. I smoked and drank—in secret, of course, since I couldn't let them know this about me. I also didn't see the world as divided between the pious and the infidels, and their harsh rhetoric often made me uncomfortable. But I admired them for their experience, for their discipline, and for the fire that burned in their love of God. He was my God, too.

Only one thing really bothered me about my new career: the Uzis. It made me sad to see all of them—Hakim, Yasin, Amin—prattle on about *umma* and *jihad* while they spent thousands on Israeli guns and Russian bullets.

This is the problem of modern Islam in a nutshell. We are totally dependent on the West—for our dishwashers, our clothes, our cars, our education, everything. It is humiliating, and every Muslim feels it. I felt it every time I thought about the Uzis. I was disappointed with Amin and Yasin for their hypocrisy, but even more disappointed in the Muslim world. Once we had accomplished so much—in science, mathematics, medicine, philosophy. For centuries we ran far ahead of the West. We were the most sophisticated civilization in the world. Now we are backward. We can't even fight our wars without our enemies' weapons.

Tarek

About four months after I arrived in Brussels, my life was turned upside down. One day, I came home in the afternoon to find the kitchen crammed full of boxes and luggage. I didn't understand what was happening, and I dashed upstairs to my bedroom. There was a huge Canon photocopier in the hallway I'd never seen before. And in my bedroom more luggage and boxes were scattered all over the place.

I ran back downstairs and found my mother. "*Maman*, what is happening? What is all of this stuff?"

"Some of Hakim's friends are coming to live with us for a while. Amin, Yasin, some others as well. They lost their apartment and they need a place to stay."

I couldn't believe my ears. But there was nothing I could do; it was my mother's house. I stormed out, slamming the door behind me.

When I came back home that afternoon, Hakim was there with Yasin, Amin, and two other men. They were all eating dinner. I sat down with the group and Hakim introduced the two new ones as Tarek and Kamal.

Tarek was by far the most striking man in the group; he looked nothing like the others. He was far more refined—elegant, European, and a bit older as well. In his late twenties, maybe. When he spoke everyone looked to him. He had tremendous charisma and took over the whole room. Kamal was much quieter. He barely spoke, but when he did I noticed his French was exquisite. But he spoke no Arabic—I had recognized this instantly from the way he mangled "*Salamu'alaykum*" when he first greeted me.

I said almost nothing during the meal, and left as soon as I had finished eating. I went up to my bedroom and lay down on my bed. Soon I heard the others come up the stairs; Tarek opened the door and came in. When he leaned down and started searching for something in one of the suitcases, I realized that he was my new roommate. I closed my eyes and pretended to be asleep. Eventually, I drifted off.

I woke up a couple of hours later. I heard noises in the room. When I opened my eyes, I saw Tarek reading his Ku'ran with a flashlight and praying quietly. I groaned and rolled over to face the wall. He woke me up again before dawn when he performed the dawn *salat*.

It was the same every night after that; I could never sleep for more than a few hours. Sometimes, Yasin and Amin would sleep in my bedroom as well, and all three of them would wake up during the night to read and pray.

I was tired. And I was furious.

During the day, Tarek and Kamal would use my bedroom as an office. Tarek was there most of every day, working on his laptop. There was a fax machine on the landing, and faxes were arriving hourly. One of the two men was always standing by the machine when the faxes came in, so I never saw what they were about or who they were from. The transmission confirmations were left lying around, though, and I'd look to see where the faxes were from. Every week on

Wednesday or Thursday a fax would arrive from London or Sweden, or occasionally from France. Tarek, Amin, and Yasin were always anticipating this fax, and talking about someone named Elias, who lived abroad. I had no idea who he was. From comments the others made, I got hints of all sorts of things: Elias had lived in France, he had lived in Sweden, he was married to a European woman. I knew only one thing for certain: Elias lived in London now.

Tarek always waited by the machine when he expected a fax from Elias. One day I waited, too, and then followed him back to the bedroom once he had taken it from the machine. "What are you doing?" I asked him, pretending just to be curious.

He looked up briefly; clearly he was in a rush. "I'm finishing *Al Ansar*."

I knew about *Al Ansar*, of course. I had been stuffing envelopes every week since I arrived in Belgium. I knew it was the newsletter of the GIA, and that the copies we sent out were going to addresses all over the world. Each copy we sent would be photocopied hundreds or even thousands of times to be distributed in mosques. I had also been reading more about *Al Ansar* in the newspapers at the Fnac. I knew from *Le Monde* and *Le Figaro* that the authorities considered it a terrorist publication, and that the police were trying to find out who was behind it.

From *Al Ansar* I learned more about what was happening in Algeria—the news of the civil war was coming straight from the front. Often it took a week or two for the European papers to catch up. The GIA was executing policemen and teachers and particularly members of rival opposition groups. They were targeting civilians, too; anyone who didn't accept their version of Islam. Also journalists, intellectuals, all foreigners—the list went on and on.

Tarek's job, I learned, was to pull together all the faxes from London and Sweden, and to translate everything from French into Arabic and Arabic into French; *Al Ansar* was published in both. He would add his own commentary as well. Kamal was always there to help him and was particularly good with the French translations. Tarek had a stamp that he would use on the final version before they photocopied it. It was a sketch of crossed Kalashnikovs, with a sword and a Ku'ran.

Sometimes, Tarek would talk about what he was writing or thinking about the GIA and Algeria. He blamed France for propping up the government in Algeria. He seemed to think the French were to blame for the civil war, that they were playing politics in the country to protect their oil interests. I disagreed with him. "Don't you think the Algerians are themselves at least partly to blame?" I asked him one day.

He was totally shocked, and asked me what I meant. I reminded him that Algeria, too, had sought a cozy relationship with France. Only a few months after Algeria proclaimed independence from France, Ben Bella, the first president of Algeria, had cut a deal allowing the French to continue their nuclear tests on Algerian soil—so long as they remained secret. Although I didn't say so to Tarek, the true scandal in my mind was not the way Western governments exploited the Muslim world. It was that the Muslim world went along with it.

Tarek barely listened to what I was telling him, and I knew I wasn't going to convince him of anything. I was exasperated. "If France is the problem," I finally asked, "then why aren't the GIA killing people there, instead of Algeria?"

"It isn't the right time now," he said without a pause. "But that time will come."

During this time I continued to buy weapons from Laurent. One day, I brought home bullets from one of our transactions. When I got back to the house Yasin told me to put the bullets in the attic. I was uncomfortable; I didn't mind buying the bullets, but I didn't want them staying in the house. But I agreed to do it.

When I got to my bedroom I pulled down the ladder that led to the crawl space above and hauled myself up, along with the bullets. It took a few seconds for my eyes to adjust to the darkness, but when they did I was shocked by what I saw. There were weapons everywhere: sniper rifles, Kalashnikovs, Uzis, bags and bags of ammunition. Some things I recognized because I'd bought them from Laurent; other things I'd never seen before. The attic was completely full—there were enough weapons for a small army.

When I came back down the ladder, I was reeling. I hadn't realized they'd been storing weapons here all along. I had assumed Yasin was taking them back to whatever safe house he and Amin were living in. I doubted even Hakim knew. He loved my mother as much as I did, and I don't think he would have put her at such risk. I couldn't believe *I* had put her at such risk.

It was becoming more and more clear to me that Tarek, Kamal, Amin, and Yasin were playing a very dangerous game. I wanted them out of the house.

Everything was accelerating. Yasin wanted bigger guns, greater quantities. More and more young men were passing through our house en route to the fronts. Often they would load their cars with weapons from the attic. More cars were coming and going every day.

Although my brother Nabil knew far less than I did, he, too, sensed trouble. One day Nabil came to me while the others were at mosque. He was more upset than I was. "What's going on? Do you think this is safe?" he asked. "What if the police come? They will arrest us all. They will arrest *Maman*."

He told me that he had a plan. He was going to push the photocopier down the stairs and destroy it so that the others would leave. Nabil was a big guy, and he could be very violent. I worried that he might actually do it.

"Don't be silly," I said. "That won't get you anywhere. It will just make them angry."

"What are we going to do, then?"

My mind was racing. He was my younger brother and it was my responsibility to take care of him and my mother. "I'll handle it," I promised.

Consulate

Actually I had no idea what I was going to do. I didn't know how to get Tarek and the others out of the house. I felt angry, and I felt trapped. And I felt like blowing off steam. And so I did the stupidest thing I've ever done in my life.

The morning after I spoke to Nabil, I stayed in bed when the others got up to go to mosque. I told them I felt sick. After they were gone, I jumped out of bed and opened Tarek's suitcase. Inside I found a passport and a picture of a woman I had never seen before. And lots of cash, in all sorts of different currencies.

I didn't take all the cash, just a little: twenty-five thousand francs. In the back of my mind I had the idea that if I took something from him, Tarek would understand that the house was no longer safe and he'd leave along with Amin and Yasin. But mostly I just wanted to get back at him. After all, I thought, he and the others couldn't really do anything to me—they needed me to buy their weapons. I was feeling cocky.

I stayed out all night that night. I had thousands of francs in my pocket, and I was happy to be away from all of them. The evening began with a long, expensive dinner at a restaurant on the Grand-Place and didn't end until the next morning. When I got back to the house, Nabil was waiting for me outside.

"Don't go inside," he said. He grabbed my arm and we started walking in the other direction. "They want to kill you. They know you took the money and they are talking about how to kill you."

"Kill me?" I was amazed. "They want to *kill* me? They talked about this in front of you?"

"Yes, of course. This is what they have to do. You're a *taghut* now—you're an enemy of the *mujahidin*. They have to kill you, it's the law."

"Hakim thinks this, too?"

"Of course. They all think it."

My mind was racing; I hadn't expected this. I had been working for them for months, stuffing their envelopes and feeding them guns for their soldiers. For twenty-five thousand francs I was suddenly *taghut*, an enemy of the *mujahidin*? It made me even angrier than I had been before. And I was angry at Hakim in particular for agreeing to this under my mother's roof.

This time, I knew instantly what I had to do. I felt it in my gut. "Nabil," I said, looking straight into his eyes. "I need you to do something for me." He nodded.

"I need you to stay home all day tomorrow. If I don't call you by noon, I need you to go up into the attic. There are two Kalashnikovs there and a bag of ammunition that didn't make it into the last shipment. I think that's all that's left. If I haven't called, I need you to take them out of the attic and put them in a bag. You need to carry them to the canal and throw them in. Do you understand me?"

Nabil looked frightened. "Yes, I understand. But what are you going to do?"

"I can't tell you," I said. "It will be better for you if you don't know."

I stayed at the house that night. No one said anything about the money at dinner, and I went to bed at the regular time. But I barely slept; Tarek, Amin, and Yasin were sleeping in my room and I wasn't sure what they would do.

In the strange space between waking and sleeping, I had a dream so vivid that I remember it even now as if it were yesterday. I was in the mountains with Hakim, walking through a valley. He was wearing a white *djellaba,* and he was almost luminescent against the black rocks. I was wearing my normal clothes—blue jeans, trainers—and I was complaining.

"Can we stop now?" I asked. "I'm tired. Can we stop here?"

"No, brother," he answered. "You are not there yet."

The next morning I got up very early and left the house. I was going to the French consulate. I knew the Belgian police wouldn't help me; to them I'd just be a terrorist and they would put me in jail. But the French cared more about the GIA because they knew they were a target. And the DGSE, France's external intelligence service, was well known for its ruthlessness. A few years earlier they had blown up the *Rainbow Warrior*, a Greenpeace ship, off the coast of New Zealand so the French could carry on with their nuclear testing in the South Pacific. I didn't think DGSE would have qualms about getting their hands dirty with someone like me.

I couldn't be sure of anything, of course. Maybe I would be arrested and put in jail. That's why I told Nabil to take the weapons. If the authorities raided the house, I wanted to make sure they didn't find anything. I didn't want my mother or Nabil to get in trouble along with the others.

I took the tram into the city center and walked towards the consulate. My stomach told me this was the right thing, the *only* thing, to do. And yet I felt awful and heavy with guilt. I thought about Hakim, about how as a child he had given me money for candy. I thought about the Uzis. I thought about the 1.6 billion Muslims around the world who felt humiliated by the failure of the Muslim world and the arrogance of the West. I thought about all these things because I felt them deeply, and knew that Hakim, Amin, Yasin, and Tarek all felt them deeply as well. So I didn't blame them for who they were, or for what they were doing. But I needed to protect my family and myself, and I had run out of options.

When I got to the consulate, I just stood on the steps and stared at the door for more than a minute. I was in a kind of trance. I knew that if I went inside my life would change forever. Images raced through my head: Tarek and the guns and Laurent and my mother and Amin and Yasin and Hakim in his glowing white *djellaba* and Nabil and the bullets and the *mujahidin* in Afghanistan and civilians in Algeria. My chest tightened and my eyes filled with tears as the images spun round and round.

And then in an instant it all fell away, and my head was clear. I opened the door and walked inside.

Gilles

Inside, I stopped at the reception desk. "I'd like to see somebody responsible for the territory and security of France," I said to the girl behind the desk.

"With regard to what matter?" she asked.

"I'm afraid I can't tell you," I said. "I'd like to see someone responsible for the territory and security of France. I have information. Do you have someone who fits the description, or should I leave?"

"No, please. Please sit down," she stammered. "I'll be back in a minute."

A few minutes later an elegant-looking man appeared. I could tell his suit was expensive. "Sir, you asked to see me?"

I nodded.

"Please follow me."

He led me into a large office and invited me to sit down on the sofa. I continued to stand. He seemed slightly surprised but then went on. "Please, what is it you would like to tell me?"

"I don't intend to tell you my story," I replied firmly. "I would like to speak to someone who is directly involved with the fight against the GIA. I have information which will be of great interest, but I want to speak to someone who is on the front lines."

He was clearly surprised and a bit angry as well. Certainly he didn't expect someone like me to place any demands on him. But then he relented. "Please go sit in the waiting room. I will be with you in a few minutes."

I left the office and sat down outside. Ten minutes later he opened the door and invited me back in. "Would it be possible for you to come back tomorrow morning at about ten a.m.?" he asked. "If it's not possible, please tell me right away."

"Yes," I agreed. "I can be here tomorrow."

"Good. When you get here, please sit in the waiting room. A man will approach you and give you directions. Then you will follow him. I can assure you that he is directly involved in the fight against the GIA."

I agreed to the plan and then left the consulate. When I got outside I immediately found a phone box and called my brother. "Don't do anything," I said. "Leave everything where it is for now."

I stayed at home again that night. I had collected my thoughts, and I realized there was no way they'd try to kill me in my mother's house. They needed it too much: for the weapons, for the young men passing through on their way to the front, for the equipment for the making of *Al Ansar*. If they were going to kill me, they would do it somewhere else.

The next morning I woke up early. Before I left the house I went into Nabil's room. "Today is like yesterday," I told him. "If you don't hear from me by one p.m., throw everything in the canal."

Nabil was clearly nervous. "Are you talking to the police?" he asked.

"No," I said. "I'm not talking to the police. It's something else, but I can't tell you what."

I was at the consulate by 9:56, and sat in the waiting area. At exactly 10:03, a man in a trench coat came out of an office and walked towards me. He was in his forties, and his face was in no way distinctive. I remember thinking that he looked like a schoolteacher.

"*Bonjour,*" he said, standing before me with his hand extended. "My name is Gilles." I shook his hand, and he continued without changing the expression on his face or the tone of his voice. "I am going to go out to the street now, and I want you to follow me in about three minutes. You'll see me on the corner. I'll start walking and I want you to follow me. Keep a good distance between us. I'll walk for about thirty minutes. After that I'll stop by the window of a store selling carpets. Please join me there, and we'll find somewhere to talk."

Gilles then turned and walked out of the building. I followed him soon after, and spotted him smoking a cigarette about fifty meters away. Then he turned right towards Passage 44 and I followed him. He turned several times, but mostly stayed on busy streets. There were lots of pedestrians and sometimes they would block my view, but I always found him again. I followed him for many blocks, though I always walked on the opposite side of the street from him.

After about half an hour I started getting tired—and angry. I knew he was trying to figure out if I was being followed, if I had brought men along with me. Every few blocks I saw the same car: a black Audi with a blond woman behind the wheel. I knew she was following me, keeping track of my every step. And there was another man in a beige trench coat whom I saw three times: once he was carrying a newspaper, once he was buying a snack on the street, once he was waiting at a bus stop. I'd spent years in Morocco watching out for undercover cops, and to me this just seemed like child's play.

Finally, after forty minutes, Gilles stopped in front of a carpet shop near the Place Rogier. I crossed the street and walked over to him, putting out my hand to greet him as he had told me to. He extended his hand as if to shake mine, but then reached behind me under the back of my overcoat and brushed his hand lightly against my back and my side.

"What are you doing?" I asked.

"I'm checking to see if you're carrying a weapon."

"Yeah, I know what you're doing, but why the hell do you think I'm carrying a gun?"

"Maybe you don't feel safe, I don't know."

"Do you think I'm so stupid that I would bring a gun to meet with an agent from the DGSE?"

At that Gilles smiled and pointed to the entrance of a hotel about forty meters away. We entered and headed straight for the elevator. Gilles told me that a second man would be sitting in on our conversation, but that I shouldn't worry about him.

We got off on the seventh floor and walked down the hallway. It was completely silent; it was a fancy hotel, with soft lighting and a thick carpet. At the end of the hallway Gilles stopped in front of a door and knocked. Seconds later a man opened it. He was young and very fit, obviously a bodyguard. He didn't say a word to either of us. He just sat down at a small table and fixed his gaze on the screen of his laptop.

The room was small. A table, a television, some chairs, not much else. Gilles and I both sat down. "So tell me," he said, leaning in towards me. "What is your story?"

"I've spent the last five months buying guns and ammunition for the GIA," I began. "But I stole money from them, and now they're trying to kill me."

"How do you know that it's the GIA you're working for?" he asked.

I reached into my pocket, pulled out a copy of *Al Ansar,* and showed it to him. "Do you know what this is?"

Gilles took the paper and studied it carefully. "Yes, we know about *Al Ansar,*" he said. "Where did you get this?"

"They're writing it and printing it in my house. I stuff the envelopes every week and send copies of it all over the world. These guys, the guys who write it, are the ones I'm working for. I've bought them hundreds of guns already, thousands and thousands of bullets."

Gilles didn't say anything, and his face remained almost expressionless. But he sat up slightly, and I could tell from his eyes that I had caught his attention. Even the bodyguard looked up from his laptop. "All right," Gilles said. "What do you want from us in exchange for your information?"

"I want you to protect my family. I want you to get these guys out of the house. I don't want my mother or my younger brother to get in any trouble because of what these other guys are doing. And I want you to give me a new identity—new life, a job, whatever. I need to get away from these guys before they kill me."

Gilles paused and studied me for a few seconds before reacting. "I can protect your family," he said, "but I can't give you everything you want. You haven't given us enough yet. If you want all these things you'll have to do more for us."

"How can I do more?" I asked. "I can't go back to them. I'm not kidding, these guys are ruthless. They'll kill me."

"Yes, you can go back." Gilles spoke slowly now. "Go back to the house and tell them that you'll return the money. Tell them all that you repent to God and that you want to return to Him. They'll have to accept you back once you say this. And then you'll win back their trust. Remember, they need you, too. They need the weapons you provide."

I was impressed. He used the French verb *repentir,* but I could tell from his language that he was referring to a specific Arabic term, *tubu lil-la,* which means "to implore the forgiveness of the Lord." I knew immediately that Gilles was a specialist in Islam, and that he knew the language of fundamentalism.

"But I took twenty-five thousand francs, and I don't have it anymore. I can't repay it."

"That's OK. I can get you the money, but it will take about a week. Go home tonight and tell them you will have it soon. Just make up some sort of excuse."

I learned a lot about Gilles in that exchange. I learned he had power within the DGSE, because he offered the money without asking anyone. I knew he would get it; he wouldn't tell me he'd come back with the twenty-five thousand francs if he couldn't do so.

I also learned that Gilles knew much more than he let on. He must have known other things to understand how valuable my information could be. And he didn't just want the information I could give the DGSE now. He wanted me to get them more information in the future. He wanted me to become a spy.

And so I became a spy for the French DGSE. After all, I was trapped. They knew who I was, they knew about my family, they knew where I lived. At least as a spy I would have some control over them. I didn't agree to it because I wanted to fight against the GIA. Later, that would come. But not during that first meeting. Really, all I wanted then was to protect myself and my family.

But first I had to take care of something else. "I need to make a phone call," I told Gilles.

"Who are you calling?"

"I can't tell you."

"We need to know," Gilles said in a firm voice.

I relented. "I have to call my brother. You see, I told him if I didn't call him by one he should throw all of the weapons in the canal."

Gilles raised his eyebrows. "Why did you tell him that?"

"Because I didn't know what you would do. You could have just arrested me, you know. And then you would have found all of this stuff in the house, and put me in jail along with the others."

Gilles smiled and laughed. "That was quick thinking."

Gilles and I would never trust each other completely—not even close. But the ice was breaking slightly. He walked with me to the phone box on the street, and I called my brother and told him not to do anything with the weapons. Then we went back up to the hotel room and he told the bodyguard to leave. Gilles wrote down a number on a piece of paper and handed it to me, and explained that I should use it when I needed to reach him. I should leave a message and tell him where I was and he would call me back right away.

Then Gilles reached into the pocket of his overcoat and pulled out an envelope. He handed it to me. "I'll get you the money for them next week," he said. "In the meantime, here's some for you."

I immediately pushed the envelope back towards him. "I don't want it," I said. "I don't want your money, I just asked for protection." I meant it. I was willing to get information for Gilles and the DGSE, but I would never let them control me. If I worked for them, it would have to be on my own terms.

Gilles looked at me strangely when I explained this. But then he spoke in a calm voice: "Don't worry. It's not a salary. I just think you should take this for the information you've given us so far. Look, I know you need money."

So I took it.

When I got home that afternoon, Hakim opened the door. I looked him straight in the eye. "Brother, I'm so sorry for what I did. I took the money and I deeply regret it. I've repented to God with all of my heart, and I've prayed to him that you and the other brothers will forgive me."

I felt awful. Hakim had done terrible things—he had even talked about killing me. But he was still my brother, and I hated lying to him. I hated the idea that I would be spying on him. But I had no choice.

"I'm ashamed of what I did," I went on. "I'll get the money back somehow. Just give me a few days. All I want is to return to God."

Hakim stared at me for a minute. I could see he was thinking very hard. I thought he was about to say something, but then he turned and walked back into the house and held the door behind him.

As I followed him in, I knew I had been forgiven. Whether or not Hakim believed me is another question, but it didn't matter. There was nothing else he could do. He knew Islamic law far better than I did, so he knew he couldn't question me when I said I wished to return to God. He wasn't allowed to speculate about my intentions. If I said I repented, then he had to take me at my word.

If I lied and sinned again, however, he could kill me.

Photos

A week later I met with Gilles again. I left a message at the number he'd given me, and he called back to name a meeting point. We went through the same routine as the first time: I followed about thirty meters behind him for over half an hour, and every few blocks I would see the same faces I had passed only minutes earlier. Like the first time, we ended up at a hotel near the Place Rogier, though not the same one as before. There was no third man in the room this time.

When we sat down, I told Gilles I knew I was being followed by his goons. "Don't be ridiculous," he said, laughing. I didn't pursue it, but I knew I was right. He went on: "I have some good news for you. I have the money. I want you to stay in the house and keep a low profile. Earn back their trust, and we will learn more later."

He gave me the twenty-five thousand francs, and we talked for a few more minutes before I left. Much later, Gilles told me that when he left that second meeting he had no idea if I was planning to give the money back to Tarek or keep it for myself. That really pissed me off.

As soon as I got home I handed the money to Hakim to give back to Tarek. I was no longer worried that they were going to try to kill me, but I knew they'd never trust me either. In fact, Amin and Yasin were staying there less and less, and I hadn't seen Tarek since the day I took the money.

Three days after I gave Hakim the money, I came downstairs to find him sitting at the kitchen table with Amin and Yasin. When I saw them I closed the door, trying to avoid them. Yasin had seen me, though, and he called me into the kitchen. I stood before him and Amin, hung my head, and repented to them as well.

They looked at me coldly for a few seconds, and then Amin spoke. "We forgive you and accept you back," he said. "The devil must have taken you over for a time, but we are glad you have decided to return to God."

Islamic law is one thing, but Amin and Yasin had another reason to forgive me as well: they needed the weapons. I had put in an order with Laurent for a number of Uzis a few days before I spoke to the DGSE, and now Yasin wanted the guns.

But of course our relationship was different now. They didn't trust me anymore. After a couple of weeks Tarek reappeared, and shortly after that the boxes and equipment started to leave the house. They even took the copier away. Clearly, they didn't feel safe with me around. They had found a new place to live.

Before they left, I took a couple of files from the boxes in the kitchen to show to Gilles. And I continued to take the confirmation slips from the fax machine as well. Amin and Yasin were always there when the faxes themselves came in. Amin and Yasin continued to come by as much as they had before they moved in. There were also lots of men still cycling in and out of the house on the way to the front. But Tarek came by only rarely, and I never saw Kamal.

I continued to place orders for Yasin with Laurent. I was buying many of the same things: bullets and sometimes guns, night-vision goggles. As time went on Yasin wanted a lot of electronic equipment as well: radio scanners, transmitters, and the like. Slowly things were returning to normal. Or at least to what they were like before Tarek moved in.

I met with Gilles every two weeks. We used the same system every time. I'd call the number he gave me, and he'd name a spot where I could find him. I'd follow him, and eventually we would meet up at a fancy hotel, usually somewhere near the Place Rogier. Each time, at the end, he'd give me about eight thousand francs, sometimes slightly more, for the information I'd given him. On this he was totally reliable. I never had to remind him or ask him for money.

He was less reliable in other ways, and it was rough at first. Gilles had the temperament of a dictator: he always wanted to be in control. He wanted to tell me what to do, what to say to Amin, Yasin, and Tarek. He was constantly pushing me to get into their "inner circle" and telling me how to do it. But I had the power—I had the information he needed—and I didn't like him ordering me around. I told him so, again and again, and I knew he was frustrated.

I was angry, too. I knew that if I let him he would take everything I had. I would cease to be an asset to him and become a liability. He would need to dispose of me, and he could put me in jail, or maybe something even worse. I wasn't going to let that happen.

And so over time we came to a kind of rough compromise. He didn't ask for specifics, generally. He would just say, "What's going on?" and I'd tell him what I'd seen. Sometimes I gave him things, like the fax confirmations, or the files from the kitchen. He seemed particularly interested in the files, which surprised me. After I took them, I'd looked inside and it was just a long list of addresses, some in France, some in Tunisia. It didn't seem particularly exciting to me, but Gilles seemed very pleased. He told me I'd done good work.

Gilles was very interested in *Al Ansar*. He wanted to know more about the stamp I'd seen Tarek use. He asked me if I'd seen anyone else use the stamp or another one like it, and I said no. He asked where we were sending the newsletters, and I told him that they were going all over the world. Not just Europe or Africa or the Middle East, but also the United States and Canada and Brazil and Argentina and Russia and South Africa and Australia—everywhere. Gilles took very careful notes on all of this, and I could tell he was concerned.

Mostly, though, Gilles and I would look at photographs. Thousands of photographs over the course of several months. He would lay batches down on the table and ask me who I recognized. At first, there were only a few I could identify: Amin, Yasin, Tarek, Hakim. But as time went on there were more: some of the men who came for dinner, others who came to pick up and drop off cars, and others who came through on the way to and from the fronts. Gilles seemed to know a lot about some of them already; he knew many of their names. Often he wanted something more from me: information about who talked to who, where each man was coming from and going to, what language they spoke, who was in charge. He wanted to know how the network functioned. My job was to fill in the gaps in the knowledge he already had.

The pictures were coming not just from Belgium. Many times he would show me photographs of some of the men I identified, particularly Tarek, in foreign countries. Pictures from France, Spain, Holland, England. I realized that each time I identified someone, the service would have that person followed.

From all this I gradually learned a bit more about the GIA. I learned that Amin was the head of political operations for the cell in Brussels. Yasin ran the military wing; he was in charge of acquiring the munitions and the logistics of getting them from place to place.

Sometimes, I also spoke to Gilles about politics. He never asked me what I thought about these things, but once in a while I told him anyway.

"You know you've already lost," I told him one day.

"Lost what?" he asked.

"Your battle against the terrorists. You've already lost your battle."

Gilles was curious and asked me why I said that. I told him that Muslims everywhere were rebelling against the dictators they lived under. In Tunisia, Morocco, Egypt, Algeria, and all over the Middle East, Muslims knew that their governments were being propped up by France, England, or the United States. It was bad enough to live under these repressive regimes, but far worse knowing that these regimes were just the playthings of Zionist and Christian nations. It enraged Muslims and made them hate the West. And it made them distrust democracy, because they saw how antidemocratic Western countries could be when it served their interests. There would always be violence, I told him, as long as Western powers continued to manipulate the Muslim world.

Gilles never said anything when I spoke to him about these things. He would just lean back in his chair and listen.

When something happened that was out of the ordinary, I would always tell Gilles. Gilles was particularly interested in Elias, the man in London with whom Tarek was in contact about *Al Ansar*. Gilles was always asking for more information about him, but since I'd never seen Elias all I could give Gilles were the confirmations from the fax machine.

So I was very interested when I overheard Yasin, Amin, and Hakim talking about Elias one day. And when Hakim asked me the next morning to go to the airport with him to pick someone up, I jumped at the opportunity.

At the airport we picked up a man carrying a small suitcase. He was young—in his early twenties. Hakim never introduced us, so even though I assumed the man was Elias I had no way of knowing.

We took him back to the house and then, a few hours later, drove him to a car park north of Brussels. Yasin and Amin had come along, and when we got to the car park everyone got out except me.

"Can I come with you?" I asked.

"No," said Amin. "You stay in the car."

So I watched them from the car. The four of them stood in a cluster for a few minutes, and then another man approached them. I didn't see where he'd come from. He was shorter than the man from the airport, and much older—in his late thirties, at least. His hair and his beard were both cut short. The others clearly looked up to him—even from the car, I could see that they treated him with great respect.

The five of them talked for a few minutes, and then the younger man handed the older one the suitcase. Soon everyone except the older man got back into the car. Then we drove the young man back to the airport and dropped him off for a flight to Stockholm.

When I told Gilles all this, he was very excited and wanted to know more about the older man, the one I had seen from the car. I couldn't tell him very much but I was able to describe him. Gilles was very excited. He smiled a lot and told me I had done great work.

Gilles was nearly as excited on another occasion, when I learned that Tarek had another name. I found this out by accident. One day, I was at the house at the same time Tarek was there picking up some faxes. He stayed for dinner. Nabil was there also, along with his friend Ali; the three of us were planning to go to the cinema that night.

After he finished eating, Nabil went upstairs to get his coat. When he was halfway up the stairs he shouted out Ali's name—he had some sort of question—and Ali looked up and answered. But I noticed that Tarek looked up also, and that he opened his mouth to say something. He caught himself, and immediately went silent. He put his head down and focused on eating and pretended nothing had happened.

The next time I saw Gilles I told him that Tarek responded to the name Ali. He smiled broadly and leaned back in his chair. "That's very good information," he said. "*Very* good."

After a couple of months working for Gilles, I got sick of all of the cloak-and-dagger bullshit. I had brought Gilles a lot of information, and he'd told me many times that I was doing a great job. So it annoyed me that no matter how many times we met, I still had to go through the same procedure as the first day. Every time, I would follow him all over Brussels for half an hour, even though we inevitably ended up at one of the hotels on the Place Rogier. Every time, I would notice at least one of his goons following me.

I confronted Gilles about this again and again. I told him I knew I was being followed and asked what the point was. Every time, he denied it. "Why would I have you followed?" he would ask.

Later, after almost a year with him, the whole thing became truly absurd. I was following him through a passage under the Place Rogier, past a spot where the same homeless man sold newspapers every day. I had walked by this spot hundreds of times, and I knew the homeless man; I had even bought his paper once or twice. The homeless man was old and frail, and his teeth were rotten and falling out of his mouth. But that day a different man was sitting in his place. This guy was middle-aged and a bit fat. His teeth were perfect.

When Gilles and I got up to the hotel room, I burst out laughing. "Come on," I said, "are you really going to tell me your guys aren't watching me? I saw that guy under the Place Rogier. That was ridiculous."

Finally, Gilles broke down. A quiet smile spread across his face. "OK, OK," he said with a laugh. "You're right. You've caught me. What can I say?"

Over the course of these months, Gilles and I spent hundreds of hours talking to each other. In fact I spent more time talking to him than to anyone else. We came to share small jokes and often I would find myself liking him. And I think sometimes he liked me, too. But then he'd do something nasty, just to show me he was in control. And I would fight back, to show him that he wasn't.

One day, he dumped a bunch of pictures on the table for me to look at. Looking down, I saw a picture of Nabil. "What the fuck is this?" I asked Gilles, holding the picture up in front of him. "You know exactly who this is. This is my brother Nabil. He has nothing to do with any of this."

Gilles shrugged and apologized, but a few weeks later the picture reappeared on the table. This time I was furious. "Take this picture away," I shouted. "I've told you this a hundred times. *Nabil is not involved in any of this.* I don't want to see this picture ever again." I was so angry I was shaking.

Gilles never showed me that picture again. But I never forgot this episode either. I had gone to the DGSE because I knew that they were ruthless, and so I knew Gilles must be ruthless, too. No matter how friendly we became, I always knew that he would throw me to the wolves, along with my brother and my mother, as soon as he had gotten everything he wanted from me.

Air France Flight 8969

On December 24, 1994, everything changed for me. That was the day four members of the GIA hijacked an Air France flight on the runway in Algiers.

Throughout the year, I had been reading a lot about the escalation of the civil war in Algeria. The GIA had taken over huge swaths of the countryside. They killed indiscriminately—women, children, even the cattle. They attacked secular schools and killed teachers and headmistresses, even students sometimes. I knew most of this from reading *Al Ansar*, which not only reported on the attacks but also justified them theologically. It claimed that these attacks on civilians were legitimate because these people were supporting the enemy regime—which meant only that they didn't support the GIA. All this made perfect sense, of course, to Amin, Yasin, and the others. But to me it all seemed very wrong.

Increasingly, the GIA was trying to draw France into the war. They were targeting French nationals in particular; earlier in the fall they had killed five employees of the French embassy.

Most of the people on the Air France flight were Muslims. The people who fly from Paris to Algiers and back again are mostly immigrants, going back to visit their families. But the GIA didn't care. They wanted to show the world that they were attacking France. It was nothing more than a symbol for them.

The hijacking began with a murder. The hijackers had smuggled Kalashnikovs onto the plane, and after a few hours they dumped the body of one of the passengers on the tarmac. He was an Algerian police officer. They had shot him in the head. The hijackers told the authorities they would kill more passengers if they weren't allowed to take off. But the Algerian authorities wouldn't let them, and soon the GIA killed another passenger and threw his body on the runway. This was all in the first few hours.

We had no television in the house. Television was *taghut*, of course. But events were unfolding so quickly that I couldn't keep pace by reading the newspapers at the Fnac. So I bought myself a small television and snuck it up to my room. I stayed glued to it throughout the ordeal.

A day after the hijacking began, the plane was still on the tarmac in Algiers. The army still wouldn't let the hijackers take off. Late at night on December 25, the hijackers shot a third passenger in the head and dumped him on the runway, as they had with the others.

It was very strange watching all this on television. For months, I had been reading all the horrible stories in *Al Ansar*, and sometimes in the French papers as well. Stories of beheadings, mass killings, car bombings. But seeing it on television was different. Seeing those bodies on the runway, imagining what was happening inside, I felt physically ill in a way I had never felt on the floor of the Fnac. I thought constantly about the people in the plane, how scared they must be. They had done nothing wrong. They were just visiting their families, and now they found themselves in this nightmare.

I was incredibly nervous as I watched everything unfold. Mostly, I stayed in my room watching television and praying they wouldn't kill any more people. But once I went downstairs to get some food, and found Amin, Yasin, Hakim, and Tarek in the living room. As they talked about the hijacking, they were very excited, happy. They were hoping for a massacre to grab the world's attention. This made me feel sicker still.

Three days after it began, the hijacking ended. The plane was allowed to take off and the hijackers were tricked into directing the pilots to land in Marseille, where the French raided the plane. There was an intense firefight. The French police and the hijackers were firing at each other in the plane with the passengers still on board. The hijackers used grenades, and many of the passengers were injured by shrapnel. One of the pilots was so desperate to escape that he jumped out a window onto the runway. When it was over, all the hijackers were dead, and many of the passengers were injured.

Later, I learned that the hijackers had carried huge supplies of dynamite onto the plane. They were planning to blow the plane up over Paris—a giant firebomb for all the world to see. And they probably would have pulled it off if they had known how to fly. Instead, they had to rely on the Air France pilots to do it for them. Years later, I found out Al Qaeda had learned from this mistake. Many of their recruits began to enroll in flight school.

The day after the hijacking ended we all ate supper together. The others were jubilant. And they were praying to follow in the footsteps of these brave *mujahidin*. "Please God, give us the strength that these brothers had. Please, make us *shahid* like them."

And then they told me something extraordinary. They told me that the hijackers were not dead, but alive and in heaven, in the arms of virgins who had been given to them as a reward for their martyrdom. I had never heard such a thing, and I couldn't believe it. I didn't know much about the Ku'ran at this stage, only what I had learned in school as a child and what Hakim had taught me in Morocco. But it didn't make sense that God would give such a prize to men who had killed innocent people.

Everything got much worse a day later. Amin and Yasin brought over a tape and we all listened to it together in the living room. It was a tape from inside the plane. It went on for more than two hours; we could hear everything. The voices of the negotiators asking the hijackers to bring the plane to the gate. The hijackers refusing and threatening to kill more passengers. The hijackers talking about fuel for the plane. And then running, passengers screaming, and the hijackers yelling about the *mujahidin*, how they would show the *al-taghut* French how the *mujahidin* were fighting in the fields of Algeria. "*Allahu akbar! Allahu akbar!*" And then the rat-tat-tat of gunfire.

It was horrible. Everything on the tape was horrible. I could only imagine how scared all the passengers must have been. They must have thought they would all die on that plane.

But for me the most horrible thing was that we had the tape at all. No one else had it; it wasn't on the television or anything. Someone with the GIA had recorded it with a scanner from somewhere at the airport in Algiers, or maybe Marseille. Someone who was working with the hijackers. Someone who knew Amin and Yasin.

It was the first time I truly felt how close I was to all this horror. I know I could have thought about it earlier, but I'd chosen not to. I bought the guns for Yasin because it was exciting, and because I needed the money. Often I fantasized the weapons were going off to Bosnia or Chechnya, that they were being used to fight legitimate wars against the enemies of Islam. Of course, I knew most of the stuff was going to Algeria, but that didn't bother me at the beginning. I had come to feel differently as I read more, and as the GIA became more vicious.

Everything was different now. The people on the plane were real to me: Arab immigrants living in Europe who loved their families and their land, and wanted to go home for holiday. The GIA had tried to kill them all. It was horrifying to me, and when I heard the tape I knew I was connected to it. I hadn't pulled the trigger, but maybe I had supplied the guns and the bullets. I was a killer, just like them.

Up to this point I had been eating from whichever hand fed me. Both hands, sometimes, since I was taking money from Gilles and still skimming my share off the deals I made with Laurent. But now I resolved to fight against the GIA with everything in me. These killings were wrong. I knew that as a human being and as a Muslim. Whether or not I went to mosque, whether or not I did the *salat* five times a day, I was a Muslim and I believed in God. These atrocities, the slaughter of innocents, this was not the Islam I knew. I could not look away anymore. Everything had changed.

Semtex

The next time I saw Gilles, I let him know how much the hijacking had upset me. I told him what I'd been reading about the GIA and that I couldn't understand why Hakim and the others didn't see what a perversion of Islam it represented. I said I wanted to play a real part in the fight against the GIA, that I wanted to do something more for the DGSE than the little jobs I'd been doing up to that point.

Gilles nodded and listened, but didn't say much of anything. Weeks later, though, he told me he believed me during that conversation, and that he saw something had really changed in me. But at the time, he seemed most interested in the tape Yasin and Amin had brought to the house. He wanted to know if I could get him a copy, but I couldn't because they'd already taken it away. He asked when we'd gotten the tape, and I told him we had it less than forty-eight hours after the hijacking ended. He seemed very surprised by that.

Gilles was even more surprised when I told him that a couple of days after the hijacking, Yasin had asked me to buy explosives from Laurent. Since I didn't know anything about explosives, I had asked Yasin what he needed, and he told me he wanted plastic explosives. I should find out what kinds Laurent could get us.

When I told Gilles about this, he seemed very tense. "You must meet with Laurent," he said. I told him that we already had a meeting scheduled in two days.

"Call me as soon as that meeting is over. I want to know exactly what he tells you."

Gilles knew more about Laurent than I did. He'd known about him even before we met. But with explosives we were entering a new territory, and I could tell Gilles was worried.

I didn't know if Laurent would have explosives or not. When I met with him, I brought up the subject carefully. "Laurent," I said. "I don't know if you deal this stuff at all, and if not you can just forget I asked. I want to buy some explosives."

Laurent was visibly surprised. "What do you want them for?"

"I can't tell you," I replied. But I knew what he meant. There are lots of different kinds of explosives. Maybe I was just looking for something to blow open a door or a bank vault. But maybe I wanted something much more powerful, to blow up an embassy or airplane. If that was the case, the explosives might eventually be traced back to him. He was smart enough to realize it wasn't worth destroying his life for a deal worth only a few thousand francs. Of course, Laurent wasn't going to admit to any of this, but I knew.

"Laurent, I give you my word," I continued. "None of it is going to stay in Europe." I looked him straight in the eyes when I said it and we held each other's gaze for a few seconds.

"All right," he finally said. "Let's go back to my house and we can talk about it."

This was something new. I hadn't been to Laurent's house before. We drove out of the city for about half an hour, on the highway towards Liège. When we turned off we were in the country. We drove for a few kilometers and then stopped next to a large villa with three satellite dishes on the roof. There were no other houses around. Laurent steered the car onto the gravel driveway and pulled around to the back of the house. I was stunned: there were ten other cars in the driveway. Ten beautiful black cars: six BMWs, a couple of Mercedes, a Jaguar, and a Porsche.

"Are you selling these cars?" I asked.

"No, they're mine."

I couldn't believe it. For months, Laurent had been driving me around in his cramped little Renault. His clothes were nothing special either: cheap, some of them clearly old. When I saw the cars, I realized that at some point Laurent had been very successful. But now he was on the way down. No major arms dealer would bother selling bullets in the small quantities we were ordering: two thousand, five thousand at a time.

We entered the house through a kind of foyer, and ahead there was a huge living room. From the minute I stepped in I could tell something wasn't right. The house smelled strange in a way I didn't recognize.

I looked around the living room. The furniture was expensive but unsophisticated. Everything was very modern but not in a way that suited such an elegant house. On the right side there was a huge television set, and a woman sitting on the couch in front of it. She was overweight, in her forties maybe. When she heard us come in, she raised her hand to say hello without looking up. She was smoking a crack pipe.

Laurent immediately walked over to the left side of the room, where there was a long table. On it sat a Bunsen burner. He sat down in front of it and got right to work. I tried to talk to him about the explosives but he was already completely distracted. For the first time since I had met him, he looked agitated. His hands were shaking. He had a glass tube in front of him with some liquid in it, which he began to heat over the flame. After a few minutes the liquid was gone, and he scraped the white residue out of the tube and put it in a pipe. I could tell it had been used a lot, because the edges of the bowl were blackened and cracked in places. Quickly, Laurent took a hit, inhaling deeply. He held the crack inside him for several seconds before finally exhaling. I could see his whole body relax.

Soon he stood up and asked me to follow him into the kitchen. He picked up a box from the floor and opened it. Inside were ten or fifteen Scorpions, Czech submachine guns. "Do you want to buy some of these?"

"I'll ask my boss," I said. "But for now I want to talk to you about explosives."

Laurent put the box down and shrugged. "All right," he said. "What color do you want?"

I had no idea what he was talking about. "Just tell me what you have," I said.

Laurent told me he could get me C1, C2, and maybe C3. I didn't know what any of this meant, but didn't want Laurent to know that. "OK," I said. "I'll have to check and see what they want. I'll let you know."

As soon as Laurent dropped me back in the city, I called Gilles from a pay phone and left a message. He called me back right away and I told him what had happened. He sounded anxious and said to call him as soon as I spoke to Yasin.

When I went home I told Yasin about my visit with Laurent. He wasn't interested in the Scorpions, and told me to find out if Laurent could get us a different kind of submachine gun, the TEC–9.

Yasin seemed very pleased to know that Laurent had access to explosives, and that he was ready to sell. "Next time ask him if he has any Semtex. Also find out if he can get us detonators."

I agreed to do it. But then something strange happened: Yasin asked me to show him where Laurent lived. I was surprised. I'd been buying from Laurent for nearly a year at this point, and he had never asked any questions about Laurent before. At the time I thought Yasin was nervous because he knew he was crossing a line. Weapons are one thing, but it is much more dangerous to traffic in explosives. Yasin had no way of knowing who Laurent was. Maybe he was a cop and the whole thing was a trap. Maybe he was going to have us all arrested as soon as he turned over the explosives. He could have been anyone.

A few weeks later I understood why Yasin was so interested in learning about Laurent. But at the time I just agreed to show him Laurent's house. I drove Amin and Yasin out there that afternoon. After that no one mentioned it again.

I called Gilles right away to tell him about the Semtex and the detonators. He was very much on edge. "Call me the instant you get any of this stuff," he said. "I'll need to see it."

When I met with Laurent I told him what we wanted. He inhaled sharply when I mentioned Semtex. "That's very hard to get," he said. "Why can't you use something else? I can get you dynamite. I can get you other kinds of plastics."

I told him we wanted Semtex specifically.

"I don't know if I can do it. I don't think so, but I'll try. The detonators will be easier." We arranged to meet again in three days.

Three days later, we met and drove out to his house again.

"I'm still not sure if I can get you Semtex," he said as we sat in his kitchen. "I can get you C3 right away, though. And here's your detonator." On the marble countertop in front of him he placed a narrow silver cylinder, four or five centimeters (about one and a half to two inches) long. I had never seen a detonator before and reached to pick it up to look at it more closely. Laurent lunged forward, grabbing my hand.

"No!" he cried. "Don't pick it up like that. You'll kill yourself, or at least blow your hand off." He explained that the detonator was very unstable. Just the heat from my hand could set it off. Laurent gave me a piece of paper and explained that I should keep the detonator wrapped in that. He named his price, and told me to let him know how many I wanted to order.

As soon as I left, I called Gilles. "I have the detonator," I told him as soon as he called back.

"OK, I'll be there in an hour." He told me where to meet him.

When I showed Gilles the detonator he knew immediately what to look for: a tiny number on the very top. He wrote it down, and then looked up at me. "Be very careful with this," he said. "Don't drop it or let it touch anything else. You could kill yourself. You were smart to put it in this piece of paper."

Then I went home and showed the detonator to Yasin. He picked it up very carefully between the tips of his fingers. After examining it for a few seconds, he nodded. "Good," he said. "How much does he want for them?"

I told him, and he whistled under his breath.

"That's too much. I'm sure I can get them from someone else for less. Tell him for now that we just want the TECs."

When I repeated the conversation to Gilles, he wasn't relieved at all. Both he and I knew that Yasin was playing his usual game to bring the price of the detonators down. This was just the beginning.

Audi

Everything was speeding up. Right around the time Yasin asked me to buy explosives from Laurent, Hakim asked me to do something even more unusual. We'd been running an errand in town, in a tiny Peugot I'd never seen before. On the way home Hakim pulled over to the side of the road and asked me to drive for a bit. This seemed strange to me but I went along with it. Once

I started driving, I immediately realized there was something wrong with the car. It kept lurching to the left and I had to use all my strength to keep it on a straight track. Soon Hakim asked me to pull over, and I did.

"What's this all about?" I asked.

"Brother, I need you to do me a favor."

"What kind of favor?"

Hakim paused, and then began to speak slowly. "There is a brother in Morocco, a very good friend of mine. I bought him a car as a favor, but he can't come to pick it up because he doesn't have a passport. So I'm hoping you'll be willing to drive the car to him."

I was stunned. "What are you talking about?" I demanded. "You know I don't even have a license."

"That's not a problem," Hakim said quickly. "There will be another brother with you. He has a license, and he can drive all the way to the port in Algeciras. You'll only have to drive yourself from the ferry dock in Tangier into the city center."

I could feel the blood rising to my face. I couldn't believe that Hakim thought I would buy his story about bringing a car to his friend as a gift.

"If you want me to do something for you," I growled at Hakim, "then you'd better tell me exactly what it is. I'm not going to take a car down to Morocco for you unless you tell me exactly what's inside. Don't try to fool me, Hakim. I'm not stupid."

My brother just stared at me and said nothing. I got out of the car and walked away.

Two nights later, Hakim came up to my room. "Come with me," he said. "I have to drop off some supplies with a friend of mine, and I want you to meet him."

There was something strange in the way he spoke, and I was curious. So I went with him to the car. We drove for about one kilometer and turned onto a residential street. We stopped in front of an apartment building and Hakim got out and opened the gate to an interior courtyard. Inside there were four garages. The light was on in one of them. We walked over and Hakim knocked on the window.

The door opened and we saw two men. One was clearly a mechanic; his jumpsuit was covered with sweat and oil. Towards the back of the garage there was a curtain, and behind it I could make out the rear bumper of a car.

The floor in front of us was covered with all sorts of supplies: piles and piles of currency, guns, radio transmitters. And what looked like bricks wrapped in white paper. It was obvious that the mechanic was taking apart the car to hide all this stuff inside.

Hakim spoke a few words to the two men and gave them a bag of groceries he had brought with him. Then we left.

On the way home he turned to me. "Will you do it?"

I didn't pause for a second. "Yes, I'll do it."

If I said no, Hakim would think that I had never really repented, that I had never come back to him and the others. But if I said yes, Hakim and the others would trust me again totally. Gilles had been telling me all along that he wanted me to get into their inner circle. I knew that this was my chance.

I saw Gilles the next day. I told him about Hakim's request, about the garage. He sat bolt upright as he asked me what I'd seen. When I told him about the bricks, he nodded and explained that it was probably Semtex.

"So are you going to do it?" Gilles asked. He was obviously nervous, but I knew that he wanted me to go. He wanted to find out how all of this worked. He wanted to get me into that inner circle.

"Yes," I said. "I already told him I would do it."

"You know this is very risky," he said. "We have no jurisdiction in Spain or Morocco. If you get arrested there, there's nothing we can do."

"I know," I said. "I don't plan to get arrested."

Gilles exhaled. "All right, then. Here's what I need you to do: I need you to tell me everything about the car. I need you to tell me when you are leaving. And I need you to call me every time you stop along the way and tell me where you are so that we can keep track of you."

Gilles was playing the bully again, and it pissed me off. I had offered to do something incredibly dangerous, and now he was trying to tell me how to do it. I wasn't going to let him. Not just because I was stubborn, although of course it was partly that. There was no way I was going to let him track me while I drove across France with a car filled with explosives. I didn't trust him; and if he wanted to he could just have the police pick me up and search the car. I'd spend the rest of my life in jail. If he tipped off the Moroccan police, it would be even worse.

"No way," I told him. "I'm not telling you where I am. I'll call you when I get there and the deal is done."

"If we don't know where you are," he said angrily, "we can't help you if you get in trouble."

"I'll take that risk."

At about three a.m. the next morning, Hakim took me back to the garage to pick up the car. The driver was already there, waiting for us. I had seen him around the house a few times before. His name was Jamal. He had a long beard, and he was very quiet. He seemed to spend most of his time reading the Ku'ran.

The car was ready. It was a green Audi. There was a trailer attached to the back and the back seat of the car was filled with all sorts of things: rugs, big boxes, electronics. We were supposed to look like a couple of immigrants traveling back to Morocco to see our families. Before we left, Hakim gave me a mobile phone number. He told me to use it when I got to Morocco to reach Yasin, who would give me instructions on finding my contact.

We headed out of Brussels towards Paris. Jamal was driving. We hadn't gotten far when we began to have car trouble. The engine temperature was rising, and Jamal was looking nervously at the gauge. About twenty kilometers past Lille we decided to stop and take a look. There was boiling water spilling out of the radiator. I had a water bottle in the car and I poured it in to cool the engine down.

We drove for a few more kilometers, and then the car started making a horrible noise. When I looked over at Jamal I could tell he was panicking; although he was silent I could see his mouth moving incredibly fast—he was praying.

I told Jamal to pull over to the side of the highway. I got out of the car and walked to the next exit, where I found a payphone in a small village and called Europ Assistance. What else could I do? We had to get the car off the road. I went back to the car and told Jamal what was happening; he looked almost sick with anxiety. He said nothing. He just kept praying.

Soon a tow truck arrived and the servicemen hooked the Audi up to it. Jamal and I sat in the Audi while the tow truck pulled us forward. We drove a few kilometers to a small village, and the driver unhooked the car in front of a repair shop.

It wasn't clear to me how we would be able to fix the car. There was something wrong with the engine, and I was pretty sure what it was: the mechanic in Brussels had stuffed every last centimeter with money and matériel. I figured he had put stuff at the bottom of the fluid tanks somehow, which would explain why the car kept overheating. But how could we get the car fixed without someone finding out what was inside?

When the man at the repair shop opened the hood, the engine was smoking. He began to look at everything, piece by piece. I had to watch him like a hawk to make sure he didn't find any of the contraband. He asked me several times if I would like to go inside the shop and sit down, but I told him no. Jamal stood next to me the entire time, praying silently.

It went on for what seemed like several hours. Finally, the mechanic looked up and closed the hood. He turned to me. "There's nothing I can do. The engine is completely dead. You'll need to have it replaced. I can get a tow truck for you tomorrow if you'd like, so you can take it back to Brussels."

We left the car there overnight, since we had nowhere else to put it. I practically had to tear Jamal away; I think he would have slept in the car if he could have. Then I called Hakim and told him what had happened. He was very upset, and told us to get back to Brussels as soon as possible so we could get the car fixed and get back on the road. I began to realize they were in a real hurry to get the car to Morocco.

Jamal and I stayed overnight in a hotel and spent the whole night fighting. I wanted to watch TV, which of course he considered *taghut*. He wanted to read his Ku'ran instead. Every time I turned on the television he would wait a few minutes, then grab the remote and turn it off. Then I would take the remote and turn it back on. I was so angry with him that I told him I'd drop him off in Brussels the next day and drive to Spain on my own. He said that the brothers would never let me do that since I didn't have a license. I told him that the brothers were stupid to let him come with me. Arab men have enough trouble with the cops in Europe, I said. His ridiculous beard made us an obvious target.

We both went to sleep angry that night. The next day we got up early and sat in the truck as it towed the car back to Brussels. We didn't speak a word to each other. When we got back to the garage, Hakim was there waiting to let us in. There was an engine already inside, and all they needed to do was switch it out with the dead one.

Hakim, Jamal, and I went back to the house that night and slept for only a few hours. When we left the house early the next morning, I noticed that Jamal had cut his beard. He hadn't shaved it off entirely, but it was short against his face. He was stubborn; he knew I was right about the beard, but he wasn't going to give in completely.

The car was ready by the time we got to the garage. We wasted no time getting back on the road.

The trip was a complete disaster. The mechanic had done the same thing to the new engine, and we had to be incredibly careful to keep it from overheating. We drove very slowly and stopped every half hour to pour water into the coolant tank. Jamal was panicked the whole time and drove without speaking. In addition to all the stops we made for the engine, he also pulled over five times a day to perform the *salat*. Each time, I smoked cigarettes instead. I could tell this made him very angry. That was the point.

The car broke down again in the south of France, and again we had to take it to a mechanic. It wasn't as bad as the first time, and he was able to fix it. Again, we both watched the entire process. We must have seemed crazy.

It broke down again just as we crossed the border into Spain, and then again as we drove up into the Pyrenees. Every time, I had to take care of everything. Jamal was totally useless, paralyzed. And every time I had to call home and tell Hakim that we had been delayed. He was getting more and more anxious. At one point, he even yelled and told me to hurry up, that I was destroying the mission by taking so long. I told him the only reason the trip was taking so long was that he and the others had hired a hare-brained mechanic.

It got a bit easier as we drove down out of the mountains. We were able to put the car in neutral and let it coast for kilometers at a time. But late that night, about seventy-five kilometers from Algeciras, the engine overheated again. We had to stop the car in the middle of the road. There was nothing I could do this time. The engine wouldn't start. I wasn't going to walk along the highway in the middle of the night, so I sat down by the side of the road and smoked a cigarette, and then another one. Jamal was so nervous that he couldn't sit down.

"What are we going to do?" he wailed. "What are we going to do?"

I was so sick of him at this point that I just ignored him and lit another cigarette. But when I looked up I saw a police car coming towards us. Jamal was beside himself.

"Where do we go?" he pleaded. "How can we get away from them?"

I told him not to worry. When the police got out of their car, I approached them first and spoke to them in Spanish. I was very friendly, and explained that we had engine trouble. They were friendly in return, and told me that I had to get the car off the road somehow.

"How?" I shrugged.

Then one of the cops smiled and said he could help. They drove the police car around to the Audi, took out some cables, and hooked the cars together. Jamal and I sat in the Audi as police towed us for about twenty-five kilometers. They dropped us in front of an auto repair shop in a small village. As the police drove off, they smiled and waved and wished us good luck.

This mechanic was into everything. It seemed like he spent an hour studying each piece of the engine. I had to tell him that I didn't have enough money to pay for any serious repairs. I just needed to get to the ferry. Just fix it so I can get the ferry. Jamal was standing beside me praying faster and faster. His hands were shaking.

At one point, I saw the mechanic reach down for the oil pan. I was afraid that there might be contraband tucked in there, so I told him I didn't want him to touch it. He looked at me like I was a lunatic.

We stayed up most of that night with the mechanic, but I didn't mind. I knew this nightmare would be over soon. It had taken us nearly a week to get here from Brussels, a drive that normally took only two or three days. But now we were only a couple of hours from the ferry.

Jamal and I left early and drove slowly, checking the engine every twenty minutes or so. As we reached the outskirts of Algeciras, he turned to me. "You should take the ferry to Ceuta," he said. "There will be less security there than in Tangier."

Of course, he was right. Ceuta was a Spanish outpost and the security was less stringent there as a result. But it was also a very small town, and much farther from Tangier. Even if I could get a tow truck in Ceuta, which I doubted, it would take hours to get the car from there to Tangiers. It hardly seemed worth it.

"I think I'll take my chances in Tangier," I said. "Given the shape this car is in, I don't have much of a choice."

Jamal kept pressing. "Really, I think you'll be better off in Ceuta." He said it three times over the course of ten minutes. I ignored him.

We got to the ferry dock around midday. There was a long line of cars inching slowly forward as the ferry was loading. Jamal steered the car around to join it. And then the car broke down again. The engine just stopped. He turned the ignition several times to try to restart it, but nothing happened. The car was dead. I looked over at him. He was staring straight ahead. He looked like he was going to cry.

"Jamal, just go," I said.

He looked at me, surprised.

"I'm less worried about security in Tangier than I am about your beard," I said. "You'll make us a target here. So just get out of the car and go."

"Really?" he asked. He looked relieved, but then a shadow passed over his face.

"Are you sure you don't want to take the ferry to Ceuta instead?"

"I'm sure," I snarled. "Just go."

Jamal looked like he was about to say something, but then stopped and shrugged. He took a roll of bills out of his pocket and handed it to me. It was the money for the ferry tickets and everything else. Hakim hadn't trusted me with it, so Jamal had been carrying it the whole time.

"May God be with you in Tangier, brother," he said. Then he opened the door and got out. When I turned around a couple of seconds later, he had already disappeared.

I sat in the car for a few minutes and lit another cigarette. It didn't take long for a policeman to come over to the car. "You need to move your car, sir. There are people in line waiting to get on the ferry and you're blocking them."

I looked up and smiled. "I'm so sorry," I said. "But the engine is dead. I can't move it."

"Then we'll have to get it towed."

"Onto the ferry?" I asked.

"No, to a shop. You'll have to get it fixed before you can get on the ferry."

"What if I push it on?"

He raised his eyebrow and looked over at the car. When I turned to look at it, I saw his point. Packed with rugs and boxes, the car was so heavy the chassis was nearly scraping the ground.

I looked around and tried to figure out how I could pull this off. I caught the eye of a Moroccan man standing by the entrance to the ferry. He was in civilian clothing, but he was standing with three other men and two of them had walkie-talkies attached to their belts. He had been watching me talk to the cop.

I looked up at the police officer. "Give me a minute. I'll get some people to help me push it."

I walked over to the men by the gate. I knew who these guys were; I had seen plenty like them during my years in Morocco. They were pretending to be customs officers or sailors or something, but they weren't doing anything. I knew they were physiognomists, trained to pick out suspicious faces from the crowds boarding the ferry.

I approached them with a smile and with my arms open to show how helpless I was. "Please excuse me," I said in French. "I am so sorry to bother you. But I am going to see my family and my car just broke down." I pointed back to it in the line. "I bought the car because I thought I could sell it in Morocco and make some money, but I've spent so much on repairs between here and Brussels that I don't have any left. I just need to get it on the ferry and my brother will meet me on the other side with a tow truck."

The men looked sympathetic. I knew I had them. I gave them my broadest smile.

"Is there any chance that you might be willing to help me push it onto the ferry?"

The men looked at each other, and one shrugged and turned back to me. "Sure, we can help."

Three of them came back with me to the Audi. It took a lot of effort, but eventually we were able to push the car—laden with explosives, guns, ammunition, and contraband currency—onto the ferry. I was laughing to myself the whole time. I had been tormented for years by the Moroccan police, and it seemed only fair that they were helping me now.

Once the car was on board, I headed up to the deck. I sat down and smoked a cigarette as the ferry pulled away from the dock. I ordered a whiskey, and then another one. I knew there were undercover police everywhere, watching everyone on board. I wanted to show them I was no extremist, just a normal guy going home to see his family.

But I also really needed a drink.

Tangier

When the ferry docked in Tangier, I waited for all the other cars to get off first. There was no way I was going to get the Audi off by myself, so I looked around the hull and saw the same group of men that had helped me in Algeciras. I went over to them and asked if they could help me again. They were cooler to me this time; they were back in Morocco now, where they had real power. But one of them offered to find some dockworkers, who helped me push the car down the ramp and off the boat.

When I got to the customs area, I was stunned. The whole place was crawling with police. The Moroccan police were carrying guns, and inspecting every car. Even the European tourists, who usually sailed through, were being stopped. The police were taking everything out of the cars, piece by piece. I saw one cop tell a British lady to take her baby out of the car seat. The baby started screaming, but the cop didn't care; he spent at least five minutes poking the seat and taking it apart before he handed it back to the mother.

At the time I didn't realize what was going on, but later I was able to put the pieces together. The Moroccan government, which had always been hostile to Islamic extremism, had gotten much tougher in the fall of 1994, when a group of Muslim extremists connected to the GIA had killed two tourists at a hotel in Marrakech. Now, after the hijacking, the government was in a state of high alert. They were desperately worried that the GIA and other extremist groups would spill over into Morocco. The government was doing everything in its power to seal the borders.

Hakim and the others had sent me straight into this powder keg with a car full of explosives. They knew exactly what was going on. The only one with even a flicker of guilt about it was Jamal, who had tried to send me to Ceuta instead.

I was livid, and I was also at a loss for what to do next. I had no protection here in Morocco; there was nothing Gilles could do for me if I was caught. If I told the authorities I was working for the DGSE, Gilles would have to deny it. If the police discovered what I was carrying in the car, they would torture me to extract the names of the people I worked for. And they would most likely kill me when they were done.

I had to think fast. I thought about the role I was playing: a tourist coming back to the country to visit some relatives. It was the end of the day, my car was busted, I was tired. All I wanted was to get to Tangier and see my family.

I began to unpack all the stuff from the car and lay it out on the pavement—the rugs, the electronics, the boxes. Soon enough, a customs official walked over. He was wearing a uniform with some marksmanship badges on the epaulets. He was clearly a high-ranking official.

"What are you doing?" he asked.

"I'm trying to help," I said. "I thought if I took everything out then it would go more quickly. I'm already the last one in line. I need to get a tow truck once I'm out of here, so I can get to my family."

"What's wrong with the car?" he asked.

I opened my hands wide and exhaled loudly in frustration. "It's dead. The car is dead. I bought it in Belgium thinking I could sell it here and make some money. But I've already spent all my money getting it repaired. I don't even know if I can get it fixed at this point. I may have to sell it for scrap."

The officer leaned in towards me and spoke quietly. "Son," he said, "if you have anything to hide, just give me two hundred *dirham* and I'll let you go through."

I looked into his eyes. I instinctively knew this was a test. With customs officers poring over everything in the cars around me, there was no way this guy
was going to let me get through for just a small bribe. So I played along.

"I just told you, I don't have any money! Now you want to charge me more
money just to get it through? Forget it. Just forget it." I had worked myself up
into a rage by this point. I kept going. "You know what? Why don't you just take
the car. Take everything in it. It would be a relief at this point. It would save me
a huge headache."

The official nodded at me and walked away. I had played my part better than
he had played his.

It still wasn't over. As the official walked away, a group of men approached: two
policemen, a soldier carrying a gun, and a uniformed customs official. There
was also another man, dressed like a civilian. He was younger than the others,
and carried a hammer and a screwdriver. He stepped forward and addressed
me: "*Assalamu'alaykum*." His face was incredibly serious.

"*Alaykum assalam*," I replied.

With that, he walked around to the front of the car and opened the hood. I
groaned in frustration. "Is that really necessary?" I asked. I was still pretending
to be angry about the car, and the delay. I gestured at all the stuff I'd taken out
and laid on the tarmac. "I've already taken everything out of the car for you to
look at. What else do you need to look for?"

He looked up. "Why do you ask? Do you have anything to hide?"

"What would I have to hide?" I asked.

"I don't know," he said with a fake smile. "Weapons, maybe?"

"Yeah, right. Come on, who do you think I am? James Bond?"

"No, of course not," he said with a wink. "But maybe you're a terrorist."

I laughed sarcastically. "I'm hardly a terrorist. I'm just a guy who got fucked
by a car dealer."

By that point, he was looking at the air filter, tapping it with his hammer to
get it open. I needed to get him away from the engine.

"Come on, brother, the car is already broken," I complained. "I've already
spent thousands of *dirham* getting that engine fixed and now you want to make
it even worse? Come on, give me a break."

The official looked up at me, then back down at the filter. He tapped it a few
more times just to show me he didn't care what I said, and closed the hood.
Then he came around to look inside the car. There was a book on the back seat

I'd been reading for a while, on the Muslim idea of the apocalypse. He picked it up. "What's this?" he asked.

"A book," I said. I hadn't meant to leave it on the back seat, but I wasn't worried that I had. After all, what kind of terrorist would be crazy enough to travel with a book about Islamic apocalyptic thought?

He looked it over on both sides. He was shaking his head, and his face was very serious. He looked me directly in the eyes. "Brother," he began, "do you really believe all of this?"

I grinned. "Are you kidding? You don't believe everything you read in the newspaper, do you?"

He smiled, threw the book in the car, and waved me towards the exit. "Get out of here," he said.

"I'm sorry but I can't," I told him. "The engine is dead. The car won't move."

He looked at me and then at the car again. And then at all my belongings out on the pavement. "All right," he said. "Put your things back in the car and these guys will help you push it through the gate." He gestured towards the policemen.

I gave him my biggest smile.

Once the police had helped me push the car through the gates and onto the shoulder of the road, I ran back to the first officer who had proposed the bribe.

"Look, brother, I know I didn't give you any money before, but could you help me now? I need someone to watch my car while I go find a tow truck. I'll give you a hundred *dirham*."

The official agreed, and I gave him half the cash. Then I ran down the street away from the port until I found a repair shop. I told the man there that I needed my car towed into the city. He agreed, and I hopped in the cab and we drove back to the Audi. The official was still standing there. I gave him the rest of the cash and he helped me hook the car onto the truck.

I couldn't help but smile to myself as we headed off on the road into Tangier. I was grateful to all these Moroccan officials who had helped me smuggle explosives and guns and ammunition and illegal cash into Morocco amidst the highest possible level of security. I couldn't have done it without them.

Hakim had instructed me to go straight to the house of Malika, one of my distant cousins, when I arrived in Tangier. He had arranged for me to stay with her. She had a fax machine, a couple of CB radios, and a videotape I needed to put in the car before I handed it over.

I'd met Malika only once, when we were both children, and since then I'd heard from my mother that she had married a junkie. When I arrived at her house, she helped me unpack everything from the car and trailer. Most of the things were for her, payment from Hakim for holding on to the electronics. Once I had unloaded everything, I found some boys playing in the street. I gave them each a few *dirham* and they helped me push the car around the corner to a garage.

Malika was still a lovely girl, very petite, with smooth skin and wide brown eyes. She was very sweet to me, and offered me food. I didn't know her, so I didn't feel comfortable asking about her personal life, and she didn't ask me about mine either.

When we finished eating, I asked about the electronics and she took me to a closet in the kitchen and showed me the radios. "Great," I said. "Where are the fax machine and video?"

She looked down at the floor and shrugged gently. "I don't have them."

I was confused. "Why not?"

She looked up at me but said nothing. Her eyes were wide and innocent but I could see they were clouding up with tears. When she spoke it was almost a whisper. "He pawned them for drug money."

This was terrible. "Do you know where the shop is?" I knew there was no time to waste, that Hakim and the others were in a real hurry for me to get rid of this car.

She shook her head. "I don't. But he'll be back tomorrow, and he can tell you himself."

Later that evening, I called the cell phone number Hakim had given me. Yasin answered. I told him I had made it into Morocco with the car, and he seemed very pleased. But he was frustrated that my contact was not in Tangier yet. He explained that he'd been held up at the Algerian border and would arrive the next day. I was relieved because it meant I had some time to get the stuff back from the pawnshop.

I didn't tell Yasin what had happened to the fax machine and the tape because I didn't want to get Malika in any trouble.

When I woke up the next morning, my boots were gone. I had taken them off before coming into the house and left them by the door. I was pissed off—they were expensive leather hiking boots.

I went into the living room. A man was sitting on the couch. His eyes were shot with red, and he was a mess. I could smell him from across the room.

"Have you seen my boots?" I asked him. He just smiled. I raised my voice. "Did you take my boots?" Still, he said nothing.

I had no time for this, so I gave up. "All right, forget it," I said. "Just get me some shoes to wear. You can keep the boots if you tell me who you gave that fax and the video to."

He shrugged and leaned back against the couch, smiling his nonsense smile. Then he gave me the name of the pawnshop, and gestured towards a pair of trainers on the floor. I put on the shoes and raced to the shop. I was there in five minutes. I took the owner by the arm and looked him straight in the eye. I told him I needed the fax and the video back. He knew immediately what I was referring to.

"I have the fax machine right here," he said, and pointed to a shelf.

"What about the video?" The man didn't say anything. "Look," I said, clenching his arm more tightly. "I know you have the video. Where is it?"

"Brother," he stuttered, "I don't have it."

"Where is it then?"

"It's not here."

"Where is it?" I demanded. "What did you do with it?"

The man looked frightened. I was holding his arm very tightly and my face was close to his. "I had the video," he stuttered. "I watched it. It was a great film; it made me so proud of what the brothers are doing in Algeria. So I gave it to a friend of mine to watch."

I couldn't believe my ears. It was incredibly dangerous to have any kind of propaganda film in Morocco at any time. But now there were police everywhere, on the lookout for any evidence of extremism. This guy must be incredibly stupid, I thought to myself.

I pulled him towards me. "You get me that tape. If you get it here in half an hour, I'll give you five hundred *dirham*. If you don't, then I'll turn you over to the police."

The man was panicked. He dashed out of the store. About twenty minutes later he came back with the tape. He bowed his head and apologized. I gave him the cash and walked out.

I sat down a few hundred meters from the shop and set the fax machine beside me. I held the tape in my hands. These tapes weren't easy to get. Even though the footage was taken in Algeria, the film had to be sent back to Europe to be edited and printed. And then smuggled back into Africa to go back into Algeria, where the tapes were used for propaganda and recruitment. It was a very dangerous trade.

I began to pull the black tape out from the spool—meters and meters of tape. I ripped it into small pieces.

I had no idea who had seen it. It could have been anyone. The police were scouring the country to root out Islamists, and they would always find people who were willing to talk. If anyone connected this tape to Malika, she would be thrown in jail. And so I had to destroy it. This tape was far too dangerous for all of us.

Cinema

The next day I called Yasin again. He told me the contact would arrive at eight that night, and asked me to pick a place to meet. I said I'd be in front of the Cinema Le Paris, chain-smoking. The contact could recognize me that way.

I arrived at the cinema at exactly eight o'clock. I was already slightly nervous because of the tape. The whole city seemed tense, too. Armed guards were prowling around in the streets. I'd spent so many years in Morocco running away from the police. When I'd left the year before, I thought I had put all of this behind me.

I stood in front of the cinema for over an hour, smoking cigarette after cigarette. No one approached me. I finished the whole pack. I didn't know what to do. My heart was racing. I began to think about the awful possibilities. Maybe this guy worked for the Moroccan secret service and he was checking me out. Or maybe Amin and Yasin had learned that I betrayed them, and were setting me up to get killed.

I couldn't keep waiting there. I was too nervous; it felt like every policeman who passed by was staring at me. I had to do something, so I found a phone box and called Yasin.

"What's going on?" I asked as soon as he came on the line. "No one showed up."

"He's there," said Yasin. "He walked by the cinema but he didn't see you."

"How hard is it?" I demanded. "I'm the only guy in front of the cinema chain-smoking."

"Just go back and wait. I'll call him and let him know you're there."

I bought another pack of cigarettes and took up my place again in front of the theater. I stood there for another forty-five minutes. Still no one. My hands were shaking. I was angry. I marched back to the phone box and called Yasin again.

"OK, just tell me what he looks like. I'll find him if he can't find me."

"I can't describe him," said Yasin. I knew why: he was worried that his phone was tapped and didn't want to give away the identity of his contact.

I didn't care. "I'll tell you what. Either you describe him to me, or I forget about the whole deal. He'll never get the car."

"I can't give it to you. You know I can't give it to you."

"Then I'll keep the car."

Finally, Yasin relented. He knew I was stubborn enough to do it, to keep the car.

"OK, fine. He's short, about 165 centimeters. Balding. He has a white beard."

I hung up the phone and walked back towards the theater. About 150 meters away from the entrance, I saw a man who fit the description Yasin had just given me. When I got closer I realized what the problem was: this man had no idea what he was doing. He was an old man, in his late sixties. From his *djellaba* I could tell that he was Moroccan. He was just standing there on the sidewalk, looking around aimlessly. He didn't have a clue.

I walked up to him and wrapped my arms around him and kissed him on both cheeks. "I am so happy to see you!" I said. "I'm so sorry I didn't find you earlier! I was looking and looking . . . "

The man stared at me, confused. I grabbed him by the arm and made him walk with me. The whole time I spoke to him loudly. "How are the children?" Then, in a softer voice: "I have a present for you. I brought it from Belgium. Do you know who sent it?"

I turned to look at him, and he looked back at me. He seemed nervous.

"Amin and Yasin?" he said. His voice trembled slightly.

I nodded. After that, we walked for a few more minutes. I kept talking, like we were old friends out for a walk.

Eventually, he turned to me. "So where is it?" he asked.

"Don't worry," I said. "It's in a safe place. We'll get it tomorrow, after we go register the car and pay the tax."

The man stopped in his tracks and looked at me. "No, brother, we don't need to do that."

"Of course we need to do it," I said. The car was registered in Morocco in my name. When any foreign car came into the country, the customs officials noted it in their database. The only way to erase my name from the system was to sell it to someone else. If I didn't, then I would be held responsible for what happened to the car and anything in it. And I was much more likely to be checked at the border leaving Morocco as well, since they would probably stop me to find out what I'd done with the car I brought in.

I explained all this to the old man, and he tried to reassure me. "Don't worry, brother. We have a man at the border. He's already taken the record out of the computer. Nothing will happen to you."

I didn't believe him. I didn't trust Amin and Yasin. They hadn't given me any warning about how tight the security was in Morocco, and clearly they weren't worried about what happened to me now that I was here. As I thought about it, I realized that it would be very convenient for them if I never went back to Belgium. They had what they needed from me: they knew where Laurent lived, and could easily start dealing with him directly. And they had never really trusted me. Particularly now, after I'd been talking about Semtex and detonators with them, it might just be easier to get me out of the way.

I stared at the old man. "Why the hell should I trust you?" I demanded. "You were standing on the square for hours looking for me. Look, I'm not kidding. Without that paper, I'm not giving you the car."

He looked scared. "I don't know what to say. You'll have to talk to the brothers."

I left him standing there and went over to a phone box to call Yasin. When he came on the line I repeated the ultimatum I had given to his contact. No papers, no car. Yasin tried to convince me that I shouldn't worry, that I should listen to the old man. There was a guy at the border taking care of it. He reminded me that we were in a hurry, that we had already lost too much time.

I wasn't buying any of it. I stood firm. "I'm serious. Either he pays the tax and registers the car, or I'm not giving it to him."

Once again, Yasin was stuck. After a long pause, he spoke. "OK," he said. "We'll see what we can do. Call back tomorrow morning."

When I spoke to Yasin the next morning, he sounded miserable. "We've done what you asked," he said. "He has the money, he'll go get the papers for you. You can give him the car."

I had never heard Yasin speak in this tone of voice. He sounded sad, resigned.

"You know," he went on, "we're practically giving this man up for dead." Yasin was right, of course. Clearly, this guy wasn't exactly a GIA soldier; he was just a runner. He wasn't going to be doing anything with the car or the stuff inside it. But if he put his name on the papers, he'd be responsible for anything that happened to the car even after he relinquished it. I understood the situation all too well: the old man had signed on for nothing more than a quick exchange. He never intended to enlist himself in the war.

Yasin kept pressing. Obviously the old man was very important to him. "He's risking his life to do this, you know. Probably his family, too. Not to mention the whole supply chain."

I was fed up—I hadn't enlisted in their war either. "Look, it's not my problem. Just get me the papers." Then I hung up.

I met with the old man later that day. When I asked him if he had the money, he nodded. "Yes, I have the money." He spoke like a dead man. His eyes were completely blank; he just stared ahead. "Let's go pay the tax and sort out the papers."

My heart sank as I looked at him. I thought about what his family might look like, how they would suffer if he was taken away from them. I thought about the police in Morocco, how they tortured and executed radicals and subversives. I admired the old man. He was willing to go put the papers in his name, no matter what the cost. He believed in what he was doing.

I put my hand gently on his shoulder. "Brother, forget it," I said. "Don't worry about the papers." I just couldn't go through with it. I just couldn't do it to this sweet old man. I took out the rest of the cash and gave that to him as well.

He stared at me in disbelief. I think he was waiting for me to take back everything I'd said. When I didn't, his eyes widened and a smile spread across his face. I smiled back at him.

I walked him to the street where I'd left the car. Earlier that morning, I'd pushed it out of the garage with the help of some neighborhood boys. I didn't want the old man or anyone he was with to know anything about me or my cousin. I explained that the car's engine was dead and he would have to find a mechanic. He nodded; it was clear he knew about this already. When we stood in front of the car, I handed over the keys.

"*Assalamu'alaykum*," I said.

"*Alaykum assalam.*" He bowed his head slightly.

I walked a few blocks and sat down in a café to smoke a cigarette and relax. But I kept thinking about the old man. I wanted to make sure he'd been able to move the car safely. So I went back to the spot where I'd left him only a few minutes earlier. By the time I got there, the car was already gone.

I left a message for Gilles right away to let him know I had handed over the car. He called back immediately and asked when I'd be returning to Belgium. I said it might take a few weeks, since I had to get a visa to get back into the country. He told me to get back as soon as I could.

Then I called Yasin, who sounded very happy and proud of me. "*Masha'allah, masha'allah*," he said. Then he thanked me for letting the old man go without making him sign for the car.

I told him that since I had given all my money to the old man, I would need more to get my ticket home. Yasin said he'd get it to me soon, within a couple of weeks. I used the time to gather my papers and apply for a driver's license. I had a contact in the consulate, an old friend of my father's, who was able to help me with the visa.

I called Yasin back after two weeks. He said he still didn't have the money, that I should stay in Tangier and wait. I knew he was lying, of course. I had spent a year with these guys; I knew how much money they had lying around. I knew then that I was right—they didn't want me to come back to Belgium.

Two things happened at the end of January. I got my first driver's license. And the GIA set off a car bomb in downtown Algiers. The streets were filled with people preparing for Ramadan, which began a day later. At least forty were killed, and hundreds injured, many of them women and children.

I don't know if the explosives I carried were used in that blast. I will never know. The GIA had lots of suppliers, of course. And yet I kept thinking about the urgency of the trip. The way Hakim yelled at me, and the frustration in Yasin's voice when I threatened to keep the car. The speed with which the mechanic replaced the engine in Brussels. Was everything timed for this attack?

I will never know the truth, but the question still haunts me.

Thierry

By the middle of February Yasin still hadn't sent the money. I wanted desperately to get out of Morocco, so I called Gilles. This time I didn't have to leave a message; he picked up the phone himself. He sounded relieved to hear from me, and anxious. "Where are you?" he asked. "When are you coming back?"

"I'm still in Morocco. I have no money. Yasin keeps promising to send it, but it hasn't come."

Gilles told me he would get me the money right away. "Come back as soon as you can," he said.

The money came the next day. Two thousand dollars by wire transfer. It was far more money than Gilles had ever given me.

It took another week or so to finalize my visa. Then I bought my bus ticket to Belgium.

The sun was setting when I got to the port. The sea and the sky were bright with red and pink. When my eyes adjusted and I looked at the line of cars and people waiting to board, I was amazed. The security was even tighter than the month before when I had come into the country. There were police everywhere, and every few meters there were soldiers standing poised with rifles and MP5 submachine guns. They're looking for me, I thought. They've connected me to the car bomb in Algiers and now they're looking for me.

The bus had dropped me off at the entrance to the ferry boarding, but it was nearly a two-kilometer walk to customs and passport control. I walked neither quickly nor slowly, and focused my eyes straight ahead. I kept a calm face, but my heart was thundering inside my chest. I could feel my lips moving in prayer, just like Jamal or Hakim.

The sun was so low and bright that it pierced my eyes. It reflected off the rooftops of the cars, casting gold in every direction. I felt dizzy. My mind was racing. Over and over, I prayed the police would not pull me over and arrest me. I knew what I had done. I knew the police in Morocco. I knew what would happen to me.

Keep walking, I told myself. Walk straight. Don't look right, don't look left. Just walk straight ahead. I focused on the sound of my feet, and squinted to keep all the gold around me out of my head. Walk straight. Keep walking.

But as I approached passport control, my heart slowed down. I became almost resigned. I knew that if they arrested me they would find out about the car and everything in it. That they would torture me until I gave them every name I knew. That my life was over.

And then I felt relieved. It was the will of God. I was in His hands now. I would give myself over to Him.

I stopped in front of the kiosk and gave my passport to the official. I was calm, and gave him a little smile. He glanced at me, and then looked down at my passport. I studied him. He had dark skin and just a bit of stubble on his face. A bushy mustache covered his upper lip.

He looked up.

"Why are you going to Belgium?" he asked.

My voice was calm. "My mother lives there. I'm going to visit her."

He nodded and looked down again. Then he stamped my passport and handed it back to me. "Have a nice trip."

I was weak by the time I got back to Brussels; I could feel a cold coming on. I called Gilles as soon as I got off the bus. Again he picked up the phone directly; there was no answering machine. I told him that I was back, that I was OK. I could tell he was pleased. He told me to get some sleep, that we would meet the next morning.

I called home after that, and Hakim came to pick me up. He smiled when he saw me. "*Masha'allah*," he said. "*Masha'allah*. I am so proud of you." Never in my life had he spoken like this to me.

When I got home, Amin and Yasin were there eating supper. They both stood up to greet me. They, too, were smiling. "*Masha'allah, masha'allah, masha'allah.*"

Everyone was in a good mood. I sat down to eat, and we talked about all sorts of things, about the trip, about what had happened while I was away. They were more open with me than ever before.

As dinner was ending, Amin looked straight at me and said, "You know everyone in Algeria is talking about this. No one can believe that you were able to do it. I can't believe it."

"Why not?" I asked.

"The border is so tight. It is nearly impossible to get anything through. Nobody else would even try." He paused. "I don't think even I could have done it."

I stared him in the eye. "Then why did you send me?" I smiled as I said it, but the anger in my voice was unmistakable.

He held my eyes and spoke slowly. "Because I knew you were the only one who could pull it off."

We held each other's gaze for what seemed like several minutes. Finally, Yasin broke the silence when he turned to me and said, "I need you to call Laurent tomorrow. We'd like to buy some detonators."

When I met with Gilles the next day, I knew from the outset that something was different. We met as we always did, and I followed him. But instead of going towards the Place Rogier as we usually did, we headed in another direction. We passed the Botanical Garden and ended up at a hotel near the Place Madou. The hotel was different also: cheap, run down. Not at all like the fancy hotels where we'd met before.

Gilles didn't explain anything, and I didn't ask. We picked up the conversation where we had left off before I went to Morocco. I told him Yasin was looking for Semtex and detonators again. He looked startled.

"Do you think they are planning any attacks within Europe?" he asked. "Have Amin and the others said anything of that sort?"

I hadn't heard anything like this, and I told Gilles so. Then he asked me a lot of questions about Morocco. Where I left the car, how I met the contact. He particularly wanted to know who the contact was, but I wouldn't tell him. I had taken a huge risk to protect the old man, and I wasn't going to betray him now.

"Can you tell me what he looked like?" he asked.

"I don't remember."

"How can you not remember what he looked like? You really can't tell me anything about him?"

"He was shorter than me, maybe 170 centimeters," I said. "Old."

Gilles didn't say anything. He never said anything when I refused to give him what he wanted. He just stared at me, his face impassive.

When I got up to leave he told me we had to meet again the next day, late in the afternoon. He would wait by the American consulate.

When I woke up the next morning, I was feeling worse. My head was clogged and my limbs felt heavy. But I went to the American consulate in the afternoon as I had agreed. I followed Gilles for a long time, longer than usual. We walked for nearly an hour, all the way to the Porte de Namur. I was so sick that it felt three times as long.

At one point, I leaned down in front of a shop to tie my shoe. I didn't need to; my shoe was laced properly. When I looked in the plate-glass window, I saw a man walking a few meters behind me. I recognized him. As soon as he saw me leaning over, he pulled his newspaper in front of his face and kept walking. I laughed to myself.

When I finally met up with Gilles in front of a hotel, I spoke to him under my breath.

"You know, Gilles," I said. "I think we're being followed."

He looked up at me. "Really?"

"Yes, I think so."

Gilles said nothing about it, and quickly changed the subject. "We will be meeting a friend of mine today," he told me. "He is from here, from Brussels. You don't have to worry about anything. He's a friend. We're just going to talk to him a bit."

I nodded and then he guided me down the street. There were lots of pedestrians all around, but about fifty meters away I saw the man who had been following me.

I turned to Gilles and directed his attention toward the man with the newspaper. "Is that your friend by any chance?"

He was surprised. "How did you know that? Do you recognize him?"

I suppressed a laugh. "No, of course not. I just guessed. I've never seen him before."

Of course, I had seen him before. He had followed me the first time I met Gilles. I thought he was just one of Gilles's spooks.

All three of us got into a car parked nearby, and Gilles introduced the man as Thierry. Thierry seemed excited to be meeting me, and I could tell that Gilles was proud to introduce us. He was smiling and sat up a bit taller than normal.

We drove far out from the city center and sat down in an empty café. Thierry took some photographs out of his bag and spread them out on the table. There weren't that many, and I had seen all the faces before. Mostly they were pictures of Amin, Yasin, Hakim, and Tarek, but also some of the other men I had seen coming and going from the house. There was also one picture of me with Nabil. I turned to Gilles. "What the hell is this?" I asked angrily. "We've talked about this. This is Nabil. He has nothing to do with it."

Gilles sat up straight. "Oh no, of course not. That picture shouldn't be here." He shook his finger gently at Thierry and told him to get rid of it.

Thierry asked me a lot of questions. Do you know this guy? Do you know that guy? Where did this guy take the car? Where did that guy come from? I had answered all these questions before with Gilles, but he wasn't saying anything.

Suddenly, I understood what was happening, and I interrupted Thierry. "You're planning to arrest them, aren't you?"

Thierry and Gilles glanced at each other and then Thierry spoke. "No, that's not what we're planning to do."

But I knew it was. I understood that Gilles had been working with Thierry from the beginning, and that Thierry worked for the *Sûreté de l'État*, the Belgian secret service. I knew Thierry had to confirm everything before they could proceed.

I was furious. I had just risked everything for Gilles, for the DGSE. I'd put my life on the line to help them stamp out these terrorists. It was quite likely I had committed a horrible crime. And now they were going to blow the whole thing by acting prematurely.

"I don't believe you," I said. "You are going to arrest them." Gilles said nothing, but he looked straight at me.

"You're making a big mistake," I said. "They finally trust me again. They're talking to me. We could go a lot further if you gave me more time."

I was pleading with him at this point, pleading with him to let me continue with my work, the one thing that gave my life any meaning. Gilles finally broke his silence. "Don't worry," he said with a tight smile. "We're not planning to arrest anyone anytime soon."

I didn't know what to think. I didn't believe that I could trust him. I asked for only one thing. "When you do plan to make arrests," I said, "promise me that you'll tell me in advance."

Gilles nodded, and spoke slowly, soothingly. He smiled at me.

"Of course I will."

Fever

I went to bed early that night. My cold had gotten worse and I had a terrible headache. I felt slightly better when I woke up the next morning, so I took a bus into the city center just to look around. It was wonderful to be back in Belgium after all those weeks in Morocco. It was the last day of Ramadan, and I was looking forward to the *Id al-Fitra* the next day. We would have a feast.

I kept going over in my mind the conversation with Gilles of the day before. I was almost certain that Gilles had lied to me, that the raids were coming. I thought about Thierry's picture of me and Nabil. Were we targets, too? Would they throw us in jail along with the others? I knew the DGSE was capable of anything. If they were willing to blow up a Greenpeace ship, they wouldn't have any qualms about destroying someone like me.

By early afternoon I started to feel sick again, worse than before. The cold had gotten through my jacket and I was shivering. I got on the bus to go home, and when I sat down I felt even more terrible. The headache had come back, and there was a ringing in my ears. I felt weak. When I got off the bus and started to walk home, my legs felt heavy.

Hakim, Amin, and Yasin were getting in the car when I reached the house.

"Where are you going?" I asked.

"Just running some errands," said Yasin.

"Wait," I said. "I want to talk to you before you go." I could hear the words come out of my mouth, but I didn't know where they came from. My head was heavy with congestion, my ears were ringing, and it felt like my mouth was moving on its own.

Yasin gestured for me to get in the back seat with Hakim. Amin was driving, and Yasin sat in the passenger's seat. They all looked at me expectantly.

"Please drive," I said. "I don't want to talk here. What I have to tell you, it's important. Just drive."

Amin and Yasin glanced at each other briefly, and then turned around. Amin started the engine. We drove for about fifteen minutes before we parked in an empty industrial area. Amin turned off the ignition, but continued to stare forward.

My ears were still ringing, louder and louder. I was beginning to sweat; I knew I had a fever. And then words came spilling out of my mouth: "I have been working with the DGSE."

Silence.

I looked over at Hakim, sitting next to me. His eyes were wide, and his lips began to move very fast. Amin and Yasin stared forward. I could only see the backs of their heads. "Since when?" asked Amin.

It was becoming real to me, what I had just said. The fog in my head was lifting just slightly, and I could feel my chest tighten. "For a while," I answered. "A few months."

Nobody moved. They seemed completely paralyzed. Yasin spoke next. "Did you tell them about Morocco?"

"Yes."

"Did you give them the name of our contact?"

"No," I told him. "I didn't tell them anything about him." This was true.

Another long silence. Still no one moved. And then Amin spoke again. "Why?"

There was no anger in his voice. I could tell he was completely calm. At the time, I was surprised by his reaction. I didn't understand why he and Yasin were so calm. Why they didn't scream at me, or try to wring my throat. Later, it would become clear to me.

I thought for a few seconds about how to explain myself. Truly, I hadn't thought any of this through before I got in the car. "I did it for you," I said slowly. "For all of us. For the *mujahidin*." My words were coming more quickly now. "I knew I could do more if I got inside. The best way to fight the enemy is from the inside. This is how I will make my *jihad*."

I could not see Amin's face, nor Yasin's. Out of the corner of my eye, though, I could see Hakim nodding gently. No one said another word. Amin turned on the ignition, and we drove back to the house. When I got out of the car, I looked at all three of them. Their eyes were wide and blank, like the eyes of dead men.

The conversation took no more than five minutes, but I've spent many years thinking about it. I don't know why I did what I did. I know that I didn't plan it in advance. I was in a trance, or something like it, when I got in the car. But it was me in that car, and those were my words.

It's true that I was sick, and that I wasn't thinking clearly. But that was not the real reason. The real reason was that I was scared, and I knew that I needed all the allies I could find. I didn't know what would happen next, but I knew that I had to be prepared for anything. Some sort of storm was coming. Everything was going to be sucked up into the sky and twisted around before dropping back down to earth. I would be sucked up, too, and I didn't know where I'd land when the storm was over.

I couldn't trust Gilles. He had betrayed me, or at least he was about to. I was sure of that. But I couldn't trust Hakim, Amin, or Yasin either. They had talked about killing me, and sent me on a suicide mission to Morocco.

I couldn't trust anyone.

Id al-Fitra

I woke up very early the next morning. I had gone to bed exhausted the night before, but had slept very badly. When I woke up I was feeling even worse. I

should have gone downstairs to eat with the others—Ramadan had ended—
and then stayed in bed for the rest of the day. But I didn't. I felt that I had to get
out of the house, though at the time I wouldn't have formulated it that way. It
was just a feeling in my gut.

I left before six a.m. and went into the city. I sat down at a café and
smoked for a bit, and then just wandered around. My head still wasn't very
clear and my heart was heavy with everything that had happened since I returned from Morocco. I had been betrayed by everyone, and I had betrayed
everyone in return.

My head was spinning with faces, the faces in the thousands of photographs
I had pored through in the past year; the old man in Morocco, the young men
who passed through our house, Gilles's face when he introduced me to Thierry,
Hakim's face when I announced I was working for the service, Malika's face
when she told me about the tape, my mother's face in the photograph, when
she was so young. All these faces were flashing before me, but there was no order to them. They were just faces.

I wanted desperately to clear my head. I decided to take the bus to the Cinquantenaire Park, where I had spent so much time as a child. It was near the
house where my family lived when we first moved to Brussels. When I came
home for the weekend or a holiday, I'd go to the museums there with my
brothers. We would run around for hours at a time, looking at the airplanes in
the Museum of the Army, the mummies in the Museum of Art and History,
everything.

When I got off the bus and walked into the park, the first thing I saw was the
mosque where I went with my family as a child. Of course I didn't go very often, because I was living at the sanitarium, but when I did come home I'd study
the Ku'ran there with my brothers. On Fridays and during Ramadan, I'd go
there with my family to pray.

I went into the Museum of Art and History. I knew the museum like the
back of my hand, I'd been there so many times. This time, I asked the lady at
the information desk if there was any Islamic archaeology or history in the museum. I didn't remember ever seeing it here as a child. She told me there was
such a section, and took out a map to show me how to get there. "It's in the annex," she said. "You'll have to go out of the building and around the back."

I was very angry. The museum had collections from all the great civilizations
of the West: Greece, Rome, Byzantium. I had seen it all as a child. But I had
never seen the Islamic collection because it was hidden away in an annex as if it
were less worthy than the others.

I went around to the annex. There was nobody else there. The light was low and the artifacts in their bright glass cases jumped out towards me from the walls. There were costumes and hats and treasures from the time of Muhammad. Spears and swords and daggers. I was transfixed. Everything else fell away. Amin, Yasin, Tarek, Gilles, Thierry, all of them disappeared. I was not even aware of my cold anymore. My head was peaceful. I was alone, and I allowed myself to be transported into this other world. I saw men in heavy armor and I could hear their horses' pounding hooves. They were warriors riding into battle, lifting their bright swords to the sky. "*Allahu akbar!*" they shouted. "*Allahu akbar!*"

But it was a world of stillness as well as motion. It was a world filled with prayer and family and knowledge, and great pride before nations, and great humility before God. I imagined Saladin, who let the Christian armies escape from Jerusalem.

It was another world. It was a beautiful world. And it was all in the annex.

When I left the museum in the late afternoon, my cold was gone and I felt much better. I took the bus back to my neighborhood. And then I did something unusual. I walked home a different way. I took a longer route, by the edge of the canal, and came towards the house from the back alley rather than the street out in front. There was no reason for me to do this; it just happened.

My mother met me at the door. Her face was red from crying. "Where have you been?" she wailed. "The police were here. They took everybody."

I went into the house with her. Everything had been turned upside down. "They looked everywhere." She was crying again. "They went through everything." I tried to hold her and comfort her. And then she said it. "They took Nabil, too. And they are looking for you."

That's when I knew for certain. Gilles was going to have me arrested along with everyone else. He had lied to me. I had worked for him for a year, I had risked my life, I had given him so much. And now he had betrayed me.

I ran upstairs and took my passport and a few small photographs of myself left over from when I got my driver's license. Then I went back downstairs and hugged my mother one more time. I left the same way I had come, through the alley, along the bank of the canal.

It would be ten years before I saw my mother again.

I took the bus to the train station and called Gilles from a pay phone, but he didn't answer. I left a message: "Hello," I said. "I'll call you again in one hour. If you don't answer, then I'll get on a train to Paris and tomorrow morning I'll be standing outside the Foreign Ministry, shouting your name. So you'd better answer." I slammed down the phone.

An hour later I called back. There was no answer. "I'm getting on the train now," I said. I put down the phone and boarded the train. I knew Gilles's men would be waiting at the Foreign Ministry the next day to arrest me. Of course, I had no intention of letting that happen.

I was still shaking with rage. I kept thinking about Gilles's promise, his assurance that he would give me warning, that he would keep Nabil out of it. I regretted everything I had done for him. I had believed him when he told me we had the same objectives, that we were fighting against the same things. But he lied to me. He had been lying to me all along.

I knew what I had to do. I had to make it impossible for the DGSE to put me in jail. If they caught me, they would arrest me and it would be their word against mine. They had pictures of me with everyone. They knew about all of the guns and explosives. About the trip to Morocco. They could lock me up for the rest of my life.

I had to make it impossible for the DGSE to deny I was an agent.

"*Passports, s'il vous plait.*" A voice snapped me out of my thoughts. A border control guard was coming down the aisle, checking all our passports. When he got to me, I handed mine to him and spoke quietly.

"You should arrest me," I said.

He looked stunned. "I beg your pardon?"

"I said you should just arrest me."

"Have you committed a crime?"

"No," I said. "But I have important information. About national security."

He looked at me skeptically, and we went back and forth for several rounds. Then I insisted on speaking to his boss. We walked to the end of the train, where the head of border control was sitting in a small cabin. Again, I explained my situation. "I want to speak to someone who is responsible for issues of national security," I said.

He looked annoyed. "I am responsible for issues of national security."

"I'm not going to speak to you. It's urgent. I need to speak to someone from the DST," I told him, referring to France's *Direction de la Surveillance du Territoire*, the DGSE's sister agency for internal security.

We argued like this for several more minutes and finally I wore him down. He agreed that I would get off at the next station and he would take me to the commissariat.

He was very angry, though. "If you're fucking with me," he growled, "you'll regret it."

"I'm not fucking with you. If you don't listen to me, you'll regret it."

When I got to the commissariat, they put me in a cell. The chief came, and I told him I wanted to speak to someone from the DST. We fought about it, but I held my ground. He relented and, later, in the middle of the night, another man came. He wore civilian clothes. He was scowling. "I was in bed," he told me. "This better be really important."

I told him it was. I asked him if he was from the DST and he said yes and showed me his identification. I told him I needed my wallet, which had been taken from me before I was locked up. Eventually, a guard came. He rifled through my wallet before handing it over. I took Gilles's phone number out, gave it to the man from the DST, and told him to call it. I told him to leave my name on the machine, along with a message that I was in custody and speaking to an agent of the DST. Then I waited in the cell.

An hour later one of the guards came and unlocked the cell. He told me to follow him, that there was someone on the phone in the office waiting to talk to me. When I got there, I picked up the phone. The voice of the man on the other end of the line was intense but warm. "Omar," he said. "How are you?"

I was surprised. It was the first time anyone in the services had spoken my name. "I'm fine," I said.

"Good, I'm glad to hear it," the man replied. "Now tell me, what have you told them?"

"Nothing. Nothing at all."

"That's good," he said. "Just stay put. We'll get you out of there right away. I'll call back in a few minutes."

The police didn't take me back to my cell at that point. They waited with me until the man called back. He told me to stay at the station overnight. The police would buy me a ticket back to Brussels. The next morning I should call Gilles, who would tell me where to meet him.

Everyone in the station was very gracious after that. The chief of the commissariat let me write my own police report, since he knew it was just for the sake of appearance. Still, I refused to sign it, and he didn't press me. Then we all stayed up early into the morning, joking and playing cards.

They knew I was one of them. And I knew that they knew. The *gendarmerie*, the local police, the DST—they all knew now that I was an agent. Gilles couldn't deny it, the DGSE couldn't deny it. Whatever power they may have had over me, they lost that night.

There was a television on that night in the commissariat, in the waiting room where we played cards. There were reports on the news about the arrests in Belgium. They weren't releasing any names at the time, but later I would learn much more.

They had captured Amin and Yasin. They went on trial in Brussels the following fall; both pled guilty to the charges and were sentenced to four years in prison. Hakim received a stiffer sentence, probably because so much—the cars, the safe houses, the bank accounts—was in his name. They had completely used him.

I learned that Tarek was, in fact, a man named Ali Touchent, a major figure in the GIA's European operations. He escaped the sting somehow, and fled to the Netherlands. But the biggest fish they caught that day was a man named Ahmed Zaoui. I had heard this name before—he had been a professor in Algeria and then a politician. In 1991, he stood as a candidate for the FIS, and would have won had the results of the election not been nullified. Gilles told me that Zaoui was the man I had seen in the car park in Brussels, the older man who came only for a few minutes to take the suitcase. Later, I learned that the authorities believed that Zaoui was the head of the GIA's European operations, and that they desperately wanted to convict him. But since Amin, Yasin, and Hakim had pled guilty to everything, it was hard for them to make their case against Zaoui. He was acquitted at first, but then convicted during a second trial. He was under house arrest in Belgium but escaped to Switzerland, which gave him sanctuary. He has moved many times since, and continues to deny that he was ever a member of the GIA.

They arrested a man named Tarek ben Habib Maaroufi as well. I had identified him in one of the photographs Gilles showed me—Maaroufi had come through the house at one point. A Tunisian national, he was a member of an extremist group with links to the GIA. Gilles later explained that the DGSE had been investigating this Tunisian group, which was why he was so interested in the list of contacts I had stolen from the boxes in the kitchen.

Maaroufi was released after only a year in prison, and went on to become one of the most important Al Qaeda organizers in Europe. In September 2001, he masterminded the assassination in Afghanistan of Ahmed Shah Massoud, the noble *mujahidin* who had become a hero to me after I watched all those films at the Pompidou Center about the Soviet invasion of Afghanistan. Since then, he had become the head of the Northern Alliance in Afghanistan, a fierce opponent of the Taliban.

Maaroufi recruited two suicide bombers in Belgium and gave them stolen passports. Posing as journalists, they met with Massoud and his spokesman. Then they detonated the explosives, killing themselves and the spokesman and Massoud instantly. Bin Laden's path in Afghanistan was clear. Two days later the Twin Towers fell.

Nouvelles Aventures

I met Gilles in Brussels the next day. The meeting was very carefully coordinated; he told me which compartment of the train I should sit in, which exit from the station I should use. There were undercover officers all over the station; I knew how to pick them out in a crowd.

When I got out of the station, I spotted Gilles and we walked together to a McDonald's and sat down. I was very angry with him. He expected this.

"You lied to me," I said. "You told me that you would warn me if there were going to be arrests." I was practically shouting. "You told me that Nabil wouldn't be arrested."

Gilles was composed, as always. But he spoke more quietly than usual, and sat a bit lower in his chair. "It wasn't my fault," he explained. "Some traffic cops pulled over Amin and they found a lot of guns in his car. They arrested him. And then we had to do everything right away." I didn't believe him.

"We did arrest Nabil," he went on. "We had to. He was in the house with all the others. But we kept him for only a couple of hours and then we let him go."

I was relieved to hear this. I was happy that Nabil was all right and also that my mother was not alone. But I was still furious with Gilles. "You were going to arrest me, too," I said.

Gilles nodded. "Yes, that's true. We were going to arrest you just so you could get more information out of them. We never would have kept you in there." Then he admitted that they were surprised I wasn't at the house with the others, because the raid was early in the morning. There had been cars waiting near my house all day, so that they could arrest me as soon as I came home. But they didn't see me because I had come through the back alley.

Gilles paused and looked me in the eye. "We'd still like you to go in with them. We'd like you to get more information for us." He told me there were officers from the Belgian secret service waiting outside, and he tried to convince me that I should let them arrest me. "Of course we wouldn't leave you in there. We'd just like to get more information. You're the only one who can do it."

I kept my composure, but I was disgusted with him. What a bastard, I thought. I had given him and the DGSE so much—I had made these raids possible. They couldn't have done any of it without me. If they could, they wouldn't have waited until I was back from Morocco. They could have just left me there. But now I had served my purpose, and he wanted to get rid of me. And he thought I was stupid enough to believe his bullshit.

I leaned across the table and stared him in the eye. "You told me we had the same goals." I could hear the anger in my voice; it was a whisper and a shout at the same time. "After the hijacking, we talked about it. I told you that you had my complete commitment. And I thought I had yours. But you've betrayed me."

Gilles's eyes were widening with every word I said. I would be as ruthless with him as he had been with me. But I still needed him. "I will tell you right now," I said. "I'll go anywhere, do anything to fight these terrorists. Give me a job and I'll do it. But I will never go to prison for you. You have no power over me, and I don't trust you."

Gilles shrank back slightly in his chair. "OK, OK," he said, sighing. "Then we'll have to figure something else out." He paused for a moment, thinking hard.

Then: "We need to get you out of Belgium. We turned your name over to Interpol last night. Once it's in the system, it takes some time to get it out." He took out his wallet and gave me some money. "Tomorrow we'll get you to France. You need to get rid of your clothes. Don't use the bus or the subway. Lie low."

I took the money. He asked me where I would stay overnight. "I'll find a prostitute," I said. I knew if I told him which friends I was staying with, he could have them arrested, too.

The next day I met Gilles at the train station. He told me to take a taxi to Antoing, a village near the French border. We met up again there, and he told me to take a different taxi and head to Rumes. From there I was to take another taxi to Orchies, a tiny village just across the border in France.

When I got to Orchies, there were two secret service officers waiting by a car next to the church. A few minutes later, Gilles arrived. He just came around the corner by foot. Obviously he had followed me from Antoing.

When he saw me, he saluted. A driver stepped out of the car and opened the door for him, and he and I and the other officers got in. After we settled into our seats, Gilles turned to me, and with a weak smile quoted the great line from the Tintin books: *"En route pour de nouvelles aventures."*

Dolmabahçe

When we got to Paris, Gilles set me up in a hotel. It was cheap, run down, and ugly, and the next time he came to visit I complained. I said I thought I deserved something better after everything I'd done. Grudgingly, he moved me somewhere nicer.

I didn't have much to do while I was in Paris, but Gilles gave me money to spend and came to visit me every few days. One day, though, he asked me to call my family. He wanted to know if they had figured out that it was me who got them arrested. I was alarmed by his request. Nabil had been arrested along with the others, and although he had only been kept for two hours it was quite possible that Hakim or one of the others had told him about my confession the day before. If Gilles found out about that, he would know I had betrayed him. I would be arrested on the spot. But there was nothing I could do, so I dialed the number.

Nabil picked up the phone, and he was furious. "Where are you?" he shouted. "Look what you've done. It's all your fault—everyone is in jail. *Maman* is devastated. If you were a man, you would come back and take responsibility for what you've done."

I was relieved. Of course, he was angry with me. Early on, I had promised to take some sort of action to get Tarek, Amin, and Yasin out of the house, so he would naturally assume that the arrests were related. But he hadn't said anything about the DGSE, and that was the important thing. Gilles already knew I had told Nabil something vague about protecting him, because he had been by my side when I called Nabil after our first meeting. Once I reminded him of this, there was no need for further discussion.

But after that phone call, we both knew I couldn't work in Europe anymore.

In fact, I didn't want to work in Europe anymore. I wanted to go to the camps in Afghanistan. I had seen so many young men come through the house on their way to the camps, and I was jealous. I was jealous when I heard Amin and Yasin talk about the time they had spent there. And I had been dreaming of mountains. I wanted to be in the mountains.

Gilles wanted me to go to Turkey. He thought that I could be useful in Turkey because the DGSE had noticed a lot of men were disappearing from France, men who were under surveillance. They would attend the radical mosques every day and then, suddenly, they were gone. They went to Turkey and disappeared. A few months later they would be back at the mosques in France, but no one knew where they had been in the meantime. The DGSE thought they were at the training camps. Gilles wanted to know what was going on in Turkey, how these men got to the camps.

I agreed to go along with it, even though I suspected that Gilles just wanted to wash his hands of me. He gave me no names, no photos, no addresses—not even the name of a city I should focus on. I knew it was a dead end, that Gilles was trying to play me yet again. But I could play him, too.

He had never taken me as seriously as he should have. But I would show him. I would infiltrate the camps. I would surprise him and the entire DGSE. I was going to make them pay attention.

Gilles took me to Charles de Gaulle airport a few days later. He had to escort me through passport control because I had no visa for France, only for Belgium. He gave me seven thousand dollars. Then he named one of the major hotels in Istanbul, where I was to meet my contact. I would give my return ticket to him. This way Gilles could ensure I wouldn't come back and hassle him or the service. He didn't say that, of course, but that's what he meant. I didn't challenge him.

It felt good to get on the plane. I was going somewhere new; I was making my way to Afghanistan. And I was looking forward to Turkey as well. I had heard so much about the Ottoman world as a child, and I had seen some of its treasures in the museum in Brussels. Turkey was the seat of the last great Muslim empire. I wanted to see the mosques and the women in their headscarves. I wanted to hear the call to prayer.

But the minute I got out of the Istanbul airport and into a taxi, I knew I had made a mistake. As we drove towards the city center, I realized I had got it all wrong. There were women in miniskirts, men in blue jeans. Bright lights and loud music. It looked exactly like Europe. I was disappointed.

A couple of hours later, I met with the contact. He was short and very fit. He introduced himself with the silly code Gilles had given me. "Hello, sir. I'm afraid Josephine cannot make her appointment today, but she sends you her best wishes." His face was very serious. I followed him into a basement and handed over the return ticket.

Then I found a taxi and asked the driver to show me the city. He was an Arab, and soon we started talking. I asked him why Istanbul was like this, what had happened to the Islamic culture and history.

"It's because of Atatürk," he said. I had never heard of Atatürk. He told me that Atatürk had secularized the whole country, wiped out the language and even the alphabet. He said that if I wanted to find the real Islam, I should go to Konya, the home of Rumi.

I had no idea who Rumi was, but I trusted the Arab. And anyway, Gilles had given me nothing else to do. So I took a train to Konya; it took nearly fifteen hours. After I had checked into a hotel and rested a bit, I asked the man at the reception desk to point me to a mosque.

I was stunned when I walked through the door. There were graves in the mosque. Only Christians have graves in their churches; it's forbidden in Islam. The mosque is a house of God, not a house of death. Hakim had taught me that in Morocco.

Once I got over my initial shock, I began to realize where I was. There were musical instruments on the floor of the mosque, which could only mean one thing: these were Sufis. I didn't know anything, really, about Sufism. Just that it had nothing to do with the kind of Islamic radicalism I was looking for. In Morocco I had seen Sufis dancing in the street: whirling dervishes. But the only Sufi I knew anything about was Cat Stevens. He had converted to Islam when I was a teenager, and as a Muslim it made me proud. But when Hakim came to Morocco, he taught me that Cat Stevens, like all Sufis, was *taghut*. Muslims do not dance, do not play music in mosque. I knew these things, of course. But I was surprised to hear Hakim say that Cat Stevens, who I considered a hero, was actually an infidel.

And so I knew I wasn't going to find anything in Konya. But I didn't have any idea where else I could find this mysterious road to *jihad* either. So I rented a car.

I spent a month driving all over Turkey, speaking with people in the streets, *a'imma,* and anyone else I could find. Ankara, Izmir, Adana, Eskisehir, Bursa— thirty-five hundred kilometers in all. I didn't find anything.

And then one day I got in an accident. A truck pushed me off the road and into a ravine. The car rolled down the cliff and landed twenty-five meters below the road. I was lucky to survive, but the car was destroyed.

The truck hadn't stopped; it just disappeared. The day after the crash a man from the rental car agency came to my hotel. Since no one could find the truck, I would have to pay the twelve-hundred-dollar deductible on the rental company's insurance policy myself. I paid the bill, but then had almost nothing left.

I went back to Istanbul and did the only thing I could: I called Gilles. I left a message on his answering machine, but he didn't call back. I left another one two days later. Still nothing. By the end of the week I was pleading into his machine. "Gilles, please call me. I got in an accident, the car was totaled. I have no money."

Still, nothing.

So I did what I had to: I went to the French consulate. When I got there, a guard asked me what my business was. I told him I was a French citizen, and that I had lost my passport. He gestured me through the door and pointed me up the stairs to an office.

I went in and stood in line. When it was my turn, I approached the woman behind the desk. I noticed that there was another office behind her, and the door was open. I glanced in. And then I saw him, the man who had taken my return ticket the first day in Istanbul. When he saw me, his eyes opened in shock. He had no idea who I was, but he knew that I was a spy. And spies don't show their faces in official buildings.

He walked towards me quickly and gestured me towards a corner. In a low voice, he asked me for a phone number. I gave him a card from the hotel, and he told me that someone would call me in two hours.

Someone did call me in two hours, but it wasn't Gilles. It was some other man, and I ended up following him through Istanbul just like I had followed Gilles in Brussels. He gave me fifteen hundred dollars and told me Gilles was very busy and would call me in two days.

When I finally spoke to Gilles, he said he was very sorry he hadn't called sooner, that he had been busy. He still thought he could bullshit me. He told me he would come to Istanbul in two days.

We met in a restaurant and I told him I was wasting my time in Turkey. I said that I wanted to get to the root of these terrorist networks in Pakistan and Afghanistan. I wanted to infiltrate the camps. He rolled his eyes. "That's impossible."

"Why is it impossible?" I asked.

"Because you can't just *go* to the camps. You'd need a letter from one of the recruiters in Europe to get in."

I brushed this aside. I knew that if I got there, I could get in.

"You'll need to get a visa for Pakistan," he went on. "It won't be easy to get."

"Why not?" I gave him a big smile. "It's not like I'm a terrorist."

I got the visa. It took me only five days, and I was only able to get a tourist visa, which lasted fifteen days. But it was enough. When Gilles returned to Istanbul a week later, he was surprised I had gotten anything at all, and impressed.

We met in the Dolmabahçe gardens. It was a beautiful spring day. We walked up the hill and found a bench overlooking the Bosphorus. He told me I had seven months. If I didn't come back in that time, he would cut me off. The phone number wouldn't work anymore. Then he gave me fifteen thousand dollars.

"You know," he said, "you're not the first one to try to get into the camps."

"What happened to the others?" I asked.

"Most don't get in. They come back with nothing. Some don't come back at all."

"I'll get in," I said. "And I'll come back."

"OK. But if you don't—well, then that's OK." He looked at me intently. "You can go wherever you want. We won't bother you."

At that moment my anger at Gilles softened. He was completely untrustworthy, but over the course of working for him for a year, I had spent more time talking to him than anyone else. And we did want the same things, ultimately, though we had to pursue them in different ways. He had to do his job. I knew that. But I also knew that in his heart, he didn't want to hurt me. He wanted to give me a way out, and he had given me a lot of money to help me start a new life.

But I didn't want a new life. I wanted the life I had, but on a bigger scale. I think Gilles also wanted me to succeed.

I looked down at my pack of Marlboros and pointed to the crest.

"*Veni, vidi, vici,*" I said. He smiled.

I stood up, and we shook hands. He stayed on the bench. Then I turned and walked out of the garden and down towards the Bosphorus.

AFGHANISTAN

Cast of Characters

Abu Anas	Takes Omar from Lahore to Peshawar
Ibn Sheikh	Emir of Khaldan
Abu Bakr	Palestinian trainer at Khaldan; Emir when Ibn Sheikh is absent
Abu Hamam	Eritrean trainer at Khaldan; leads training run on Omar's first day
Abu Suhail	Yemeni trainer at Khaldan; trains Omar on guns
Abdul Haq	Moroccan trainee from London at Khaldan
Abdul Kerim	French Algerian trainee at Khaldan; reappears at Darunta
Assad Allah	Visits Khaldan briefly; reappears at Darunta as explosives trainer
Abu Yahya	Yemeni trainer at Khaldan; trains Omar in explosives; reappears at Darunta
Abu Hudayfa	Saudi trainee at Khaldan; subjected to interrogation upon arrival
Hamza	Young Egyptian trainee raised in Canada; brother of Osama
Osama	Young Egyptian trainee raised in Canada; brother of Hamza
Abu Said al-Kurdi	Takes Omar from Peshawar to Darunta
Abu Zubayda	Makes arrangements for Omar in Peshawar
Abu Mousa	Iraqi Kurd; lives at Darunta
Abu Jihad	Emir of Darunta

Timeline

March 1991: *Mujahidin* forces capture the strategic town of Khowst from Afghan government, led by Mohammed Najibullah.

April 1992: Najibullah resigns as president of Afghanistan.

June 28, 1992: Burhanuddin Rabbani takes office as president of Afghanistan.

Fall 1994: Taliban emerge as political force within Afghanistan.

December 24, 1994–January 3, 1995: Russian troops attack Chechen capital of Grozny and are repulsed.

January 19, 1995: Russians capture Grozny, after prolonged war of attrition.

February 7, 1995: Ramzi Ahmed Yousef, a suspect in the 1993 bombing of the World Trade Center towers, is arrested in Pakistan.

July 11, 1995–July 16, 1995: Bosnian Serb troops enter Srebrenica and massacre an estimated seven thousand unarmed Bosnian Muslims.

July 26, 1995: Bomb explodes in RER train under the Saint Michel station in Paris, killing eight people and wounding over one hundred.

November 11, 1995: Dayton Peace Accords signed, ending the war in Bosnia.

November 19, 1995: Car-bomb attack on Egyptian embassy in Islamabad kills eighteen people and injures seventy-five.

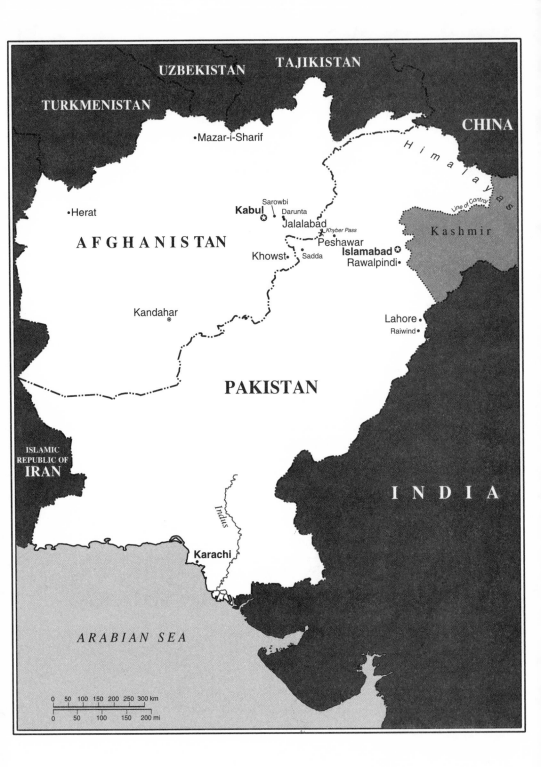

TURKMENISTAN

UZBEKISTAN   TAJIKISTAN

                                                    CHINA

•Mazar-i-Sharif

                              H i m a l a y a s

•Herat   Sarowbi   Line of Control
            Kabul   Darunta
AFGHANISTAN   ✪   •Jalalabad   Kashmir
                  Khyber Pass
            Khowst• •Sadda Peshawar
                           Islamabad ✪
                           Rawalpindi•

                                    Lahore•
            Kandahar   Raiwind•
               ◉

            PAKISTAN

ISLAMIC   I N D I A
REPUBLIC OF
IRAN

                           Indus

            Karachi

ARABIN SEA

    0 50 100 150 200 250 300 km
    0   50   100   150   200 mi

Pakistan

On my last night in Istanbul, I took myself to the fanciest restaurant in the city. I ordered the most expensive bottle of wine on the list, drank it, and then ordered another one.

When I woke up the next morning I was tired. I had breakfast in my hotel and finished my pack of cigarettes. I knew I wouldn't be smoking another one for a very long time.

I took a taxi to the airport for my flight to Karachi. I was early, so with time to burn and lots of money in my pocket, I headed to the duty-free shop. I ended up buying a pocket flashlight and a small Swiss Army knife with all sorts of different blades. They seemed like the sort of things I would find useful in the camps.

Then I headed to the gate and sat down. I looked around the room at the others waiting for the flight, but I was still weary and it took a few minutes for everything to come into focus. Then, in front of me, I saw something interesting: a man wearing a turban. I couldn't see his face since he was sitting with his back to me. But instinctively I wanted to know more. I got up and walked around so I could sit facing him, about three rows away.

I could tell he was young, in his thirties, but he had the face of a much older man. His skin was brown and parched from the sun, and there were deep wrinkles around his eyes. He was dressed like an Afghan, with a dark vest over his *shalwar kameez*. He held a *siwak* in his mouth. His lips were moving.

After a couple of minutes, a businessman came and sat next to me. He lit a cigarette and began smoking. As I stood up, a young woman came towards me. She wanted my seat and asked if I would be coming back. She was beautiful, quite sexy, wearing a short skirt and an open blouse. I shook my head and walked away. I headed over to the man in the turban, and sat down next to him.

"Muslims who smoke," he said under his breath as he looked at the businessman, "aren't true Muslims. They're *tawaghi*." He spoke English with a Pakistani rather than Afghani accent.

"And so are Muslim women who dress like that," I replied, gesturing towards the woman in the skirt.

He nodded, and then continued to pray. We sat together in silence until the flight boarded.

As I settled into my seat on the plane, I thought about how my life was about to change yet again. I would be playing a very different role from here on out. But in fact it wasn't really a new role, or even a role at all. As a young child I had dreamed of fighting—fighting the Japanese, fighting the Germans. Later, in Paris, I had dreamed of fighting the Russians in Afghanistan. And then later of fighting in Bosnia, and still later in Chechnya. Now, finally, I was on my way. I was excited.

An hour into the flight, I felt a hand on my shoulder. I looked up; it was the Pakistani man. "Which way is Mecca?" he asked.

I was surprised; there was a flightmap on every screen in the plane. I pointed to the one in front of us and showed him how to read it. I told him Mecca was on the right side of the plane.

He thanked me and walked forward a few rows. Then he took off his jacket and laid it on the floor in front of him. A stewardess saw what he was doing and spoke to him.

"You can't stand here," she said. "You musn't block the exit row." The man ignored her, and she raised her voice. "Sir, I have to ask you to move. You can't block the emergency exit door."

He finally looked up. "I must make my *salat*."

She shook her head and spoke to him in a low voice. He stood up, but soon their voices became louder; they were arguing. "Nothing will stop me from making my *salat*," he said. "I don't care where I am, on a camel or on a plane. I will do it."

The stewardess shook her head, and said something else to him. Then he took a paper out of his pocket and waved it in her face. "Fine, here's my ticket," he shouted. "Give me my money back, and I'll get off the plane right now."

The stewardess looked confused and frightened. He didn't seem to be kidding; he really seemed to think that he could get off the plane mid-flight. I shot out of my chair and went over to them. I smiled at the stewardess.

"Why don't you let him pray?" I said in my friendliest voice. "It will only take a couple of minutes. I can stay here in case anything happens."

She looked at me for a long time, saying nothing. Finally, she shrugged her shoulders. She turned to him, scowled, and walked away. The Pakistani looked at me and bowed his head slightly. I could tell he was very grateful. Then he turned and made his *salat*.

When he was done, I returned to my seat and he came and sat down next to me. "Why didn't you make the *salat*?" he asked.

"I am practicing the *sunna*," I said. According to the *sunna*, Muslims can be exempted from bodily prayer when traveling far from home. One makes the *salat* internally instead, in the mind. The Pakistani nodded, and asked me where I was going.

"Karachi."

He looked surprised. "Why Karachi?"

I looked at him carefully. His eyes were very bright, intense.

"I want to make my *jihad*," I whispered.

His eyes opened wide. "But then why Karachi, brother?"

I shrugged my shoulders and smiled. "I don't really know very much about Pakistan," I told him. "So I just got a ticket for Karachi."

"Brother, no. You must not stay in Karachi. It's very dangerous right now, not safe for foreigners." He paused. "You should go to Islamabad instead."

He took out a piece of paper and pen from his bag and started writing. I didn't recognize the language. When he finished he looked up and handed me the paper. "I know someone who can help you. He lives in Rawalpindi, just a few kilometers outside of Islamabad. When you get to Islamabad, show this address to a taxi driver and he will take you there." Then he leaned in very close to me. "Whatever you do, brother, do not mention *jihad* to anyone. It is very dangerous. You must be very careful."

I nodded gratefully. "*Al-hamdu lil-lah*," I said earnestly, thanking him for his help. "You must have been sent to me by God."

He smiled at me and leaned back in his seat.

It was still dark when I got off the plane in Karachi, but the heat was already unbearable. I crossed the tarmac and went into the terminal to buy a ticket to Islamabad. When I was done, I glanced out the window. The sky was getting lighter, so I hastened to the airport mosque to make the dawn *salat*. It was very easy to slip into the rhythm of this life, into the patterns of my upbringing.

When I arrived in Islamabad, I immediately found a taxi and showed the driver the paper the Pakistani had given me. As soon as I sat down, I realized how tired I was from the long flight; my whole body ached. But as I leaned back and stretched, my eyes focused and I began to pay attention to everything around me. I realized that I was in a world totally different from anything I had seen before. The music playing on the radio in the taxi was exotic, Indian. The streets were chaotic: there were donkeys and carts and people surging in every direction, alongside cars and trucks of all sizes, each one honking at the others. The houses were tiny, patched together out of stone and metal and who knows what else. Lingering over everything was an odd, unsavory smell I had never encountered. And dust everywhere. Dust in the roads, spit up by the wheels of trucks. Dust on the animals in the streets. Dust on the people's clothes. Dust in my eyes, my throat.

We were in Rawalpindi in less than an hour, but then we drove out of town again on a very rough dirt road. I was watching every turn the taxi made and committing it to memory, to make sure I could find my way back on my own if I had to. Soon, the driver pulled over to the side of the road. He asked me for the paper, then he got out of the car. I stayed inside and looked around. I could see a gate, and behind it a minaret and several buildings. I didn't know if I was supposed to get out of the car or not. Maybe the driver was just stopping to ask for directions.

He knocked on the gate. Soon, a young man in Pakistani dress opened the door. The driver handed him the paper, and the young man disappeared for a few moments. When he returned, there was a much older man behind him. He spoke to the driver briefly, and then the driver walked back to the car.

"We're here," he said. I paid him, and he pointed to the gate. The young man was still standing there, and he ushered me inside the compound as the taxi turned to go. He said nothing, but gestured towards an open courtyard. There were about thirty men there of different ages, all wearing the Pakistani *shalwar kameez* in white or cream.

Across the courtyard I could see several young boys in a kind of makeshift classroom. There was a teacher walking among them, carrying a stick. The boys were shouting out verses from the Kur'an, and their faces were twisted with concentration. They were learning *tajwid*. Like most Muslims, I had learned the Kur'an the same way, phonetically, before I knew any Arabic. And my teachers, like theirs, would hit me with a stick if I mispronounced any words. Although Muslims speak hundreds of different languages all over the world, there is only one Kur'an. Islam does not permit any innovations, accidental or otherwise.

I turned my attention back to the young man standing next to me. He was handing me a sleeping bag. I moved to unroll it so I could lie down. He shook his head and pointed towards a door off the courtyard. Behind it there was a small, empty, air-conditioned room. The young man left me there, closing the door behind him. I spread out my sleeping bag and lay down. Within seconds, I was asleep.

A few hours later, the young man woke me up and handed me some clothing. It was a white *shalwar kameez*, like the others were wearing. After I put it on he guided me towards another area, near the mosque, where I made my *salat* along with the others.

Then he took me into another room, much larger than the one where I had slept. In the center was an old man sitting on some cushions. His beard was white, with streaks of red henna. My piece of paper was on the ground in front of him.

He began to speak to me in English, but his accent was so heavy I could barely understand him. He said something about thanking God for me and for the brother who sent me. And then something about going to Lahore the next day with the other brothers. This made me nervous. I wanted to go to Afghanistan, and Lahore was in the opposite direction. But there was nothing I could do; there was no way we would understand each other if I asked him a question. Soon he gave me back the paper. I thanked him and went back out to join the others.

It was getting dark and slightly cooler. I sat in the courtyard with the other men and looked around. I noticed that some of them were very old, seventy or eighty. It all seemed very strange to me, and I had a feeling in my gut that something was wrong. I had come to make *jihad*, but *mujahidin* don't wage war with small children and old men.

I didn't understand the language the men were speaking, but soon a few approached me and asked in halting Arabic where I had come from. Morocco, I told them. They nodded. One of the men said he was from Peshawar, another from Faisalabad, another from Islamabad.

We spoke about other things, but because none of us had strong Arabic we couldn't say much to each other. No one spoke of *jihad*, certainly, but the man on the plane had told me how dangerous it was to speak of such things inside Pakistan, so I thought maybe that was why.

I was still exhausted and went to bed early that night. As I lay down, I felt slightly uneasy. I wasn't in the camps yet, and I wasn't sure if I was getting closer or farther away. But I knew I would get there eventually. For the time being I was just happy to be in Pakistan. I fell into a deep sleep.

Tabligh

The next morning, we awakened before dawn and performed the *salat*. Then we gathered our belongings and walked outside the compound, where a truck was waiting for us. The other men threw their things into the back and started to climb on board, and I joined them. But suddenly I felt a hand pulling me back. "No," a voice said. "Come down."

For just an instant, I panicked. Had they found me out? Had they somehow learned I was a spy? But then I turned around and saw a man with a broad smile on his face. "Sit there," he said, pointing towards the cab. "You're our guest in Pakistan."

At first I was grateful not to be in the open back of the truck. There was so much dust flying up from the road, and even this early in the morning I could feel the heat searing through my clothes.

But when we got on the highway, I realized it was the worst possible place to be. I had never seen such driving in my life. The highway was very narrow, and there were all sorts of vehicles on it: bicycles, cars, trucks, donkey carts, men pushing wheelbarrows.

There was no order to it at all. Our driver seemed to choose which side to drive on based on nothing more than whim. When he overtook the vehicle in front of him he would lean on the horn and blast forward without looking ahead. Usually, there was another car coming, if not a truck. It was a game of nerves, and his seemed unusually strong. Often, he would force his opponent to veer off the road entirely. It felt like I had fifteen heart attacks in the first hour.

But it wasn't just our driver—the roads were filled with madmen just like him. Every few kilometers I saw wrecked cars, twisted bicycles, and pieces of trucks by the road. I longed for the orderly highways of Europe.

A couple of hours later, we stopped at a small mosque by the side of the road to make our ablutions and perform the *salat*. When we returned to the truck, I tried to get in back with the others. But they smiled and waved me away. "No, you are our guest," said the same man as before, gesturing towards the front. I sighed and took my place next to the crazy driver.

We drove all day, through the night, and into the next morning, stopping every few hours along the way to make our *salat*. We finally got to Lahore, where we switched to a different truck and continued on out of the city.

The truck stopped in a dusty village not far from Lahore and we all got out. The first thing I noticed was the heavy stench of human waste. It hung over everything. I saw a canal by one side of the road carrying a constant stream of raw sewage. On the other side were many colorful shops selling clothes, food, incense, and cassettes. Almost all the people on the street were dressed in the same white *shalwar kameez*. It seemed illogical given the incredible storm of dust all around us.

A huge mosque towered over everything in the village, with several other buildings clustered around it. There was a large, open space between the buildings where hundreds of men sat under the beating sun. They were all wearing the same white clothes.

Our small group walked towards the door of the compound. Two men guarded the entrance, each holding a large wooden rod. They asked us where we were from and we told them. Suddenly, a guard appeared and escorted me away from the rest of the group. He led me into a large, air-conditioned room, much cooler than the entrance hall. It was an incredible relief after being outside under the scorching heat.

There were about thirty men scattered around the room, some lying down, some sitting up or standing in small groups, talking. I could hear them speaking in many different languages, though I didn't recognize them all. From their clothing, I knew many of them were from Saudi Arabia. There were also some north Africans—Moroccans, Tunisians—wearing street clothes. None of them wore the white *shalwar kameez*.

And then I understood that I was here in this room because I was a foreigner. The men I had come with were all Pakistanis, so they had been taken outside to the huge courtyard I had seen from the entrance. They were roasting in the heat while I was cool. I knew at that moment that this place had nothing to do with *jihad*. In the camps, everyone was equal. I knew this from the films I had seen, and from talking to Amin and Yasin. And I knew enough about the Kur'an to know that true Muslims don't discriminate in this way. I would not be staying long in this place.

Suddenly, a voice snapped me to attention. An old man was sitting in front of me behind a desk. "Please give me your passport and your wallet," he said in English.

I was surprised, and wary. "I can give you my money," I told him. "But I'd like to keep my passport."

He smiled very gently. "Don't worry," he said. "All of the pilgrims do this. It is our way of keeping the papers and the belongings of our guests safe. We will return them to you when you go."

I didn't see any way around it, so I handed over my passport and eight hundred dollars from my money belt. I left the rest of the money in the belt. Then the guard led me into another room, and I put my things on the floor. I looked around and noticed that everyone had the same sleepy, vacant eyes. When I picked up the smell of expensive perfume on some of the men, I knew for certain that these were not *mujahidin*. In fact, they weren't even devout Muslims; perfume is forbidden because it contains alcohol. These were just rich men on some sort of bizarre holiday.

The guard escorted me into another room, a kind of library. A group of older men sat on cushions on the floor. They all had long beards laced with henna. One was clearly in charge; he sat in the center and his cushion was slightly higher than the others'. He had several books scattered in front of him, but no Kur'an.

The guard passed something to this man. As he held it up to inspect it, I saw that it was the same paper the turbaned man had given me on the airplane. He glanced at it, then looked up at me and gestured for me to sit. "Welcome," he said. "How long will you be with us?"

"Thirteen days," I said. At that moment I was grateful that I had only been able to get a tourist's visa in Istanbul. The man nodded and began to speak. I confess I don't remember what he said. In my mind I had already moved on. This was some kind of sect, and these men had little connection to Islam.

Over the next couple of days I would learn more about this place. I learned that I was in Raiwind, the headquarters of Jama'at al-Tabligh. Every day we had lessons not on the Kur'an but on the teachings of Muhammad Ilyias, who had founded the movement. Mostly, the group was interested in proselytizing, finding Muslims who had lost their way and who needed to be brought back to the faith. In Arabic *tabligh* means "message." This is all they wanted to do: deliver their message. They were opposed to any kind of violence.

As a new recruit, I was supposed to attend class every morning. But there were so many people there, no one cared what I did. Mostly I just wandered around. I talked primarily to the foreigners, since many of them spoke Arabic or sometimes English.

Everyone was very friendly, but so soft. Many of them smoked, and once I even saw one of the Saudis take a small vial out of his pocket and distribute white tablets to some of the other Arabs. I was stunned.

Sometimes I would speak to them about *jihad*. When I said that *jihad* for me was the fight of the *mujahidin* against the Russians, or the Bosniaks against the Serbs, they looked horrified. Oh no, brother, they would tell me. *Jihad* means love. *Jihad* means bringing the lost to God. *Jihad* means saving souls.

On the third day, I cracked. "Really?" I said "Really, this is *jihad*?" I was raising my voice. "We're only a few miles from the border with India. If the Hindus come across tomorrow to kill us, what will you do? Hold your Kur'an in the air while they aim at the target on your chest? This is your *jihad*?" The men just nodded blankly and murmured about *tabligh*.

There was one person at Raiwind I liked, a man from Chechnya who was about my age. He was there with his teenage son. He arrived a couple of days after me, and I could see immediately that he was different. He wasn't rich; I could tell from his clothes. And he wasn't soft, like the others.

That afternoon I saw him speaking with one of guards. I could see the Chechen was very upset. When the conversation was over, I approached him and asked what was wrong. "My son needs supplies for school," he said in English. "But I don't have any money. I spent it all getting here."

He told me he had brought his son from Chechnya to protect him from the war there. The only way to get him out of the country was on a student visa, and Pakistan was the cheapest place to go. But he knew that if he sent his son to university, the boy would be recruited and sent to the camps and then back to Chechnya to fight. He told me how awful the war had become in Chechnya, that the Russians were destroying the entire country, just like they destroyed Afghanistan. He wanted to save his son. There were tears in his eyes as he spoke.

That night, the Chechen and his son came over to where I had laid out my sleeping bag. They put theirs down next to mine. I watched the father speak gently to his son, and even though I didn't understand his words I could see how much he loved him. He smiled as he helped his son prepare for the night. But the son was cold, hard. His eyes were dead, and he said almost nothing.

After his father fell asleep, I could hear the son tossing back and forth. After I few minutes, I whispered to him. "You can't sleep, can you?"

"No," he whispered back.

I waited for a minute to see if he would say anything else, but all I could hear was the sound of him turning over again and again. "It's hard for you in Chechnya, isn't it?" I asked.

There was a long pause, and then through the darkness he whispered to me in halting English. "I want to kill them all."

The next morning, I took four hundred dollars out of my money belt and gave it to the boy's father. He didn't say anything to me, nor I to him. But his eyes were filled with tears.

Soon enough, I was taken to Lahore for *khurooj*, a kind of mission to share the *tabligh*. Twelve of us went deep inside the slums. The people there had clearly seen groups from the center before. They approached us and offered us food and invited us into their homes.

We spent three days in Lahore, walking through the markets and streets. I had never seen such poverty in my life. There were slums in Morocco, but nothing like this. There was raw sewage running through the streets, and even the adults were walking through it in bare feet.

I was supposed to talk to people about the Six Principles of the movement, but I hadn't paid any attention to the lessons so I didn't know what they were. I just made it up as I went along. There was a guide with me to translate.

I saw many men and women with mouths red from chewing *pan,* a narcotic leaf available on the streets. It made me angry; I told them it was a drug, *taghut.* Later that day, when I was sitting by the mosque, a man sat down next to me and asked if he could join our group. I looked at him. He had an amulet on a leather strap around his neck. "No, you can't come with us," I told him.

He was stunned. "Why not?"

"Because of that," I said, pointing at the amulet.

"What's wrong with it?" he asked. "It protects me."

"It protects you?" I asked. "How does that protect you? Only God can protect you. And you dishonor Him by wearing that."

The man's eyes opened wide. And then he reached around his neck and removed the necklace.

By the end of the third day, our group of twelve had expanded to twenty-six. I had recruited most of them myself. It was such a successful mission that when I returned to the compound the elders called me back into the library.

"We're very proud of you," said the man in the center. "We heard about your *khurooj*, about how many people came with you. We think you have a very good future here." But then his face darkened, and he went on. "But we've heard from the others that you've spoken about the armed *jihad*. We are worried about this. That is the wrong path. The only true *jihad* is the *jihad* of the Tabligh." He told me not to talk about the armed *jihad* again.

I told him I was not well educated in Islam, and that when the people I knew spoke about *jihad* they meant something very different than the people at Raiwind. He nodded, and then told me they would like me to stay on as long as possible, and to continue with the *khurooj*.

"It will be impossible for me to stay," I told him. "I have only a few days left on my visa." He told me not to worry, and said that he could help me extend it. He would make a call and then I should go to Lahore the next day. He wrote down an address and handed it to me.

The next day, I changed back into my street clothes and retrieved my passport from the old man who had taken it on the first day. I took a taxi to Lahore to the Regional Passport Office. They sent me to another office to extend my visa. In just a couple of hours my visa had been extended from 15 days to three months.

I went back to the compound and packed my things. I went to the old man at the desk and demanded my money back. He looked completely stunned. "What do you mean? Where are you going?"

I'm getting out of here," I said. "I'm going to Peshawar." He picked up the phone to call someone but in the meantime a group of men had gathered around me. They told me not to go, that it was the wrong way, that Peshawar was dangerous. That I should stay with them and work in peace.

I shooed them away. There was no way they were going to convince me of anything, and I told them so. Eventually, the old man got off the phone. With a long face, he handed me my eight hundred dollars. "You are taking the wrong path," he said. I laughed. It was the right path for me. I had wasted two weeks here, but I had gained three months on my visa. It wasn't such a bad deal.

As I walked out of the compound and into the bright sun, I was assaulted again by the stench of sewage. I thought about the legend I had heard over and over again inside. That Muhammad Ilyas had been living in India, but he smelled the perfume of paradise coming from across the border and brought his followers with him to Raiwind.

I laughed. The whole place smelled like shit.

Abu Anas

I knew I had to get to Peshawar. I was certain that if I got there I could find my way to the camps. I knew this because I had seen *Rambo III*. On his way into

Afghanistan, Rambo stopped in Peshawar to pick up weapons. So I knew there was a border crossing near Peshawar, and figured that's where the weapons were going also. Peshawar was the best place, I reasoned, to find the road to *jihad*.

So after I left the Tabligh center in Raiwind, I took a taxi to the train station in Lahore. There was no train to Peshawar for another seventeen hours, and the ride would take two full days. I took a taxi to the airport instead, and bought a ticket for a flight at seven o'clock that evening. I would be in Peshawar by nine.

It was mid-afternoon by the time I bought my ticket, and soon I would need to make my *salat*. I had seen a small mosque near the airport parking lot, so I headed there. I was still fifty meters away from it when I saw a swarm of people in the white robes of Tabligh. I cursed under my breath; these were the last people I wanted to see. But I needed to make my *salat*, so I put my head down and headed towards them. I was wearing my street clothes, and hoped they wouldn't recognize me.

Of course, one of them did. "Omar, where are you headed? Are you going back home?"

I looked up. I didn't recognize the man who called out to me. He was smiling at me with that slightly vacant look everyone had at the center. "I'm going to Peshawar," I grumbled.

Immediately, a cloud passed over his face. "Why would you go to Peshawar?" he asked, his voice deep with concern.

I didn't have time to answer him; we needed to perform our *salat*. But when we were done with our prayers a large group clustered around me. They asked me to sit with them for a few minutes. I conceded and we all sat down in front of the mosque. There was an old man in the group, and he spoke first. "It was God who brought you to Tabligh," he said. "And it was God who gave you your gift for bringing people back to Islam. Why do you want to run away from your destiny?"

The others murmured in agreement and looked at me with their wide, stupid eyes. I had already had enough, and stood up to go. "My destiny is in Peshawar," I said, turning to walk away.

Behind me, they began to wail in sad voices. "No, no, please come back. Sit with us. Come back to us. You're making a huge mistake. Please come back."

I was annoyed. I had already endured two weeks of this, and I wanted to end it for good, so I turned back to them and spoke in a loud voice.

"My philosophy is not the same as yours. You fight your *jihad* with a Kur'an in your hand. I fight mine with a Kur'an in my belt, and a Kalashnikov in my hand."

Then I turned away and walked back towards the airport. I hadn't taken five steps when another voice rang out.

"Omar."

Shit, I thought. They're never going to give up. I turned back and saw a man sitting alone by the side of the mosque. He was wearing light beige robes, like the others, but he hadn't been standing with the group. He raised his hand and beckoned me over. I was curious, and took a few steps towards him.

"Don't worry," he said. "I'm not one of them." He spoke in Arabic, which struck me. All the others had spoken to me in English.

"*Assalamu'alaykum*, brother," I responded as I walked over to where he was sitting. I spoke to him in Arabic. "But if you're not one of them, then how did you know my name?"

He gestured to me to sit down next to him, and I did. He said his name was Abu Anas. "I was in the Tabligh center with you," he explained in a flat, calm voice. "But I am not one of them. I've been watching you."

"What do you mean?"

"I watched you. I listened to what you said. I saw that you were not like the others, that you wanted to make a real *jihad*. But I couldn't speak to you there. It's too dangerous."

I said nothing.

"I can help you," he said. "I'm on the same flight as you to Peshawar this evening."

He knew I was going to Peshawar, which meant he had been following me in the airport. I was suspicious of this man, and tried to get a fix on him. He wore a *Pakol*, the traditional Afghani hat I knew from pictures of Massoud. But he wore a Pakistani *shalwar kameez*. It was old; the cloth was worn and it had holes in it. If he's so poor, I thought, how can he afford to take a plane from Lahore to Peshawar? I didn't know who this man was or who he was working for, but I knew that Pakistan was infested with spies and secret police. I had to be extremely cautious. When I didn't respond, he spoke again.

"We have a few hours until our flight," he said. "Let's go back to the airport and sit down and talk. It's cooler in there, and we can get something to drink. It's not safe to talk out here."

I nodded, and we walked back to the terminal. We sat down at the café and we both ordered a Fanta. Then, without speaking, he took a paper out of his bag and put it on the table. "Do you know what this is?" he asked.

I was stunned by what I saw when I looked down: a copy of *Al Ansar*. I picked it up to examine it and realized immediately that it was the real thing; I recognized Tarek's stamp. I looked at the date and saw that it was only a couple of weeks old.

I could feel tears welling up in my eyes. I was excited, of course, because I immediately grasped that Abu Anas was for real, that he was going to help me get into the camps. I knew at that moment that it wouldn't be long before I was in Afghanistan.

But seeing the copy of *Al Ansar* also made me sad, because it reminded me of my family. Of Hakim, who had completely lost his way. Of Nabil, who had lost both Hakim and me on the same day. And of my mother, whose family had been ripped apart along with her house.

"This is incredible," I said, shaking my head. "Incredible." I looked up, and I knew Abu Anas saw that my eyes were wet.

"Brother, you have no idea." I said. "I came from Belgium. We printed *Al Ansar* in my house. We mailed it all over the world. But then the police raided the house and arrested everyone. I escaped, and that's why I'm here. I'm here to make my *jihad*."

Abu Anas opened his eyes wide for just an instant—I could tell he was impressed. Then he looked at me intently and spoke in a soothing voice. "Yes, brother, I heard about the arrests. *La hawla wa-la-kuata ila bi-allah*." There is no power apart from God.

He was clearly affected by the emotion in my voice and the tears in my eyes. I knew he thought that I was upset that my family had been arrested, which I was, of course. But as any actor knows, the best performances always draw on real emotions.

Abu Anas leaned in and spoke quietly in his affectless voice. "It was risky to try to get to Peshawar without an address, the name of a contact." He paused and stared at me intently. "If you come with me, I can bring you to some of our Arab brothers in Peshawar. They will train you, and help you get into Afghanistan."

I couldn't believe my luck. "*Allah malikoul'hamd*," I said. "I am so fortunate that God has brought you to me." I was genuinely grateful to Abu Anas, just not for the reasons he thought.

He told me that as soon as we got up from the café, we should pretend not to know each other. We would sit apart on the plane. When we arrived in

Peshawar, I should go straight to the taxi rank and wait for him there. We would spend the night at the Tabligh center in Peshawar, and then meet the Arabs the next day. I agreed, and we parted without another word.

As the plane took off from Lahore, I gazed out the window and thought about how fortunate I was. I had been in Pakistan for less than a month, and already I had found my introduction to the camps. I had a fleeting wish that Gilles could see me now and realize how wrong he and the DGSE had been about me. But then I pushed it aside. I had to put Gilles, the DGSE, and that whole part of my life out of my mind if I was going to succeed in the camps.

Peshawar

When we landed in Peshawar, I headed straight outside to the taxi rank. Every few seconds a different driver would approach me and try to lure me into his car with an offer of the lowest price. After about twenty minutes, Abu Anas finally emerged from the airport. There was a Pakistani man with him. Abu Anas explained that this man would be our driver and take us to the Tabligh center where we would spend the night.

During the ride, Abu Anas explained that it was far too dangerous to travel to the refugee camp that night. We would go the next day to meet the Arabs there. I had to be careful not to arouse any suspicions, Abu Anas warned. He told me the Tabligh centers were overrun with *mukhabarat,* the secret service. Much later, I learned that a group of army officers had tried to overthrow the government the previous fall. After they were arrested, it emerged that they had links to *Jama'at al Tabligh*. Abu Anas told me none of this, he just warned me to speak as little as possible as long as we were inside the center, and not to speak a word of Arabic.

It was the spring of 1995, a dangerous time to be an Arab in Pakistan. Islamic extremism was on the rise, and Benazir Bhutto, the prime minister, had been trying for years to stamp it out, particularly after the United States threatened to put Pakistan on its list of terrorist states. But she seemed to be losing the battle: a year earlier, two American employees of the U.S. consulate in Karachi were murdered on their way to work. And just a few months before I arrived in Pakistan, Ramzi Ahmed Yousef, the mastermind of the 1993 World Trade Center bombings, had been arrested in Islamabad, focusing the world's attention on the country's role in breeding Islamic extremism. Bhutto was

determined to show the world she was tough on radical Islam. And she was especially determined to prove it to America. She was in the midst of negotiating
for the purchase of several F–16 fighter planes, and the deal had been held up
due to U.S. sanctions.

Bhutto's government was particularly tough on Arabs, who they blamed for
inciting extremism within Pakistan. A year earlier, the government had ordered
Arab veterans of the Soviet-Afghan war to leave the country. When they didn't,
the police began a series of aggressive raids to draw them out. By 1995, the
crackdown on Arabs was intensifying as the war in Bosnia was coming to an
end, and more Arab fighters were streaming back into Afghanistan and Pakistan
from that conflict.

It was a dangerous time to be an Arab in Pakistan.

We spent the night at the Tabligh center outside Peshawar. It was just like Raiwind; there were hundreds of people sitting on the floor, all with the same
glazed look on their faces. By now I loathed them, these weak, lost people with
their philosophy of inaction.

Abu Anas and I did not speak at all that night. We made our ablutions and
performed the *salat* and ate dinner, then went to bed very early. The next morning I put on my white *shalwar kameez* and Abu Anas and I made our *salat* along
with the others. We left the center and had breakfast at a café nearby, and then
got on a bus to the refugee camp in Peshawar. We drove for several kilometers on
a road so filled with shops, people, animals, and vehicles of all kinds that it could
hardly be called a road. And everywhere there were armed police, dressed in
their uniform: a black *shalwar kameez* and a beret.

At one point, Abu Anas gestured to me and we got off the bus and began to
walk. We were in the midst of the refugee camp. There were shops, stands selling food, and people everywhere. Tent after tent after tent. At one point, Abu
Anas stopped to buy some bread and meat. He told me he had a wife and five
children, and needed to bring food because he hadn't been home for a week.

For a week. Factoring in the travel time, he could only have been observing
me at Raiwind for a few days, I calculated. My mind went back to the man I had
met at the airport in Istanbul, the man who sent me to Tabligh. Originally, I
thought he was a member of the sect who just wanted to recruit me, but now I
wasn't so sure. He hadn't been wearing white like the others, and he was wearing an Afghan turban. And now here was Abu Anas, who fit in with the Tabligh
in both Raiwind and Peshawar, although he clearly wasn't one of them. Was it
coincidence he had found me at Raiwind? Or had he been sent to find me?

We walked through part of the camp and then out onto a dusty track. Abu Anas pointed ahead at the dark mountains that rose in the distance. "That's Afghanistan," he said. Then he pointed to a valley. "There, that's the Khyber Pass."

As we continued walking, he pointed out a cluster of houses. The houses were far bigger than anything in the refugee camp. They were sturdy, made of brick. He said Arab families lived there, mostly the families of the men who had been martyred in the war against the Russians. Some of the men were still alive and in Afghanistan, he explained, fighting against the government of Burhanuddin Rabbani in Kabul.

The terrain was changing as we walked. The camp was set on completely flat ground, but here there were small hills and the ground was much rockier. About five hundred meters from the perimeter of the camp we reached a group of houses. We stopped in front of one, and Abu Anas told me to wait while he went inside and asked his family to prepare a room for me.

A few moments later he emerged from house and led me inside. He took me to a room with a bed and told me to rest for a couple of hours. He said he would wake me for the midday *salat*, and that in the meantime he would try to reach Ibn Sheikh by radio. I had never heard that name before, but I didn't think about it. I just shut the door and lay down on the bed.

As I stared up at the ceiling, I thought about the dream I had in Brussels. Hakim and I were walking through the mountains. My legs were tired and I wanted to stop; I wanted to begin my *jihad*. "No, brother," he said. "Not yet. You're not ready."

As I drifted off to sleep, I spoke softly to myself. "I'm ready now, brother. I'm ready now."

Ibn Sheikh

The room was bright with sunlight when Abu Anas came to wake me up. It was time for the midday *salat*. As we were heading out the door of his house, he turned to me. "We'll go to the mosque now to pray," he said, "but you must not speak to anyone. Not a word. When you're done with your prayers, go outside and sit by yourself." Then he went on to say he had made contact with Ibn Sheikh who would be meeting us at the mosque. I was excited. I had no idea who Ibn Sheikh was, but I was sure he could help me get to the camps.

Abu Anas took me to a small mosque where we made our *salat*. There were about ten other Arabs and two black Africans there. No one spoke to anyone else. When we were done, I went outside and sat on a rock and read my Kur'an. After about twenty minutes, I heard a voice behind me. "Which one do you think is Ibn Sheikh?"

I turned. It was Abu Anas. He was pointing up the road towards the refugee camp. There were two men coming into view. One was short, the other tall. "I have no idea," I said.

Abu Anas sat down next to me and smiled. "Brother, at least make a guess."

I looked again at the two men. The short one was incredibly fit. Even under his clothes I could tell he was made of pure muscle. His skin was dark and dry from the sun. The other man was quite thin and seemed more ethereal. There was something almost regal about him, like a Masai warrior. He had a black beard, and very light skin. He looked nothing like a *mujahidin*. "I think he's the shorter one," I told Abu Anas.

"Brother," he replied. "You're mistaken. The tall man is Ibn Sheikh." Then he stood up and walked towards the two men. The three of them spoke briefly, and then the shorter man peeled off to the side to wait while Abu Anas and Ibn Sheikh spoke to each other alone.

After a few minutes, I saw Abu Anas walk off with the short man, back in the direction of his house. Ibn Sheikh approached me. "*Assalamu'alaykum*," he said.

"*Alaykum assalam*," I replied.

Then he sat down next to me and began asking me questions. "Where are you from?" His voice was calm and quiet, like Abu Anas's voice.

"Morocco," I told him.

He smiled. "No, brother, I meant where did you come from to get here?"

"From Belgium," I said.

"Really?" he asked. His face barely moved as he spoke, but I could see that his eyes held a fierce intelligence. "Why did you leave Belgium? Did someone send you here?"

Before I responded, I paused for a few seconds. My body was completely wired. I had already told Abu Anas my story, and I was traveling under a passport with my own name. If Abu Anas read *Al Ansar*, then Ibn Sheikh surely did as well. So he certainly knew about the raids in Brussels. The only question was whether or not he knew about my role in them. In those short seconds, my mind raced through the possibilities. Maybe Hakim and the others believed my explanation of why I had joined the DGSE. Or maybe they had had no chance to tell anyone about my confession because they were arrested so soon after. But what if they had? What if Abu Anas had figured out who I was and brought me here to have me killed for betraying the *mujahidin*? Anything seemed possible at this moment, but there was only one thing I could do.

I took a deep breath. "I left because I had to escape." I paused. "You've probably already heard about the raids in Brussels." I paused again and looked at him, but he said nothing. He gave no indication of what he did or did not know. And so I continued. "A couple of months ago there was a crackdown on the GIA in Belgium. The police came to our house. We were printing and distributing *Al Ansar* there. They arrested all of the brothers." I looked again at Ibn Sheikh. Still nothing. Just the same cool gaze

I went on. "The police were looking for me, and so I had to get out of the country. I flew to Turkey first, and then came to Pakistan to join the *jihad*."

Ibn Sheikh listened intently as I told him my story, but nothing I said seemed to surprise him. He asked only one question. "What were the names of the brothers in Belgium?"

I responded immediately. "Amin and Yasin." I had no way of knowing if they had ever met Ibn Sheikh, but I knew they had been in the camps. I was almost certain that Tarek had not been; he was too slick, too European.

As soon as the words were out of my mouth, Ibn Sheikh smiled at me and stood up. It was as if I had flipped some switch. "Come, brother, let us go back and collect your things. Then we will go together and I will introduce you to some of the other brothers."

Ibn Sheikh and I walked back to Abu Anas's house. He was waiting for us at the door. I saw Ibn Sheikh make a tiny gesture to him, and Abu Anas darted back inside. When he came out, he was holding my bag. As he handed it to me, he gave me a warm smile.

"*Allah hafazak*" he said. "May God protect you, brother."

I never saw Abu Anas again, but much later Ibn Sheikh would tell me the two of them had fought side by side in Afghanistan in the war against the Russians.

Interrogation

After saying goodbye to Abu Anas, Ibn Sheikh led me back down the road and into the refugee camp. It was a strange and disorienting place. There were houses, tents and other structures, all pressed up against each other with no apparent logic. Along one side there was a long wall, broken up by doors. In some places the doors were ten meters apart, in others twenty-five. There was no order whatsoever.

We were in a different section of the camp than the one I had walked through earlier that day with Abu Anas. Here it was much quieter, less crowded. And the faces I did see were Arab, not Afghani.

Ibn Sheikh stopped in front of one of the doors and knocked. Someone opened the door from behind, so I couldn't see who it was. Ibn Sheikh turned to me and told me to wait where I was for a few minutes, and then went into the house. When he emerged, he spoke to me. "Please go inside and join the brothers. I'll send someone to get you in a couple of hours."

With that, he turned and walked away. I didn't know what to expect, but I had no choice but to step through the doorway. The house was cool inside, and dark. As soon as my eyes adjusted, I saw there were seven Arab men sitting on the floor. They were all very young, in their late teens or early twenties. They all wore street clothes—jeans, tracksuits. As I set my bag down, I could feel their eyes burning into me.

"*Assalamu'alaykum,*" I said.

"*Alaykum assalam,*" they all responded.

They gestured for me to join them on the floor. I sat down, and they began to talk to me. They all spoke quietly and calmly, and smiled a lot. I noticed several had strong Algerian accents. They asked me where I was from and how my trip had been. They made me feel welcome.

Then they began to ask me questions about Belgium. They continued to smile and speak in the same calm voices, but I soon realized they were testing me, that Ibn Sheikh had left me there to be interrogated. He knew I had been involved in the GIA, and so he had chosen a group of Algerians to grill me.

I told them the same story about Belgium that I had told Abu Anas and Ibn Sheikh. I told them about *Al Ansar* and about the arrests. No one said a word in response, and I had no way of knowing what they made of it; they all maintained the same placid expression throughout the conversation. They asked questions about my year in Brussels, but not about anything specific. They were direct and elliptical at the same time: they referred to no one by name, and they asked questions out of order. I realized I had to be very careful, very precise in the way I answered.

One asked me about the war in Algeria, and what I thought about the FIS and the GIA. I had heard so much about this from Amin and Yasin that I knew instantly how to respond. The FIS was *taghut*, I told the group, because it wanted elections. Only the GIA was fighting a true *jihad*. My interrogator said nothing, and then one of the others jumped to another topic.

I was getting nervous. I had no way of knowing what these men knew about me, or why Ibn Sheikh had brought me here. Their questions seemed arbitrary, and they offered nothing in return for my answers. No response at all. The same gentle smile no matter what I said. I wanted it to end.

"What is your name, brother?" one of them asked.

"Omar Nasiri."

And then silence. Total silence. Their expressions changed completely as the words came out of my mouth. They were all in shock.

Time stood still for me. It was like a bomb had gone off in the room. Did they know who I was? Had they heard this name from someone in Belgium? The men turned to each other with anxious looks, but everything and everyone was moving in slow motion. I was paralyzed.

It dawned on me that I was a dead man. I could tell from the looks on their faces that it was over. They knew I was a spy. They knew I had caused the raids in Brussels. They were going to kill me. And yet after all these weeks of anxiety, I found the realization somehow liberating. I knew my fate; I was in the hands of God now, and nothing could change my destiny. I was going to die here, as God had willed it. And so it seemed almost inevitable when I felt a hand press on my back.

"Brother, is that your real name?" The voice came from my right. The man next to me had placed his hand on my shoulder blade.

I turned to him. "Yes, that's my real name." There was nothing to be done at this point. They'd found me out.

Then the man spoke again. "Brother, we never use our real names. When you come here, you must leave everything behind—your home, your family, your identity. You must take a new name."

It was like a dam had broken; all the tension poured out of my body. This was why they were so stunned: I had failed to use a code name. I had no idea I needed to. I had been rescued only seconds before my execution. I thanked God that he had spared me.

"I'm so sorry," I said. "I didn't know that. I only have my real name." The others laughed quietly, and the man to my right told me I should choose a new one.

I decided to take the name Abu Bakr, the Prophet's close friend and the first elected caliph of Islam. The others nodded in assent, then began to stand up. The interrogation was over, and I was still alive.

Chemicals

As soon as the questions were over, one of the young men in the group told me to take my things and follow him into another room. There he asked me to show him what was in my bag. I opened it and dumped the contents on the floor: a sleeping bag, some street clothes, a pair of Ray-Bans, my new Swiss Army knife and flashlight, and some toiletries—a razor, a toothbrush, and so on.

First, he picked up the Ray-Bans. "You won't need these in the camp," he said. "You'll need to learn to fight without them." He took away most of my clothes as well, setting aside only one sweater and some underwear for me to take along. He rejected the sleeping bag. "You'll have to get used to the cold in the mountains where you're headed." Then he took up the Swiss Army knife and held it before me with a look of reproach. "You can't carry the cross of Christians when you fight under the flag of Allah." Finally, he took up my razor, and smiled gently. I realized I hadn't shaved since I arrived in Pakistan. I had already grown a short beard. "You certainly won't need this in the camps," he said. We both laughed.

The man collected all my remaining belongings and put them back in my bag. He said the rest would be waiting for me when I returned. Then he told me to leave my passport and any other forms of identification I had with me. I said I didn't want to give up my passport, and he just shrugged and let me keep it.

Then he told me to say goodbye to the other brothers in the house; he was taking me somewhere else to spend the night. After I spoke to the others, we stepped back out into the bright sunlight and walked for several minutes through the narrow streets of the refugee camp.

Soon we stopped at another door. He knocked, and an Arab man let us in. There were five other Arabs inside; they seemed older than the men in the first house, and more serious. They were all sitting quietly on the floor, reading. I looked around the room; there were books and files everywhere.

My guide greeted the other men and introduced me. They looked up briefly, greeting us in return. Then he led me to another room and told me I would be spending the night there. He said he'd come back to get me later in the afternoon. Before he left, I asked him if I could use the library and he told me I could look at anything I wanted to.

I put my things down and walked back to the front room. The other men were still reading. I went over to one of the shelves and took a few of the files. Nobody even looked up.

I went back to my room, sat down on the bed, and opened the first file. Inside, there was a degraded photocopy of some kind of training manual. It was hard to read in some places because it was clearly a copy of a copy of a copy. But the letters at the top were clear: United States of America.

It was a manual on urban warfare. It spelled out a scenario in which the Russians attacked a West German city, and outlined how the Soviet army could be repulsed by guerrilla tactics. It went on for pages and pages, and was extremely detailed. It explained how to position snipers on buildings, how to set traps, how to use buildings for cover. It explained how to hold a gun in an urban setting, and how to target the enemy in close quarters.

There was a second dossier in the same file. It was all about the use of explosives. Instructions on how to lay antitank mines and how to set booby traps by placing bombs in dead bodies. There were instructions as well on how to make bombs, but there were too many chemical formulas for me to understand most of it.

I picked up a second file and looked through that, too. It, too, was from America: a manual on kidnapping, with illustrations showing a big house and instructions on how to overcome the guards standing outside. But then I stopped reading because I heard noise in the other room. The others were getting up to perform their ablutions. It was time for the afternoon *salat*.

The guide from the first house returned shortly after the *salat*, and asked me to come with him to meet someone. As I followed him out of the house, he explained that the man we were going to see was Egyptian. "He's very nice. You'll like him. He fought in the war against the Russians. He lost an arm and a leg there. Now he studies chemicals." We were going to meet a bomb maker.

When we arrived at the house, a man in his thirties opened the door. He was wearing thick glasses, but behind them his eyes were bright and active. He had a white mask hanging around his neck. He had a prosthetic leg and arm, and smelled very strongly of chemicals.

The Egyptian looked surprised to see us at first, but then greeted us warmly and invited us in. He led us out to a small, cool garden at the back of the house, where we all sat down. I said very little in the course of the conversation that followed. Mostly, the Egyptian spoke to my young guide. Listening to them, I learned that the guide had been in Afghanistan just recently, and that he was going back in a few days. But mostly they just gossiped. I didn't recognize the names, and I couldn't follow the entire conversation because my Arabic still wasn't very strong.

After about twenty minutes, we all stood up. The Egyptian smiled and congratulated me. "I wish we had more brothers like you," he said. Then the guide and I walked back out into the afternoon heat.

Gaslight

The next afternoon, a young man came by the safe house to pick me up. I had never seen him before, but he told me Ibn Sheikh had sent him. I said goodbye to the other brothers, and then the young man and I took a bus from the refugee camp into the main part of Peshawar.

We got off in downtown Peshawar and then took a taxi to another part of the city. The area was unlike anything I had seen in Pakistan up to that point. It was very clean and lush. Over the walls, I could see that the houses were very grand.

The taxi stopped and we got out to walk. "This is Hayatabad," my guide told me. "Many Arabs live here, men who fought the *jihad* against the Russians."

I was confused. These hardly seemed like the homes of *mujahidin*. I wondered aloud if they had won their money by pillage in the war, but my guide explained that they had brought money with them when they first moved to Pakistan. Many had married Afghani women, and had stayed on when the war was over. Others were killed in the war, but their families didn't leave because they had made Pakistan their home.

It was late afternoon by this point, so the guide led me to a beautiful mosque nearby. It seemed to be made entirely of marble. There was a large open area with a fountain in the middle where we made our *salat*. The other men in the mosque looked different from any I'd seen in Pakistan since my arrival. Their clothes were finer, their skin less rough. I could even smell perfume on some of them.

Shortly after we were done with our prayers, two young boys approached us. They seemed to know my guide, and they greeted us with great enthusiasm. They spoke in Arabic. I could tell from their faces and their accents that they were Egyptian.

"Are you taking him to the *madrasa*?" one of them asked, his eyes wide.

The guide scowled, and spoke sharply under his breath. "Never speak like that in public. I will tell your father on you. You must never say such things."

The children, whose eyes had been so bright up until that moment, suddenly looked crestfallen. They darted away.

The guide then turned to me and told me to wait where I was. He needed to speak to someone. When he came back ten minutes later, something had changed. He was more somber now, less open with me. "We need to buy some Afghani clothes for you," he said. So we took a taxi to a huge textile market nearby. He picked out a green *shalwar kameez* for me, along with a *pakol*.

We ate dinner at the market. Then, as the sky was growing dark, we found another taxi and drove deeper into Hayatabad. The houses were even bigger here, on long blocks. When we got out of the taxi, the guide started down the block and I followed him. He stopped after a minute or so and turned back to make sure the driver was gone. Then we turned around and walked back in the direction we had come from.

I followed him for several blocks. We cut back and forth as if someone were following us. It was dark by now, and the only light came from the few street-lamps that dotted the neighborhood. After a few minutes we arrived at the door of a large villa. The guide stopped and knocked several times. Knock. Tap-tap-tap. Knock-knock. It was some kind of code.

The door opened, but I couldn't see anyone standing there. When I stepped inside, though, I saw a man with glasses standing behind the door. The guide handed him a piece of paper and then the two men exchanged a few words. They spoke so quietly and quickly that I couldn't understand any of it. Then the guide said goodbye to both me and the other man. He scurried out of the house so fast that I didn't have time to reply.

The house was almost completely dark inside. The only light was coming from the small gas lamp the man held in one hand. I squinted and studied the man and I saw that his beard was closely cropped to his face. It was not the beard of a *mujahid*.

He indicated that I should follow him further inside the house. It was completely silent—the two of us were alone there. He led me to a room, held his lamp inside, and told me that we would sleep there. There were two beds on the floor and a small table, nothing else. On the table was a copy of the Kur'an.

My host asked me if I had Afghani clothes. I showed him the *shalwar kameez* from the market, but he only shook his head and left the room. He came back carrying other clothes. He held them out to me and I saw that this *shalwar kameez* was much older, more worn.

Then it was time for the evening *salat*. He pointed me to one of the bath-rooms, where I made my ablutions, and then we prayed together. When we were done, he sat on the bed and picked up some papers. He pointed me to the Kur'an. We sat silently in our beds reading by the light of his lamp. Eventually, I set the Kur'an aside and lay down while he continued to read. I quickly fell into a deep sleep.

My host woke me before dawn and guided me into another room, where we performed the morning *salat* together. Before the sunlight began to creep into the house, he walked over to a desk and wrote a letter. Then he turned to me: "In a few minutes a man will come to take you into Afghanistan and to the *mukhayyam*."

Mukhayyam means "camp." It was the first time anyone had actually said I was going to one of the training camps. I felt a slight shiver, not just because I was excited, but also because I realized I was in the presence of someone very powerful. His voice was serene like the voices of the other men I had met in the refugee camp, like the voices of Amin and Yasin. But there was an intensity in him when he spoke that I had never experienced before in anyone. I will never forget the perfect clarity of that moment.

"You must not say a word to the guide," he went on. "If he orders you to do something, you must do it. You must not ask him any questions, or tell him anything at all." I nodded in assent.

Soon, there was a knock on the door. "Come with me," he said. "Take your things." He opened the door and there was a young Afghani standing outside. My host passed the Afghani the letter he had just written. As I left the house, the man asked me to remember him in my *du'a'* supplications, my personal prayers. Then he bumped his chest and shoulder against mine.

I had seen the others do this in the refugee camp. Most Arabs, when they greet someone or say goodbye, show great affection; they will even kiss each other. But the *mujahidin* do nothing of the sort. Their greeting is aggressive and respectful at the same time.

It was my first salute as a *mujahid*.

Borderland

I followed the guide from the house. We walked for a little bit and then took a taxi for a few kilometers. The sun was just inching over the horizon. The taxi dropped us off by the side of the road and we stood there for a few minutes. Soon, I saw a pickup truck in the distance coming towards us.

The guide and I climbed in the back of the truck. There were bags of meal in the bed of the truck and we sat on those. There were a few men and women, all Pakistanis, with us, and chickens also.

We drove south from Peshawar for six or seven hours. I didn't speak a word during the journey, but I studied the face of my guide. He was young; even though his skin was ruddy from the sun, it had not yet been etched by the deep wrinkles I had seen on some of the other men. He had a broad forehead, and his nose was almost Asiatic, not as slender as the typical Afghan nose. Perhaps because of what the other man had said to me that morning, or perhaps for other reasons, I didn't quite trust him.

There were several checkpoints along the way, each one controlled by a different tribal militia. This was a dangerous journey; these were Shiites, and I was an Arab Sunni traveling with an Afghan Sunni. I was happy I had a beard at this point, because it helped conceal my appearance.

At one checkpoint we were stopped by four men. They were all dressed in black and held Kalashnikovs. They ordered two of the Pakistanis to get off the truck, and began to argue with them about what was in their bags. Eventually, they arrested the two men, and we drove on without them.

Somewhere near a town named Sadda, the truck stopped. The guide ordered me to get out and we got into a Toyota pickup which took us up a smaller, unpaved road. We drove for several kilometers. At one point the guide pointed forward. "Do you see those two trees?" he asked. He spoke in Arabic. "Behind them there is a hill. That is Afghanistan."

Soon we arrived at the border, though at first I didn't understand that it was a border because there was no sign or building to mark it. There were two Pakistanis in military uniforms standing under the shade of a tree.

My guide ordered me to give him my belongings and walk straight through the crossing without stopping. If anyone asked me anything, I should keep walking and he would follow behind to speak with the officials. I must not speak to anyone.

When I got to the guards, they were busy inspecting the other people who were crossing in both directions. I looked at the other travelers and noticed that all their clothes were worn and covered with dust. I understood then why the man in the house had taken my new *shalwar kameez*. I would have stood out like a light.

Most of the people crossing the border were carrying large packages and sacks. It was quite clear that the guards had no interest in what was inside the packages, only in how much money they could get for allowing these people to pass. Their hands were constantly shooting in and out of their pockets. They were far too busy to notice me when I walked by.

There were several taxis—trucks and four-wheel-drive vehicles—parked on the Afghan side of the border. The guide got into one of them, and I followed. We drove deeper into Afghanistan, on narrow roads snaking through the arid hills. By now it was midday, and the sun was bright and hot. It shimmered off the black rocks of the Afghan mountains.

We had driven for about forty minutes when we passed a cemetery. Tall stakes, some as high as six meters, rose from the ground next to some of the graves. Each one was adorned with a piece of bright fabric in red, white, or green. These were the tombs of the *mujahidin*. I recognized them from all the films I had seen.

We saw many more of these cemeteries as we drove. As we were drawing near to one of them, I noticed a group of five men in white turbans. They were standing next to a pickup truck with a huge antiaircraft gun inside. There was a rack on the roof of the truck with hundreds of black ribbons hanging from it, glimmering as they rustled in the slight wind. I knew instantly these were bands of audio- and videotapes. This was the Taliban.

The men stood in the road and forced the driver to come to a halt. As one of them walked towards the car, I was struck by how young he was, no more than sixteen years old. He held a Kalashnikov in one hand and a stick in the other. He leaned inside the truck and poked his stick at the stereo on the dashboard, and began to speak to the driver. The driver leaned forward, plucked a cassette from the glove compartment, and stuck it into the tape deck. The tape began to play; it was a recitation of the Kur'an. The young *talib* smiled and waved us on.

As we drove onward the terrain began to change. The road was less dusty, and there was more vegetation. Soon, I saw a village ahead of us, and a river. There were children playing in the road, and girls in the river doing the washing.

The guide said something to the driver, and he stopped and let us out. From here, the guide and I continued on foot out of the village and up into the hills. As we pressed on, he moved more and more quickly. Soon, I was practically running. I knew that I mustn't speak to him, so I couldn't ask him to slow down. After a couple of kilometers, I was really struggling and began to wonder if he was running away from me on purpose. I wasn't at all sure I could trust him.

Soon, he was so far ahead of me, I couldn't see him anymore. I was alone among the black rocks. I began to wonder, is it possible that he knows I'm a spy? That the last few days have all been an elaborate ploy to kill me? I remembered the film in the Pompidou Center in which the *mujahidin* ambushed the Soviet convoy, and wondered if I should continue following this man. I knew nothing about him, or where he was taking me. I briefly considered turning around, but then forced the thought from my mind. I was here for a reason. I would press on no matter what.

I was sweating all over from walking so fast in the bright heat, and my legs were tired. I stopped to put my head down to take some breaths and recover. When I looked up, I saw the guide standing on a ridge far ahead of me. "Hurry," he shouted back at me. "Or we'll miss lunch."

From that point we continued on together. We headed back down into a valley. It was like an oasis among the black hills. Everything was green and lush, and I could see the glimmer of water in the distance.

Suddenly, a loud noise. *Bam. Bam. Bam.* I didn't recognize it immediately. Soon, there were other noises. *Boom. Boom. Tat-tat-tat-tat.*

Then I realized what it was: guns, explosions, mortar fire. The guide grinned at me. "Here we are, brother," he said. "This is Khaldan." It was the first time I had heard the word *Khaldan*.

I followed the guide down the hill to the bottom of the valley, where I could see some buildings nestled in a gorge between two high mountains. A river ran down from the mountains, flowing into the valley and across the camp. To my right was a wide, flat space. High in the distance on the left were the remains of some sort of watchtower.

We stopped in front of the first building. The guide turned to me and looked me straight in the eye. "Stay here," he ordered, as he pointed to my feet. He wanted me to stand in this exact spot. Then he ran up the path and disappeared behind the building.

I stood there for what seemed like an hour. The sun was beating down and sweat was dripping into my eyes, mingling with the blinding rays of the sun. I wished that I had my Ray-Bans. I was weak and dizzy from the walk; I had not eaten anything all day. Suddenly, everything seemed surreal, threatening. The merciless sun had drained all the color from the sky, and the black rocks seemed menacing against the hazy white backdrop.

I had no idea what was going to happen next. A guide who I did not trust had left me standing here by myself. I hadn't seen any other people for several kilometers. What was in store for me here? I had put myself in great danger. It wouldn't be hard for them to find out that I was a spy. But then I began to reason with myself that if they wanted to kill me, they could have done so in Peshawar, or even earlier. Abu Anas could have murdered me in Lahore.

Gunfire snapped me out of my reverie. *Tat-tat-tat-tat-tat.* From this spot deep in the valley, I could hear the shots ricochet between the mountains. Every explosion multiplied in the air with its own echo. *Bang. Bang. Bang.*

I could feel the explosions in my body. I began to experience the same primal thrill I felt when I fired guns with Édouard for the first time. I realized that I had dreamed of this moment for years. I was in the mountains of Afghanistan and there was gunfire all around me. *Tat-tat-tat-tat-tat.*

I pushed away all the dark thoughts inside my head, realizing I had accomplished my objective. I was ready to begin my *jihad*.

Khaldan

In reality, I had not been standing there for more than five minutes when a man came running down the path towards me. He was young, in his early thirties. He held an assault rifle in his right hand; it looked like a Kalashnikov, only more compact. His body was incredibly taut, powerful. He moved like a cat, quietly but with tremendous precision.

I was so struck by his extraordinary physical presence that I did not realize until he was standing right in front of me that he was in fact quite short, maybe 165 centimeters, no more. I could tell he was Palestinian. The faces of Palestinian men all have something in common, a kind of blankness that reflects both an acceptance of loss and a commitment to destiny. I had seen it on television a thousand times.

The man stopped in front of me. "*Assalamu'alaykum,*" he said.

"*Alaykum assalam.*"

Then he took my bag out of my hands and dropped it on the ground. In one swift motion he searched my entire body with the light touch of his hand. His movements were precise, controlled. The whole process took no more than a couple of seconds.

Under my *shalwar kameez* he discovered my belt, which contained my passport and money. He took it from me. "Do you have anything else with you?" he asked.

I told him no, and he counted the money in front of me. He told me that later he would give me a paper to sign for my belongings. Then he put his hand on my arm. "Brother, what is your name?"

"Omar Nasiri," I said.

He stepped back, surprised. "Is that your real name?"

I could feel the blood rising to my face; I was ashamed of myself. I had responded instinctively; I hadn't yet gotten used to my new name, and this strange man had disoriented me. I rushed to correct myself. "My name is Abu Bakr," I stuttered.

He smiled. "That name has already been taken by another brother," he said. "You'll have to choose something else."

I thought for a second and then asked, "Abu Imam is OK?"

"Yes, that's fine," he said. Then he led me up into the compound, past several buildings. As I followed him, I noticed again how controlled each step, each movement was. Every piece of him seemed activated. His body was completely wound up, like a lion preparing an attack.

He led me into the center of the compound, to a brick building with a metal roof. He explained that this was the mosque, and that I should sit there and wait for the others. Before he took his leave, he leaned in to me and spoke in a voice that was calm yet intense. "You must always remember that you are here to make your *jihad*," he warned me. "You are not here to talk to the others. We do not ask questions of the brothers. We do not reveal anything of ourselves. You must stay focused on your mission."

I nodded, and he went on. "Also, you must never speak to any of the Afghanis—the guides, the guard, the cooks. Not a word."

I nodded again to show him that I understood. Then he turned and disappeared as quickly as he had come, his feet skimming the ground like a dancer's.

I sat down alone in the mosque and let the dark, cool air wash over me. I felt my body relax slightly. My eyes were no longer tearing from the burning sun. The explosions and gunfire continued to echo in the hills, but I was already growing used to it.

After few minutes, everything suddenly fell quiet. It was totally silent in the mosque: no bird cries, no explosions, nothing. I could hear the sound of my breath and the beating of my heart, which was beginning to slow down after all of the exercise and anxiety.

Suddenly, the door flew open with a loud noise. Five huge men lurched into the mosque. They were all in their twenties, with white skin and light eyes. Each had a Kalashnikov strapped around his chest, and wore a belt strung heavy with grenades and ammunition. They all had the same dark circles under their eyes as I had noticed on Amin and Yasin.

When the men saw me sitting there, they smiled and approached me. I could tell from their accents that they were from Chechnya, so I spoke to them in English. They introduced themselves by the names they had adopted: Abu Enes, Abu Omar, and so on. We greeted each other in the typical manner, by pressing our shoulders against each other's. I could feel the brute strength of their bodies.

It was the time of the midday *salat*, and soon the mosque began to fill up. There were about sixty men in all. I could tell from their faces that these men were from all over the world: North Africa, the Middle East, Central Asia.

As the prayers were about to begin, I realized that I hadn't made my ablutions. I turned to the man next to me and asked him where the bathroom was. He touched my arm and gently guided me out of the mosque and across an open space, down to the edge of the river. Then he pointed up to a cluster of cabins amidst a group of large rocks. He told me to take a bucket of water from the river and make my ablutions there. I dipped my hand in the water. Although the sun outside was scorching, the water was freezing cold. I realized it was coming straight from the snows in the mountains.

After I finished my ablutions, I returned to the mosque to perform the *salat*. I noticed the men who had Kalashnikovs had placed them on the ground between their legs while they prayed. Once we had finished, the man who met me when I arrived at the camp stood up to introduce me. "This is Abu Imam," he said. "He is your new brother. He has joined us today in our *jihad*."

I smiled as all of the men in the mosque greeted me and cheered. *"Masha'-allah! Masha'allah! Masha'allah!"*

We left the mosque and walked over to the cantina, which was the first building I had seen at the entrance to the camp. The building was made of stone, but the roof was constructed out of dried leaves that looked like palm. I had seen these plants on the walk into the camp. Inside, the roof was covered with plastic to keep the water out.

We all sat on the floor and ate a kind of stew made of beans. It was disgusting, but I was famished so I ate it anyway. When we had finished our meal, another man came to me and told me to follow him. He handed me a thin sleeping bag and some blankets, then guided me across the camp to a cluster of small buildings and led me inside one of them. He told me that this was where I would sleep. I looked around and saw that several other people were living here as well. Their things were neatly stacked around the edges of the room. There was no floor, just the hard earth of the Afghan mountains.

That evening after dinner, we divided up into small groups to practice the *tajwid,* the recitation of the Kur'an. We were assigned to groups according to the level of our spiritual knowledge. My group included five Chechens and an Algerian. We were all beginners.

One of the men explained to me that the man who had introduced me in the mosque was the emir of the camp, Abu Bakr. I laughed to myself that I had inadvertently chosen the same name in Peshawar. The man then explained to me that Abu Bakr was only emir when Ibn Sheikh was away, and that when he returned he would be emir.

After we finished our studies, we gathered again in the main square in front of the mosque. Abu Bakr called us to attention. He gave his instructions to the night guard, and told us that night's password. Then he chose one of the brothers to lead the call to prayer the next morning.

Abu Bakr then reviewed the events of the day. Without naming anyone directly, he praised particular achievements and criticized certain failures of some of the brothers. One had been in the bathroom when his group was leaving for training. Abu Bakr reminded everyone that this was careless and not the correct behavior for a *mujahid.* A *mujahid* is constantly mindful of his brothers. It is a matter of life and death.

When Abu Bakr finished speaking, I headed up to the dormitory and lay down on the cold earth. The temperature had dropped considerably when the sun set, and cold had seeped through my clothes and into my body. It took me several minutes to warm up under the sleeping bag and blankets.

Soon, my heart began to slow. My body relaxed, and I began to think about everything that had happened. I had woken up in a different country that morning. I had been in Istanbul less than a month earlier. And now I was here, in a training camp with the *mujahidin.* Everything seemed strange and yet totally familiar at the same time. It was exactly what I had expected and longed for after watching all those films, after reading about the war against the Russians, after listening to Amin and Yasin talk. I thought about the gunfire that I had heard and the Kalashnikovs the brothers carried, and I realized I was going to enjoy myself here.

I was excited and eager for the dawn. But in the final moments before I fell asleep, I forced myself to reflect on my mission. That night, and every night that followed for the next year, I reminded myself that I was a spy.

Abu Hamam

I didn't get much sleep that night. After what seemed like only an hour or two, I was awakened by the sounds of the others rustling about in the dark. When I opened my eyes, it was still completely dark. As I began to focus, I realized it must be time for the first *salat*. It was summer, and the sun rose very early.

We made our ablutions and walked over to the mosque to pray with the others. It was very cold still. When we were done, the entire group assembled on the square in front of the mosque. Abu Bakr divided us into three groups and assigned each group to a different trainer.

Then we all ran out to the front of the camp, where there was a large, flat area. The sun was just peeking over the mountains and my body was still chilled from the night before. We performed exercises as a group to warm up our muscles. I noticed that the others were all extremely fit, I began to worry. It had been years since I had taken any kind of exercise.

That morning, I was assigned to a group with a trainer named Abu Hamam. He was Eritrean, and his skin was much darker than the others'. His movements were elegant, but in a different way than Abu Bakr's.

I didn't have much time to consider Abu Hamam before our exercise began. Without saying a word, he began running towards one of the large mountains behind the camp, and we followed him. Soon we were at the mountain, and running straight up the side.

At first, the movement felt good. I could feel my body warming up, overcoming the chill of the night before. But after about a hundred meters, I began to feel a sting in my quadriceps. The others were pulling far ahead; I was already the last man in the group. There was one other man nearly as slow, but he was quite fat and was wearing a bullet-proof vest that must have weighed twenty kilograms or more. No one else was wearing a vest; I assumed that this man had been told to do so because he needed to lose weight. Slightly farther in front of us were two Saudis. They were clearly much older than the others, well into their forties. My heart was pounding so loudly that I could hear it. Clearly, my training wasn't off to a good start.

After about fifteen minutes, the rest of the group, including the fat man and the two middle-aged Saudis, disappeared behind a large outcropping. When I got there a few minutes later, I saw them all standing together hundreds of meters higher up the mountain. Abu Hamam was giving directions and the brothers were all stretching their bodies.

I was so glad at the prospect of a rest that I sprinted as fast as I could. But I was so far behind that it took me several minutes to reach the others. As I was pulling closer, I heard Abu Hamam shout at the top of his lungs. "*Takbir!*"

The others responded as a chorus. "*Takbir! Allahu akbar! Takbir! Allahu akbar! Takbir! Allahu akbar! Takbir! Allahu akbar!*"

Just as the echoes were receding, I caught up to the group. I finally stopped running, but my heart was still pounding and my legs felt dead under me. I bent over to catch my breath, and when I brought my head up Abu Hamam was standing right in front of me.

"*Masha'allah*, Abu Imam," he said.

I tried to say something in return, but hadn't caught my breath. No sound came from my mouth. But it didn't matter; he had already turned around. He immediately began running again and everyone followed him.

My heart sank. I didn't know how I could go any farther; I had no energy left. All I had eaten the day before was that terrible stew for lunch and dinner, and none of us had had any breakfast that morning before beginning our exercise.

I stayed put for just a few final, precious seconds, and then I began to run again. Within a minute, I was already well behind the others. The sun had risen by now, and it was hot on my back. The heat and the exertion were beginning to make me dizzy.

After about half an hour, I turned a corner and saw that the group had stopped again. I prayed they would stay put long enough for me to have a rest, but just as I got to them, Abu Hamam turned to start off again.

"Abu Hamam," I cried. He turned and looked at me quizzically. "Abu Hamam," I sputtered, trying to catch my breath. "I just got here yesterday. Could we stay here for just a few more minutes so I can rest?"

He gave me a broad smile, his teeth bright white against the dark of his skin. "Abu Imam," he said, "in combat, the group can't be held up by one person." His voice was soft and lilting.

I pleaded with him. "Before a *mujahid* can fight, he has to train. I just got here yesterday, and now you seem to want to kill me before I even become a *mujahid*." Abu Hamam smiled again and laughed softly. Then he turned and began sprinting up the mountain.

Abu Hamam kept running, and the group kept running behind him. Nobody seemed to wear out, not even the fat man with the vest, or the old Saudis. Of course, they got rests in between. The farther I fell behind, the longer the group rested each time Abu Hamam stopped. And because I couldn't rest, I got slower and slower. With every step, I prayed that Abu Hamam would turn and head downhill, back towards the river and the camp. But of course he didn't.

We ran for nearly four hours that morning. By the time I got back to camp, I was a complete wreck. The others were standing next to the cantina waiting for me to arrive. Once I did, Abu Hamam called out the name of each member of the group. When he had accounted for all of us, we were allowed to get water and eat our breakfast. It was only tea and bread, but I devoured it.

As I learned in the coming days, this was a normal morning at Khaldan. Every day we would have the same routine. We would wake before dawn to pray, then immediately head out for callisthenics on the field and then exercise in the mountains.

I didn't always run in Abu Hamam's group; we had different trainers at different times. It wasn't always the same run; sometimes we did other things as well: jumping, crawling, and swimming in the frigid river. Carrying weapons with us, not just to add weight and increase the level of difficulty, but so that we could learn to transport matériel to the front. One day we carried rockets up into the mountains. Some of them were huge, more than a meter long. These were for a smaller version of the Katyusha, or Stalin Organ, a multiple-rocket launcher the Soviets fielded in World War II. That day no one was running. It was all we could do to remain standing under their massive weight.

Often we ran without shoes. Not just in summer; we ran barefoot even when there was frost on the ground in late fall. It was awful at first; the rocks were sharp and rugged, and I would come back to camp with my feet covered in blood. Over time, Abu Bakr would teach me how to move on the rocks, how to measure them with my eyes so I would know where to step. He taught me how to shape my foot to each stone so that I could glide over the ground without feeling a thing. This is how I learned to walk like Amin and Yasin.

Abu Hamam ran differently. His body wasn't as wound up as Abu Bakr's, and his motions were less precise. There was something regal in the way he moved, but also relaxed. He never seemed to look at the rocks in front of him. Once I thought about it, it made a great deal of sense to me that he was comfortable in this terrain in a way the others were not. He had grown up fighting in the mountains of the Rift Valley in the guerilla war against Ethiopian rule.

Abu Suhail

I was on my own in the camp, which was unusual. Most of the others came and went in groups of three or more: Chechens, Tajiks, Kashmiris, Uzbeks, Saudis, Algerians, and so on. These groups would train together. I had no one to train with, so after breakfast the first morning Abu Hamam told me to join Abu Suhail's group. Abu Suhail was already working with a group of young Chechens who had arrived several weeks before.

Abu Suhail was from Yemen. He was young, in his early twenties. He was very thin, and his skin was light. He was quiet and intense.

Our classroom was a small building several hundred meters upriver from the cantina. We sat while Abu Suhail instructed us at a blackboard. The first day, he began by teaching the Chechens something about surface-to-air missiles. He was showing them how to make the calculations necessary for correct targeting. I sat and watched, but I was coming into the lesson in the middle and didn't understand most of it.

We interrupted our class to return to the mosque for our afternoon prayers. When we returned, Abu Suhail left the Chechens to study on their own. He spent the rest of the afternoon teaching me about handguns. But I didn't touch a gun that first day, because there was so much to learn. That day, as every day, the instruction was incredibly detailed. For each gun, Abu Suhail would first teach me the name of the weapon and explain what kind of ammunition it required. Then I learned the safety procedures for each gun. I would also have to memorize the manufacturer and even the name of the inventor: Makarov, Kalashnikov. I learned the specifications of every gun: the size of its chamber, its weight and length, its barrel capacity, its range. The situations for which it is best suited: assassinations, urban warfare, and so on. How to calculate the trajectory of the bullets it fires. How to take it apart and put it back together. How to clean it.

I had to learn all these things before I could even pick the gun up. I was impatient. Every time I learned about a new weapon, I wanted to get my hands on it right away.

I was a quick study. Partly because Abu Suhail spent a great deal of time working with me alone, since the Chechens were far ahead of me. And partly because I already knew so much from my time with Édouard.

During that month, I would learn to use a huge variety of weapons. Abu Suhail introduced me to guns I had never seen before. Most were German and Russian weapons from World War II. In the first weeks, I trained on the Makarov PM, a Soviet semiautomatic pistol invented in the 1940s; the Tokarev TT, a semiautomatic pistol the Soviets used during World War II; the Walther PPK, a German pistol used by the *Luftwaffe* (I liked the Walther PPK, it was the gun James Bond carried); the SIG-Sauer, an updated version of a pistol the Germans had invented during the Nazi era; and the Luger, designed by the German Weapons and Munitions Works at the beginning of the twentieth century. Its real name is the Pistol Parabellum. The "parabellum" part comes from the company's Latin motto, *Si vis pacem, para bellum.* If you seek peace, prepare for war.

Once I had learned those, Abu Suhail taught me how to use the larger machine guns. First I trained on the Uzi, the gun I hated most. A lightweight submachine gun, it was designed by Uziel Gal in the wake of the 1948 Arab-Israeli war. After that, I trained on two more Soviet military guns: the Degtyarev DP, a light machine gun from the 1920s, and the RPD, which was introduced much later. It is a belt-fed machine gun with a built-in bipod.

Abu Suhail finally taught me the legendary weapons invented by Mikhail Kalashnikov. First the Kalashnikov AK-47, a gas-operated assault rifle. It was named after the year of its invention. This is the gun the Soviets handed out to its client states all over the world; the Vietcong used it, as did the Sandinistas in Nicaragua. In some parts of Africa, parents name their male children Kalash in honor of the gun and its inventor.

And then I learned how to use the famous PK and PKM. These are fully automatic machine guns, fed from an ammunition belt. They have bipods, and can be fired by hand or mounted to a vehicle. I loved the PKM in particular; it is an incredibly accurate gun. I could fire at and hit targets a kilometer away.

Finally, we moved on to larger artillery. By now I had caught up to the Chechens, and we were training together. First, we learned the Dushkas: the DShK and DShKM 12.7. We started with the DShK, and spent several days learning about it in the classroom. It's an incredibly heavy, big gun; it can only be transported by trolley. It's the gun the Soviets installed in the turrets of their tanks.

When it was time to try out the DShK in the field, Abu Suhail asked for a volunteer to take the first shot. We all raised our hands—we were all so eager to try it. Abu Suhail picked one of the Chechens, the youngest member of our group by far. He was thirteen or fourteen years old; he still had the body of a boy, not a man.

The boy positioned himself behind the gun. The tripod was as big as he was, and he had to reach his arm above his head to place his hand on the trigger. Abu Suhail told the rest of us to stand back but not to cover our ears.

None of us was prepared for the sound when the Dushka fired. It was like nothing I had ever heard before. The explosion filled the canyon and reverberated against its walls. We all leapt back several meters, as far as we could get from that monster of a gun.

When the sound died down, we all raised our heads. The Chechen boy was standing exactly where he had been before he fired. He was still holding his hand above him, and his finger was still wrapped around the trigger. But he was screaming at the top of his lungs. His face was contorted with pain. He only let go of the gun when Abu Suhail came over to him and gently unwrapped his hand from the trigger. After that, there were no more volunteers.

After the Dushkas, we learned the RPGs, Soviet-designed antitank rocket launchers. We trained on the RPG-7, an early version first used in the 1960s, and then the RPG-18, a lighter, short-range version, which was easier to carry because it was collapsible. Finally, we learned how to use the RPG-22, a version invented in the 1980s. It is so powerful it can penetrate a meter of concrete or four hundred millimeters of armor.

We had all these weapons at Khaldan, and were able to practice on every one of them. But we didn't learn about just the weapons at the camp; Abu Suhail taught us about all the enemy weapons as well. In combat, the enemy might leave weapons behind after a defeat. Or maybe we would raid an enemy camp and steal their weapons. Whatever the situation, we needed to learn about every kind of weapon on earth.

Abu Suhail would show us photographs of guns—guns from America like the M16—and teach us all the same things we learned on the other weapons, but this time only theoretically. He also taught us what made the enemy weapons distinct; how the American mortars, for instance, fired different rounds than the Russian ones we were using.

When I finished learning everything there was to know about a particular gun, I was allowed to use it at target practice. There was a large space still farther upriver from the classroom where we all practiced against the side of a mountain. With each gun, I had to learn how to target instinctively, without a sight.

I learned how to inhale and exhale at exactly the right time, because on the exhale the body is most steady and the hand most accurate.

I liked the handguns the most, the Makarov and the Walther PPK especially, because they were the hardest to fire. Most guns can only be fired with both hands, but I liked to fire the hand guns with just one, the way Éduoard had taught me. I liked to challenge myself.

I also liked the tests Abu Suhail would give me, because I always did well. When he taught me the Kalashnikov, he timed me to see how long it took me to take apart the gun and put it back together with a blindfold on. On their first try, most recruits took about two minutes. I took less than sixty seconds. I could tell he was impressed. "*Masha'allah*, Abu Imam," he said. "*Masha'allah*."

I think Abu Suhail realized from the way I handled guns that I had been around them in the past. But he never asked me anything. Those were the rules of the camp. We didn't ask each other questions.

Over the course of these weeks I grew very attached to Abu Suhail. He was skillful and smart and very helpful. He pushed me hard, but had a gentleness to him I hadn't seen in any of the other trainers. And a sadness as well; he didn't joke like the others, or laugh as much. There was resignation in his face, an emptiness, almost. I grew convinced that he had lived through something terrible, and that by nurturing me and the others he was trying to heal himself as well. His praise meant an enormous amount to me, partly because I knew it meant a great deal to him also.

I loved the training. I loved almost everything about it. I loved the feeling of holding a gun in my hand, the kickback after I fired. I loved feeling that I had mastered each weapon, that I knew it totally. And I loved the noise of the target practice. So much noise! Many different groups would be firing at the same time; groups at all different levels of ability. There would be handguns and assault rifles and mortar fire all blasting against the mountain. It sounded like a kind of chorus, almost, and sometimes I shivered and praised God for having brought me here.

We never had to conserve ammunition, and there was always something new to try. The munitions were stored in caves next to the camp. There were three caves in all for weapons, and I went into two of them. Both looked small from the outside, only about one meter wide. I had to crawl to get through the opening. But once inside, the caves were huge.

The first cave contained just ammunition: thousands and thousands of different kinds of bullets and mortar shells. They were stored in wooden crates stacked high to the roof of the cave. Many of the boxes were stamped with numbers and words in Russian. The second cave contained nothing but mines, all different kinds of mines. Like the ammunition, they were stacked in crates, and I could tell from the writing that they were mostly from Russia, Italy, and Pakistan. The supplies were endless.

There was a third cave as well, the biggest cave at the camp. But I was never allowed to go in; it was forbidden to most of us. And because it was forbidden, I desperately wanted know what was inside. The trainers were allowed to go in, and a few other brothers as well. I badgered them constantly to tell me what they had seen, but they spoke in hushed tones and that said they weren't allowed to talk about it.

One of the people allowed in the cave was Abdul Haq, a Moroccan brother. I saw him go into the cave several times while I was there, but he never spoke about it. I didn't know Abdul Haq well at all. He was young, in his twenties, but he had already lost much of his hair. He was the shortest brother in the camp. The only thing I knew about him was that he and his sister lived in London.

Night

After we finished our weapons training, we would perform the sunset *salat* and then assemble in the cantina. We always ate together. There were two Afghanis who cooked for us; they lived next to the cantina, near the entrance to the camp. Right behind their hut, in the base of the mountain, there was a small cave where they baked bread. One of the cooks was both deaf and dumb, but since we were all under strict instructions not to speak to the Afghanis, this hardly was a problem.

The problem was that the food was terrible, and the same every day. We were always hungry; every one of us lost a lot of weight while we were at Khaldan. For lunch and dinner we almost always ate a kind of stew made of beans. We rarely ate meat, even though there were chickens running around the cooks' house and they would cook one from time to time. We knew from the smell.

Early on, I noticed that everyone put huge amounts of salt on their food. At first I thought this was to mask the taste. Later, I realized it was because our bodies desperately needed the minerals. Without meat, we weren't getting the nutrients that we needed to support what our bodies were going through. The trainers reminded us, of course, that we wouldn't be eating meat on the battle-field either.

There was always religious instruction after dinner. The emir and the trainers reminded us constantly that this was the most important part of becoming a *mujahid*. Before we began fighting for God, we needed to understand what he had called us to do.

Some nights we practiced *tajwid* and other nights we would study the Kur'an and the *hadith*, the traditions established by the words and deeds of the Prophet Muhammed. Sometimes, we were taught by the trainers. Other times, we were taught by other recruits, mostly Arabs, because they were by and large the most educated.

We learned a great deal during these lessons each evening, but most of all we learned about the laws of *jihad*. There are more than a hundred fifty verses in the Kur'an about *jihad*, and hundreds of references in the *hadith*. I had read a lot of justifications in *Al Ansar* for some of the most grotesque practices of war. But it wasn't until I got to Khaldan that I started learning for myself what the Kur'an actually had to say about *jihad*.

There are many different kinds of *jihad*, of course. There is the inner *jihad*, which is something every true Muslim practices constantly. There is the *jihad* of knowledge and scholarship. There is the *jihad* of the tongue, which takes all kinds of forms. It can mean proselytizing, as I had seen at Tabligh. Or it can mean speaking out politically, through sermons or through protest, or even through propaganda such as *Al Ansar*. There is the *jihad* waged through actions, such as making the *hajj* pilgrimage to Mecca, or even giving money to support the ultimate *jihad*, the *kutila fi sabilillah*. The holy war.

We talked almost entirely about this last form of *jihad*, of course. We learned all the rules of engagement. Force is to be avoided unless it is absolutely neces-sary, and even then it is to be used only in proportion to the strength of the en-emy. But once force becomes necessary, no one can shirk his duty. If one woman halfway around the world is raped or taken from her family, all Muslims must come together to fight until the injustice is righted. It is required by God.

Before he fights, a brother must prepare himself. First and foremost, he must prepare himself spiritually. With faith, an army can vanquish an opponent ten times the size. "How many a little company has overcome a mighty host by God's leave! God is with the steadfast."

Other kinds of preparation are vital as well. A *mujahid* must be morally pre-pared; he must avoid all sins and make himself pure before God. He must also prepare his body and make it as strong as possible. And every brother must learn everything he can about science and technology, so that his superiority over the enemy is total.

Once in battle, a *mujahid* must obey very strict laws. There must be no slaughter of innocents. No indiscriminate killing, no killing of women and children, no mutilating the corpses of the enemies. No destroying of schools or churches or water supplies or even fields and livestock. No killing of anyone during prayer, regardless of whether those prayers are Muslim or Christian or Jewish or anything else.

I learned how important it is to fight for the right reasons. A *mujadid* must fight only for God, not for material gain, not for politics. He fights with righteousness on his side, and he fights to serve God's creation. The deeper his faith in God becomes, the greater his ability will be to honor God's work.

True believers are those whose lives God has bought in exchange for the promise of paradise. They must not flee from battle, even if they are facing certain death. A man who turns his back on the unbelievers and runs, it says in the Kur'an, "has indeed incurred God's severe punishment, and his final refuge is the Fire; how evil a homecoming and a destination to arrive in."

I was surprised to learn how specific the laws of *jihad* actually are—far more so than any of the human rights conventions dreamed up in the West. In fact, our teachers told us again and again that these principles are what differentiate Muslims from non-Muslims. The infidels are the ones who murder indiscriminately, lawlessly. They lay waste to whole cities, even entire populations. They bomb churches and mosques and schools.

We learned about the British and the French, who conquered peoples all over the world and stole their land for their colonies. We learned about Hitler and his concentration camps. We learned about how the Americans had slaughtered the Koreans and the Vietnamese. We learned about Hiroshima and Nagasaki and the carpet bombings at the end of World War II. And of course we learned about the horrors the Israelis had perpetrated in Palestine, but all of us already knew about that. The infidels massacred and bombed and destroyed everything in their path. They were animals.

Of course, learning all this made me think again about what I knew about the war in Algeria. The GIA had done so many of the things forbidden in Islamic law. They had murdered civilians, even shot up whole schools. But over time I learned something about the laws of *jihad*: there is room. There is room within the boundaries of the law for all sorts of interpretation.

There is room particularly when it comes to defining who the enemies are, and who the innocents. It seems simple, of course—the enemies are the ones with the guns. According to the laws of *jihad*, however, the definition of "enemy" can be expanded to include the entire supply chain: anyone who supports the enemy with money or weapons, or even food or water; even to those who provide moral support—journalists, for instance, who, write in defense of the enemy's cause. But how far, I wondered, does the supply chain extend? To anyone who votes for an enemy regime? What about those who don't take sides at all? How far does it go?

Women are generally thought to be innocent; yet they, too, can be the enemy. If a woman prays to God to protect her husband, then she is not an enemy. But if she prays for him to kill a Muslim, then she is. It is similar for children. A young boy can be forgiven for his prayers; he is too young to be responsible for that. But if he carries food or even a message to an enemy fighter, then he becomes an enemy.

I came to understand how, in the mind of an extremist, almost anyone could become the enemy.

Al-Jum'a

Fridays were different from all the other days. There was no running, no weapons training. In the morning, we would do just an hour or so of exercise on the field in front of the camp. Then we would assemble on the square and the emir would separate us into groups. He would assign a chore to each group: cleaning the mosque, gathering wood for the cooks to use, filling the large tanks of water by the cantina. But there was one task the emir never assigned to anyone: cleaning the toilets. Instead, he would ask for volunteers. None of the brothers ever raised his hand because it was a filthy job. Except for me.

Everything we did in camp was guided by the principles of the *sunna,* the forms of behavior rendered legitimate by the practices of the Prophet Muhammad during the years of his ministry. Muslims believe these customs were dictated directly to the Prophet Muhammad by God. The *sunna* prescribes rules for every aspect of daily life, from the way to greet another person to personal hygiene.

Abu Hurayrah is the *sahabi,* or companion of the Prophet Muhammad, who is quoted most often in the *hadith.* He reports that when one is traveling in the desert or lacks water for some other reason, it is acceptable to clean oneself with pebbles. "Allah's Messenger (may peace be upon him) said: When anyone wipes himself (his anus) with pebbles (after answering the call of nature) he should make use of an odd number of pebbles." And so the bathrooms were littered with pebbles. Pebbles covered with shit.

I certainly didn't enjoy cleaning the bathrooms, but I could do it very quickly. It took me no more than fifteen minutes to sweep off the stones in every bathroom and then rinse them with buckets of water from the river. When I was done I had time to spend by myself. I could read or listen to the radio, or just watch the others carrying wood or heavy buckets. Those jobs took hours. I volunteered to clean the toilets every week.

After the chores were done, we would all wash ourselves and our clothes in the river. I was always very careful about washing my sleeping bag. The bags were old and stained, and I knew why. In the films about the Soviet-Afghan war, I had seen *mujahidin* carrying corpses from battle. The bodies were often wrapped in sleeping bags. Since then they had been used by any number of *mujahidin*. So it was hardly surprising that during their time at Khaldan, many of the brothers got terrible rashes and skin diseases.

Friday was *al-Jum'a*, the day of gathering. Instead of performing the *salat* at midday, we would gather in the mosque for the sermon. Sometimes, one of the trainers would be the *khatib*, the speaker. Abu Suhail and Abu Hamam often spoke, but just as often the sermon would be delivered by one of the trainees. Nobody was chosen as *khatib*; anyone could prepare a sermon and volunteer. Generally, though, it was the Arabs who put themselves forward. They were more fully indoctrinated than the others, and more educated.

Sometimes, the sermons were about the history of Islam. Brothers spoke about important and influential *imams*, for instance. But generally the lectures were political, about the different *jihad* Muslims were fighting around the world, about the theft of Muslim lands by the infidels.

In the evening, after the sermon, we would gather for discussion. We could ask the *khatib* about anything he had said, even if the emir had given that day's sermon. This was one of the most striking things about the camp: everyone was equal. Of course, we had to obey the emir when he gave us specific orders, but if something seemed strange or irrational we were always allowed to challenge him and make him explain himself. It was like this with everybody; we could disagree and argue whenever we felt like it, which we did for hours at a time. There was no real hierarchy, no sense of authority, no feeling of subjection. It was the most democratic place I had ever been.

On Friday evenings, Abu Suhail would hold classes on the theology and ideology of Sayyid Qutb, the Egyptian theologian. I always attended. Abu Suhail would read to us from his work, particularly *Fi zilal al Qur'an* and *Ma'alim fi-l-Tariq*— *In the Shade of the Kur'an* and *Milestones*—his two most important books.

I was absorbed by these classes, by the gentle way in which Abu Suhail taught us, but also, more importantly, by the ideas. In Qutb, I heard a language that made sense to me. His writings struck me as fiercely intellectual; Qutb was a real scholar. Abu Suhail explained that Qutb had attended university in Cairo, and even had a master's degree from a university in America. He had a profound respect for the teachings of Islam, but was able to write about it in a way that seemed modern and real. He wrote about the world I lived in, not the world of centuries past.

Qutb wrote about Islam as something more than a religion. For him, it was a complete social system that incorporated everything in the world. Only through complete submission to God could we solve all the problems on earth— ignorance and injustice and poverty. His philosophy was highly political. God was his only sovereign. Theocracy was the only legitimate form of government; everything else was *taghut*. Muslims living in countries with secular governments were obliged to resist those governments. Qutb believed in revolution.

Abu Suhail explained to us how Qutb had lived according to his beliefs. In 1948, in the wake of Egypt's humiliation in the Arab-Israeli war, a young army officer named Gamal Abdel Nasser formed something called the Free Officers Movement, with the goal of overthrowing the monarchy. In 1952, he succeeded. Qutb supported Nasser at first, and he was given the position of cultural advisor to the Revolutionary Command Committee in the new government. But the relationship quickly soured. Like many others, Qutb had expected Nasser to establish an Islamic state. When he didn't, Qutb switched his support to the more radical Muslim Brotherhood, which opposed the regime.

In 1954, when a member of the Muslim Brotherhood tried to assassinate Nasser, the government declared the organization illegal. Qutb was imprisoned along with many others. It was during this time that he wrote both *In the Shade of the Kur'an* and *Milestones*. After ten years, Qutb was released from jail. But he was rearrested only a few months later, in August 1964, and subjected to a show trial. He was sentenced to death and executed in 1966 by hanging. He was *shahid*, a martyr to his faith.

We didn't have electricity at Khaldan, of course, so at night everything was lit with gas lamps or candles. And so it surprised me when, several months after my arrival, a television appeared. It emerged one Friday evening, hooked up to a diesel generator.

That night we watched a number of speeches delivered by Abdullah Azzam. Azzam, we were told, was born in the West Bank but emigrated to Jordan after *Al-Naksah* (known in the West as the Six-Day War) in 1967. He joined the *jihad* against the Israeli occupation, then went on to get a doctorate from the University of Cairo, where he became friends with Qutb's family.

As the 1970s wore on, Azzam distanced himself from the Palestinian *jihad* and moved to Saudi Arabia. He began to focus on the global *jihad* instead, and grew convinced that the *umma* needed an organized military force to conquer the infidels. When the Soviets invaded Afghanistan, he emigrated to Pakistan with his family to be closer to the fighting.

Azzam ended up in Peshawar, where he founded the *Maktab al-khadamat*, an organization dedicated to assisting the *mujahidin* fighting the Soviets across the border in Afghanistan, and to training the new recruits who were spilling into Pakistan from other countries. He also traveled to Afghanistan to witness the heroism of the *mujahidin*.

Before he was assassinated in 1989, Azzam became one of the most important propagandists for *jihad*. And through his books and teachings, he lived on in the hearts of Muslims, particularly young Muslims, all over the world.

As we watched the tapes that night, I could see why. He was deeply articulate but also fiery and passionate. He spoke about the destruction of Israel, and about the global *jihad*. One statement, however, made the greatest impact on me. "Love of *jihad* has taken over my life, my soul, my sensations, my heart and my emotions," he proclaimed. "*If preparing is terrorism, then we are terrorists.*"

The *al-Jum'a* prayer was always the most intense of the week. We had been running and fighting and working all week with our brothers, and on Friday we came together to rest and worship God as one. Sometimes, a brother would be so overcome by faith that tears would well up in his eyes.

I was overcome, too. Standing amidst these *mujahidin*, I could feel the spirit of God fill me completely. I was as swept up as the others by the feelings of love and fellowship and brotherhood. I was part of a community, a community of complete devotion to God.

As the weeks passed, it became harder for me to separate myself from my brothers. It took more and more effort each night to remember that I was not one of them. To remember that I was a spy.

Abdul Kerim

There were only two Algerians at Khaldan while I was there. One, Abdul Kerim, was in my group for the evening study of the *tajwid*, and he also slept in the same dormitory with me. Like me, he hadn't come with a group; he was on his own. And his Arabic was terrible, far worse than mine. But his French was perfect.

When I first got to the camp there was another Algerian there as well, Abu Jaffar, who was slightly older than Abdul Kerim. I saw the two of them talking together several times, but then Abu Jaffar left and Abdul Kerim was alone again.

One Friday, early in the summer, I finished cleaning the toilets early and headed to the northern entrance to the camp, far upriver from the cantina. There was a small waterfall coming off one of the mountains where we collected our drinking water. I brought my flask to fill it up; it was very hot that day.

On my way to the waterfall, I passed the mosque and saw Abdul Kerim sitting by himself under a tree. I waved to him and asked if he would like me to get him some water. Smiling, he said yes, please, and handed me his flask.

It was the sort of gesture we were always making at the camp. We all looked out for one another because we were all there for the same reason. We brought one another food and water, and supported one another when we were weak or tired or sick. When one of the brothers left the camp, he would leave almost everything he had behind: his coat, his boots, his radio. Whatever he had, he gave—to his brothers.

When I returned to the mosque and approached Abdul Kerim, I saw that he had a tiny stove in front of him. He was heating a pot of water. There was a jar next to the stove: Nescafé. I hadn't had coffee since Peshawar—we had only that dreadful tea at breakfast—and my mouth began to water.

But then I noticed something else. Abdul Kerim was cleaning his Kalashnikov, and he was doing it all wrong. I knew Abdul Kerim knew how to clean it. I didn't have my own Kalashnikov yet, but Édouard had taught me how to clean a gun and I had practiced it hundreds of times.

It would not have taken a specialist, however, to recognize that Abdul Kerim was not cleaning his gun correctly. He was scraping it down with sandpaper. This is the worst possible thing for a gun, because it creates tiny little scratches on the metal inside the gun which could collect moisture and then rust. And a gun with rust inside would clog, or misfire.

Everything about this seemed wrong to me. We were always taught to treat every weapon with great respect, because the other brothers who would follow us would use the same equipment. So Abdul Kerim was doing something very selfish. And I could tell from the way his hands and eyes darted about that he knew it. There was something furtive about his movements. He was clearly on edge.

I sat down next to him. "Brother," I said, "that's not the right way to clean a gun." I reached my hands out. "Here, let me show you how."

"I know it," he mumbled. "I don't care anymore. Whatever I do, it still won't be good enough for Abu Bakr."

I smiled. I knew that the further a brother got with his training, the tougher the trainers would be. Particularly when it came to the maintenance of guns. In the later stages of training—the tactical training—the brothers were shooting constantly. The more rounds they fired, the dirtier the guns would get. And so the trainers spent even more time inspecting them to make sure the recruits were taking good care of their weapons.

I left the subject of the guns. I wanted a cup of coffee and asked him if I could have one. He said of course, but he asked me not to tell anyone. He was the only one in the camp allowed to drink Nescafé, and the emir had told him to keep it a secret.

The Nescafé told me something: Abdul Kerim was someone important. There were no special privileges in the camp, and no secrets. If he was allowed to drink coffee when the others were not, there was almost certainly something about him that made him unusually valuable.

Abdul Kerim was eager to talk. Because his Arabic was so poor, he couldn't talk to most of the other brothers. But I spoke French like he did, and that made him happy. Very quickly, he began to speak about the GIA. Soon he was on to the subject of *Al Ansar*. I reminded him that we weren't supposed to talk about our previous lives, but he couldn't help himself. It was spilling out of him, and I could tell from the movements of his hands that he was getting more and more agitated. His eyes were darting back and forth, as if he were afraid of something.

Then suddenly, he turned towards me. "You," he seethed. His eyes were so large they bulged out of their sockets. "You're a spy. I know it. The French sent you here to get me."

My heart nearly stopped. How did he know? And what was I going to do? He was sitting there with a Kalashnikov in his lap. I had nothing. We were alone, hundreds of meters from the other brothers. My mind was racing—I had to say something.

So I laughed at him. "*Astaghfur Allah*, brother," I said. May God forgive you. "Do you really think you're so important that the French would bother sending an agent all the way to Afghanistan just for you?" Then I stood up.

"No," he said. "No, of course not. I am so sorry. Please, come. Sit down and have some coffee with me." He explained that he had lived in fear while he was in France, that he was being followed constantly. When he heard me talk in French about the GIA, it reminded him of everything he had gone through.

I sat down again and laughed to myself. I knew this guy wasn't going to let go of the only person he could talk to in the entire camp.

Abdul Kerim was different from everyone else at Khaldan, that was clear. At first, I wondered if he was a heroin addict. I had seen heroin addicts on the streets in Morocco, so I knew their faces and movements and the deep paranoia in their eyes. Of course, there were no drugs in the camp, and I wondered if he was allowed to drink Nescafé to help take the edge off the withdrawal.

Whether or not I was right about this, it was certainly true that Abdul Kerim was an exception to all sorts of rules. The wild variations in the tone of his speech, the jittery motions, the rapid mood swings, the stream of information he poured forth without any solicitation—another brother would have been kicked out of camp for any one of these. Though it would be some time before I understood why, I knew even at this early point that Abdul Kerim was going to be particularly interesting. They were letting him stay for a reason.

That day, and in the days that followed, I came to learn more about Abdul Kerim. He spoke mostly about the GIA; like the French language, it was something we held in common.

Abdul Kerim told me he had a wife in France. He was divorcing her because she was not pious. But together they had a small daughter, and the wife had taken her when they split. He wanted to get the daughter back so that he could raise her as a true Muslim.

Later, he would talk more about politics. It became clear to me that Abdul Kerim was a real extremist. "*Insha' Allah*," he would tell me, "one day all of France will be Muslim." And after that Europe as well. The *kafir*, the infidels, would be wiped off the continent.

One day, we talked about the raids in Europe. I desperately wanted to learn what he knew, but I couldn't ask him directly. But with Abdul Kerim there was no need; he just leapt into the subject on his own. He ranted about how terrible the raids were, how unfair. I agreed, and nodded sympathetically. I told him about my own experience, that they had raided my mother's house and taken my brother, and tried to capture me as well.

Then, innocently, I asked him a question. "Who tipped the police off? Do you have any idea?"

Maybe I would have been anxious if I had been forced to wait for his response. But I didn't. Abdul Kerim immediately gave me the name of a French Algerian I had never heard of. It was a huge relief for me to hear that. Maybe I was safe after all.

Over time, Abdul Kerim and I became friends, of a sort. We spent lots of time sitting and talking in French and drinking coffee. It was nice for me, too, to have someone who spoke my native language and who understood the world I had come from.

One night, Abdul Kerim and I were sitting by the mosque by ourselves. We had to be careful to meet when no one else was around; we couldn't let the others see us drinking our Nescafé. Suddenly, we heard a noise. It was coming from the radio transmission station, a small building near the cantina where the emir and the trainers would gather at night.

BAM.

We both stood up and saw someone firing his Kalashnikov into the sky. BAM BAM BAM BAM. There were several guns going off at once, and the sound of people celebrating. We heard footsteps running towards us, and soon one of the trainers appeared. "Turn on the radio," he said. "There has been an attack in Paris."

We turned on the radio and heard the first reports coming in on RFI (Radio France Internationale). Just an hour earlier, a bomb had ripped through an RER (*Réseau Express Régional*) train under the Saint Michel station near Notre Dame. There were confirmed casualties already, and more expected. Hundreds were injured, and there was chaos at the scene.

By now, others had heard the gunfire and run out to join us. We were celebrating on the square in front of the mosque. Nobody said a word about the GIA because we didn't have to. Everyone knew immediately that they were responsible.

Abdul Kerim was beaming. "*Masha'allah!*" he rejoiced. "*Toute la France deviendra musulmane!*" He grinned at me as he said it. All of France will be Muslim.

"*Insha' Allah*, brother," I said. "*Insha' Allah*." And then I forced myself to smile.

In the coming days and months, we would learn more about the bombings. Eight people were killed, and hundreds injured. It was the first of a series of attacks in France that summer. In August, a bomb went off at the Arc de Triomphe. In the same month, the police found a bomb on the railroad tracks outside Lyon. Another bomb went off in Paris in early September, and a few days later a car bomb exploded at a Jewish school in Lyon. In October, two more bombs were detonated in train stations in Paris. Scores of people were injured in the course of the bombing campaign, but luckily no one was killed after the first explosion at Saint Michel.

I spent a lot of time thinking about the Paris bombing, and the reaction of the others in the camp. I was struck by one thing in particular: no one ever asked about the people on the train. Surely, these were innocent bystanders—not enemies? What was the justification for this kind of attack?

Abu Bakr

Abu Bakr was absolutely extraordinary; at times, he seemed almost superhuman. The more I watched him, the more impressed I became by his discipline as well as his physical strength and agility. He was constantly in motion; every minute he was awake, he was training. During the sermons, I would watch him as he played silently with his fingers, bending them back and forth to make them more flexible. He could bend them so far back over his hand that his fingernails nearly touched his wrists.

Once, I watched Abu Bakr leap off a cliff at least seven meters high. He didn't flinch when he jumped, and when he landed he didn't tuck his body or land in a ball and roll forward, like the others. He just bent his knees slightly and walked away. Several brothers followed him off the cliff that day, and many broke legs and ankles. A couple of them wore casts for weeks.

Even though we weren't supposed to talk to each other about anything outside the camp, we often did. I learned many things about Abu Bakr this way. I learned that he was a Jordanian of Palestinian origin. I learned that he was emir of the camp only sometimes, when Ibn Sheikh was away. I learned that he was extremely brave—the brothers spoke constantly of his courage in battles in Tajikistan and Kashmir.

I never trained with Abu Bakr because, for the most part, he trained recruits in special operations. Most of the men who came to the camps were there for six or seven months, for the full course of training. But sometimes groups would come for just one or two weeks, and train for a specific mission.

But sometimes he would direct special exercises for the entire camp. He loved to lead nighttime runs into the mountains. Several times during my months at Khaldan, he ordered us awake in the middle of the night. We collected on the square, and then he sprinted into the mountains in the pitch black and we would follow.

I hated all the runs, but I hated the night runs the most. I was always tired and disoriented. And the nights were always cold, even in the summer. It got worse and worse as we headed into autumn. And the runs were dangerous. Many nights, the sky was overcast and we didn't have even the light of the moon or stars to guide us. We couldn't see anything at all; we had to guide ourselves solely by the sound of the brothers in front of us. Often, we ran along narrow trails that clung to the side of a mountain. At every moment, there was the danger of falling into a ravine. One false step, and I could die.

One night, the sky was unusually clear as Abu Bakr led us on a run up into the mountains. We ran for nearly an hour by the light of the moon until we reached a plateau, and then he halted us. "Can anyone point in the direction of *qibla*?" he asked, meaning the way to Mecca. Scores of recruits raised their hands and pointed in different directions. Abu Bakr was not impressed.

I raised my hand. "It's in the opposite direction from where the moon rises." I knew he didn't want to know where Mecca was. He wanted to see how our minds worked. I knew a lot about the planets because of my childhood obsession with science fiction, which had matured into a more general interest in science during my time in Paris and Brussels. I knew the sun, like the moon, rose in the east. And because we were in Afghanistan, Mecca was to the West. When I explained this to the brothers, Abu Bakr nodded. "*Masha'allah*, Abu Imam," he said. "That's a good answer."

After Abu Bakr had completed that test, he began running again and we followed him. After about half an hour, he stopped us again. "When I say 'hide,'" he explained to us as we hovered close to each other in the cold night air, "I want you to drop to the ground immediately. You have five seconds." He explained how important it was to hide if we heard a helicopter overhead, and that we were less likely to be spotted if we spread ourselves out as much as possible. We should leave a minimum of five meters between ourselves and the next brother. Ten meters was ideal.

Then he began running again. And running. It was at least forty-five minutes before he gave us the signal. As soon as he did, we all dropped to the ground. We probably did fall closer together than we should have, but it was so dark it was hard to see where the others were. There was a ravine to the right of us, so no one wanted to run too far from the group. And we had been running in a tight formation to begin with, no more than two feet between each of the brothers, so it was hard for us to fall too far apart.

I had been lying on the ground for only a couple of seconds when I heard a sharp noise and felt something whiz past my right shoulder. And then another noise, and something hit the dirt just to my right, throwing dust into the air. Suddenly, I realized they were bullets. Abu Bakr was shooting at me.

Then I heard a voice say my name. I peeled my face from the ground and looked up. Abu Bakr was standing right above me. TAT-TAT. He fired two more times, just inches away from my shoulder. "Move, Abu Imam," he commanded. "You're too close to your brother." Then he turned away and moved on to the next brother, and started firing at him.

Later that same night, he did it again. We had been running for nearly five hours in total when he gave the signal. By now, everyone was completely exhausted. A few of the brothers didn't drop to the ground at all; they had forgotten his instruction.

TAT-TAT-TAT-TAT. Abu Bakr immediately began to fire his gun at the men who remained standing. Bullets were flying to the right and left of them; some came within six centimeters. I could see that some of them were completely paralyzed with fear.

But now I understood that a bullet from Abu Bakr's gun would never touch any of the brothers. He was an exquisite marksman, totally confident of his abilities. This was just his gentle way of reminding us to follow his orders.

Abu Bakr was a perfectionist in everything he did. He was also a rigid disciplinarian. One day, I saw some of the men from the group he was training crawling down the riverbed. It was well into the fall, and the water was achingly cold. But there they were, holding their Kalashnikovs out in front of them as they navigated across the rocks and through the frigid water.

So sharp were the rocks that some of the brothers were covered with blood when they emerged from the river. I asked one of them what they were doing and he explained they were being punished because they had not cleaned their guns properly the night before.

Suddenly, I understood why Abdul Kerim was so angry with Abu Bakr on the day I found him cleaning his gun with sandpaper. As if crawling through a frigid river weren't bad enough, Abu Bakr was punishing his recruits by making it much harder for them to clean their guns that night. Each brother would have to wipe out all the water from the inside of the gun and then re-oil the entire mechanism. It would take hours. Abu Bakr was tough.

Once, Abu Bakr disappeared for a couple of days. I asked one of the trainers where he was and he told me Abu Bakr was ill. So I went to visit him in the cottage where he lived with some of the other trainers. I wanted to see if there was anything I could do for him.

Abu Bakr looked awful. He was sprawled out on the bed with his eyes closed, and could barely move. He had contracted malaria, which was rampant in the camps. There were mosquitoes everywhere.

I sat down by his side. "*Assalamu'alaykum*," I said. "I didn't know you were sick until just now. How are you feeling?"

"Good, brother," he replied. "I am feeling good." But he was groaning and moving his head from side to side as he said it.

There was a syringe lying on the ground next to him, filled with some sort of liquid. I picked it up. "What is this for, Abu Bakr?"

"It's medicine," he answered. "Someone is supposed to come and inject it. Would you mind asking the doctor?" He was referring to one of the brothers who presided over the small infirmary in the camp.

"I can do it myself," I offered. I had spent so much time in hospitals in Belgium and had been injected with so many medicines and painkillers that I knew exactly what to do.

He looked up at me with gratitude. "You know how?"

I nodded, and he told me to go ahead. I plucked up the syringe, found an artery, and injected the medicine very quickly. He looked surprised when I told him I was done.

He smiled at me. "Brother, I have had so many injections since I've been in Afghanistan," he told me. "This is the first time it hasn't hurt. Thank you."

I was very happy that I had been able to help him. As I stood up to go, I looked around the room. That was when I noticed something magnificent:

a huge sniper. I knew all about sniper rifles from Abu Suhail, but had never seen one at the camp. I wanted desperately to try it out.

Abu Bakr must have noticed the look of excitement on my face. "Brother, I'm sorry," he said. "But it's from America. We don't have the right cartridges for it."

One day, a group of us were sitting outside the mosque when Abu Bakr told us that he and Abu Suhail would be leaving in a few days for a mission with a group of Tajiks he had been training. Ibn Sheikh would be coming to replace him.

I was sitting next to Abu Bakr, and at one point he turned to me. "Do you want to come with us?" he asked with a smile.

I didn't know what to say. I assumed he was kidding, since I hadn't trained with the Tajiks and knew nothing about their mission. "Sure," I stammered.

Abu Bakr kept smiling. "If you come with us," he continued, "would you be able to cut the head off a Russian soldier?"

"Of course," I said firmly. I had seen it in the films, and I knew this was the right answer. And anyway, I knew I wouldn't have to do it since I realized Abu Bakr was just testing me.

"What if I bring a Russian soldier back to the camp with me?" he asked with the same smile. "Would you be able to cut his head off right here on the square?"

My heart stopped. I wondered if he was actually going to do this, if I would have to cut someone's head off to prove I was a true *mujahid*. I thought to myself, What the hell am I doing here? But I answered the only way I could.

"Of course, Abu Bakr. Of course."

Explosives

The next stage of our training was in explosives. We trained with Abu Yahya, who was from Yemen. This section of our training lasted for about two weeks. Like the gun training, it was both theoretical and practical. We spent a great deal of time in the classroom learning everything there was to know about the major explosives—TNT, dynamite, and all the plastics: C1, C2, C3, C4, and Semtex. We learned that the Americans were trying to retrieve Semtex from the *mujahidin* in Afghanistan, because it was so dangerous. Unlike other explosives, Semtex was almost completely undetectable.

We learned the consistency and appearance of each explosive. We learned to identify the different explosives by smell and taste; we'd put just a tiny bit on our tongues. Some, like dynamite, tasted sweet because of the glycerin.

We learned about all different kinds of land mines, and the different kinds of explosives used in each one. We learned how to arm a mine, and how to defuse one. We learned how to lay a minefield. We learned how to rig a mine so that anyone who tried to defuse it would be blown up instantly.

We learned about all the different kinds of grenades, and which ones to use depending on our position in a battle. We learned when we should attach timers to them, and when we should let them explode on impact.

We learned about the different kinds of detonators, and Abu Yahya reminded us constantly how dangerous they were. He taught us how to handle them very gently so that they wouldn't blow up in our faces.

We spent a great deal of time learning about safety procedures. How to calculate a blast zone based on the amount of explosive we were using, and how far away we should stand. Abu Yahya explained that if we stayed in contact with certain kinds of explosives for too long we might experience health problems, including infertility.

Aby Yahya taught us the chemistry and physics of explosions. We learned the difference between high- and low-intensity explosives, and how to calculate the impact of a bomb based on its velocity of detonation. He taught us the chemical composition of each kind of explosive, and also explained the reactions it underwent after it detonated. He explained the different kinds of trauma it would inflict depending on how far away the victims were standing.

Just as Abu Suhail had during gun training, Abu Yahya also taught us about weapons we didn't have at the camp but might someday use. One day, he taught us everything we needed to know about nuclear explosions.

There was an endless supply of mines in camp, and sometimes we would practice with live ones so that we could study the power and effect of the explosions. We began with the antitank mines, which were generally filled with TNT. They always exploded from the ground up, unlike the antipersonnel mines, which could explode in either direction.

We learned about blast mines, which exploded from below, and bounding mines, which were buried underground and set off by a trip wire. When a bounding mine detonated, it would leap several feet into the air and explode at head or chest level, scattering shrapnel with incredible force. They were very effective for attacking infantry divisions, where lots of people are clustered together.

We practiced laying minefields, which is an operation that allows for no carelessness whatsoever. First, we mapped out the minefield with very precise coordinates. Then we laid the mines. A few days later, we would have to come back to the site and find them. We knew that we had to draw our maps very carefully, and place the mines at exactly the right coordinates. If a *mujahid* were sloppy at either stage, he stood a very good chance of blowing himself up on a mine he had laid himself.

I really enjoyed the explosives training. I loved the precision it required, and the intense concentration it took to do everything just right. I was transfixed by the bright flash that appeared milliseconds before the explosion, and the huge noise that ricocheted endlessly off the canyon walls.

I will never forget the first day Abu Yahya allowed our group to set off a real explosion. We spent the afternoon digging fifteen holes in a open space behind the camp and filling each one with Semtex. We connected them with a detonating cord, the kind engineers use for controlled explosions. We filled the holes with dirt, and then Abu Yahya led us high onto the mountain above.

When we were all sitting on a precipice, Abu Yahya turned the crank on the hellbox to generate an electric charge. Then he pushed down hard on the handle to release the charge into the detonating cord. Seconds later, there was a flash of blue. Then another blue flash, and another. Fifteen in a row, just milliseconds apart, like flashes of lightning leaping out of the ground. And then BOOM BOOM BOOM as the Semtex detonated. Fifteen claps of thunder bursting forth from the canyon floor. It was mesmerizing.

One day during our explosives training, we were charged with solving a practical problem at the camp. It had been raining heavily for several days, and some boulders had fallen loose from the mountain into the river in front of the camp. They were blocking the flow, and water was pooling up behind them.

Abu Hamam took us out that day to remove the rocks with TNT. Next to the boulders we placed twenty-five kilograms of TNT, a far greater volume of explosives than we had ever used before. It was much more than we needed, but Abu Hamam wanted us to see what a real explosion looked like.

To prepare the explosion, we pressed the detonator into a small amount of Semtex and stuck it on the TNT. Then we attached the whole thing to an electric cable, which we rolled out about thirty meters to a huge boulder upriver.

We all gathered behind the boulder. Abu Hamam told us not to cover our ears. We needed to learn to withstand the noise of these explosions on the battle-field. Then he ordered us to connect the cable to the battery. He looked up once more to make sure that no one was near the TNT, and ordered us to blow it.

One of the Chechens began cranking up the hellbox. We were all waiting breathlessly; the others enjoyed the explosions almost as much as I did, and this was going to be the biggest blast we had ever seen. After a few seconds, the Chechen rammed down the handle.

And . . . nothing. No explosion. We stood up, mystified, and looked down-river to see what had happened. The TNT was still there. Abu Hamam checked the cables and looked at the battery in the hellbox. Everything was in order. He took the crank in his own hand and began to turn it. We all crouched down and waited for the blast. Abu Hamam pushed the handle and again, nothing.

Abu Hamam looked puzzled. He stood up and faced us. "So, which one of you wants to be *shahid?*" he asked, jokingly. Which one of us wanted to become a martyr. Which one of us wanted to volunteer to dismantle the explosive by re-moving the detonator. We looked at each other and smiled nervously. It was a serious question.

I raised my hand. "I'll do it," I said. If anyone was going to be *shahid*, it would be me. The Chechens looked at each other, then at me; they were dumbfounded. Even Abu Hamam seemed surprised. But he shrugged slightly and reminded me to be careful in handling the detonator; it had been charged, and was far more dangerous than it would be normally. Of course, I knew—if I touched it the wrong way, it could ignite the TNT. I would be blown to pieces.

When Abu Hamam finished, I turned to the others and saluted each one. "*Assalamu'alaykum,*" I said.

"*Alaykum assalam wa-rahmatu liahi wa-barakatuhu,*" they replied. May the peace, the blessings, and the mercy of God be upon you. The peace and the blessings; this was normal. But the mercy of God? To me it sounded like a prayer before death.

I turned and walked across the rocks and down the river towards the boul-ders and the TNT. I wasn't really thinking at that moment. I was fairly certain I would die, and I accepted it. And yet even then there was a tiny part of me that also believed this wasn't my real destiny. That I would be back in Europe some-day. That my time had not yet come.

I didn't have more than a few seconds to think all this through before I was in front of the boulders, kneeling next to the TNT. It was silent at that moment, peaceful. I was away from the camp and from my group, and there were no voices at all, just the gentle sound of water. I knew that I could die at any second, that I probably would die. But I wasn't panicked.

I leaned forward, and with the tips of two fingers I very carefully removed the detonator. It was scorching hot. I briefly held it in my hand, then gently placed it on a nearby rock to cool off. I raised my hand and signaled to the others that it was safe.

I still can't quite explain why I volunteered that day. I volunteered without thinking, really. At that moment, I felt it was critical to my mission. But which mission—my mission as a *mujahid* or my mission as a spy? Both, I suppose.

I had grown very attached to my brothers in the group at this point, and had spent months talking and thinking about the mandates of *jihad*. I felt that it was my responsibility as a *mujahid* to sacrifice myself to God in order to help my brothers. There was no other choice, and I wasn't afraid to die. But of course I also realized that if I pulled it off, it would remove any doubts anyone in the camp might have about my commitment.

My two missions, spy and *mujahid,* were now one and the same. I had lost myself totally in my role. But that's what any spy must do to succeed. No one can lead a double life for long and expect to get away with it. I had to immerse myself completely.

And yet it was so easy for me. The minute I landed in Karachi I had gone straight to the mosque as if I had made my *salat* five times a day for my entire life. Here at Khaldan I often fantasized about going back to Chechnya with the men in my group and using everything I had learned to exterminate the Russian invaders.

So which was it? Was I a good spy because I could lose myself so completely in my role as a *mujahid*? Or was I a good *mujahid* who just happened to be a spy?

Tactics

After we finished with the explosives, we moved on to tactical training, which lasted for several months. In tactical training we learned how to fight in real-life situations. We learned how to operate radio transmitters and use Morse code.

We learned how to signal in code at night, using light. We learned how to gather information about the enemy's plans, and how to spread false information about our own. We learned how to prepare an ambush in cities and in mountains. We learned how to react when the enemy ambushed us. We learned how to coordinate multiple groups for an attack. We learned how to use camouflage to approach a target. We learned how to stage false attacks to draw the enemy into a trap. We learned how to give medical assistance to our brothers on the field, and how to transport them off the field if necessary. We learned how to storm a house and how to defend it. We learned how to kidnap and assassinate, and how to kill with our hands.

We learned different skills from different trainers. Trainers moved back and forth from group to group. Sometimes trainers would be gone for weeks at a time. Sometimes trainers would come from other camps and stay for just a couple of weeks. Sometimes whole groups went off to other camps, and came back a few weeks later. We never knew where they were going, because we weren't allowed to ask questions.

Once a group of seven Chechens left the camp. Six weeks later, five of them returned. One of them had burns all over his body. None of them said a word about what had happened, and no one asked. But it was obvious: they had been doing advanced training with explosives, and two of them had blown themselves up.

Ibn Sheikh had come to the camp a few days before Abu Bakr and Abu Suhail left for Tajikistan, and he trained our group in assassination. We trained out on the open field in front of the camp. We set up elaborate courses to simulate real situations in which we might find ourselves once we returned home. So in one case, for instance, we learned how to assassinate someone in an outdoor café on a busy street. I would sit behind one of the Chechens on a motorbike as he drove towards the target. As we got closer, he would slow down and I would jump off. I would run towards the target and stop and fire my gun, then leap back onto the motorbike to get away. It was hard to get the timing exactly right, and we practiced it again and again.

It was even harder when both the gunman and the target were moving. There were wires strung across the field, and targets that could be pulled from side to side. We would practice firing at them from inside a moving truck, or from the back of a motorbike. Before we even tried it, Ibn Sheikh spent hours with us in the classroom teaching us how to calculate all the variables: the speed of the bullet, the distance between the shooter and the target, the speed of each vehicle.

There was an almost infinite number of variations, and we trained for each one. I really enjoyed the challenge of it, and I loved the feeling of finally getting it right after practicing over and over again. I also really liked working with the Chechens. I admired them tremendously. Athough they were much younger than I was, they were totally dedicated to learning everything they could.

In time, we learned to work as a team. We always knew instinctively where our brothers were, and learned to coordinate our movements with precision. At times, it felt like we were a single body moving together. A single lethal body.

The Chechens learned many things more quickly than I did, which surprised me. I had spent years training with guns when I lived with Édouard, whereas they had just begun. And they were very young; the oldest could not have been more than eighteen. But I came to see they had a far deeper passion than I for their homeland. They were desperate to go home and kill Russians.

I never asked them any questions, of course, and they didn't ask any of me. But over time they revealed themselves little by little. They were all haunted by things they had seen in Chechnya. Each one of them, in his own way, described the constant presence of death in his village, and often in his own family. Some of them talked about the horrific battle in Grozny the winter before. They talked about the carpet bombing and the destruction and the corpses lying in the streets.

The Chechens had not known each other for very long. They met in Islamabad. They had been sent by their families, who wanted to keep them out of the war. But none of them wanted to be kept out of the war. As soon as they arrived at the university in Islamabad they were recruited to come to the camps. They were so grateful they had been taken here, and so angry at their parents for trying to keep them away from the front. After they explained this to me, I understood that awful tension I had witnessed at the Tabligh center, between the Chechen father and his son.

The youngest boy, the very small one who was the first to fire the DShK, was the fiercest by far. He was a sweet-looking child, with blond hair, white skin, and wide blue eyes. He was different from the others, more serious. He never smiled or laughed with the rest of us. He rarely spoke, but when he did he was vicious. While the others spoke about going home to kill Russian soldiers, he talked about slicing off their heads.

I felt sorry for the boy, and wanted to help him. I took care of him as much as I could when we were training, and tried to coax him out a bit when we weren't. Still, it took several months before he told me his story. The Russians had come to his village and there was a terrible battle. One day, the Russians fired a mortar into his home. Everyone inside was killed immediately, his entire family. Not just his parents and his brothers and sisters. His *entire* family. Fifteen of them.

Several different trainers came from other camps to teach us specific skills. For two weeks, we did specialized physical training with an Algerian named Assad Allah. He was enormous. With his green eyes and red hair, he looked like an Irish rugby player.

Another time, a trainer came for three weeks to teach us hand-to-hand combat. The brothers in the camp whispered that he had been a colonel in the Egyptian army, in the special forces division. He taught us all sorts of things. How to evade arrest. How to escape if captured. How to turn small objects into weapons that can kill. How to disarm an enemy and then use his weapon against him.

He taught us how to kill someone silently by approaching from behind, to stick the knife in just the right place to rupture the lungs so he suffocated instantly. He taught us how to kill with no weapons at all, just using our hands or feet. We practiced all this on each other, and there were a great many injuries in the course of those weeks.

We spent days learning surveillance tactics. We learned how to surveil a building in advance of a bombing. We had to know if there were guards or video cameras, what the building was made of, where the structure was most vulnerable, where the building was most heavily trafficked and at what times of day.

We also learned how to surveil human targets, because surveillance is an essential part of planning a kidnapping or an assassination. Once, we were given the name of a brother in the camp and told to surveil him for four days, keeping notes on every move he made and at what time. We couldn't let the brother leave our sight, but we also had to make sure we weren't spotted. Abu Yahya showed us a plant that grew an edible fungus on the underside of its leaves, so we could eat enough to sustain ourselves without letting the target escape from view.

Abu Yahya taught us how to use our surveillance skills to carry out a kidnapping. He explained that it's always best to kidnap someone in his own house, so there would be no witnesses. But first it is essential to find out what goes on inside the house. Who the target lives with. When he leaves in the morning and when he returns. When he's awake and when he's sleeping. How he moves in his house. Whether or not he owns any weapons. We learned how to stake out a house to gather this information, but Abu Yahya told us it was always best to gather accurate intelligence by bribing or threatening members of the household staff.

Abu Yahya then taught us how to stage the actual kidnapping. How to get over walls or through gates without been seen. How to kill the guards and get into the house. How to come up behind the target and restrain him, and how to subdue him by covering his face with a rag soaked in chloroform. He warned us not to leave the rag on for too long, the victim could die. Then he would be of no use.

Abu Yahya taught us all this from a huge training manual. All the trainers had the same book; the cover was red and green with two Kalashnikovs and some writing in Arabic. It was thousands of pages long, and it contained instructions for every kind of military and guerilla operation, from defusing a trapped land mine to targeting an airplane with a surface-to-air missile.

There were illustrations in the manual, and sometimes the trainers showed them to us to help us understand some aspect of the class. I still didn't speak perfect Arabic, though I was getting better and better, and the Chechens didn't speak perfect English either. So the pictures could be very useful.

One day, Abu Yahya asked us to gather around him to look at the illustrations in the kidnapping section, which laid out the process step by step. I was amused when I saw the pictures he set before us. I had seen them before: they were the pictures from the American training manuals I had plucked off the shelves in the safe house in Peshawar.

Emir

Between the time I met Ibn Sheikh in Peshawar and the day he came to Khaldan, I had learned a great deal more about him. Everyone at the camp talked about Ibn Sheikh, even through we weren't supposed to gossip. I learned he was the emir of Khaldan and of several other training camps as well. I learned that he was from Libya and known as Ibn al-Sheikh al-Libi. I learned that he had fought in the war against the Russians in the 1980s.

Afterward, Ibn Sheikh continued fighting against Mohammad Najibullah. Najibullah was president of Afghanistan during the final years of the Soviet occupation and, even after the Red Army withdrew, the Soviets continued to support him. He was ruthless in his efforts to rid the country of the *mujahidin*, who hated him. He was finally forced to step down in 1992, when rival *mujahidin* factions took control of Kabul. They raided the government's vast weapons supply, and the *mujahidin* became more lethal still.

Ibn Sheikh was very tough, like all the trainers. Everyone looked up to him, including Abu Bakr. Ibn Sheikh was the most powerful man in the camp, but he was also gentle in his way. Once, when I was sick, he took care of me. In the morning he cooked eggs and brought them to me in the dormitory, and came by during the day to check up on me. He brought me chicken soup, and explained that chicken was full of vitamins and minerals and that it would help me recover. It didn't go on forever, of course. After three days, he commanded me to start training again. I told him that I still felt sick, but he didn't care. He said the fresh air would be good for me.

He was very strict as a trainer, but not sadistic like Abu Bakr. He demanded a great deal from us, but never said anything harsh. And he spoke about *jihad* in a way the others didn't. He didn't say anything about fighting for a particular group or against a particular enemy. For him, the *jihad* was global. Whatever we did, wherever we fought, it was for the entire Muslim *umma*.

It was during tactical training that we each got a Kalashnikov of our own. It was incredibly exciting. Abu Hamam handed them out to me and the Chechens, and gave us a long lecture about how to handle them. He explained that the gun was *amana*, property that did not belong to us, but for which we were totally responsible.

"You must guard your gun like your eyes," Abu Haman said. "It's like your body. It will break down if you don't take care of it. You must clean it carefully every night. Remember, this gun is your life. If you lose your gun, you will lose your life. It is everything—it is your son, it is your wife. Don't ever forget."

Soon, my Kalashnikov became almost a part of me. I slept with her in my sleeping bag at night and brought her to mosque when I prayed. I knew where she was every second of every day. But she was never loaded; that was a rule. Unless we were on guard duty, we had to keep our ammunition separate from the gun. Otherwise, we would have ended up killing each other.

One evening, I was sitting by the mosque talking with Ibn Sheikh and a few others. The whole time, I was playing with my Kalashnikov, just moving the charging handle up and down slightly. But I wasn't paying attention, and at one point I pulled the charging handle all the way back, and the gun made a loud click. Nothing happened; there was no ammunition inside, and even if there had been I would have had to pull the trigger before the gun fired. But it didn't matter. Ibn Sheikh heard the click and immediately turned to me. "Abu Imam," he said sternly. "You know you're not supposed to play with your gun." Then he ordered me to run up and down the mountain.

"For how long?" I asked.

"Until I tell you to stop," he replied.

I ran up and down the mountain for over an hour. I was exhausted already from the training that morning, and I was miserable. Eventually, I heard the whiz of a bullet and a loud noise as it hit the rock face about fifteen meters away from me. My punishment was over, and I headed back into camp.

I got punished a lot during my time at Khaldan, more than anyone else. Unlike the other trainees, I wasn't intimidated by Ibn Sheikh or the other trainers. Early on, I came to be known as something of a class clown. When I translated Arabic into English for the Chechens during training, I would always inject little jokes. The Chechens would laugh and the trainers would get annoyed. Ibn Sheikh scolded me for this, and scolded me for doing the same thing during the lectures in the evenings. The Chechens would burst out laughing in the middle of our religious instruction, and Ibn Sheikh would scowl at me. I kept doing it anyway, and eventually he wouldn't let me translate for them anymore in the evenings.

I was bad in other ways as well, though it was never anything serious. I would find shortcuts during the morning runs, and Ibn Sheikh would take me to task for it. Again and again, he and the other trainers punished me with extra runs and other exercises in order to make me behave. When Ibn Sheikh disciplined me, he put his face very close to mine and stared me straight in the eye. It was a challenge; he wanted to see how much I could take. I always stared right back and never gave him any sign that I was upset.

In the evenings, when Ibn Sheikh handed out assignments, I was almost always chosen for night guard duty. It was a horrible job; it was freezing cold, and it meant I couldn't sleep at all. I was given guard duty so many times that after a couple of months, it became a joke. When Ibn Sheikh prepared to announce the names for the night watch, I would step forward before I was even called. The brothers laughed at that, too, which only made him Ibn Sheikh angrier.

The one plum assignment at Khaldan was leading the call to prayer. The *muezzin* could stay at camp all day and relax while the others were training. I got this job only once, but my voice was so bad the brothers complained. I was never chosen as *muezzin* again.

Over and over again, Ibn Sheikh and the others would explain how important it was for every brother to be part of a group. The group was essential because it made each brother stronger. Without it, we would falter very easily.

It was true, of course. When I was with the Chechens I felt completely committed to the group. Even though I joked sometimes, I gave everything I had to the group and to our training. The more I learned about how they had suffered in Chechnya, the more I wanted to go back with them and exact revenge. Their *jihad* had become mine.

But in important ways, I wasn't like the other brothers. I had grown up in Europe, with all the individualism that implies. I thought for myself and spoke up when I disagreed with something. I was free in a way that the others were not.

One Friday, I finally got sick of cleaning the toilets. They were always disgusting, but as the weather got colder they became even more wretched because the brothers didn't want to go down to the river to clean themselves.

That night, after the prayers were over, I decided to say something. Abu Bakr must have sensed this, because when he stood up to ask if any of us had questions he looked straight at me. I raised my hand immediately.

"OK, Abu Imam. What is it you want to say?" Abu Bakr rolled his eyes slightly as he said it, and some of the brothers laughed quietly.

I stood up and turned to face the group. "*Bismi'allah Arahman Arahim wa Asalt wa Aslam Ala Rasoul Allah, Sayedna Muhammad Sala Allah Alihi wa Salam,*" I intoned with a false earnestness. Then I launched in. "My dear brothers, tonight I would like to talk about all of this shit you're leaving for me to clean up. The Prophet says that you can use stones to clean yourself if there's no water. But there's water five meters away from the bathrooms! You just don't want to use it because it's too cold, and so every Friday I have to clean your shit off the stones."

Everyone fell silent as I sat back down. The brothers' eyes darted back and forth from Ibn Sheikh to Abu Bakr and back to me. Nobody ever spoke like this in the camp, and they were waiting to see how I would get punished this time. But nothing happened. Ibn Sheikh and Abu Bakr exchanged a glance, but neither said a word.

Later, right before I left Khaldan, Abu Bakr told me that when he and Ibn Sheikh were alone later that evening, they had recounted the story again and again. He said he had never in his life heard Ibn Sheikh laugh so hard.

Tajikistan

One day, a man arrived at camp by himself, without a guide. We were all in the cantina when he stopped in front of the camp; we looked at each other but said nothing. Ibn Sheikh rose from his seat and walked outside, and we watched him talk to the new man for a few minutes. The man was African, Somalian or Ethiopian or Eritrean, it wasn't clear. But I could tell from the way he moved his eyes there was something not quite right about him.

Soon, two of the other trainers went outside and spoke to him while Ibn Sheikh came back into the cantina. Ibn Sheikh warned those of us with our own Kalashnikovs to be very careful and to keep our guns nearby.

We went off to training after lunch, and by the time we returned the African was gone. We learned Abu Bakr had pinned him to the ground and put him in handcuffs, and that they had radioed for a four-by-four to take him back to Pakistan.

That night Ibn Sheikh explained that the man had come without papers. He had been in the camp once before, but he had returned to Pakistan. Now he wanted to come back. I was surprised that he had sent away a brother who had already been at the camp, and in such a dramatic fashion, so I asked about it. At first, Ibn Sheikh explained he had to be very careful, that he couldn't allow anyone into the camp who didn't have the right papers. But then he went on to say there was something wrong with the African, something not right in his head. It was very important to keep such people out of the camp because they could be dangerous. Once he had seen a brother go mad very suddenly from battle fatigue. One day, he picked up his Kalashnikov, walked into the mosque, and started shooting. He killed four brothers and seriously injured ten more. Ibn Sheikh had to be very careful.

Battle fatigue was real. Sometimes it made people crazy, and sometimes just careless. One day, Ibn Sheikh pointed out to me a spot in the training area at the back of the camp. He told me that just a few months before I had arrived, a group of seven Chechens were training there with mortars. One of them had accidentally picked up a booby-trapped rather than a regular one. When he put the mortar inside the cannon, it blew up instantly and killed the entire group.

At times I thought I was going crazy, too. One Friday, shortly after Ibn Sheikh arrived at the camp, I was taking a nap in front of the entrance to one of the caves when I had an incredibly vivid dream. I dreamed that I was lying in front of that very cave, and that Abu Suhail was standing over me with a handgun pointed at my forehead.

Just as he was about to pull the trigger, I woke up. It took me several seconds to realize Abu Suhail wasn't really there—not standing over me, not even at the camp. He was still in Tajikistan with Abu Bakr. It was a nightmare, nothing more. But I was sweating nonetheless, and my heart was racing.

Only a few days later, Ibn Sheikh told us he had heard from Abu Bakr via radio. The previous Friday, Abu Suhail had gone crazy. During their mission, the group had to cross a dangerous river. Three of the Tajiks had drowned. As soon as it happened, Abu Suhail went mad and still hadn't recovered.

I was stunned that all of this happened on the same day as my dream, and it struck me then that there was something almost palpable connecting me to these brothers. But I wasn't entirely surprised about Abu Suhail. I remembered how intensely he had cared for us during training. He loved us all, and wanted us to succeed. I could imagine how he must have felt when those Tajiks died, how much pain it would have caused him. I could that see it would be enough to drive him insane.

Abu Bakr didn't return to camp for several weeks after Abu Suhail went crazy. When he did return, Abu Suhail was with him. But he was at the camp for only a few hours before he was taken away again, and sent back to Pakistan to recover. I never saw Abu Suhail again.

I knew it must have been very dangerous for Abu Bakr to cross Afghanistan with Abu Suhail, who could no longer fend for himself. It was an extremely dangerous trip anyway, with the civil war raging in Afghanistan. I admired Abu Bakr very much for his courage and for his loyalty.

Abu Bakr never spoke to me directly about what had happened in Tajikistan, but over time I heard stories about it from the others. After Abu Suhail lost his mind, Abu Bakr left him in the temporary care of some Afghanis near the border. Then he had gone off with the Tajiks to help them on their first mission. He had killed several Russians while he was there, and some of the brothers that whispered that he had cut off their heads.

Abu Bakr went off many times with the groups he had trained from Kashmir and Tajikistan. He understood that practicing in camp wasn't the same thing as real battle. He wanted to make sure that his students remembered everything they had learned and that they knew how to implement their skills on the front. Over time, I came to see that this was Abu Bakr's way of giving love.

Arabs

About two months after I had arrived at Khaldan, Abdul Kerim left. I never said goodbye to him. I came back from training one afternoon and his things were gone. That was it. There was nothing unusual about Abdul Kerim's departure. People were coming and going all the time, and we rarely got to say goodbye. No one was sad about it. We all knew we were there for a reason.

Many of the recruits stayed for several months, like I did. But others came for only a couple of weeks to learn very specific skills: how to attack a convoy or blow up a bridge. These groups were generally from Tajikistan, Uzbekistan, Kyrgyztan, Kashmir, and Chechnya; that is, places fairly close to the camps. They would train apart from everyone else, usually with either Abu Bakr or Ibn Sheikh, and we never saw what they were doing. Sometimes, the same group would go away and then come back again to learn something new.

After Abdul Kerim left, I spent more time talking with brothers from other places. I liked the Kashmiris very much. They talked about their war, and described the Indians as a vicious and merciless enemy. But mostly, they told me about their land and how much they loved it. I have never heard people from anywhere speak with such intensity about the beauty of their land—the lakes and the rivers and the mountains that brushed against heaven.

The Kashmiris also talked about their route to the camps. They didn't come like I did through Peshawar. First they trained with a unit of the Pakistani military, which then sent them on to the camps. Every one of them told me the same thing.

The Tajiks were fighting the Russian occupation of their homeland, and they hated the Russians with the same passion as the Chechens. One of the most intense brothers I met at the camp was a Tajik. He did extra training on his own in addition to everything he did with his group. He pushed boulders and climbed up the treacherous cliffs every day to make himself stronger. His hands were always bleeding by the time he got back to camp for dinner.

This Tajik was no more than fourteen years old. The other men in his group were in their twenties, so whatever free time the boy had he spent on his own. There was a kind of open-air gymnasium by the river near the bathrooms, and I would see him there by himself. There were some makeshift barbells made of thick metal rods with rocks at either end held together by concrete. I would see him lifting them for hours at a time. They looked much heavier than he was.

I was drawn to the boy, and felt sorry for him; he seemed so lonely. I tried to talk and joke with him, but he was terribly earnest and never smiled. Eventually, I approached one of the men in his group and asked him why the young boy was training so hard. The Tajik explained the Russians had forced the boy to stand and watch as they shot his entire family at close range.

I was proud of the young Tajik. He had taken his destiny into his own hands. He refused to accept the slaughter of his family. Even at such a young age, he understood his duty as a Muslim. But still, I could never get used to these stories, to these children who had suffered so much. I didn't feel sorry for the older *mujahidin*. Like me, they were prepared to die. They had made that choice. But it broke my heart that these children were forced to sacrifice their lives so early, before they had eaten an ice cream cone or kissed a girl.

I never said goodbye to the Tajik boy either. He left one day with the rest of his group. Like so many others I met at Khaldan, he is probably dead now.

Some Arab *mujahidin* passed through the camp on their way back from the war in Bosnia. All summer, we had been hearing news reports about Bosnia on RFI and the BBC World Service. But they mostly reported on the diplomatic efforts in Washington, Paris, London, and elsewhere.

The Arabs returning from the front told us about the reality on the ground. We heard about the massacre in Srebrenica, where the Serbs forced tens of thousands of Bosniaks from their homes. We heard about the atrocities that followed at Potočari, where the refugees had fled and the Serbs had followed. We heard about the rapes and the killings and the truckloads of men who were separated from their families, executed, and dumped in mass graves. We heard how the Serbs rounded up the men and forced them into buildings, then threw in grenades to kill them all at once. We heard about the men who escaped by running for days through the forests, about how they arrived in safe territory covered with blood and completely deranged from the horrors they had seen.

We heard that the UN forces had done nothing to protect the Bosniaks. We heard that the commander of the Dutch peacekeeping forces was seen eating and drinking with Ratko Mladić, the Serbian general. We heard that they abandoned the Muslims and allowed them to die.

But although the Arabs hated the Serbs, they didn't really like the Bosniaks either. They said many of the same things about the Bosnian Muslims I had heard from Amin and Yasin. They said that the Bosniaks weren't really Muslims because they drank and listened to music, and because the women didn't wear scarves on their heads.

As the summer turned into fall, more Arabs came to the camps filled with rage at the Bosniaks. They had betrayed the *mujahidin*. The Arabs were furious that after they had offered up their lives for their Bosnian brothers, they were being kicked out of the country or arrested. A few even told stories of Bosniaks killing the Arabs who had fought alongside them.

It was the rapes, though, that bothered the Arabs most. The Serbs raped thousands and thousands of Bosniak women, and many of them became pregnant. The Bosniak men wouldn't touch these women. They hated the Serbs so much that it was impossible for them to imagine raising a child who was half enemy. But the Arabs believed that it was their duty to marry these women, and to raise their children into *mujahidin* who could go on to slaughter the Serbs whose blood they shared.

One day during the morning run, I ended up speaking to one of the Arabs who had returned from Bosnia. We were both at the rear of the group throughout the run, and by the end we were so far behind that we could no longer see the brothers. So we decided to walk the rest of the way, and while we were walking he told me he had seen something new on the battlefield. It was some sort of compass that used satellites for accuracy; the Arabs used it for targeting. It sounded really useful, and I asked him why he hadn't brought one back with him for us to use at the camp. He smiled and said that as soon as he got his visa and was allowed to go home, he would send one back.

I forgot all about that conversation, and was surprised when Ibn Sheikh appeared three months later with a package from the Arab. "Do you know what this is?" he asked me as he held it up.

"Yes, of course," I replied. "The Arab told me all about it. It's called a GBS." I was very pleased with myself for knowing something Ibn Sheikh didn't. Ibn

Sheikh's eyes twinkled, and he thanked me for thinking to ask the Arab to send it along.

The next day I saw Abdul Haq playing with the new device, and I was furious. It had come with an instruction manual in English, and he was learning how to use it. I thought it was terribly unfair. After all, it was only because of me that we had the thing in the first place. Ibn Sheikh should have let me use it first.

A few days later, I learned why he didn't. It was called a GPS, not a GBS. Ibn Sheikh had been testing me, and I had failed.

There were many other Arabs in the camp, of course, from all over North Africa and the Middle East. But the Saudis stood out. Groups of Saudis would come to Khaldan for short periods; they were unlike anyone else there. They were much older, in their forties or even fifties, and they were soft.

It was obvious immediately that these men were rich. They didn't really come to train, like everyone else. They were there for a holiday. They didn't have to run with us in the morning, so most of them slept in and only came out in the afternoon to play with the guns.

We didn't mind having them there—quite the opposite. Whenever they came, the food was much better. There were no insects in it, as there normally were. We had butter and honey with our bread, which we never got otherwise. Some days, we'd even have meat.

They weren't *mujahidin*, but they were always very gracious and kind. One night, I had a very high fever. I was sitting out by the mosque feeling dreadful when a clutch of Saudis spotted me. They immediately sat down and began to take care of me. They brought me water and reassured me that I would feel better soon. Then one of the men put his hand on my forehead. With his other hand, he held open his Kur'an and began to read. It was so soothing, the coolness of his hand and his gentle voice pronouncing the words I had heard so many times before.

After a while, the group began to get up to go to bed. The man finished reading the passage in the Kur'an, closed it, and took his hand away. "No, please," I said instinctively. "Please stay. Please stay and put your hand back on my forehead. It feels so good." I was practically begging. As his friends turned in for the night, the man quietly sat back down, put out his hand, and began to read again.

These were the things I missed about Khaldan after I left: the kindness, the sense of community. We were all brothers there, and we did everything we could for each other. It was wonderful to know that every one of the brothers would lay down his life for me, just as I would for them. I had never felt so loved in my life, so taken care of. And I wanted to take care of them as well. Once, I gave Ibn Sheikh some money to buy a sheep so that we could eat it at the camp. I told him not to tell anyone where the sheep came from, because I didn't want anyone to know. But a few days later, when we ate the meat, it was wonderful to see the brothers so happy. After that, I gave Ibn Sheikh money for all sorts of things whenever he needed it: food, ammunition, other supplies.

In the summer, we would all go swimming in a pool in the river. We looked really silly. Many of the brothers swam with their clothes on, and the rest of us covered ourselves from our navels to our knees. But I still loved the water as much as I had as a child in Belgium, and I was happy there. The others looked up to me because I was strong and could dive from rocks high above the river.

Everything we did at Khaldan was for a single purpose: to prepare ourselves for *jihad*. So we were training even when we swam. I was the best swimmer by far, and would show off by carrying heavy rocks across the river at its deepest point. The others would try to copy me, but they weren't strong enough and always dropped the rocks in the water before reaching the other side.

Soon enough, the brothers got annoyed with me and tried to knock me over. But I could swim faster than them, so they could never catch me. One of the Chechens had a better idea: he dove underwater and tried to pull me down from below. I could feel his hand on my ankle and lost my balance. The rock fell into the river and my body began to sink.

The whole thing lasted for only a few seconds, but what struck me most was how gently the brother pulled me in, how he let go of my leg just as my head went under. He wasn't trying to hurt me; he just wanted to show me he had figured something out. I was very touched by it, particularly when I thought about my own brothers. When we went swimming together during our summers in Morocco, they would try to push me under the water and drown me, and I did the same to them. We went for the kill.

We weren't a family at Khaldan, that was certain. We were something much better.

Chechnya

Ibn Sheikh was brilliant in every way. He had been a commander in the war against the Russians, and he knew everything there was to know about weapons and battle. But he was also an intellectual; it was obvious that he had read and thought very deeply. He spoke more intelligently and eloquently than anyone else at the camp. And he had extraordinary charisma. When he spoke, all the brothers listened to him with rapt attention.

During our discussions in the evenings, Ibn Sheikh spoke mostly of *jihad*, and the duty of Muslims all over the world. He explained the difference between the *faridat al-jihad* and the *kifayat al-jihad*—the obligatory or defensive jihad and the offensive or preemptive *jihad*. All of us, he explained, were fighting the *faridat al-jihad*, the battle to reclaim the lands of the caliphate from the infidels. Only a caliph could proclaim a *kifayat al-jihad* and thereby command Muslims to attack the *kafir* in non-Muslim lands, to either kill or convert them. But the caliphate had ended when the Ottoman Empire collapsed, and so there was no caliph to deliver such an order. Every battle we would fight, Ibn Sheikh told us, was part of the bigger battle to restore the caliphate.

The battle to reclaim Palestinian land from Israel was by far the most important battle any *mujahid* could fight in his life. Jerusalem was the heart of Islam. Faced with danger, every man protects his heart first; only later does he protect the rest. Palestine was not the only *jihad*, of course, but it was the most crucial one.

The *jihad* against the Hindus in Kashmir was also vital. The Hindus were idolaters. They worshipped the cow, just as Aaron and his followers turned their backs on Moses and worshipped the golden calf. The Hindus were the descendants of a Jewish tribe that had wandered to India many centuries earlier.

The Shiites were another great enemy. They were innovators, the worst thing of all. There is no innovation in Islam. There is only the Kur'an, the *sunna*. This was why every Muslim child learns to pronounce the words of the Kur'an phonetically. This was why the laws of the *sunna* dictate the behavior of every Muslim. Iran was a primordial enemy to Islam, a greater enemy than America or Russia or even Israel. The others were infidels, but the Shiites were far more dangerous. They were trying to destroy Islam from within.

Bosnia, Chechnya, Uzbekistan, Tajikistan—all these were essential. In all these cases, the *mujahidin* were battling the *kafir* for control of Muslim land. This was clear to everyone. Even clearer was the importance of overthrowing secular governments in Muslim lands. Theocracy was the only acceptable form of government for an Islamic nation. But of course at this time Iran was the only theocracy, and since Iran was Shiite it was no consolation at all. Everywhere else—Morocco, Algeria, Tunisia, Libya, Jordan, Egypt—all these countries were governed by infidels because they were governed by men and not by God.

But these regimes were enemies of Islam for another reason as well. Everyone knew that these rulers were just the puppets of other powers: Russia, America, France, England. Their hands were all over the Muslim world, propping up corrupt leaders to serve their own interests. The *jihad* against these secular regimes was in every case a crusade against foreign influence.

One night, one of the brothers asked what the next *jihad* would be. Ibn Sheikh didn't hesitate: Iraq. Iraq was rich with oil, and the government was weak. The Gulf War and the sanctions had left Saddam Hussein almost powerless. The people were ready for a revolution because they had been oppressed for so long under Saddam. Of course, there was another reason to go after Iraq: if the *mujahidin* won Iraq, then Iran would be surrounded. It was a tantalizing opportunity.

There were two Muslim countries, however, that we didn't discuss much at all: Afghanistan and Pakistan. We were guests of both. Afghanistan we called the "land of jihad" because she had welcomed us and allowed us to stay and train for our battles around the world. Pakistan was an ally as well; many of us came through Pakistan and had been helped by Pakistanis along the way. And of course the Kashmiris had been trained by the Pakistani military.

There was no government in Afghanistan. Burhanuddin Rabbani, the president and the head of the Northern Alliance, was holding on by his fingernails as rival factions laid siege on Kabul. And we were careful not to criticize the Pakistani government either. The only one we did talk about was Benazir Bhutto—we despised her. When we talked about her, it was never just "Bhutto"; it was always "that whore, Bhutto." Mostly, we hated her because to us she was a Westerner; she had lived in America and was educated there. And now she was a puppet of the American government. But I suppose it was the fact she was a woman that made us feel so free to attack her.

We talked about America, of course, because America was the great Satan. We all knew that. But America wasn't really America; it was controlled by Israel. That, too, was obvious to everyone. Everything America did made sense in these terms. Its support of Israel, of course, but also the way it behaved in the rest of the world. We knew, for instance, that America had sided with the Serbs in Bosnia. They wanted to render the Bosniaks completely powerless, so they let the Serbs kill as many as they could, and surround them. Only then, when the Bosniaks were completely helpless, did America come to their aid, in exchange for a vow from the Bosniaks that they would drive out or arrest all the Arab *mujahidin* who were their only real protectors. Obviously, the Jews were pulling the strings.

I knew that Palestine was the most important *jihad*, but I didn't want to go there. I wanted to keep fighting, and I knew that I wouldn't be fighting for long if I went to the Middle East. I would strap a bomb on my chest and blow myself up, and it would be over.

It's not as if I didn't care about Palestine—far from it. Before everything else—before the Soviet invasion of Afghanistan, before the Serbs in Bosnia, before Russians in Chechnya—there was Israel. One of my first memories is of watching the news with my father when the Egyptian army overran Israeli forces to take control of the Suez Canal in 1973. My father was so happy that he threw a cushion into the air.

And then there was the endless war in Lebanon. Like everyone else, I was horrified by the siege of Beirut in 1982. The Israelis were brutal. They attacked by land, they attacked by air, they attacked by sea. They killed more than ten thousand civilians in their attempt to rout the PLO.

Israel destroyed Beirut, but even that wasn't enough. And when the Americans came and removed the remaining PLO, that wasn't enough either. A month later, Israel sealed off the refugee camps at Sabra and Shatila in West Beirut. They armed the Christians, the Lebanese Phalangists, and let them loose in the camp, with orders to kill everyone in their path. They said that they were looking for the PLO, but they were really just looking to kill Muslims. And they did—women, children, everyone. The killed them with guns and hatchets and knives.

The Israelis waited just outside on the perimeter of the camp and set off flares so that the Phalangists could continue their slaughter through the night. And when it was all over, the Israelis sent in bulldozers to mop up the hundreds of dead bodies lying in the streets.

At first the PLO fighters were heroes to me; they were fighting to reclaim Muslim lands. But then Arafat betrayed Islam in the Madrid conference in 1991, and later with the Oslo Accords in 1993. After that, the PLO held no allure for me. During my summer in Paris, I had watched a documentary about the war and it was clear to me that the PLO fighters were nothing like the *mujahidin*. The PLO was just a political party with guns. They weren't fighting for the Muslim *umma*. They were fighting for purely political objectives.

Whenever the PLO came on screen in the footage I saw at the Pompidou Center, there was music in the background. Even the Christians seemed more pious. Many of them had tiny crucifixes affixed to their assault rifles. But the PLO listened to music. No, these were not *mujahidin*.

Most of the brothers knew where they would go after they left the camp; they would go back wherever they came from and make their *jihad*. But I hadn't come from anywhere, or with any group. I could choose my own *jihad*. I could fight wherever I wanted to.

So one night, when Ibn Sheikh asked me where I wanted to go after leaving Khaldan, I didn't have to think for even a second before I replied. "Chechnya," I told him. "I want to go to Chechnya."

Night Guard

One night, I was awakened by the sound of gunfire. It was very near the camp. I sat up in my sleeping bag and reached for my gun. But she was gone.

BAM. BAM. BAM. Tat-tat-tat-tat. There were explosions, and more guns firing. It was very dark, with only the sliver of a moon for light. I felt all around me for my Kalashnikov, but I couldn't find her anywhere. I panicked. If I lost my gun, I would be in terrible trouble with the emir.

Then I snapped out of it. BAM BAM. Tat-tat-tat-tat-tat. BAM. The guns were getting closer and closer. Whether or not I was going to get in trouble, we had a much bigger problem on our hands. The camp was under attack, and I had no gun. Neither did any of the other brothers in the room, it turned out. Someone had come in while we were asleep and taken them all. We were defenseless.

Suddenly, a man burst into the room. My eyes had adjusted by now and I tried to look at his face, but there was nothing to see. He was wearing a mask. He could be an American, he could be a *talib*, he could be anyone.

Without saying a word, the masked man lurched at one of the brothers and threw something over this head. With just one movement, he circled his arm around his prey. He lifted the brother from the floor and dragged him outside. Before I could react, they were gone. The remaining brothers and I looked at each other in stunned silence. The whole thing had taken no more than a few seconds.

The gunfire continued for another minute, and then it stopped. An eerie silence settled over the camp. We looked at each other, but no one knew what to do. Then one of the trainers appeared in the doorway. "Move now," he said. "They've taken our guns. We need to get new weapons."

We all crouched low to the ground as we ran across the camp and up towards the armory. Almost all of the brothers were there, but the night guards and a few others were missing, including Abu Bakr. Some of the men looked completely dazed, and others were rubbing their eyes. The enemy had used stun grenades to blind them during the attack.

Quietly, and as quickly as we could, we headed up into the mountains to plot our next move. It wasn't safe to go back into the camp now, in the dark of night. We would wait until the dawn.

The next morning we learned that the whole thing was fake. Learning how to stage a raid was part of the training, and the rest of us needed to learn what to do if our camp came under siege. So one of the other Chechen groups had gone away for a couple of days to plan their attack. Once they were ready, the trainers removed the triggers from the night guards' Kalashnikovs so they couldn't kill anyone. And as soon as the rest of us had fallen asleep, they took our guns as well.

During the attack, they had taken the guards and some of the brothers hostage. They dragged them up into one of the caves and interrogated them all night. Hostage-taking and interrogation were also part of the training.

The next morning, Abu Bakr told us how they had tried to break down one of the brothers, a boy of no more than seventeen. He had been on duty as a night guard when the camp came under attack. The assailants wanted to know what kind of weapons the camp had, but the boy wouldn't tell them anything. The Chechens held their guns to his head and slapped him, but he wouldn't talk. And so they fired their guns within centimeters of his feet and told him they would kill him if he didn't talk. Finally, he cracked.

"We have seventy-five tanks," he said. "And thousands and thousands of guns. We have fifty stingers. There are more than three hundred of us, and the whole area around the camp is mined."

Abu Bakr laughed as he told the story. The boy had done exactly the right thing: he had given his interrogators more than they wanted, and made his army sound much stronger than it really was.

I was assigned to night guard duty many, many times as a punishment. One night, however, I was chosen to be the chief guard. It was an honor, because it meant that I was responsible for making sure the other guards were doing their jobs correctly.

Every night, there were four guards assigned to different sectors of the camp. The chief guard supervised all of them. That night, there were two Chechens, a Tajik, and a Kurd on guard duty. I knew the Kurd slightly, and I liked him. So I decided to play with him a bit. His job was to guard the front of the camp, beginning at the river, all the way across past the cantina, past the entrance to the camp and into the area behind the cooks' hut.

I waited for a couple of hours so that the Kurd would settle into the rhythm of his patrol. Then I hid behind the cantina and waited for him to approach. As soon as I heard his breath, I shouted. "*Dresh!*" It was the Afghan word for "stop"—we had all learned as soon as we arrived at the camp.

I heard the Kurd shout out, and I peeked around the corner and saw him pointing his gun in my direction. He looked panicked. From behind the cantina I spoke the night code we had been given, and said my name. Then I came out and faced him. The Kurd had lowered his gun and was scowling at me.

"I got you!" I said with a laugh.

"You won't get me again," he grumbled. He didn't see anything funny about it at all. He turned and walked off to continue his patrol.

Of course, I couldn't let that stand. I had to get him again. So I walked up along the river for over a kilometer, far back into the camp. I climbed about a hundred meters up the side of the mountain to the right of the river. I headed back towards the camp along the face of the mountain until I was just above the cooks' hut, then began to sneak back down. There were low bushes everywhere and I could feel the thorns cutting at my feet.

Eventually, I got to the area behind the cooks' hut. It was a strange part of camp, and no one ever went there except when they were on guard duty. It was haunted. When the *mujahidin* used the camp during the war against the Russians, they put the toilets there because it was close to the lowest part of the river. But one day, while several of them were making their ablutions, the Russians had stormed the camp. They entered from behind the mountain I had just descended, and so they fell upon the toilets first. They killed everyone inside.

But it was not just the deaths that rattled us. Muslims believe that devils live in toilets; there is even a prayer for warding them off. The toilets were gone now—they had been moved to the other side of the camp. But somehow the devils were still haunting this place, along with the ghosts of the slaughtered *mujahidin*. Every one of us had felt their presence at one time or another.

I prowled through the underbrush for several minutes until I heard the Kurd approaching. Very slowly, without making a sound, I walked towards him. He kept moving—he didn't hear me. I got very close to him, and then closer still. I was no more than fifty centimeters from his face when I shouted, "*Dresh!*"

The Kurd screamed at the top of his lungs. He was scared to death; he must have thought the devil had come to take him away. But then he quickly realized that it was just me, and he gave me an ugly, angry look.

"You should really be more careful," I told him. "If I were your enemy, you'd be dead now."

Clearly, the Kurd didn't appreciate my insight. He just frowned.

"You're a very dangerous guy," he said, before turning on his heel and heading back in the other direction.

There was one full-time guard at the camp, but no one spoke to him because he was an Afghani, and we all knew we weren't supposed to talk to the Afghanis. During the day he slept in a small building right near the cook's hut. He came out only at night and prowled around the camp by himself with his Kalashnikov at the ready.

He had three dogs at the camp with him: two big shepherds, one black and one brown, and a white bitch who was a bit smaller. They wandered around during the day. No one knew the dogs' names, since no one talked to the guard. But over time the brothers had given them names of their own. We called the black one Bush and the brown one Reagan. The white bitch was Thatcher.

Spy

One day, about a month after I got to Khaldan, we were training with explosives at the back of the camp when we saw Abu Bakr and one of the other trainers escorting a man up towards the caves. The man was wearing handcuffs and a blindfold.

Two days later, the same man was presented to us as a new recruit. His name was Abu Hudayfa, and he was from Saudi Arabia. That night, Abdul Kerim explained to me that he had been taken into the cave for interrogation because of a radio transmission from Peshawar. Ibn Sheikh had learned there was something not quite right with the man's papers, so before they let him into the camp they had to be absolutely certain that he wasn't a spy. Apparently, Abu Hudayfa had said all the right things, because now he was among us. Nobody asked any questions.

A couple of days later, Ibn Sheikh ordered Abu Hudayfa to teach me *tajwid*, and so I spent a lot of time with him. I began to notice things about him that made me suspicious; tiny things at first, but they began to add up. I noticed he was very fit, much more so than the other Saudis, even the young ones, who came to the camp. There was always something a bit soft about the Saudis because their lives were so easy. But Abu Hudayfa's body was braided with muscle.

Over time, I began to realize that many of Abu Hudayfa's mannerisms were slightly strange as well. For instance, one day I saw him in the doorway of his dormitory. There was another brother right behind him. Abu Hudayfa held the door open from the inside and let the brother go ahead of him. It was just a tiny gesture, but it was a Western gesture: a real Arab would have walked out first, then held the door open behind him.

But the most telling thing about Abu Hudayfa was his boots. Everyone at the camp wore leather boots except him. His were tan canvas. I had seen the boots before, and I knew where they had come from. They were American army boots. At the beginning the Gulf War, there were lots of television reports about how the American troops were struggling because they were all wearing the same heavy black jungle boots made for soldiers in Vietnam. They were designed for trudging through muddy rivers and forests, and were horrible in the sand and heat of the desert. The black leather became incredibly hot in the sun, and the boots didn't breathe at all. So the army rushed to commission hundreds of thousands of pairs of light canvas desert boots for the soldiers. Abu Hudayfa was wearing those boots.

It was perfectly clear to me: Abu Hudayfa was a spy. But there was nothing I could do. Even though I was certain of it, I had no proof. And we were taught again and again at Khaldan that *mujahidin* never speculate. They make judgments solely on the basis of what they know, because no one can ever enter someone else's mind. And so even though it bothered me, I never spoke to anyone else about Abu Hudayfa.

Sometimes, when a group of brothers came close to finishing their training, they would stage a demonstration at night out in the field in front of the camp. They would show us their targeting skills, perform hand-to-hand combat, and make rings out of branches, which they would set on fire and jump through. It was always thrilling to watch, to see how attuned these brothers were to one another, how they had learned to move together like a single body. The fire was breathtaking against the dark sky, and the guns would emit sparks that looked like tiny firecrackers. It was a kind of circus.

One night, I decided to watch the performance from high up on the mountainside. As I peeled away from the group, Abu Hudayfa spotted me and asked where I was going. I told him, and he decided to come with me.

We walked up to an outcropping and sat there watching the brothers run and leap and tumble down below us on the field. Neither of us said a word for a few minutes, but then I turned to him. "Abu Hudayfa," I said calmly. He turned to me and I looked him straight in the eye. "Abu Hudayfa, I know who you are. I don't have any evidence, so I won't tell the others. But I want you to know that I know who you are."

He held my gaze but did not say a word in response. Then he turned his head and continued watching the performance.

The heavy silence between us was interrupted a few minutes later, when a bullet whizzed past us and smashed into the rock face about ten meters away. And then another one. And another. Abu Hudayfa turned to me; he looked anxious. I looked down at the field and saw the brothers were firing up at a sheer cliff face to the left of where we were sitting. I wasn't worried, though. They had spent months training with these guns, and they knew what they were doing.

Abu Hudayfa wasn't so confident. "Abu Imam," he said. "Don't you think we should go down now?"

I looked at him. "Why?" I asked. By now, the bullets were striking the rocks continuously, setting off tiny sparks.

"Because of the bullets, Abu Imam. They might hit us." I could see from Abu Hudayfa's face that he was scared.

"No," I said calmly. "I'm going to stay up here." Then I smiled. "After all, I came here to make my *jihad*. If one of their bullets hits me in the head," I said, gesturing down at the brothers, "then I'm already *shahid!*" I was joking with Abu Hudayfa, but I wasn't kidding. He knew that.

Abu Hudayfa stared at me for a second. Then he stood up. Without a word, he turned and began to scurry down the mountain.

Flashlight

Topography was the final stage of our training. In this part of the course, we learned how to target objects and people at long range. We studied topographical maps and learned complicated mathematical formulas so that we could figure out the correct angle to fire. Some of the cannons could hit a target accurately at three kilometers, but only if we were very careful in our calculations.

The mathematical calculations were difficult because there were so many variables to consider: altitude, wind speed, the extent of bore wear, the type of propellant charge, and so on. I had studied mathematics all through high school in Belgium, so I caught on quickly. But what impressed me was that many of the other brothers caught on quickly, too. Of course, many of the Arabs were well educated; but the Tajiks, the Uzbeks, and the Kashmiris generally weren't and yet they were always able to keep up somehow. In fact, they were often better than the rest of us. They seemed to understand the science instinctively.

One day, after we had spent a week in the classroom doing calculations, Abu Hamam took us out for target practice. We carried a mortar behind the camp and up the side of the mountain. Across a broad valley, there was another mountain and on it was a pile of large boulders. Someone had placed it there as a target.

We had done the calculations in the classroom already and we had our notes with us. We dug a small hole in the ground to stabilize the base of the mortar, then spread the bipeds to fix it in place. We lined up, and one by one each of us took turns adjusting the angle of the mortar tube and firing at the target.

We all missed the first time around, and Abu Hamam told us to note where our shells had actually landed so that we could adjust our calculations. We scribbled away on our papers and lined up again. Again, all of us missed. We were getting frustrated. We had been training for months at this point, and we felt invincible. And yet here we were. We had been calculating for a week just to get to this moment, and now none of us could finish the job.

We went back for a third try, and the first two brothers missed again. I decided not to use the paper this time, just the targeting lens. The trajectory of the shell was a simple ellipsis, and since my shell had landed high above the target the time before, I knew I had to point the muzzle slightly higher. All the other variables remained constant, so there was no need to recalculate everything.

This time, the shell hit the target. When I turned around, I could see the others were impressed. But then something caught my eye: Ibn Sheikh was sitting on the hill above us, watching. I had not seen or heard him arrive and was surprised to see him there, observing us. When our eyes met, he gestured for me to join him. I went up and sat down beside him.

"Why didn't you use your notes?" he asked. As he said it, one of the Chechens fired the cannon. His shell landed about fifty meters to the left of the target.

"It's like throwing a stone," I said. "You don't need all the calculations." As I began, Ibn Sheikh put his finger on his lips to indicate I should speak more quietly. I assumed he didn't want me to distract the others. So I continued in a whisper, "You can make adjustments just by throwing it harder or softer, or by throwing it higher up or lower down. The cannon works on the same principle."

Ibn Sheikh smiled at me gently, then whispered in my ear. "Very good, Abu Imam," he said. "But don't tell the others. I want to see if they can figure it out on their own."

His comment struck me as very strange. Ibn al-Sheikh had told us again and again to share everything we had with our brothers, to help them at every opportunity. As a group, we were more than the sum of our parts because each brother contributed different skills and special knowledge. We taught each other new things all the time.

Ibn Sheikh stood up and walked towards the brothers, who continued to fire at the target and miss each time. I wondered why Ibn Sheikh wanted me to keep my discovery to myself.

One night, Ibn Sheikh came to the door of our room only an hour or two after we had gone to sleep. He ordered us to assemble in front of the mosque. We were not to wear shoes or a jacket, he said. And anyone who brought a flashlight would be punished severely.

As I headed out the door, I saw that the sky was pitch black. There was no moon that night, nor any stars. I went back inside and rustled around in my bag until I found the tiny pocket flashlight that I bought at the airport in Istanbul. I tucked it inside my trousers and groped my way over the rocks and towards the mosque. I couldn't see anything at all, but I could hear noises. I heard brothers behind me, and I could tell some of them were stumbling and falling as they pawed their way through the darkness. I could hear many voices speaking in front of me, so that I knew I was headed in the right direction.

As soon as I got off the rocks and felt the flat ground in front of me, I knew I was nearing the mosque. The voices were getting louder, so I threw my hands up in front of me. Eventually, my hand touched the face of one of the brothers and I knew I was in the right place.

As we stood there waiting for everyone to arrive so we could get our orders, I realized I was shivering. It was well into the fall at this point. The days were colder, and the nights were almost unbearable. Once we were all assembled, Ibn Sheikh spoke. He ordered us to line up, one behind the next, and to put our hands on the shoulders of the brother in front of us. I couldn't see even as far as the neck of the person in front of me, but I imagined us as a kind of snake made up of nearly one hundred *mujahidin*. I was near the tail end, with only a few other brothers behind me.

We began to walk. None of us could see where we were going, but I could feel the grade shifting dramatically after the first few hundred meters. We were headed up a mountain. I couldn't know anything but what I felt beneath my feet, and all I felt were rocks. They were very painful on the soles of my feet because I couldn't look ahead before I planned each step.

We must have walked for three hours like that. At first we were headed west; I knew that from the direction we took when we left the camp. But after a while, I lost track even of that; it was impossible to stay oriented without any points of reference. I knew we were going very high up, since the path was steep and the wind was getting stronger and stronger, lashing through my thin shirt.

After a while, my other senses began to compensate for my lack of sight. I could hear the gentle rustling of clothes in the wind, and distinguish more clearly between the rocks under my feet. Some were harder, some were softer. Each one was a slightly different temperature. My body had warmed up from the exercise, and I could feel my hands relaxing on the shoulders of the brother in front of me as I settled into the pace of our strange, blind march into the mountains.

Suddenly, my body crashed into the brother in front of me, and the brother behind me lurched into my back. The line had come to a halt. At first I couldn't understand what happened, but then I heard a gentle rustle coming from in front of me. I thought it was the wind, but as it got louder and louder I realized it was the sound of voices whispering. The brothers were speaking one to another, passing a message down the chain. I couldn't hear what they were saying until the Kashmiri in front of me turned and whispered, "Ibn Sheikh orders Abu Imam to the front of the line."

I was confused, but I had my orders. Using my feet, I felt around to either side of me. I could tell the mountain was going down to my right, so I stepped to the left of the brothers and brushed my hand against each one as I picked my way slowly over the rocks towards the front of the line.

After several minutes, I reached the head of the snake. I heard Ibn Sheikh's voice, although I could not see him. "Abu Imam, give me your flashlight."

Shit. How did he know I had my flashlight with me? My mind began to spin as I remembered what he had said earlier: anyone caught with a flashlight would be punished severely. Ibn Sheikh had punished me many times, and it was never gentle. What did he consider a *severe* punishment?

But there was nothing I could do. I put my hand inside my trousers and pulled out the light. I groped my way towards Ibn Sheikh's voice, and when I was in front of him I felt for his hand and put the flashlight in his palm.

Ibn Sheikh immediately turned the flashlight on and pointed it down to the right of the group. I understood immediately: one of the brothers had fallen. We had been walking along the edge of a very steep ravine, and he had tumbled about fifteen meters downhill. He was lucky: two large boulders had broken his fall. His body was wedged between them.

Several of us at the front of the line rushed down to help him. Ibn Sheikh led the way, flashlight in hand. When we got to him, I saw it was one of the Chechens. Not one in my group, but one of the older ones I had met in the mosque on my first day at the camp. Now, he was covered in blood and moaning softly. He wasn't moving at all.

We quickly constructed a stretcher out of some stray branches, took off our shirts and tied them in between. We heaved the Chechen onto the stretcher, and with Ibn Sheikh leading the way with the flashlight, raced back towards the camp.

It was nearly dawn by the time everyone had spilled back down off the mountain. We made our morning *salat*, then headed to the cantina for breakfast. After a few minutes, one of the trainers joined us and told us the brother had broken both an arm and a leg. They were taking him to a hospital in Khowst.

Ibn Sheikh walked into the cantina just as we were finishing our breakfast. As he began to walk towards me, my heart sank. I prepared myself for a horrible punishment; I had disobeyed his direct orders. Everyone else in the cantina fell silent as well. They, too, were waiting to hear what he was going to say.

And then Ibn Sheikh did something unexpected: he handed me the flashlight. "Thank you, Abu Imam," he said. "Thank you for lending me your flashlight."

The other brothers were as startled as I was. I could see their eyes darting from person to person as they tried to figure out what had just happened. But Ibn Sheikh gave no further explanation. He just sat down and began to eat his breakfast.

Taliban

We were sealed off from the rest of the world at Khaldan, and I liked that. We had none of the pressures, none of the distractions of normal life there. We had only one focus: becoming *mujahidin*.

We did have radios, however. Secretly, late at night, I would sometimes try to find music. Strange bits would come through from China, India, and elsewhere. There was always a lot of static, so it was hard to hear. Usually, it would disappear as quickly as it came. Only once did I hear a song from beginning to end: "Zombie" by the Cranberries.

But we could always hear the news. BBC and RFI always came through clearly, and the brothers and I were always eager to hear what was happening in our home countries. In the summer and fall of 1995, there was always lots of news about Afghanistan as well. Rabbani was president of the country at that point. He and Ahmed Massoud, his military commander, held the capital, Kabul. But just barely; the city was under constant siege. With the support of Pakistan's secret service, the Taliban were gaining ground across the country and moving on Kabul. Gulbuddin Hekmatyar and his *Hezb-i-Islami* faction had been waging war against Rabbani and Massoud for years, and now they were fighting the Taliban as well.

No one at the camp liked the Taliban. We didn't talk about it openly, because we were discouraged from talking about the politics of our host country. But there were whispers, of course, and off-hand remarks. The trainers and the other brothers said many of the same things I had heard from Amin and Yasin already: the Taliban were overreaching in their application of *sharia*; they were too strict; they were innovators.

I hated the Taliban. When I was in Belgium, I had read about them and seen them on TV. They were vicious, completely uncivilized. I was disgusted by the public executions and decapitations, and the way they held the country in fear. And I also hated the Taliban because they were the enemies of Massoud. He was still my hero, a noble *mujahid* who had earned the respect even of his enemies.

I never spoke about any of this, of course. None of us did. The Taliban had taken over huge swaths of Afghanistan, and we needed Afghanistan, the land of *jihad*. We needed to stay and train.

One day, as we were all leaving the mosque after the evening *salat,* one of the trainers came running towards us. He told us to leave our guns in the mosque.

We put our guns down and headed out to the front of the camp, curious to see what was happening. Ibn Sheikh was speaking to an Afghan man from the village. They were talking in low tones; it was clear that something was wrong. Then Ibn Sheikh turned and walked quickly into the cantina.

All of a sudden, we heard the sound of a motor. A four-wheel-drive truck was making its way slowly down the side of the mountain towards the camp. Farther behind, I could see a small cluster of men heading towards us on foot. A few minutes later, the truck reached the camp and came to a halt. Six men stepped out. They had Kalashnikovs and RPGs strapped over their shoulders. Soon nine others walked up to the camp as well.

It was an extraordinary group, nothing like the young *talib* we had passed on the way into the camp. These men were older, in their late twenties at least. And they looked like hell. Their clothes were filthy and their faces were creased with dirt and wrinkles. I felt myself recoil from them instantly.

It was a strange scene, all of us standing there without our guns facing down these battle-hardened mercenaries. None of the brothers showed any emotion. Mostly, we were curious. The *tullab* were not hostile when they approached us either. Three of them smiled; it was obvious they were the commanders. The others just looked sullen.

As the trainers walked out to greet them, I turned to look into the cantina. Ibn Sheikh was hurrying to prepare for their arrival, and I asked if I could help. He looked grateful, and together we laid out a large sheepskin carpet and set out plates for dinner.

I left as the *tullab* began to file into the cantina. Ibn Sheikh came out briefly to tell the brothers we would not be eating dinner that night. We hovered for a few moments, and then walked away. But before I left, I took one last glance inside the cantina. Ibn Sheikh was sitting at the head of the circle of *tullab* with Abu Bakr beside him. One thing struck me: Abu Bakr was still holding his gun.

That evening, as we were sitting around waiting to see what would happen, one of the trainers told me that the Taliban had come once before, about six months earlier. They hadn't reached the camp that time because one of the villagers had come down to warn Ibn Sheikh that they were on the way. Along with some of the villagers, Ibn Sheikh had gone out to meet them.

The Taliban were coming for one reason: they wanted weapons. They had been sweeping across southern Afghanistan, going from camp to camp, demanding that the emirs turn over all their guns. And they got them, because the emirs were afraid. But they didn't get to Khaldan that night because Ibn Sheikh intercepted them. The trainer told me that he had spent six hours talking to the Taliban, using one of the villagers to translate. By the end, he had convinced them to leave Khaldan in peace. Khaldan was not training anyone to fight in Afghanistan, he explained. It was preparing *mujahidin* to fight in the rest of the world. The brothers at the camp were fighting the same *jihad* as the Taliban, but in a different place.

After a few hours, the Taliban left. Neither Ibn Sheikh nor Abu Bakr ever talked about what had happened that night. But that Friday, one of the brothers asked Ibn Sheikh if the *jihad* of the Taliban was legitimate. Ibn Sheikh paused, and then answered curtly. "None of you is here to fight with the Taliban," he said. "You are here to train to fight in your own countries."

The brother pressed him again, and Ibn Sheikh went a bit further. It was clear that he was choosing his words carefully. He said that the Taliban were not well educated like we were, meaning they did not understand *sharia* as we did. But Rabbani, he said, wanted to see democracy in Afghanistan, whereas the Taliban wanted Afghanistan to be an Islamic state. For this reason, the Taliban were worthy of some support.

"If any one of you chooses to fight with the Taliban one day," he said, "it would not be wrong." He paused before continuing. "But it would be far better for you to make your *jihad* against the occupiers in Jerusalem or the murderers in Chechnya."

Infirmary

One day in the fall, I was walking past the mosque when Ibn Sheikh stopped me. He called me over and asked me to sit down with him. Once we were settled, he began to speak. "Abu Imam, you are not going to Chechnya with the brothers. We need you for other things."

I was dumbstruck. I hadn't been expecting this at all. For months, I had been training with the Chechens with the idea that I would be going to Chechnya with them when we were done. We had all talked about it. I had hated the Russians ever since they invaded Afghanistan when I was a teenager, and I hated them even more after I heard what they had done to the brothers in my group. I had dreamed many times of becoming a *mujahid*. Every time I fired a gun or set off an explosive or practiced some tactical procedure, I did it with the expectation that I would soon be using my skills against the Russian invaders. Chechnya was a war I believed in.

But there was nothing I could do. I could always challenge something Ibn Sheikh said if he was unclear, or if I didn't understand what he was doing. But this was a direct order, so I said nothing. I just nodded and walked back to the dormitory.

That afternoon, I walked into the mountains by myself. My mind was reeling. I was devastated and confused. I walked farther and farther up until the camp was almost out of view, then sat down on some rocks and stared at the setting sun. I wrapped my arms around myself as protection against the cold autumn wind. And then I called out to God. "God, why won't you let me go to Chechnya? Why won't you let me be *shahid*?"

There was no answer, of course. Just the sound of the wind whistling through the canyons. "If you won't let me go to Chechnya, then let me lead a normal life," I cried out. "Let me have a wife. Let me have a child. Let me have a home."

My face was numb with cold. I realized I was crying, and that the tears were freezing against my skin. And then I saw her, right in front of me. A beautiful, fair woman with long brown hair and a gentle smile. God had heard me and answered my call. But then, just as quickly, she disappeared and I was all alone.

The next day, Ibn Sheikh told me I would be running the infirmary. An Ethiopian brother had been running it for the past few months, but he was leaving and they needed to replace him. I had no medical training at all, but maybe they thought I did because I had given Abu Bakr his shot.

The infirmary was near the mosque, in front of one of the caves. It wasn't big, but it was heaped full with all sorts of medicines, bandages, antiseptics, and surgical tools. There were also many books and manuals in English explaining the treatments for different kinds of injuries and illnesses.

I wasn't training with the Chechens any more so at first I had a lot of free time in the infirmary. I still exercised with the rest of the brothers in the morning, but I had most afternoons to myself. I spent the time organizing all the medical supplies on the shelves, and reading the books.

Soon enough, though, the patients started to come. Many of the brothers contracted malaria in the camp, and there were all sorts of skin infections also. Afghanis from the nearby village would come for treatment as well, usually because they had stomach problems from drinking the water.

Sometimes, there were as many as five people sleeping in the infirmary at night, and it was my job to take care of them. It wasn't hard; I had spent so much time in hospitals when I was young that I didn't feel uncomfortable around sick people. If I didn't know what they needed I could always look it up in a book. I missed training with the Chechens, though, and I was bored.

I was in the cantina one afternoon when one of the trainers rushed in and told me to go to the infirmary. He said that Ibn Sheikh was waiting for me. When I got there, one of the Afghani cooks, the one who could speak, was standing there with Ibn Sheikh and two boys from the village. One was about twelve years old, and he was holding a much younger boy in his arms. The little one was no more than six or seven.

The younger boy's head was covered with a cloth, and when the older boy lifted it I saw he had a huge gash on his skull. The older boy was trying to explain what had happened, and the cook was translating. The younger boy had fallen and cracked his head open on a rock.

I sat the younger boy down on a chair in the doorway to the infirmary so that I would have enough light to examine him. The gash was very deep. I could see pieces of his skull. Blood was spilling from the wound. Both the boys were covered with it, and soon I was, too.

The boy was completely out of it. His eyes were glazed with shock and his head was rolling from side to side. I had to brace his neck with my hand to keep his head steady while I examined the wound. He felt tiny in my hands.

"Abu Iman," Ibn Sheikh said. "You'll need to suture the wound."

I had my orders, but I had no idea what to do. I had done little more than administer painkillers and apply antiseptics up until this point. I certainly hadn't performed any surgeries. The only thing I had ever sewn in my life was a hole in a pair of blue jeans.

I had to think fast. I remembered that one summer in Morocco I had fallen off my bicycle and cut my leg open. My mother took me to the hospital. I struggled to remember exactly what had happened there. I knew the first thing the doctors did was give me a tetanus shot right in the stomach. So I ran back to the supply shelves and grabbed the tetanus and a syringe. I injected the boy in the stomach, just like they had done to me. I thought for a second and then remembered what came next: I had to clean the wound. I grabbed some distilled water and began to wipe the blood and dirt from his scalp.

But as I touched the boy's head, he began to scream. I told the cook to tell the older boy to calm him down, but there was nothing he could do either. I needed to give the boy a painkiller. I raced back inside and took a bottle of Lidocaine from the shelf, along with a needle. I had used Lidocaine before to treat a brother with a rash, but I had no idea how much to give to a child.

I didn't know if I could inject Lidocaine into an open wound, but I had to do something. The boy was shrieking in pain and I hadn't even begun to put in the stitches. So I injected a small amount straight into the boy's head at one end of the wound. I waited for a few seconds to see if he had a negative reaction but he seemed fine, so I injected more into the other side.

After about a minute, the boy stopped screaming. His head kept rolling from side to side, as it had before, but his eyes were slightly droopy now, and his sobs were more like whimpers. I laid him out on a table. The materials—the needles and the thread—were there in the cabinet, but I didn't know what to do with them. So I took one of the books off the shelf. It had lots of pictures, including a complete series of photos outlining the steps to suture a wound. I spread it out in front of me on the table next to the boy, and began to follow the instructions.

At first, I tried to do it exactly what I saw in the pictures, because the book said it was important to use a special kind of stitch that wouldn't leave any scar. But I couldn't figure out how to do it that way and it was taking far too long, so I ended up using the same kind of straight stitches I used to sew my jeans.

I was incredibly hot. It was freezing cold outside, but I felt sweat dripping from my forehead. I gestured to the cook to wipe my brow with a cloth. I didn't want my sweat to infect the boy's wound or cloud my eyes as I operated on him.

As the Afghani pressed a rag against my forehead, a strange image shot through my mind. It was an image I had seen again and again on European television shows: a handsome doctor performing surgery surrounded by sexy nurses. They wiped his brow and did whatever else he told them to. It all seemed very surreal in that instant. The Afghani cook was about the furthest thing I could imagine from a sexy nurse.

Seconds later, the boy jolted and began to scream again. He was waking up, and I was only halfway through stitching the wound shut. He began to thrash about on the table and the older boy was having trouble holding him still. So I grabbed the Lidocaine and filled up the needle. I didn't measure the amount this time, and I didn't care. I was panicked.

I jabbed the needle straight into his scalp just as before. In less than a minute he stopped screaming. He was out cold; his little body lay completely still. His head dropped to one side and his tongue fell out of his mouth.

The older boy looked up at me with fear in his eyes. I was terrified; I had given the boy too much anaesthesia. Or maybe he had lost so much blood that he was going into a coma. I leaned down to check to see if he was still breathing. He was, so I finished the stiches as fast as I could. The whole time, I was praying to God that the boy wouldn't die.

When I was done, I looked at him again. All the color had run out of his face. His eyes were slightly open now, but they seemed to be just rolling around in his head. I cleaned his scalp with Betadine to disinfect it and covered it with a bandage. And then I waited. And prayed.

After about fifteen minutes, the boy woke up slightly. He still looked very weak, and his eyes weren't focusing on anything. He was beginning to whimper again, however, which I took as a good sign. I called the older boy over, along with the Afghan cook. I took a bottle of antibiotics off the shelf and had the cook explain that the boy should take them every day for two weeks, and then come back to the infirmary for a checkup. The older boy nodded solemnly.

We waited for a few hours until the boy had regained enough strength to sit up. Then the older boy took him in his arms and carried him out of the infirmary into the cold night. My heart wasn't racing as fast as it had been, but I was still scared.

When I walked into the cantina a few minutes later, Ibn Sheikh looked up at me expectantly. "Will he be all right?" he asked.

"*Insha'Allah*," I replied. God willing.

The next few days were the most stressful of my life. I was terrified that I had killed the boy. He was so tiny and vulnerable. What had I done?

And then, one day, I was sitting in the infirmary when he came bouncing in along with the older boy. It had been less than two weeks since I operated on him. I called for the Afghani cook to come and translate. The older boy said he was fine: he had been sleeping and eating well and didn't seem to have any problems.

I took off the bandage and saw that the wound was healing. I disinfected a pair of scissors and gently removed the stitches. It didn't seem to hurt the boy at all. When I finished, I put a new bandage on his head. Then I told both boys to come back and visit soon. They smiled and then ran out of the infirmary, across the field and back up towards the village. I could still hear their laughter as they disappeared into the dusk. It was one of the happiest days of my life.

The Chechens left a couple of weeks after that. I went out with Abu Hamam one afternoon for some special training, and when I came back the Chechens were gone. I never said goodbye to them. I wonder if any of them are still alive.

Osama

One day, two boys arrived at the camp. They were even younger than the youngest Chechen in my group, or the very intense Tajik child. The oldest boy was no more than twelve, and the younger one about ten.

Ibn Sheikh stood up to introduce them in the mosque that night. "Please welcome your new brothers. This is Hamza," he said, pointing towards the older one, "and this is Osama." When I looked over, I instantly recognized them: they were the ones who had approached my guide at the mosque in Hayatabad in Peshawar. My guide scolded them when they asked if he was taking me to the *madrasa*.

As we all welcomed Hamza and Osama, I noticed the greeting was more solemn than usual. The boys were beginning their training very young, and the brothers were impressed.

Hamza and Osama weren't put in a group like the other brothers. Mostly, they spent their afternoons with a trainer learning about guns. But sometimes they would tag along with me. I had finished all my training at this point, but some days Abu Hamam would take me out for extra training, usually with explosives. I spoke to the boys in English, and I noticed they both had strong American accents. But I didn't learn much about them at first, because they hated each other and fought constantly. Not just bickering the way brothers do, but really fighting.

One day, a group of us were sitting on a hill near the camp. Hamza and Osama were practicing on the firing range with one of the trainers. Hamza was shooting a Kalashnikov and Osama was practicing with a PK. They were both terrible; they clearly didn't know anything about guns. They had obviously already forgotten everything they had learned in the classroom.

As usual, they were less interested in the training than in fighting with each other. After a few minutes, they stopped firing at the targets and turned towards one another. Even though we were far away, we could hear them yelling. Suddenly, Osama lifted his PK and pointed it at his brother. Hamza immediately pointed his Kalashikov back at him. We were all shocked. We never turned our guns on each other this way. The boys were screaming more and more loudly. Their fingers were on the triggers of their guns.

I think every brother on that hill believed that the boys were actually going to kill each other. And they probably would have if the trainer hadn't jumped in between and pushed them apart. When it was over, we all turned to each other in dismay. We had never seen anything like this at the camp. They had broken all the rules we had learned since our first day of training. Soon, we were laughing about it, even though it wasn't funny at all. It made us nervous.

One day, the boys' father came to Khaldan. He stayed for only a few hours. He arrived in a four-by-four with a few other men, but before I had a chance to study them, Ibn Sheikh whisked them off to the explosives laboratory.

Nobody ever talked about the explosives laboratory. It was behind the mosque, near the entrance to the munitions caves. We were strictly forbidden to go inside. In fact, we weren't even supposed to look at it. But the building had glass windows and it was easy to see all the equipment—beakers, test tubes, everything, just like a laboratory at school.

The only other person I had ever seen go into the laboratory was Assad Allah, the red-headed Algerian trainer who came to Khaldan for two weeks. I saw him go into the laboratory with Ibn Sheikh several times. The rest of the time we just pretended it wasn't there.

The two boys were constantly hurting themselves, and they came to the infirmary many times. They were very different. Osama was almost hyperactive; he bounced around constantly and never stopped talking. His brother was much quieter, more cautious.

Soon, Osama started telling me about his family. I learned the that boys' father was Egyptian, and a scientist. The brothers had been raised mostly in Canada, but they lived in Peshawar now. They had been with their father in Khowst in 1991, during the ferocious battle that ultimately drove Najibullah from power.

Osama bragged about his father constantly. He was very important, he told me, and knew lots of people. "My father is one of Zubayda's closest friends," he told me.

"Who is Zubayda?" I asked. I had never heard the name before.

Osama looked at me curiously. "Didn't you meet him when you were in Peshawar?"

"I don't know," I told him. "What does he look like?"

As Osama began to describe him, I realized who he was referring to: the man I had stayed with on my last night in Pakistan, in that strange, dark house. The one who had given me the old *shalwar kameez*, and handed me over to the guide who took me into Afghanistan.

"Zubayda is very important," the boy babbled on. "He gets all the Arabs in and out of the camps."

One day, Osama asked about someone else. "Do you know Osama?"

"Of course I do," I said. "You're Osama."

"No, not me. The *other* Osama."

"Who is he?" I asked. I knew the boy wanted to tell me.

"He's very important," the boy said. "He's one of my father's best friends. He pays for all of the food here."

Over time, I would learn a little bit more about Osama. I learned that he was very rich and that he had built roads all over Afghanistan after the civil war ended.

"Where is Osama from?" I asked one day.

The boy began to say something, but then he stopped himself. He was blushing. "I think he's from the Emirates . . . I don't know. I can't remember. Maybe that's wrong . . ."

It was the first time I ever saw him try to conceal something. He was very bad at it. But at the time, I only registered that Osama must be someone important if the boy was trying to hide information. It would be another two years before I learned why.

Hamza rarely spoke. He almost never had a chance to, because his brother was babbling all the time. But one evening, Ibn Sheikh ordered him to the infirmary because he had a high fever and pains in his stomach. Hamza ended up spending the night there, and I stayed with him.

That was when he told me what he had seen during the battle in Khowst. Night after night he saw the sky burning with mortar fire and rockets. Once, a bomb fell near where he and his father were standing on a public square. But it didn't explode. Everyone stood by for a few minutes waiting for something to happen, but nothing did. The bomb just lay there.

He said that once it was clear the bomb wasn't going to explode, several Afghanis rushed forward to salvage the metal and the explosive material inside. The people were desperately poor, and fed themselves by selling bits of ammunition and other matériel back to the *mujahidin*.

The Afghanis clustered around the shell, and one began to hit it with a hammer to crack it open to get at the components inside. The shell exploded. There was a giant fireball, and when the smoke cleared all the Afghanis were dead. There were body parts and pieces of clothing scattered all over the square.

Hamza smiled as he finished the story. "Isn't that stupid?" He laughed and shook his head. "The Afghanis are so stupid." But I could tell from his eyes that, five years after it happened, the story still upset him.

Khyber Pass

And then one day it was my turn to leave Khaldan. There was no advance warning. One of the trainers came to the infirmary and told me Ibn Sheikh wanted to speak with me, so I walked over to his cottage. He was standing in front with an Afghani I had never seen before. Ibn Sheikh saluted me, and then spoke. "Go get your things. You're leaving in one hour." He handed me a sealed letter. "You're going to another camp, where you'll receive advanced training in explosives. When you get to Peshawar, give this letter to Abu Zubayda, and he'll take care of the rest."

I took the letter and went back to the dormitory to assemble my things. I didn't have time to think about what was happening. All the others were off training, so there was no one to say goodbye to. I carried my bag out to the front of the camp, where Ibn Sheikh and Abu Bakr were waiting for me along with the guide. We saluted each other, and Abu Bakr said, "Pray for us, brother." His face was warm and kind.

At that moment, I had an overwhelming sense that I would see both of them again. "I will come back to you," I said. "*Insha'Allah.*"

The guide took me back into Pakistan, though we took a different route this time. When we arrived in Peshawar, we went to make our *salat* at the same mosque where I had first seen Osama and Hamza several months earlier.

When we were done with our prayers, we took a taxi into a section of Peshawar I had never seen. It was fancy, like Hayatabad. Soon, the guide stopped the driver and waited for him to disappear. Then we walked for a few hundred meters until we arrived at the gate of a large villa. The guide rang the bell, and soon a man carrying a Kalashnikov came to let us in. The three of us walked up through a lush garden and into the house. It was beautiful inside, very European, like pictures I had seen of estates in the English countryside. There were several men prowling around with assault rifles.

We walked upstairs to a large room, where two men were sitting on cushions on the floor drinking tea. The guard who had let us in told me to sit down and wait. He then escorted the Afghani guide out of the room.

A few minutes later, a blond man walked in. He had fair skin and blue eyes. At first I thought he was German, but then he introduced himself. "*Assalamu'alaykum*," he said. "I'm Abu Said al-Kurdi." The man was Kurdish. I introduced myself and he told me to get my bag and follow him.

We took a taxi to a bus stop and then rode into the refugee camp. Abu Said took me back to the same safe house where I had stayed my first night in the refugee camp, and told me to leave my things there. We left the house and went to the section of the camp Abu Anas had pointed out to me on my first day there, the large houses where the Arab fighters and their families lived. The houses were set off slightly from the rest of the camp, and they were much nicer. Larger, made of brick.

We stopped in front of one of them and Abu Said rang the bell. A guard let us in. Inside, in the living room, I saw the man with whom I had spent my last night in Pakistan before going to Khaldan. The man with the glasses and the short beard. I knew from Osama and Hamza that this was Abu Zubayda.

Abu Zubayda guided me into his office, leaving Abu Said in the living room. Once he had closed the door, I passed him the letter Ibn Sheikh had given me. After he read it, he put his hand on my shoulder and smiled at me. "*Masha'allah*," he said. "You did a very good job at Khaldan. I'm proud of you. Tomorrow you will be going to a new camp near Jalalabad, where you'll begin your training with explosives."

Abu Said and I stayed at the safe house that night. There were several men there, but I didn't recognize any of them from my first visit.

The next morning Abu Said and I took a four-by-four taxi up into the mountains, towards the Khyber Pass. I was getting more and more excited. I was bored during my final weeks at Khaldan, and I was looking forward to doing something new. And I was eager to learn more about explosives. They were my favorite part of the training at Khaldan.

As we climbed into the Khyber Pass, the scenery became more and more majestic. The cliffs on either side of the road rose hundreds of feet into the sky, and there were forts and ruins everywhere. I was looking forward to my new adventure.

I had read so much about the Khyber Pass that being there felt almost unreal to me. The greatest armies in history had passed through here. Darius had swept through with his Persian troops, and then Alexander the Great and Genghis Khan. Armies of Mongols, Tartars, Turks, Moguls, and Afghans all followed. And then the British. As I stared out the window, I imagined the successive generations of warriors marching across this dry, unforgiving terrain.

Abu Said snapped me out of my daydreams as we approached the border crossing. He told me that if the guards stopped me, I shouldn't speak to them. Instead, I should pretend I was crazy. Roll my head from side to side. Pretend to have an epileptic seizure. Whatever happened, I must not speak a word of Arabic. He would handle everything.

When we reached the border, I could see that this would be much more dangerous than my first border crossing into Afghanistan. There were people, cars, and trucks everywhere, and many, many police. And there was a customs office, where I might have to show my papers. I hadn't seen my passport since the day I arrived at Khaldan, when I left it with Abu Bakr. Of course, it wouldn't have helped me at all—just the opposite. I was dressed like an Afghan but my passport was Moroccan, and my visa had expired months ago.

I stood in the huge line behind the customs building. The crowd was slowly pressing through the doorway. As I got closer to the guards, I could see that they were generally stopping people just to check for weapons and contraband. Some they stopped for longer, in order to examine documents.

When I reached the guard, I held my arms out so he could frisk me as he had the others. I waited for him to say something, but before he could, I was thrown forward by a push from behind. Someone was yelling. My body was carried forward as people began to shove.

Soon, I was well past the guard. I didn't understand what had happened, but I knew I was lucky, and kept walking. When I looked back, I saw Abu Said yelling at the guard in a language I didn't understand. I realized that he had engineered the whole thing.

Once we were both on the Afghan side of the border, Abu Said and I took another taxi. We stopped in Jalalabad briefly so that Abu Said could pick up some supplies. Jalalabad was a bustling market city, and the streets were lined with shops selling all different kinds of merchandise. I was surprised to see all sorts of electronic equipment for sale—televisions and stereos. I asked Abu Said why the Taliban hadn't put a stop to this, and he explained that Jalalabad was a kind of no-man's-land in the civil war. Neither Rabbani nor Hekmatyar nor the Taliban controlled it.

Once Abu Said finished picking up what he needed, we got into a different four-by-four taxi and drove on for a few more miles, until we arrived at a small village. Abu Said told me the village was named Darunta, which was also the name of the camp we were going to.

The taxi dropped us off there, and we proceeded on foot through the village. Ahead of us, the road disappeared into a high mountain. "That's the road to Kabul," Abu Said told me. We continued walking. There was a river to the right, and soon we arrived at a bridge. I quickly realized from the noise that it was in fact the top of a dam, and when I looked behind me I saw a large reservoir.

There were two guards at the entrance to the bridge. They glanced at us but did nothing. At the other end of the bridge, there was a small, dusty road. As we walked along it I saw the rusted remains of all sorts of Soviet military vehicles scattered in the hills. Farther on, I saw what looked like large houses. But as we got closer, they came into focus and I realized they were not houses but rather two enormous tanks. It was a checkpoint.

The checkpoint was guarded by several Afghanis. Abu Said began to speak with them, and it was clear that they all knew each other. While I waited for them to finish, I studied the armored vehicles. I saw that they were two types, both of which I had studied at Khaldan, though I had never actually seen either. One was a BMP–1, a Soviet infantry vehicle that fires high-explosive antitank missiles. The other was a ZSU–23–4, known as a Shilka. It is even bigger than the BMP–1, and contains an antiaircraft system guided by radar.

I felt proud of myself as I stood there in front of the tanks. I had graduated from Khaldan and now I was on to something much bigger. The tanks were here for a reason: we were very near the front lines of the civil war. Clearly, whatever lay beyond the checkpoint was worth guarding.

Darunta

As we walked farther up the road, Abu Said explained that Darunta was actually made up of several distinctive camps for different *mujahidin* groups. There was one camp run by Arabs; another was run by Kashmiris. We would be going to the *Hezb-i-Islami* camp. *Hezb-i-Islami* was Hekmaytar's faction.

The sun was setting as we approached the camps, so we stopped first at the Arab camp to make our *salat*. Abu Said told me this was not the camp where I would train. We would leave after we finished our prayers. He warned me to be cautious, and to tell the brothers at the camp nothing about myself.

We went straight to the mosque to pray, and when we were done the Arab trainees smiled and greeted us. They clearly recognized Abu Said. They were all young and fresh; they reminded me of the new recruits who arrived at Khaldan.

Abu Said took me inside the main building to meet with the emir of the camp. We sat and drank tea with him, and he and Abu Said spoke to each other in Arabic. I didn't understand everything they were saying, so I let my mind wander along with my eyes.

I began to study these *mujahidin*. They were all so young. I tried to imagine their futures. I thought about them bombing consulates, kidnapping officials, hijacking planes.

I had never looked at anyone at Khaldan this way, although of course they were just as young and had the very same futures in store for them. But we were focused all the time on our training, and when we weren't we were too ex-hausted to think. There was little room left for imagination.

It was different at Khaldan for another reason as well. There, I didn't think of myself as separate from the brothers. I was one of them. But here, I was on the outside. I knew I wouldn't be training with these men. And so, for just a sec-ond, I was able to see them through the eyes of a spy.

With a gentle tap on my shoulder, Abu Said signaled that it was time for us to leave. We saluted the emir and then headed back out of the camp and farther down the road. Once, Abu Said pointed ahead at a heavily fortified bunker. He told me it was a television and radio broadcasting station for Hekmatyar and *Hezb-i-Islami*.

As we turned into the *Hezb-i-Islami* camp, Abu Said stopped and spoke to me.

"This is where you are going to train," he explained. "The Arab fighters within *Hezb-i-Islami* own this camp, and many of them come here from the front to rest. But you are not one of them. You are not part of Hekmatyar's group. You are here for a different reason. The emir of the camp has no control over you, except to organize who will cook and clean and guard the camp each day. Otherwise, you can do what you want."

Abu Said's speech seemed very odd to me. At Khaldan, every minute of our time was planned for us, and the emir had complete power. The kind of freedom Abu Said was describing sounded tantalizing to me. Abu Said went on, "I just learned from the emir back there that your trainer won't be here for a few more weeks. He was injured, and he's been taken to Peshawar for treatment." Now I was very confused. What would I be doing here, with no real emir and no trainer?

I looked around as we walked into the camp. There were some storage sheds at the entrance, and then some barracks a little farther inside. But what really caught my eye was the BMP–1 sitting in the middle of the camp. Fifteen meters away I spotted a T–55 tank. The T–55 was iconic. I had seen one in almost every *mujahidin* video I had ever watched. It began to dawn on me that even without a trainer, I would have plenty to do at Darunta.

Abu Said gestured me towards a small brick building at the center of the camp. It was the mosque. There were two men sitting inside already, and Abu Said introduced me to them. One was Abu Mousa, an Iraqi Kurd, and the other was Abu Hamid, from Jordan. They both lived at the camp. They seemed to be in their early thirties, and they were extremely friendly. I looked around the mosque and saw it was filled with books. There was a television against one of the walls.

Abu Said then stepped out for a minute, and when he returned there were two men with him. One was Abu Jihad, the emir of the camp. He was from Algeria. The other man came as a surprise to me. It was Abdul Kerim, my friend from Khaldan. He was clearly surprised to see me as well, but the emir began to speak before we could say anything to one another.

Abu Jihad repeated many of the things Abu Said had already told me—that the camp belonged to Hekmatyar, and that brothers from the front would be coming in and out. Everyone would share responsibilities for the daily chores. But there were only the five of us at the moment: Abu Mousa, Abu Hamid, Abu Said, Abdul Kerim, and me.

Then Abu Jihad spoke directly to me. "You may have heard that Assad Allah, your trainer, was injured today. We spoke to our brothers in Peshawar just a few minutes ago, and unfortunately it will be another month or so before he's able to return. You can spend the time until he comes back training on the tanks here, along with any of the other weapons you're interested in."

I laughed to myself. It felt like the beginning of a summer holiday: no classes for a month, and all these amazing weapons to play with. And Abdul Kerim was here, so I could speak French again. This was going to be much more fun than working in the infirmary at Khaldan.

We stood up once the emir had finished. Abdul Kerim came over to me with a broad smile on his face. "*Al-Hamdu lil-lah* that you were sent here, brother." Praise be to Allah. Then he guided me towards a mobile infantry kitchen near the center of the camp. There was a stove inside, and he told me that the electricity for it came from the dam I had walked over on my way in. As we were talking, Abdul Kerim boiled some water and made us each a cup of Nescafé.

Fishing

Adbul Kerim and I spoke for several hours that first night. Abdul Kerim told me about Assad Allah, the explosives trainer, who had injured himself earlier that day while preparing RDX. I asked him if this was the same Assad Allah who had come to Khaldan, the Algerian trainer who had spent so much time in the explosives laboratory. Abdul Kerim told me it was.

We caught up on the months since we had last seen each other. Abdul Kerim told me that after he left Khaldan, he had stayed in Peshawar for a couple of months learning how to forge documents—passports, credit cards, identity papers. He had arrived at Darunta about a month before me. Since then, he had been studying with Abu Mousa, the Iraqi Kurd I had met in the mosque. He was learning how to make remote-control devices to detonate explosives.

Abdul Kerim and I ended up sleeping in the same room at Darunta. It was Assad Allah's room also, but there was extra space now that he was gone.

During the weeks that followed, I would sometimes sit in with Abdul Kerim as Abu Mousa trained him in electronics. At Khaldan, we had learned very basic things, like how to set off an explosive using a watch or a cell phone. But Abdul Kerim was learning something much harder. He was learning how to make remote-control devices from scratch. There were all sorts of components at the camp: microprocessors, mother boards. But the work itself was painstaking, and required immense concentration. Still, Abdul Kerim was eager to learn. He had an enormous textbook, and he would study it late into the night.

There were all sorts of weapons at Darunta, many of them far more sophisticated than the ones we had at Khaldan. And they were everywhere. The two storage sheds at the entrance were filled with them, and there were many more supply sheds behind the mosque filled with all sorts of guns, mines, and grenades.

Abu Jihad, the emir, trained me on many new weapons during those early weeks. I learned how to use the AT–4 Spigot, an antitank weapon so large it required three people just to carry it. The gunner lies prone to fire and the missile shoots out at an incredible speed. Once in flight, it travels nearly two hundred meters per second. A long wire connects the missile to the sight, allowing them to communicate. The launcher can guide the missile with incredible accuracy to targets two kilometers away.

I trained on the SPG–9 also. The SPG–9 was a Russian gun that fired antitank missiles, just like the BMP–1 I had seen in the front of the camp. It made a horrifying noise when I fired it, but there was nothing I could do to protect my ears. I just had to get used to it.

I liked the snipers most, though. I had never fired one at Khaldan; the closest I had come was the one I had seen in Abu Bakr's room the day I went to give him a shot. But there were a great many Dragunov sniper rifles at Darunta. I was excited to finally to use one. I had bought Dragunovs for Yasin in Belgium, but they were always disassembled when Laurent gave them to me. The Dragunov was a marksman's weapon, and I loved the precision.

We never ran out of ammunition at Darunta. There was an endless supply in the sheds, and Abu Jihad let us use whatever we wanted. And so we did. There wasn't much else to do.

One night, Abdul Kerim and I decided to take a grenade and go fishing. We went down to the lake and launched it into the water. But our timing was off. The grenade was set to explode after ten seconds, but we threw it too early and by the time it detonated it was far below the surface. The next time, we decided to use Semtex. We used a blasting fuse and it worked perfectly. Hundreds of dead fish rose to the surface, and Abdul Kerim and I swam out into the lake with buckets to collect our dinner.

Once, we used Dragunovs to hunt ducks. It worked in one sense: we were able to kill them easily. But we had made the mistake of using armor-piercing bullets, and when we went to pick them up the ducks were blown to shreds. We couldn't really eat them that way.

Even though we had fun together, I could tell something had changed for Abdul Kerim. He was calmer than he had been at Khaldan, but much sadder, too. Often, I would walk into our room and find him sketching idly in the margins of his textbook when he was supposed to be studying.

Abdul Kerim was a wonderful artist. He drew marvelous, detailed pictures of people. He particularly liked to sketch antique warriors like the ones I had seen in the museum in Brussels: the early *mujahidin* in their full battle regalia. But all the people he drew had one thing in common; none of them had faces.

Many times, I asked Abdul Kerim if something was wrong. Usually, he brushed me away. But one night he admitted that he was depressed because he had been sent to the camps by the GIA in France in order to become a *mujahid*. He wanted desperately to be a martyr, he said. But there was one thing holding him back: his daughter. If he died, his daughter would be raised by his ex-wife, who was *taghut*. There would be no one to raise the child as a Muslim.

Abu Jihad

Abdul Kerim already knew the camp, so he showed me around. On one side of the camp, there were several sheds dug deep into the ground. They were filled with components for explosives. The components were stored in separate bins, to prevent them from reacting with on another. Inside the sheds, each bin was carefully labeled: acetone, nitric acid, sulphuric acid, ammonium, cellulose, aluminium powder, wood composite, and so on.

The laboratories were about fifty meters past these sheds, near the edge of the camp. One was for explosives training, and another one for poisons. Behind them there was a hutch filled with rabbits.

But there was no one at Darunta to teach us explosives, and so we had most of our time to ourselves. Sometimes, we would go into Jalalabad and visit the market. Other times, we would watch films in the mosque. There was a huge array of propaganda videos we could watch at any time. I had always loved watching movies, and I realized that I had missed watching television when I was at Khaldan. I spent a lot of time in the mosque during those early weeks, going through the huge collection of films about the *mujahidin* during the Soviet-Afghan war.

One day, I found myself in the mosque with Abu Mousa, the Iraqi Kurd. We were watching a film I had first seen in the Pompidou Center, the one with the dramatic *mujahid* standing on the turret of a tank shouting "*Allahu akbar*" as he raised his Kalashnikov over his head. I told Abu Mousa it was one of my favorite films ever.

"Yes, it's a great film," he agreed. "That tank is amazing." Abu Mousa was laughing as he said it, though, and I asked him why. "Don't you recognize it?" he asked. "That's my tank!"

And then I realized what he meant: it was the T–55 near the front of the camp. He told me he had won it during a battle in Kabul, and that he was driving it when the film was shot. I was stunned. This image from the film had been seared into my mind half a decade earlier. And so when Abu Mousa asked me if I wanted to learn how to use it, I jumped at the chance.

Abu Mousa taught me everything there was to know about the T–55: how to drive it, how to crank the engine, how to work the gun. When he thought I was ready, he let me take it out it by myself. I took it out on a flat area near the camp while he watched. The tank was very heavy and hard to maneuver. I quickly found myself veering up a hillside, towards the camp where the Kashmiris lived. Out of the corner of my eye, I saw Abu Mousa gesturing wildly for me to stop. I pressed down on the brakes as quickly as I could. When Abu Mousa got over to me, he explained that the hillside was littered with landmines left over by the Soviets. I could have blown myself up.

Later, I consoled myself. I could hardly be blamed for steering off course, I thought. After all, I had only gotten my driver's license a few months earlier.

For several weeks, Abdul Kerim and I were the only two Arab trainees at the camp. The only other people we saw were the *Hezb-i-Islami* fighters who would come in for a few days from the front. We avoided talking to them, though, because we had been told we were not part of their mission, and we shouldn't get involved in their politics.

The *Hezb-i-Islami* fighters ate with us and prayed with us in the mosque, so of course we often heard what they were talking about. Most often, they talked about the Taliban. It was in the late fall of 1995, and we had been hearing on the radio about the pitched battle for Kabul. Rabbani and Massoud were holding on, but the Taliban had made huge advances. Many people believed, however, that the Taliban could never win the capital on their own, that they would have to ally themselves either with Hekmatyar and his troops or with the Uzbek warlord General Rashid Dostum, who still controlled large sections of the country.

The *Hezb-i-Islami* fighters all thought Hekmatyar should join forces with the Taliban. They hated Rabbani and saw the alliance as an opportunity to get rid of him for good. But they all knew that Abu Jihad, the emir, opposed it. He was completely loyal to Hekmatyar, and Hekmatyar didn't want to ally himself with the Taliban.

Abdul Kerim and I were on the emir's side, of course. We knew that the Taliban were innovators. But we had nothing to do with Hekmatyar, and so we kept our thoughts to ourselves. Neither Abu Mousa nor Abu Hamid, the Jordanian, seemed to care either way.

The tension soon erupted. The fighters decided they wanted to replace Abu Jihad with a new emir. They took a vote, but were torn about it because the vote wasn't unanimous. A few of us hadn't voted at all, and that bothered them. It didn't matter, though, because Abu Jihad soon found out about the whole thing. He wasn't angry; he just took to his bed. He stayed in his room and had his food brought to him. He let it be known that he was sick.

After a few days, Abdul Kerim and I went to check on him. When we walked into his room, it was clear there was nothing at all wrong with Abu Jihad. He was just upset that the brothers had turned against him. He didn't understand why they didn't like him, and his feelings were hurt. This went on for a week, and even those who opposed the emir began to worry. Abu Jihad hadn't been pushed out; he was still the emir of the camp, and someone had to be in charge. So a group of *Hezb-i-Islami* fighters gathered together and went to see him in his room. They told him how much they wanted him to be emir, and begged him to return.

A few hours later, Abu Jihad reemerged, and life went back to normal. The drama was over. I couldn't help but think, however, that this was a strange way for an emir to behave, particularly one only a few kilometers from a war zone.

One day after the midday *salat*, Abu Jihad told us he was going over to the Kashmiri camp. He asked if any of us had any messages to transmit to Peshawar or the other camps, or if any of us would like to accompany him. I was curious, so I decided to go along.

Even though the Kashmiri camp was only about four hundred meters away from us, to get there we had to drive all the way around back past the Arab camp, down a long road, and back up onto the hill where it was located. The area in between our camp and theirs was covered with landmines, and we couldn't go near it.

The commander of the camp greeted us when we arrived, and led us back towards a small building fitted with a radio transmitter. Abu Jihad called to Peshawar and then to other camps in Sarowbi and Khowst. While I sat by and listened, a young Kashmiri brought us cookies and tea. Then Abu Jihad called Ibn Sheikh. They talked for several minutes, then Abu Jihad handed the phone to me.

"*Assalamu'alaykum*," I said. "How are you doing?"

"*Assalamu'alaykum*. How is the training?" He sounded happy to hear from me.

"We're waiting for Assad Allah to return," I told him.

"I see," he said. "You know, you left us with a big problem here, Abu Imam." For a second I clenched up; I was so used to being scolded by Ibn Sheikh. But then he continued. "You're famous in the village," he said. "Since you saved that boy, everyone there is coming to the camp for medical care. We don't have anyone to treat them, and they've already run us out of aspirin!"

I could hear him laughing on the other end of the line, and I laughed, too. I missed Ibn Sheikh.

Sarowbi

We were in the mosque one day when Abu Jihad asked us if we would like to join him on a trip up to the Lataband plateau. Two tanks had just fallen into a ravine when Massoud and his army were forced to retreat from their position by Taliban advances. Abu Jihad and Abu Mousa were going up to scavenge equipment from the tanks. There was an infrared targeting system that Abu Mousa wanted for himself. We would stay for a few days at the *Hezb-i-Islami* camp in Sarowbi.

I had been listening to the radio, and I knew all about Sarowbi from reports on the radio. It was Hekmatyar's main base, because it was such an important position strategically. Sarowbi was about seventy-five kilometers or so from Kabul, and it was home to a huge dam that generated all of Kabul's electricity. There had been fierce fighting around Sarowbi throughout the fall.

Abdul Kerim and I leapt at the opportunity to join Abu Jihad; we wanted to see the front lines. We began the journey early the next morning. Abu Jihad drove a Toyota pickup truck, and Abu Mousa sat alongside him in the cab.

Abdul Kerim and I sat in the back, in the open air, along with two of the *Hezb-i-Islami* fighters.

I have never been colder in my life than I was in the back of that truck. It was late fall, and there was a fierce wind whipping through the canyons. The roads were completely unpaved: sometimes there was no road at all. Huge segments had been destroyed by bombs and mines. There were checkpoints along the way, but the guards just waved us through.

I knew this road—the road from Jalalabad to Sarowbi—from my reading and from the documentaries. It was the site of extraordinary ambushes during the war with the Soviets. I could see the evidence of those battles everywhere. The deep gorge below the road was littered with the wreckage of Russian tanks and artillery. In my mind, I could see the *mujahidin* crashing down like thunderbolts on the Soviet invaders.

We arrived in Sarowbi in the late afternoon and drove through the village and to the camp just beyond it. There were two Afghanis guarding the entrance, and they signaled us to stop. Abu Jihad spoke to them for a minute, and then they opened the gate and waved us through.

Abu Jihad told us that Hekmatyar might be at the camp. If he was, we would meet him. He said that when he was in Sarowbi, Hekmatyar slept in a bunker at the base of the dam. But even more exciting than the prospect of meeting Hekmatyar was the incredible array of weapons and artillery spread out before us. Tanks like the T–55 and the newer T–64, multiple Shilkas, many large missile launchers and huge missiles to go with them. These were real weapons for a real army.

There were only Afghanis in this part of the camp, and so we drove on to another part of the camp for the Arab *Hezb-i-Islami* fighters. We crossed a bridge and saw the dam to our left. It was enormous, and the sound of the water pouring over it was almost deafening.

Soon, we arrived at some barracks. I was shivering as soon as I got out of the truck. Abu Jihad led us to one of the buildings, where we were greeted by several Arab *mujahidin*. We made our *salat* together in a small mosque nearby and then ate dinner and talked as the dam roared in the distance.

The next day, we drove up towards the Lataband plateau along with several of the Arab fighters from the Sarowbi camp. The road was so heavily mined that we couldn't use it; we had to drive along a dried riverbed instead.

We came upon a large truck as we began our ascent to the Lataband plateau. As we got closer, I could see there were three armed guards surrounding it. Abu Jihad pulled over to the side and I looked inside. The truck was filled with mines and all sorts of other weapons.

There was a man standing next to the truck. When he spotted Abu Jihad he smiled and waved. He had a metal claw where his right hand should have been. He and Abu Jihad spoke cheerfully for a few minutes and then we drove on. Abu Jihad explained that the man was a famous mine-hunter who made money by extracting the explosive material inside and selling it back to the *mujahidin.*

It took us about five hours to reach the tanks. We could see them from the road; they had fallen down into the gorge, about twenty meters below us. They were brand new T–55s.

We all got out of the truck, and the others huddled by the edge of the road to look down into the gorge. I was desperate to relieve myself, so I sprinted up the hill and squatted behind some rocks. When I was finished, I stood up. Abu Jihad was waving his arms at me and yelling. "What are you doing up there, Abu Imam?" he shouted. "Why did you leave the group?"

"I had to!" I yelled back. "It was urgent!"

"Abu Imam, there are mines all over that hill! Massoud was just here!"

Suddenly, I understood. Massoud's retreating army had mined the road to cover its flank. There wasn't much I could do at this point, though. I just walked down the hill and hoped for the best.

The hillside down to the ravine was extremely steep, so retrieving the equipment from the tanks was a precarious task. There were eight of us altogether, but two of the brothers stayed with the truck while the rest of us scaled down a thick rope to the tanks. While Abu Jihad and Abu Mousa extracted the electrical components they had come for, I peered inside the tanks. They were both covered with drying blood.

On the way back to Sarowbi that night, we stopped at a *Hezb-i-Islami* station on a high plateau. "Let's get out," Abu Jihad said. "We can see Kabul from here."

As the others talked to the Afghanis stationed there, Abdul Kerim and I walked over to the edge of the cliff. There were mountains in front of us and then a broad plain. Far in the distance, we could see bright flashes of artillery

fire. The sound of the explosions took several seconds to travel across the landscape to where we were standing.

It was the first time I had ever seen live warfare. Abdul Kerim and I stood
there for several minutes, until Abu Jihad called to us. We performed our *salat*
with the Afghanis, and then headed back to the camp.

Afghani, Afghani

We stayed at Sarowbi for about two weeks. We never did meet Hekmatyar, but
we had fun with the Arab *mujahidin*. It was a whole new level of artillery. My
favorite was the FROG–7, a huge rocket launcher. The missiles were enormous;
each one weighed over five hundred kilograms.

Mostly, though, I learned more about the politics of the war. I learned how
deeply the *Hezb-i-Islami* fighters hated Massoud, which upset me. They laughed
at him for the way he wore his *pakol* tilted back on his head. They were convinced that he was a puppet of the French because one night they had heard
him over the radio speaking French to one of his men in the field.

One of the men told me they had talked to Massoud a few days earlier. They
heard his voice on the radio and tuned in to the same frequency. They broke
into the conversation and began to insult him. Massoud waited until they were
done. Then told the Arabs to leave Afghanistan. The war was not a *jihad,* he
said, but simply an internal battle for land and power. There was no reason for
the Arabs to be involved.

The *mujahid* who told me the story laughed at Massoud's stupidity. After
Massoud finished the speech, he said, the group resumed their insults. The *mujahid* did admit, however, that throughout the exchange Massoud remained
very polite.

The *Hezb-i-Islami* soldiers didn't trust the Afghanis at all. Occasionally, they
would visit the Afghan camp down the road, but for the most part they kept to
themselves. They told stories about the battles over Kabul in the early nineties,
and talked about how the Afghanis would shift their loyalties in an instant.
They said they had seen Afghanis kill Arab *mujahidin*, even when they were
fighting on the same side. Never trust the Afghanis, they warned us. I had heard
a few comments like this at Khaldan, though no one ever said it outright. I be-

gan to understand why we were always forbidden to talk to the Afghani guides and the guard or the cooks.

So strong was the distaste of the *Hezb-i-Islami* fighters for the Afghanis that even Hekmatyar himself was not safe from their insults. Sometimes the men would laugh about the war, shrug their shoulders, and chant *"Hekmatyar, Rabbani—Afghani, Afghani."* The meaning was clear: it didn't matter who took Kabul; in the end, they were all the same.

At first, I was confused by these men. Why were they here at all? Clearly, years of battle had made them hard and cynical. They were much older than the young men I had met at Khaldan, in their thirties, at least. Their eyes were hollow. They had all fought against the Soviets, and they spoke of that war with pride and nostalgia. But now they seemed to be in love only with war; they talked of little else. They would describe in great detail battles they had witnessed between the Taliban and the Northern Alliance. They hated the Northern Alliance and they hated the Taliban, yet they seemed exhilarated when they talked about their deadly clashes. It wasn't the ideology but the fighting itself that turned them on.

At night, we would sit together in the barracks and talk. We had only gas lamps for light, because the Northern Alliance had been bombarding the area. We would shroud ourselves in blankets to stave off the bitter cold night air, and the *mujahidin* would tell us stories from the front lines. I was transfixed by these stories, by the detailed descriptions of famous battles I had only read about.

But one night, one of the *mujahidin* told a story about an airplane that broke up over Kabul a few months before Najibullah's government was toppled in 1992. As the plane fell from the sky, the Afghani pilot ejected. As he floated to the ground with his parachute, he held his hands in the air to surrender. The Arabs fired on him anyway. The pilot was injured, and when they got to the place where he landed they captured him immediately.

The *mujahidin* were discussing the best way to execute the pilot when they received a radio transmission from *Hezb-i-Islami* headquarters. They were told to keep the prisoner alive; he might have valuable information. The Arab fighters beat the pilot brutally while they waited for the interrogators to arrive. By the time they got there, the pilot was in such bad shape that they ordered the Arabs to take him to the hospital. The fighters didn't want the pilot to survive, so on the way there they injected engine oil—sticky, black engine oil—directly into his body.

The interrogators arrived at the hospital shortly after the Arabs. The *mujahidin* told them the pilot had been so badly injured when he ejected from the plane that he was on the brink of dying. The interrogators examined the pilot for a couple of minutes and decided he was useless, so they authorized the Arab fighters to execute him. So they threw the pilot in a hole in the ground and all fired on him at once. The bullets shredded the pilot's body to pieces. His intestines exploded out of his stomach, spreading rice everywhere.

"The *taghut* had rice for lunch!" That was the punch line, and everyone laughed. It was the most disgusting story I had ever heard.

A few nights later, another one of the *mujahidin* told a story that had taken place as the Soviets were retreating from Afghanistan. Just before dawn, he had snuck up on one of Najibullah's garrisons and launched a grenade through a window. But just as the grenade left his hand, he heard a voice from inside call out, "*Allahu akbar!*" It was time for the sunrise *salat*.

Seconds later, the grenade exploded, killing everyone inside.

At first, the man said, he was worried. He was troubled by the fact that he had killed Muslims during prayer. So troubled, in fact, that he sought out a highly respected scholar of the Kur'an. The scholar reassured him. "Brother," he said, "you are fighting under the flag of Islam. They are fighting under the flag of infidels. In the end, God will decide." The scholar's advice must have come as a relief to the *mujahid*. After all, he was still here.

Assad Allah

When we returned to Darunta, there were several more people there than when we had left. I recognized some of them from Khaldan: Abu Yahya, the Yemeni trainer, along with two Saudi trainers I also recognized. They had all come to train with explosives, just as I had.

Abu Yahya told me that Assad Allah, the explosives trainer, was feeling better and would be returning to Darunta very soon. He arrived about a week later, with three Kyrgyztanis in tow. They, too, would be training with us.

We began explosives training the next day. There was a kind of classroom in one of the barracks, and Assad Allah would write formulas for us on the blackboard or perform demonstrations on a large table. Before anything else, he taught us safety procedures. We spent days on this, memorizing the proper temperature and humidity at which to store different components, and learning the different safety equipment—gloves, gas masks, goggles—to use with the various chemicals and explosives. Assad Allah also taught us what to do if an experiment went wrong.

He gave us the same warning again and again. "You have a visa here, and you bring it to class with you each day. But I can take it away from you at any time. If you violate any of the safety procedures, I'll send you home immediately." We knew he wasn't kidding.

We were either in the classroom or the laboratory for about ten hours each day. We broke only to eat and to perform the *salat*. We used complicated mathematics and chemistry, and the work required intense concentration. We learned to make every explosive from scratch. That was the point: wherever we were going, we weren't going to have access to military-grade explosives or industrial materials. We would need to make do with what we could find on our own.

We learned how to make all kinds of things: black powder, RDX, tetryl, TNT, dynamite, C2, C3, C4, Semtex, nitroglycerine, and so on. We learned how to construct each of these from products we could find in shops or steal from school laboratories. Corn syrup, hair dye, lemons, pencils, sugar, coffee, Epsom salts, mothballs, batteries, matches, paint, cleaning products, bleach, brake fluid, fertilizer, sand—each of these contained components of different kinds of explosive material. We learned how to break down each of these products and more, and how to build them back up into bombs. I even learned how to make a bomb out of my own urine.

We tested the explosives outside, near some ruins at the edge of the camp. We almost always used very small quantities, but we would measure the velocity of explosion to calculate what the effects would be with much larger batches. We talked about how and where to use different kinds of explosives. We learned which materials we should use to blow up a train, how much of the explosive we would need, and how to position it on the railway tracks for maximum impact. We learned how to blow up cars and buildings.

We talked a lot about airplanes. These were hard to blow up because of airport security. Semtex was easiest to get on board, we learned, because it was almost impossible to detect. But Semtex was hard to obtain, Assad Allah reminded us. So we learned about liquid explosives as well.

We took notes on everything in the small notebooks they gave us at the camp. But ultimately we were expected to know the material by heart. When it came time to use the explosives, we weren't going to have a training manual in front of us. We needed to know what to do instinctively. And so we rehearsed the formulas over and over again until we could repeat them in our sleep. And every Sunday, Assad Allah gave us a test to make sure we knew it.

There was no joking around in Assad Allah's class. He never smiled, and he demanded our complete attention. I knew I couldn't play the class clown here if I wanted to succeed. The naughtiest thing I ever did was passing notes in class to Abdul Kerim. He, in turn, drew pictures in the margins of my notebook and wrote funny captions beneath them.

One day, we were in the laboratory when one of the Kyrgyztanis spilled a glass of water on one of the trainees. As a joke, he pretended it was sulphuric acid. Assad Allah saw the whole thing, and immediately banished the Kyrgyztani from the laboratory. Within an hour, he was on his way back to Pakistan. Assad Allah was right, of course. Explosives are extremely dangerous, and any one of us could have killed the entire group with a small mistake.

One day, Assad Allah told us about an accident that had occurred during his own explosives training. His group was learning how to make nitroglycerine, and one of the brothers wasn't paying attention. He let the materials get hotter than he should have. Luckily, the trainer looked over just in time and saw from the thermometer that the material was on the brink of exploding. There were seven other people in the laboratory, and it could have killed every one of them. "It's going to explode!" he shouted at the brother.

There was a sink full of ice right next to the trainee, and he should have poured the materials on that to cool it down. But instead he rushed towards the door with the liquid time bomb in his hands. Just as he got outside, the mixture exploded. It blew both his arms straight off, and destroyed one of his eyes.

"Did the brother survive?" I asked.

"Yes," Assad Allah replied. "He lives in London now, and preaches in the mosques. His name is Abu Hamza."

I had no idea who the man was at that point, and no way of knowing how important he would become in my life.

Mustard Gas

One day, Assad Allah took us down near the lake to practice preparing a really big explosion. There was a destroyed Russian truck on the hillside, and we dragged it down to water level. Then we filled it with explosives. We used fifty kilograms of ANFO—ammonium nitrate/fuel oil—and eleven anti-tank mines.

We connected the detonator to a long fuse. We had already calculated that it would take exactly one minute and fifteen seconds for the fuse to burn down completely. Assad Allah ordered one of the Kyrgyztanis to stay with the truck and ignite the fuse. The rest of us walked about two hundred meters uphill and gathered in a tight cluster behind the rocks to watch the explosion.

Assad Allah waved at the Kyrgyztani on the truck to signal him to light the fuse. We all held our breath as the brother leaned down. As soon as he stood back up, he bolted away from the truck and up the side of the mountain. He ran like he was escaping from an army of devils—I had never seen anyone run so fast in my life. A cloud of dust flew up all around him. When he got up to the rocks where we were standing, he hurled his body on the ground beside us.

Just as he landed, the truck exploded. It began with the blue light I had seen so many times, but this flash was more intense than anything I had ever seen before. Then, BOOM. A giant fireball burst forth from the truck, followed by a cloud of thick black smoke that rose up to the sky in the shape of a perfect mushroom. The noise filled the entire valley.

We all stood there in shock for a few moments as we absorbed the immensity of what we had just seen. And then we raced down the hill to examine the place where the truck had been. The explosion had left a crater five meters wide and two meters deep. It was littered with tiny pieces of metal from the truck. We were all extremely impressed when we realized that only six of the eleven mines had exploded.

Abu Said al-Kurdi came and went from the camp. He'd stay for a few days at a time and then leave for a week and come back. Often, he brought new trainees with him. But on and off, over the course of several weeks, he and Abu Mousa worked on a complicated project. They were using a laboratory right next to where Assad Allah was training us, and we could see them through a window. Often they were there for hours at a time.

I figured they were probably doing something with poisons. Abu Said had taught us a little bit about poisons early on. We had learned how to make cyanide from apricots, and then we tested it at different strengths on the rabbits. When Abu Said injected cyanide straight into one of the rabbits, it died almost instantly. Then we put a bit on some carrots and let the rabbits eat them. It took longer to kill them that way, nearly twenty-four hours.

One night, Abu Said and Assad Allah were discussing their project in the mosque, and I listened in. I learned that they were trying to weaponize mustard gas, and that they were having trouble combining the components in the mortar shell. In the weeks after that, I saw the two of them firing mortars over and over into the valley. Nothing ever happened, though, and so they would wait for a couple of hours and then trudge down the hill in their protective gear to recover the mortars and find out what went wrong.

But one day, it finally worked when the shell landed in the valley and exploded, emitting a thick cloud of smoke. When Abu Mousa and Abu Said saw what had happened, they leapt up and cheered—"*Takbir! Allahu akbar!*"—four times over. They grabbed their guns and fired wildly into the air, and everyone in the camp ran out to celebrate with them.

A few weeks later, I had a vivid dream that I was walking through the streets of London. I had never been to London in my life, but in my dream I knew I was there. I was approaching a huge white church. In front of it, stood four Indian imperial soldiers dressed in the military regalia of the nineteenth century: turbans, broad sashes, elegant jackets. But everything they wore was pure white.

The men were not guarding the church. They were trying to blow it up. Each man had a cannon in front of him, and they were all firing at the church again and again. But their shells never hit the target. The Indians were getting frustrated, and I was frustrated watching them. I knew I could do it easily. "Let me try," I said. "You don't know what you're doing."

I placed a shell in the cannon and fired it. It hit the church right under the steeple, and the building buckled and fell to the ground. A cloud of black smoke exploded into the air, debasing the bright white sky.

I woke up shaking, and when Abdul Kerim awoke I told him about the dream. He saw that I was upset, and told me there was a brother at the Arab camp who knew how to interpret dreams. Abdul Kerim gave me the name of the brother, and said I should go to him.

That afternoon, I walked over to the Arab camp, and when I asked for the dream reader by name, one of the brothers pointed me to a small building. There was a young man inside wearing a white *djellaba*. His legs were crossed beneath him and he was reading. I cleared my throat to get his attention and he looked up. "Can you help me with a dream?" I asked.

"Of course," he said. "Close the door and sit down. Tell me about your dream." After I told him everything, he asked me a question. "Are you sure it was a church," he asked, "and not a mosque?"

"Yes, I'm sure," I said. "I saw the cross."

The brother stood up and walked over to a large pile of books stacked by the wall. He picked one up and began to read to himself. Then he looked at me. "This is very good news, brother," he said.

"Why?" I asked.

"You will be going to the land of infidels. You will fight them, and you will succeed."

Abu Khabab

One day towards the end of the fall, we were outside testing some calculations. We were learning how set off a bomb on a railroad track using a conic-shaped charge when I saw a Toyota four-by-four driving into the camp. Assad Allah looked over his shoulder and then turned to the group. "Ah, here is Abu Khabab," he said.

We had all heard the name before. Many times during the course of our instruction, Assad Allah had told us we were learning techniques and formulations devised by a man named Abu Khabab. All of us were excited to see him in person.

Five men and two small children got out of the car. I recognized one of the men instantly: it was the Egyptian with the prostheses I had met months earlier in Peshawar. He was carrying a backpack. There was another man with him who was a bit older, in his forties at least. He was distinctive looking; instead of the traditional *Pakol*, he was wearing a black turban. He wore glasses, and his beard was colored with henna. The three other men stuck close by the older man. They were clearly bodyguards. Two of them had Kalashnikovs strapped across their shoulders, and one was carrying an RPG.

We all greeted the guests, then Assad Allah told us lessons were over for the day and dismissed us. As I was walking away, I heard a voice behind me. "Abu Imam! Abu Imam!" I turned and saw the older man gesturing at me to join them. I walked back over to them. "How are you, my son?" asked the older man. He had a strong Egyptian accent.

"*Al-hamdu lil-lah*," I replied. Praise be to God.

Then the Egyptian with the prostheses spoke. "We've heard very good things about you, brother." I wondered what he meant. I had only been at Darunta for about a month, so he must have been referring to Khaldan, where I was known primarily for getting punished more than anyone else. He continued, "Brothers like you are always welcome in *al-Gama'a*."

I knew about *al-Gama'a*. It was a militant group in Egypt that had broken with the Muslim Brotherhood when it renounced violence in the 1970s. I knew from the radio at Khaldan they had claimed responsibility for an assassination attempt earlier that summer on Hosni Mubarak, the president of Egypt.

The older man whispered something to Assad Allah, who frowned slightly. Then the Egyptian with the prostheses guided me towards the ruins where we tested explosives. The older man came with us, along with two of the bodyguards. The third guard stayed near the car with the children. I saw Assad Allah skulk back to the laboratory by himself.

When we got to the ruins, the young man opened his backpack and took out a small metal box. Inside were several smaller containers, each no larger than a matchbox. He leaned down to place one of the small boxes at the base of the ruin.

"What is that?" I asked.

"It's ANFO," he replied. "We're testing it."

I was impressed. We always practiced on small quantities of explosives and then calculated from what the effects would be in larger quantities. But I had never seen anyone test a quantity this small. He gestured us all back, and the older man and I sat down on a rock. The bodyguards hovered behind us. Then the Egyptian set off a small explosion, and leaned down to examine the results.

Meanwhile, the older man spoke to me. "Abu Imam, where would you like to make your *jihad*?" He continued to look straight ahead as he spoke. His eyes were focused on the man with the prostheses.

I didn't know what I was supposed to say, so I told him the truth. "I want to go to Chechnya."

The man nodded silently, and continued to stare forward. Soon, the younger man walked back towards us and said he had finished his work. The older man stood up, so I did, too. As we all walked back towards the four-by-four, the older man turned to me. He was smiling. "When you have finished your training, I hope you will come visit us." Then he climbed back into the car with the others and drove away.

A few days later, as we were walking out of the classroom in the late afternoon, Abu Jihad and Abu Mousa came running towards us. They stopped by the mosque and began firing their Kalashnikovs in the air. "*Takbir!*" they shouted in unison. "*Allahu akbar!*"

Abu Jihad was grinning. "They did it!" he said. "They blew up the Egyptian embassy!" Then he ran back inside to radio the other camps.

Within minutes, there were explosions coming from every camp. Shilkas, BMPs, antiaircraft guns—everything was firing at once. Hundreds of strings of blue and green were flying up into the darkening sky. For an instant, I imagined this was what it would look like if Darunta were ever attacked by airplanes.

"*Takbir! Allahu akbar!*" The voices echoed from every side.

That night, and in the days to come, I would learn more about what had happened. Suicide bombers had blown up the Egyptian embassy in Islamabad. They had driven cars filled with explosives into the building. The first bomb got everyone's attention; people rushed outside from all the buildings near the embassy to see what had happened. Then the second car exploded in a huge blast, scattering shrapnel everywhere.

The explosion brought down one whole side of the embassy and left a crater three meters deep. Many people were crushed when the concrete collapsed on them. In the end, eighteen people were killed and another seventy-five injured.

Al-Gama'a immediately claimed responsibility for the attack. They demanded the release of their spiritual leader, Sheikh Omar Abdel Rahman. Sheikh Ramhan, allegedly the mastermind of the 1993 plot to blow up the World Trade Center, was awaiting trial in a prison in the United States.

Over the next weeks and months that followed, we heard on the radio that Benazir Bhutto had initiated a massive crackdown on Arabs. There were police raids all over the country. Many fled into Afghanistan, and a couple even came to Khaldan. They were no longer safe, they said, across the border in Pakistan.

Shortly after the Islamabad embassy bombing, a Canadian engineer named Ahmed Khadr was arrested in Pakistan. He was accused of funding the embassy attack with money he had filtered through a Canadian charity. Khadr claimed he was innocent, and was released from prison a few months later. The Canadian prime minister had put pressure on Bhutto during a state visit to Pakistan.

I would learn much more about Khadr after 9/11, when the United States put his name on a list of suspected terrorists. I learned he had been a close associate of Osama bin Laden's since the 1980s, when the two had funded the *mu-jahidin* in the war with the Soviets. Khadr had gone on to become one of bin Laden's top fundraisers.

In 2003, Khadr was killed in Afghanistan in a shootout with the Pakistani army. His youngest son, Abdul, was with him, and during the attack was paralyzed from the waist down. Khadr's other sons had also been in Afghanistan at the time. The oldest son, Abdullah, was indicted in Massachusetts in February 2006. He was charged with buying weapons for Al Qaeda, plotting the murder of American soldiers, and conspiracy to use weapons of mass destruction. Another son, Omar, was captured in 2002 after it was said he killed a U.S. Army medic with a hand grenade. Now he is in captivity at Guantanamo Bay. His older brother Abdurahman was arrested in Afghanistan in November 2001. He was handed over to the Americans and taken to Guantanamo Bay. At some point, he flipped and began to work for the CIA, at first in Guantanamo, and then in Bosnia. He told his story on television in 2004, and now Hollywood is making a movie about his life.

Ahmed Khadr was the man I saw going into the explosives laboratory at Khaldan with Ibn Sheikh. Abdurahman was the son I knew as Hamza, who told me about the Afghanis killed in front of him in Khowst. Omar was his younger brother, whom I knew as Osama. He was the noisy one, who always talked about his father's important friends.

An Egyptian man named Abu Khabab al-Masri was widely thought to have masterminded the embassy bombing. Abu Khabab was, of course, his *nom de guerre*. His real name was Midhat al-Mursi. He was said to have recruited the two suicide bombers from the camps at Darunta.

After 9/11, I learned that al-Mursi was Al Qaeda's top bomb maker, an expert in chemical and biological weapons. It was said he had plotted the Islamabad attack with a man named Ayman al-Zawahiri, who is now Osama bin Laden's second in command. When bin Laden took control of the camps in the late nineties, al-Mursi was put in charge of developing unconventional weapons for Al Qaeda.

At Darunta, al-Mursi trained an Algerian recruit named Ahmed Ressam, who was captured in 1999 at the U.S.–Canadian border. He was driving a truckload of explosives, and was going to use them to blow up the airport in Los Angeles on the eve of the millennium. Al-Mursi also trained the shoe-bomber Richard Reid, and Zacarias Moussaoui, the "twentieth hijacker," who is now serving a life sentence. It is thought al-Mursi also trained the bombers who in 2000 attacked the USS *Cole* in Yemen.

In January 2006, al-Mursi was killed by a U.S. Predator drone in Damadola, Pakistan. The Americans had hoped to kill al-Zawahiri, who was supposed to be with al-Mursi at the time. There was a five-million-dollar bounty on al-Mursi's head at the time of his death.

There are no pictures of al-Mursi, at least none that I have seen. And so there is no way I can declare with certainty that he was the man I saw at Darunta that day. But it seems very likely.

Psychological Warfare

By the time Ramadan began that winter, I was growing restless. We had finished our explosives training early in the winter. One day, Assad Allah told us that we were done, congratulated us, and then left the camp along with all the trainees. Abdul Kerim and I were alone with the *Hezb-i-Islami* fighters.

We didn't have much to do after that except for going back over the things we had learned during training. I still spent hours each day practicing with the guns, but I wasn't learning anything new. I spent a lot of time hiking just to pass the time; we didn't have to exercise at all if we didn't want to. Every Friday, we would play soccer over at the Arab camp with the young recruits. It was fun to watch the brothers run around the field in their *shalwar kameez*, but I spent most of my time on the sidelines. I had never really learned to play soccer.

Without anything to do, I spent a lot of time thinking. I thought about the bombing in Pakistan quite a bit. I kept seeing the face of the Egyptian man. "*I hope you will come visit us. I hope you will come visit us.*"

It was like a nightmare. I knew that he had wanted me to become one of his suicide bombers. He must have heard the story about how I had volunteered to defuse the bomb in the river, and thought I was desperate to become *shahid*. I had dodged fate that time, but I was certain I would be recruited for another mission soon. They must have plans for me, otherwise why were they keeping me at Darunta? And next time, would I be asked to join a mission—or *ordered* to?

I was worried about other things, too. The longer I stayed here, the more likely it was that I would be found out as an agent. There were Algerians everywhere. Eventually, someone would talk to Amin and Yasin and figure out who I was. I thought about the horrible story I had heard at Sarowbi, about the pilot who had been injected with engine oil and then torn to shreds by gunfire. I didn't want to end up like him.

And once in a while, I thought about Gilles. I remembered what he told me in the garden in Istanbul. I had seven months; after that I would be cut off. My seven months had already expired.

One day, Abdul Kerim and I walked into the mosque and saw someone hanging from the rafters by his ankles. His eyes were covered by a blindfold, and he was screaming. There were several brothers standing all around him, I recognized some of them from the Arab camp. They were shouting at the prisoner, and one was pointing his gun at the prisoner's head.

I felt chills as I watched. This is what they do to spies, I thought. This is what will happen to me if I get caught. My stomach lurched, but I had little time to dwell on this before Abu Mousa came up behind us and ushered us out of the mosque. "Come," he said. "This is not for you."

"What's going on?" I asked. I was more than curious.

"They're from from the other camp," he said. "One of the brothers is going on a mission. The others are preparing him for interrogation, in case he gets caught."

"Why can't we watch?" asked Abdul Kerim.

Abu Mousa shook his head. "Because we don't know what he'll say. He might reveal something about his mission, and you mustn't know anything about it."

He must have realized how disappointed we both were, because after a few seconds Abu Mousa offered to give us a book about interrogation. But when we opened it, we saw that it was in Arabic. The text was far too complicated for either Abdul Kerim or me to understand; neither of us was really fluent.

Abu Mousa agreed to read parts of it to us aloud. We went back to our room and sat down, and he began the book. From the first sentences, the lesson was fascinating, and incredibly detailed. The book began by running through all different stages of an interrogation: from the arrest through the early questioning to the threats and soon to torture. And then came the list of all the different things the interrogators might do: hang you upside down in your cell, beat you with their hands or sticks or electrical wire, make you stand naked for days on end, tear out your fingernails, burn your skin with cigarettes or open flames, attack you with dogs, hit you in the groin, or apply electrical shocks to the genitals. The list went on and on, and Abu Mousa told us that of all these techniques had been used on brothers in different countries.

The first lesson was simple: a *mujahid* must keep everything to himself. The best way to prevent secrets from being revealed was not to have them in the first place. I realized that this was why, from the very first day, we were all ordered never to speak to each other about anything outside the camps. It wasn't just because they were afraid of spies. It was because they wanted to make sure none of the brothers could reveal too much if he cracked under pressure.

But faith, not secrecy, was by far the most important weapon at the *mujahid*'s disposal. A true *mujahid* can withstand anything if he is suffering for God. He must prepare for interrogation and torture just as he would prepare for any other kind of battle. Abu Mousa was very clear on this: interrogation was a form of psychological warfare. And as in real warfare, there was no way a brother could lose. Either he vanquished his enemy, or he died a martyr.

But there were concrete steps as well. Before going on a mission, the brother must discuss with his commander what to say to his interrogators if he was captured. He must never deviate from that plan. He must never give out any information, and he must understand that nothing could be gained by doing so. It would only lead to more torture, because the interrogators would realize that the prisoner had secrets to reveal. But the interrogators would never kill him, because he would be of no use to them dead.

As Abu Mousa explained it, interrogation was a great opportunity for a brother. He could learn more about the enemy and spread misinformation that would help his group obtain its objective. This kind of manipulation required skill, and a brother must train for it, just as he would train to use a gun. He must learn to draw out his interrogators. The longer the interrogation went on, the more information the interrogators would reveal about their knowledge and their strategy. The brother could use that information to shape his own responses, to tell the enemy lies that sounded true. For a *mujahid*, counter-interrogation was just another battle tactic.

That afternoon, after Abu Mousa finished reading to us, I thought about what I had learned. I understood better why Abu Bakr was so pleased with the brother he had taken hostage during the night raid at Khaldan. The brother had used the interrogation process to the advantage of his group. He was trying to frighten the enemy so that they would retreat.

Many years later, I would think about this lesson again, when I began to learn more about Ibn al-Sheikh al-Libi and his role within what has come to be known as Al Qaeda. Ibn Sheikh continued to run training camps in Afghanistan throughout the 1990s, and was close to bin Laden. He was captured early on when the Americans invaded Afghanistan after the 9/11 attacks, and he was flown to Egypt where he was tortured by the CIA. There he told his interrogators that Saddam Hussein had given Al Qaeda information about building chemical weapons. It was Ibn Sheikh's information that George W. Bush and Colin Powell were alluding to when they said they had proof that Saddam Hussein was connected to Al Qaeda. They used what Ibn Sheikh told them to justify the invasion of Iraq.

Later, Ibn Sheikh said that the story about Saddam Hussein was not true. In fact, the CIA had known Ibn Sheikh's story was not reliable long before Colin Powell referred to it in his famous speech in front of the UN. But by the time this fact emerged, it didn't matter anymore. America was already at war.

Many say that Ibn Sheikh lied to his captors out of desperation, because he was being tortured so brutally. I know that isn't true. He ran these camps, and everything we learned there Ibn Sheikh had learned long before. He had prepared himself for interrogation just as the brother in the mosque was preparing himself. He knew what to do.

No true *mujahid* is afraid of pain, certainly not one as zealous as Ibn Sheikh. Pain is nothing. You can train yourself not to feel it. And no true *mujahid* is afraid of death. Dying for God is the purpose of life.

No, Ibn Sheikh did not crack under the pressure of torture. He handled his interrogators with the same skill that he used to handle his gun. He knew what his interrogators wanted, and he was happy to give it to them. He wanted to see Saddam toppled even more than the Americans did. As he had told us at Khaldan, Iraq was the next great *jihad*.

Somewhere, in a secret torture chamber, Ibn Sheikh had won his battle.

Propaganda

I was so bored that one day I decided to organize the storage sheds near the entrance to the camp. Abu Jihad and I had gone inside to look for some munitions and I saw how messy they were. I asked Abu Jihad if I could tidy them. He seemed surprised by my request, but told me that I was welcome to.

The next day, he gave me the keys to the shed and I began to sort through everything inside. Mostly, there were lots of weapons divided into different bins depending on who owned them. At Khaldan, all the weapons belonged to the camp, but at Darunta, they were the property of the various *mujahidin*. On the battlefront, the *mujahidin* could claim whatever they captured from the enemy. We were all allowed to use them, but it was clear who owned them.

There were several wooden boxes inside the shed as well. One of them caught my eye. It belonged to an Arab filmmaker who had come to Darunta a few weeks earlier. He had stayed at the camp for only one night, and in the evening we had all sat together in the mosque while he showed us some of the films he had made. I was surprised, because I had seen so many of them before in Europe: films about Afghanistan, Bosnia, and Chechnya.

Later that night, one of the *Hezb-i-Islami* fighters explained to me that the filmmaker was famous. He had made hundreds of propaganda films. They were printed in Europe and sold in the mosques after the Friday prayers.

The filmmaker had brought a box with him to the camp. Before he left, I saw him lock it in one of the sheds at the front of the camp. There was a storage area inside as well, where the *Hezb-i-Islami* fighters left their things when they went off to the front. I had forgotten all about the filmmaker's box, but now I was desperate to go through it. I felt it in my gut: I would be leaving Afghanistan soon. I had to get back to Europe before Gilles cut me off. And I thought I should try to gather some concrete information before I saw him. I had been in Afghanistan for nearly a year, after all, and I had yet to learn the real name of a single *mujahid*.

After I finished tidying the shed, I looked around to see if anyone was watching. Then I pried open the lock on the filmmaker's box. My heart was pounding. I would be killed on the spot if anyone caught me. We weren't even supposed to ask each other questions. Going through someone else's belongings was a complete violation of every principle we had learned. The image of the pilot and the engine fuel flashed before me yet again.

I could feel the sweat on my forehead as I opened the box. Inside there were videotapes, a 9 mm Makarov, and several different passports from Europe and the Gulf, each with a different name. There was nothing particularly useful to me, and so I quickly closed the box and put it back inside with the others. I could feel my body shaking as I walked over to the barracks to return the keys to Abu Jihad.

Instead of just taking the keys, Abu Jihad asked me to walk back to the sheds with him so he could look at the job I had done. I could tell that he thought I might have stolen something from another brother. But once he counted all the weapons and boxes, he realized that nothing was missing. Then he thanked me for my work.

A few weeks later, the filmmaker returned to the camp. He had been in Chechnya. The night he arrived, he showed us some films he had shot during his stay, including one of Shamil Basayev. I knew all about Basayev—he was a great hero. I had learned all about him at Khaldan, from listening to the news on the radio.

The summer before, Basayev had led a small group of *mujahidin* into a hospital in the Russian town of Budyonnovsk. There were fifteen hundred Russians inside, and Basayev and his men took every one of them hostage. Twice, the Russians tried to storm the hospital and free the hostages. But Basayev and his fighters repelled them. Eventually, Basayev managed to negotiate an agreement with the Russian prime minister. In exchange for freeing the hostages, Russia was forced to grant Basayev free passage back to Chechnya. They also agreed to halt their military operations on Chechen soil.

In the film the Saudi filmmaker showed us, Basayev was showing off a new machine gun. It had a silencer on it, and when he fired it we could hear only a tiny clack in the barrel. Basayev spoke through an interpreter, and said the gun was the latest Russian model. At one point, he turned to the camera, waved, and sent his greetings to all the brothers in the training camps in Afghanistan. He must have known the filmmaker was coming back to Darunta, since he singled us out for special mention.

The filmmaker was still there the next day. I saw him at the morning *salat*, and again at midday. But I could tell something was wrong the second time; he had a sour look on his face. My senses immediately went on high alert.

After the midday *salat*, Abu Jihad stood up and spoke to us in a grave voice. "This morning we discovered that someone opened our brother's box in the storage shed," he began, glancing over at the filmmaker. "As you can imagine, we're very upset."

I stared straight forward with no expression, but my heart was racing inside my chest. I was hardly surprised when Abu Jihad turned to me.

"Abu Imam, you were in the storage sheds for several hours by yourself. Did you open the box?"

I was ready with my answer. "No, brother, I did not," I said in a calm voice. "Don't you remember that you checked the shed with me after I reorganized everything? If I had broken into a box, surely you would have noticed."

I could see the blood rise to Abu Jihad's face. "Yes, of course I remember," he said, trying to force a smile. "You are right, Abu Imam. I'm sorry." Then he turned to the others and, in a show of false strength, told them that from now on no one would be allowed into the sheds unless he was present.

After that, all the *Hezb-i-Islami* fighters were incredibly friendly to me. The tension between the *mujahidin* and Abu Jihad had only gotten worse over the course of the winter, as the Taliban continued their march on Kabul. All the brothers were very happy that I had put the emir in his place.

The Land of the Jihad Is Wide

I was in the kitchen washing the dishes one evening when I saw a four-by-four truck drive into the camp. Several men got out and Ibn Sheikh was one of them. I set the dishes aside and walked over to him, and we saluted one another. I was happy to see him.

Soon, the others emerged from the barracks and we all went into the mosque to talk. Ibn Sheikh told us about his journey and how difficult it was. They had to drive on perilous roads through the snow-covered mountains to avoid crossing over into Pakistan on the one side, and the war zone on the other.

After he was done with his story, he turned to me. "Abu Imam, why don't we go for a walk?" I followed him out of the mosque, but as soon as we were outside we were hit by the blistering wind. We ended up sitting together in the front of his truck.

"Abu Imam," he began, "it's been nearly a year since Abu Anas brought you to us. And in that time you've learned many different ways to fight the *tawagheet*." I nodded, and he went on. "I remember when you were at Khaldan, you talked about wanting to fight your *jihad* in Chechnya?"

"Yes," I said. "That is what I want."

Ibn Sheikh exhaled. "Abu Imam, the land of the jihad is wide. But the most important is the *al-jihad 'ila al-quds al-sharif*. There, in Jerusalem, the enemies of God are inflicting great suffering on our Muslim brothers and sisters."

Ibn Sheikh had said this many times at Khaldan: Jerusalem is the heart of Islam, and the first priority for the *mujahidin*. But I didn't want to go to Jerusalem. I had never wanted to go there because I didn't want to make my *jihad* by blowing myself up in a market or on a bus. Surely I hadn't gone through all this training for that?

But then Ibn Sheikh explained. "We must fight the Zionists efficiently; we must hit them where they are most vulnerable. We need brothers who can live among them, who can watch them, surveil them. We need blueprints and photos of their clubs, their synagogues, their banks, their consulates. Anywhere they gather in large numbers.

"We can't send just anyone to do this job," he continued. "We need a brother who can resist all temptation, and remain pure in himself while he lives amongst the *kafir*. We need someone with unlimited resources of patience and determination. It will take time to assimilate, to find a job, to get the right documentation. It will take time to find a group of brothers, four or five Muslims to join the mission."

I knew what was coming.

"Abu Imam," he said, leaning close to me. "You lived in Europe for many years, and you speak several languages. You are smart, you are courageous, you are independent. For all of these reasons, we believe that you can best serve the *umma* by going back to Europe."

"Ibn Sheikh," I said, "I will always follow any order you give me. But why can't I go to Chechnya?"

I said it, but I didn't mean it. Of course, if Ibn Sheikh had come to me that day and told me to go to Chechnya, I would have gone. I believed in that *jihad*. But at that moment, what I all I really cared about was getting out of Darunta. I wanted to do something—*anything*—new and bigger than what I was doing there.

But I was surprised to realize how excited I was when Ibn Sheikh told me that I would be going back to Europe. For nearly a year, I had suppressed this part of myself. In fact, I had almost completely annihilated it. I was a *mujahid*; I couldn't afford to think about anything else. If I had, I would have cracked. Life would have been intolerable, and the others would have seen through my guise.

Everything came back at that moment, all at once. I missed my life in the West. I missed wine. I missed cigarettes. I missed good food and newspapers and soft sheets. More than anything, I missed sex. And so this time, when Ibn Sheikh told me I could not go to Chechnya, I was not devastated. I was relieved.

"The brothers in Chechnya do not need you fighting with them on the field," Ibn Sheikh continued. "They need money. The best way for you to help them is by supporting them financially, by sending money to camps through the *Maktab*." He paused. "And what we all need most is to have more brothers in the land of the *kafir*."

Ibn Sheikh was done. He had given me an order, and I nodded in assent.

Then Ibn Sheikh's tone shifted. "Can you travel with your own identity, or have you been in trouble with the authorities?"

"I think I could travel to Turkey," I said. "I could buy a passport there."

"Good," he said. "We'll make arrangements when we get to Peshawar. Your passport and your other things are there with Abu Zubayda. We will go tomorrow. But you must know, Abu Imam, that it is a very dangerous time for Arabs in Pakistan." His tone was dark. "The police have raided houses all over the country. They're arresting any Arab without a visa."

I thought about my passport, and the visa that had expired eight months earlier.

"Now, Abu Imam, bring me your notebooks." He was referring to the notes I had taken during the classes with Assad Allah.

I ran over to the barracks to pick up my notebooks and brought them back to the truck. As I handed them to Ibn Sheikh, he reached into his jacket and pulled out a stack of bills.

"Here, this is for you," he said, "It is a gift from the sheikh to each of the brothers." Then he got out of the truck and walked back to the mosque.

As I headed back to the barracks, I looked down at the money. He had given me Pakistani rupees, about four hundred dollars' worth. At the time, I had no idea to whom he was referring when he told me the money was from the sheikh. Now, of course, I assume that he meant Osama bin Laden.

When I got to my room, Abdul Kerim was there. He had received the four hundred dollars as well. When I told him I was leaving, he looked sad. "But you came after me, and now you are leaving before me!" he said. He seemed as eager to leave Darunta as I was.

"Are you tired of the *jihad*, Abdul Kerim?" I asked.

"No, no," he replied. "It's not that. I just want to get to the front lines. I want to go back to Europe, I want to begin my mission."

I understood, of course. It was what I wanted, too, in my own way. "Don't worry, brother," I reassured him. "Your time will come soon enough. *Insha' Allah*."

He smiled. "*Insha'Allah.*"

I felt peaceful as I prepared for bed that night, more peaceful than I had felt since my final night in Istanbul. I was nervous, of course, because of what Ibn Sheikh had said about the dangers of the journey through Pakistan. But in my stomach I felt I would make it, that my destiny was leading me back to Europe.

I considered what Ibn Sheikh had told me about his decision to send me back to Europe. I understood better than I had before why he treated me differently than the others at Khaldan. Why he allowed me to stay and then even promoted me despite the fact I took shortcuts when I ran, talked back to the trainers, and carried my flashlight when I shouldn't have. Tonight, Ibn Sheikh had revealed himself: he saw my independence as an asset. Unlike most of the *mujahidin* at the camp, I thought for myself. I didn't need other people to prop me up. In battle, a *mujahid* must think with his brothers, and must depend on them completely. But if I was going to form a cell in Europe—and that was certainly what he was asking me to do—I would need to function on my own.

It was all numbingly ironic: for Ibn Sheikh, I was the perfect *mujahid* for this assignment because I was an individual. But I was an individual because I had grown up in the West, with all of her freedoms. Ibn Sheikh wanted to destroy the West with its own weapons.

Crossing

The next morning, we were all standing near the mosque when a blue Toyota four-by-four drove up. It was painted like an ambulance, with a red crescent on the side. One of the *Hezb-i-Islami* fighters told me the truck belonged to Hekmatyar. Ibn Sheikh stepped out of the truck and saluted all the brothers. Then he turned to me. "Abu Imam, it is time to leave."

I said goodbye to everyone and promised to remember them in my prayers, and they said the same to me. Then I climbed into the truck with Ibn Sheikh. There were three other men inside. The first one I noticed was the Afghani guide who had led me to Khaldan that first day. There was a driver as well. And on the floor in the back there was an African man laid out on a stretcher.

Ibn Sheikh explained that the patient had been taken hostage during Hekmatyar's attempted coup against Rabbani in 1994. He had only just been released. Ibn Sheikh told me the man had gone mad during his ordeal, and that he would not be safe on the front.

Ibn Sheikh handed me two syringes, a bottle of chloroform, and some pieces of cloth. He told me that it was my job to make sure the brother stayed asleep throughout the trip to Peshawar. I should use the chloroform until we got near customs at the Khyber Pass, and then I should inject him with one of the syringes. I should use the second syringe when we reached the last police checkpoint before the refugee camp.

We drove out of the camp, and fifteen minutes later the patient's eyes began to open slowly. I opened the bottle of chloroform and carefully wet the cloth with it, just as I had learned during our kidnapping training at Khaldan. As I covered the patient's nose, his eyes snapped wide open. They were bright and ferocious. I realized after a few seconds that he was holding his breath, and so I pushed the cloth down harder against his nostrils. I could see the strain in his face as he resisted inhaling. I had to make him go back to sleep, but I also remembered from training that if I held the cloth against his face for too long, I could kill him. As soon as his eyes dimmed just slightly, I pulled the cloth away.

Every half hour or so I had to the repeat the process. Every time he fought me, and every time I had to hold the cloth against his face longer. There was clearly something wrong with this man. I understood why the brothers didn't want him on the front—he was a psychopath.

We had ascended high up into the pass when Ibn Sheikh told me to inject the patient with the syringe. He was already asleep when I did it, so he didn't resist. Then the driver pulled to a halt and Ibn Sheikh, the guide, and I all got out. We were about two hundred meters from the checkpoint.

"We'll cross the border by foot," Ibn Sheikh told me. The Toyota would drive through along with the other vehicles. Ibn Sheikh reminded me not to speak at all. One word of Arabic would be enough to get me arrested.

There were crowds of people as we approached the crossing. They were all surging towards the checkpoint. I got in line and soon I began to feel my body pressed forward by the people lining up behind me. I was more confident this time than I was on the way in with Abu Said. I knew that Ibn Sheikh must have some plan to get us past the guards.

"Abu Imam!" I heard a voice behind me and I turned to look. "Abu Imam!" It was Ibn Sheikh. He and the guide were still standing fifteen meters behind me. I hadn't realized they had stopped. They were both waving their hands frenetically, signalling me to come back.

I quickly turned back to look at the checkpoint, and just as I did two guards let go of the man they were searching and started to run towards me.

They were shouting at me in a language I didn't understand. I had been trained to handle this situation: I stopped in my tracks and raised my hands in the air. All of a sudden, I felt a sharp pain in my leg. One of the guards had clubbed me with his nightstick. The other one lifted his Kalashnikov and pointed it straight at me.

I looked forward and saw that two other guards had apprehended Ibn Sheikh and the guide. They were pushing both of them towards me. The guards were pummelling both of them with their sticks and kicking them viciously. Neither one called out; they were both completely silent. We had all been trained to respond this way if captured. But I had never seen it play out in real life before, and I was struck in particular by Ibn Sheikh. He was perhaps the most vital man I had ever met; there was always a fierce energy at work behind his serene gaze. Now, in the hands of the guards, it was as if all of the life had evaporated from his body. His eyes were completely empty. He had transformed himself completely.

I didn't have time to think about this. We needed to escape. I caught the guide's eye and nodded my head towards the pocket of my coat. I could tell from the guide's face that he understood: I had money in there. The guide whispered something to the guard restraining him. The guard let go of the guide's arms and he edged towards me. He reached into my pocket and he took out about half the bills inside: the money Ibn Sheikh had given me the night before. Discreetly, he passed it to the guard.

The guard looked at the bills, said something under his breath, then shoved the guide back towards me. Clearly, the guard had seen the money and now he wanted more. As the guide took the rest of the money from my pocket, I looked over at Ibn Sheikh. The guard was holding him with one hand, and using the other to hit him again and again with his stick. It was horrifying to watch; it must have been incredibly painful. But still Ibn Sheikh made no sound. He smiled contentedly as the guard continued to batter him, which only infuriated the guard more.

Once the guide had handed over all the money, the beating came to a halt. The guards let all of us go, and gestured us through the crossing. Ibn Sheikh went first, glaring at me as he passed by.

I scolded myself harshly as I crossed through the checkpoint. It was all my fault that this had happened. I realized that Ibn Sheikh had never intended to go through the checkpoint. He and the guide had just walked to the barrier to make sure the truck got through. They must have had some other, secret route in mind, but I had blown it because I wasn't paying attention. I was angry at myself. I had let Ibn Sheikh down.

But I learned something that night—something important. I had never fully understood the way Amin and Yasin had reacted back in Brussels when I told them I was working for the DGSE. By all rights, they should have killed me. It was the second time I had betrayed them, and they owed me no mercy. But instead they had said nothing, done nothing.

That night, in the empty eyes of Ibn Sheikh, I understood their strange reaction that day. Amin and Yasin knew that they were trapped. Maybe I was wearing a wire. Maybe there were police surrounding the car, waiting to arrest them. At the very least, they were being watched. Amin and Yasin had been in the camps and had trained for moments just like this. I realized they hadn't believed one word of my explanation. They just knew to stay silent because as far as they were concerned, the interrogation had already begun.

Ghost Town

We got to Peshawar and drove towards the refugee camp. I was shocked when I looked around: there were police everywhere, and road blocks one after another. As we got closer, Ibn Sheikh nodded to me to indicate that I should inject the second syringe into the patient. By the time we approached the final road block, he was out cold.

Just before the road block, Ibn Sheikh and I got out of the truck and walked towards the Arab section of the camp. I was stunned when we got there. I had been here twice before; this time everything had changed. It was eerie; there was no one in the streets. Ibn Sheikh explained that most of the houses were empty now, that after the attack on the Egyptian embassy the police had surrounded the camp for a week and arrested many brothers. Some were lucky and managed to escape across the border into Afghanistan.

Ibn Sheikh guided me back to the safe house where I had stayed both times I had been in Peshawar. He told me that I would be staying here for two weeks and guarding the house. Then he took some keys from his pocket and we walked around to three other houses. He said that I should check each of them every day to make sure nothing happened to them. All the houses were empty, apart from a few boxes and suitcases. He told me that I should carry these back to the safe house where a brother would come to pick them up in a few days' time.

Then we went to a fourth house, just across the street from the safe house where I would be staying. Ibn Sheikh opened the door and we poked our heads inside. There were two Saudis whom I recognized from Khaldan, and a Pakistani boy no more than fifteen years old. We all greeted each other, and then Ibn Sheikh explained that I should come here for lunch and dinner each day.

Ibn Sheikh and I then returned to the safe house. He went into one of the closets and pulled out a holster and Makarov and passed them to me. He told me if anything went wrong I should tell the Saudis in the other house, and they would reach him through Abu Zubayda. Then he smiled, saluted me, and walked out the door.

It was late afternoon by the time Ibn Sheikh left, and it was time for the sunset *salat*. I made my ablutions and then walked across the street. The Pakistani boy opened the door for me.

This time I was able to look around. I quickly realized this had been the home of a wealthy family: there was a kitchen with a microwave and a freezer, and in the living room a large television and a VCR. There was a garden in the back of the house, concealed from the street by high walls. There was a vegetable patch in the corner and a small football pitch. There were rabbits everywhere.

After we made our *salat,* we all ate dinner together. The Saudis told me how happy they were to see me, and explained that they hadn't left the house in nearly three months. When dinner was over I returned to my house. As I lay down to sleep, I realized that it was the first time in nearly a year that I would sleep in a room by myself.

I spent the next two weeks in Peshawar. My first task was to search through the boxes and suitcases before someone came to pick them up. I wanted to see if there was anything inside I could tell Gilles about when I saw him again. I waited until nightfall, and then rummaged through each one with my flashlight. But there was nothing of interest, mostly just clothes and other personal belongings.

I spent a lot of time with the Saudis. We played badminton in the garden, and watched videos together. They had a huge supply of videos, most of them for training. There were films about kidnapping, about surveillance, about bombmaking. There were also lots of propaganda videos: GIA battles, the assassination of Anwar al-Sadat, the 1983 bombings of the U.S. Army barracks in Beirut.

Once, I asked the Pakistani boy if the Egyptian was around, the one with the prostheses. He nodded, and I asked him if he could go ask him for some more films on explosives. He ran out of the house and returned half an hour later with five training videos. Each one contained step-by-step instructions on how to fabricate high explosives.

Every day, we beheaded a couple of rabbits and ate them for dinner. I hoped that none of them had been used for testing poisons or chemicals, like the ones at Darunta. I couldn't be sure, though, because one day as I was snooping through the house I found some silvery powder on the floor in a back room. I touched it with my finger; it was aluminum power, which we had used in Darunta to make bombs. A few days later, in the garage of one of the other houses, I found some traces of ammonium nitrate. Combined with fuel oil, it becomes ANFO.

Clearly, everything, or rather almost everything, had been scrubbed clean before the police came. But prior to that, I thought, the whole Arab section of the refugee camp must have seemed like one giant weapons laboratory.

One day, the Pakistani boy came by the safe house. He told me that we all had to leave, that it was no longer safe for any of us in the refugee camp. I quickly gathered my things and went outside with him. The Saudis were there waiting, and all four of us headed towards the main road.

We took a bus to Peshawar and then another one back out. We ended up in a modest residential area of town I had never seen before. When we got off, we walked to a large house where the Pakistani boy rang the doorbell in code. The door opened and inside stood Abu Said al-Kurdi, the brother who had taken me across the border and into Darunta. He led the four of us to the back of the house, to a room that looked like an office. There was a laptop on the table, and several passports.

Abu Zubayda and Ibn Sheikh were sitting in chairs towards the back, and they rose to greet us. Then Ibn Sheikh led the others out of the room so that Abu Zubayda could speak to me alone. "Abu Imam" he said, "tomorrow you will go to Islamabad. I will give you the name of a brother at the university who will help you to get your papers in order. You need to leave the country right away. It's too dangerous for you to stay any longer. They could arrest you at any time, and with an expired visa they will throw you in jail." He paused. "They won't let you out."

Abu Zubayda handed me some money for my airline ticket, and then handed me my passport. I had not seen it in a year, since I left it with Abu Bakr my first day at Khaldan. Then he wrote three numbers on a piece of paper. "The first two are mobile phones. Once you get to Europe, you can call me on these. You can usually reach me on Fridays. Don't use the third number until you have tried both of those. That's the number of a brother at the university here in Peshawar. You can give any messages to him."

Then he wrote down the addresses of two different post boxes and also the number of a bank account. He told me that once I was settled in Europe and earning a salary, I should begin wiring money back to that account. He also wrote down a radio frequency number. He told me that it was the one they used to communicate with and between the camps. If I had powerful radio equipment, he said, I could use it to communicate from Europe.

Finally, Abu Zubayda opened his desk drawer and held out a notebook. It was mine, from Darunta. "I will send you this," he said, "as you soon as you have established yourself and can send us a secure address." Then he and I talked about where I should go. He didn't seem to have any particular place in mind. England, France, Belgium, Germany—any of these, he said, would be useful.

Abu Zubayda stood up then and opened the door. He called out to Abu Said al-Kurdi, who was talking with the Saudis. "Abu Said will take you into the city now to buy some new clothes," he said, "You need to look like a Pakistani from now on."

Abu Said took me into Peshawar, where he bought me a new Pakistani *shalwar kameez*. Then he took me to a barber for a shave. As I sat down in the chair, I looked at myself in the clouded mirror in front of me. There were no mirrors in the camps, so it was the first time in almost a year that I had a chance to study my own face. I barely recognized myself. My beard was fifteen centimeters long, and my skin was cracked and dark from the sun.

But it was the circles under my eyes that struck me the most. They were so dark that they looked almost like face paint. I realized that I had not had a solid night of sleep since Turkey. The predawn prayer, the exercises late at night, the constant stress—it was all imprinted on my face. I had seen these eyes so many times before, on Amin and Yasin, on all the brothers at the camps. I had never imagined their eyes could become my own.

When my beard was gone, Abu Said and I walked back to the house. He showed me to a room with several sleeping bags, and when I looked on the floor I saw the suitcase I had carried with me from Europe. I opened it up and everything was there: my clothes, my razor, my Ray-Bans. The only thing missing was the Swiss Army knife, the one with the cross.

The next morning, it was time for me to leave. After we made our *salat*, we all gathered at the door: Abu Said, Ibn Sheikh, and Abu Zubayda and me.

"Remember, don't speak to anyone," Ibn Sheikh reminded me. "It's not safe." I nodded and smiled. I had grown used to this command. Then he and the others saluted me and wished me a safe trip out of Pakistan. They told me they would remember me in their prayers, and I told them the same.

I leaned down and took my Ray-Bans out of my suitcase and put them on. When I stood up, Ibn Sheikh was laughing. "Look at you," he said warmly. "You already look like one of them."

I laughed, too. Then I turned, opened the door, and walked out into the early morning light.

LONDONISTAN

Cast of Characters

Gilles DGSE officer who handled Omar in Brussels

Fatima Young woman Omar meets in Paris

Daniel Officer of the British secret service

Abu Qatada Cleric at the Four Feathers Youth Club

Abu Walid Abu Qatada's second in command at Four Feathers

Khaled Young Algerian with ties to GIA; attends Four Feathers and later takes Omar to Finsbury Park mosque

Samir Young Algerian man with ties to GIA; friend of Khaled

Abu Hamza Cleric at Finsbury Park mosque

Omar Bakri Mohammad Cleric who supports Abu Hamza during debate with Abu Qatada

Ali Touchent "Tarek" from Brussels; alleged mastermind of 1995 Paris metro bombings

Alexandre DGSE officer; replaces Gilles in London

Mark British secret service officer; replaces Daniel

Penny British secret service officer

Abdul Haq Moroccan trainee from Khaldan

Timeline

November 4, 1995: Rachid Ramda arrested in London in connection to the July 1995 Paris metro bombings.

November 1996: Statement by GIA emir Antar Zouabri circulates announcing the imposition of *sharia* law in Algeria.

November 1996: Ali Touchent reportedly sited in London.

Fall 1996: Abu Hamza begins preaching at Finsbury Park Mosque; Abu Qatada denounces the GIA

December 3, 1996: Bomb explodes in a RER train under the Port-Royal station in Paris, killing 4 people and injuring nearly 180.

March 1997: Abu Hamza takes over the Finsbury Park Mosque.

August 29, 1997: GIA massacre hundreds in Algerian village of Sidi Moussa.

October 1997: Abu Hamza denounces the GIA.

November 23, 1997: Trial of 39 Islamic militants suspected of connections to the 1995 Paris metro bombings begins in Paris.

February 13, 1998: Algerian government authorities announce that Ali Touchent was killed in Algeria in May 1997.

February 18, 1998: Paris court convicts 36 people in connection with 1995 Paris metro bombings; Ali Touchent is sentenced in absentia to ten years in prison.

February 23, 1998: Osama bin Laden and Ayman al-Zawahiri issue a *fatwa* advocating *jihad* against U.S. military and civilian targets around in the world.

March 5, 1998: Farid Melouk arrested in Brussels after shoot out with Belgian police

May 26, 1998: Police in France, Belgium, Germany, Italy and Switzerland seize scores of suspected GIA militants in a series of raids.

August 7, 1998: Attacks on American embassies in Nairobi, Kenya and Dar es Salaam, Tanzania, kill 271 people and wound thousands more.

Galata Bridge

It was a beautiful spring evening and I was drinking wine on the Galata Bridge in Istanbul overlooking the Golden Horn. Tourists were bustling about. There were sailboats in the Bosphorus, and fishermen above me on the top level of the bridge. Their lines caught the sun as they were cast out into the water.

A week had passed since I had left Ibn Sheikh and Abu Zubayda in Peshawar. It was one of the most perilous weeks of my life. The road to Islamabad and the city itself were infested with police and spies searching out Arabs for arrest. I came very close to getting arrested myself when I made the mistake of letting a hotel clerk see my passport with the expired visa. But with a great deal of anxiety as well as help from a very naïve official at the Moroccan embassy, I was able to obtain the necessary paperwork.

I was so desperate by that point to get out of Pakistan that I took an absurdly long flight from Islamabad to Istanbul via Abu Dhabi and Cairo. I didn't mind at all; I found the stillness inside the plane incredibly relaxing after a year of constant stress. I think I scared the flight attendant on the first leg of the trip because after I ate my in-flight meal I ordered four more, one after the other. To me, they tasted absolutely delicious.

I called Gilles as soon as I landed in Istanbul. Or at least I tried to—the phone number I had always used had been cut off. I wasn't surprised.

I had only a few dollars in my pocket. I had spent all the money Gilles had given me at the camps. I had given it to Ibn Sheikh to buy food and supplies and weapons. So I went to the hotel where I had stayed before. I thought they might recognize me, and I was right. I explained to the man at the desk that I needed to go to the bank to get some money before I could pay, and he let me go straight up to the room.

Then I went to the French consulate. I did everything exactly as I had the last time I was in Istanbul and needed to get hold of Gilles. I explained to the guard at the door that I was a French citizen and had lost my passport. I went to the very same room I had gone to before, and immediately spotted the very same man. He looked extremely surprised to see me. He ushered me over to the corner of the room and in a low voice asked for a phone number where I could be reached.

Two hours later, Gilles called me at my hotel. "How are you?" he asked. "How was your trip?" His words were friendly but his voice was filled with disbelief.

"I'm fine, thank you. The trip was great. A bit long, though." I spoke as if I had been away on holiday for a couple of weeks. "I've run out of money."

"You don't have any more money?"

"Only about ten dollars," I told him.

"I can take care of that," Gilles said. "Let me call you back in half an hour."

When Gilles came back on the line he told me that cash was on the way. He also said that he had some pressing business to attend to and that he would come to Istanbul in three days' time.

"You should get some sleep between now and then," he said. "Relax."

An hour later, reception rang up to tell me there was a package waiting for me. I went downstairs and the attendant handed me an envelope. There were hundreds of dollars inside.

And so that evening I found myself relaxing on the Galata Bridge at sunset, eating a delicious dinner of lamb and fish and drinking Turkish wine. I felt like I was on top of the world. No one had believed in me; no one thought I had anything to offer. The DGSE had been ready to throw me in jail and wash their hands of me. Then they tried to pay me off to disappear. But now here I was, just back from the Afghan training camps with vast stores of information. They wouldn't try to get rid of me this time. Now they needed me.

I slept straight through for sixteen hours that night, and when I woke up I went to a *hamam*. I told the man near the door that I would pay twice the normal amount if I could get a really thorough bath. He gestured to one of the attendants, who guided me to the dressing room. I took off my clothes and walked into the hot room. It was heavy with steam.

As the attendant began to scrub down my skin with a rough sponge, I realized that I should have paid him ten times the going rate. It was the first real bath I had taken since I arrived in Pakistan. Of course, we had washed in the river at Khaldan and the lake in Darunta, but I was never remotely clean the entire time I was in the camps.

It took the attendant more than an hour to scrub my whole body. I stared at the water as it washed down the drain—It was thick and black.

I was exhausted when I emerged from the *hamam,* and I went back to the hotel and slept for several more hours. Then I walked through the city and found a restaurant overlooking the Ataköy marina.

As I ordered my first bottle of wine and lit a cigarette, I reflected on how easy it had been to leave behind my role as a *mujahid*—nearly as easy as it had been to enter it. I had begun smoking again during my last days in Pakistan to prove that I wasn't an Arab extremist. But of course I *wasn't* an Arab extremist. I was a European.

Here in Istanbul, I was quickly settling back into the rhythms of life in the West. The wine, the food, the clean sheets. I had been watching television from the moment I arrived: CNN, BBC, whatever I could find. I realized how starved for news I had been at the camps. There we heard only snippets over the radio, and on the rare occasions when we got a newspaper it was already weeks old. In the camps, we had marked time with only the passage of the sun across the sky and the slow turning of the seasons. We were in a world of our own.

At first, I imagined it as a switch, the thing I turned on and off inside of me when I needed to enter a role. Every spy needs this switch, this ability to shut down whole parts of himself for months if not years at a time. I had flipped this switch at the airport in Islamabad a year earlier.

It was both easier and harder to flip the switch back. Easier, because I loved my life and my freedom in the West. And as much as I hated myself for it, I loved the luxuries as well, all of the material things I had renounced as a *mujahid.*

But this transition was harder, too, because I had changed while I was away. I had learned something essential about myself. I had learned that at my core I was a Muslim. Of course, I had known this all along. I had always believed in God. And since my earliest years at the Catholic school outside of Brussels, I had realized that as a Muslim I was something different, something special. But that feeling only went so far.

In Belgium, I had mocked Hakim and the rest for their pieties and pretensions. Now I wasn't so sure. In the camps I had met men from so many different nations and classes and ethnic groups who all held one thing in common: they were all driven by the same hot fire of love for Islam and for her lands. This fire drove me, too. At times, it had nearly engulfed me.

I was educated in the West, and I went to Afghanistan as a spy. I was there to fight against these terrorists, these men who slaughtered women and children in the killing fields of Algeria. If the fire burned in me despite all of this, then how must it scorch the hearts of young Muslims everywhere?

I knew that I would never be able to go as far as some of the men I had met in Afghanistan. Certainly, I would never go as far as those men at Sarowbi, who had tortured and killed a fellow Muslim even after he had surrendered. It was the excesses that turned me off in the end—the huge gap between the theology we learned and the battles fought on the ground.

But still I understood these men, even as I distanced myself from their methods. I understood their rage and their anguish as more and more of their land was stolen from them. Jerusalem, Afghanistan, Bosnia, Algeria, Chechnya—it was all the same to them. These were just the latest manifestations of a war that had been going on for centuries, a perpetual war against Islam. The *mujahidin* were not born killers. They were born Muslims, and as Muslims it was their responsibility to defend their land.

On the third day, the last one before Gilles came, I walked around Sultanahmet, the old city of Istanbul. The old city is one of the most beautiful places on earth: the cobbled streets, the glorious Topkapi Palace, and most of all the Hagia Sophia and the Blue Mosque facing each other across the rich, green park. During my first trip to Istanbul, I was racing to begin my mission and I didn't see anything of the city. But now I was between assignments, and I had plenty of time.

I wandered in to the Hagia Sophia in the late afternoon, and the sheer size of it awed me. But as the interior came into focus, I noticed the beauty of the architecture: the glorious dome above hovered almost weightless above arched windows. Golden light spilled everywhere.

It was the most beautiful mosque I had ever seen. But it was a church, too, and that is what struck me most. The rich mosaics of Jesus and Mary and Saint John of Chrysostom; they were all still there. They shouldn't have been: The representation of any human form is considered blasphemous by Muslims. And so when the Ottomans took Constantinople and transformed the church into a mosque, they plastered over the mosaics. But from time to time, over the course of the centuries, Ottoman architects removed the plaster, cleaned and restored the mosaics, and then covered them up again. The Ottomans could have destroyed these images, but they didn't. They chose to keep them alive.

Reunion

I waited for Gilles at noon outside the train station in Eminönü, as he had told me to do. A few minutes later, I spotted him at a distance. As usual, he was smoking a cigarette.

He began to walk and I followed him, just as I had done so many times before. He led me first along the Golden Horn and then up the hill through alleys crowded with vendors. We walked through narrow passageways and empty streets and bazaars thick with the smells of spices. A half hour passed, and then another. Of course, I was being followed. The DGSE had no reason to trust me anymore; I had just come back from Afghanistan, and they must have wondered whose side I was on.

Eventually, we wound our way up into the old city. We had walked for nearly two hours when Gilles finally stopped on a cobbled street behind the Hagia Sophia. I walked up beside him.

"Do you think someone is following you?" he asked. He was smiling, and his eyebrow was arched.

I laughed. "No, of course not!"

"You're sure?"

"Absolutely."

Then we both laughed and shook hands and began to walk side by side.

Gilles and I walked for hours that afternoon, through the old city and through Gülhane Park to the water and then back up again. I told him the story of my journey, beginning the morning after I left him in the Dolmabahçe gardens: the man I met on the plane, my stay with the Tabligh, my meeting with Abu Anas, and then Peshawar and Khaldan and Ibn Sheikh and Abdul Kerim and Sarowbi and Darunta and the mustard gas and the Egyptian embassy and Abu Zubayda and the phone numbers and all the steps I had gone through to get back here to Europe.

Mostly, I spoke. Gilles showed no reaction to anything I told him, and he said almost nothing. He did, however, ask me three times to walk more slowly. I had been training in the mountains of Afghanistan, and he could barely keep up.

Eventually, we sat down at a café. "You don't need to tell me anything more for the time being," he said. "In two days, we'll meet with a friend of mine and he will ask you more questions."

He handed me a thick envelope filled with cash. We talked for a few more minutes and then he stood up to go. "Bring your passport with you next time," he told me. Then he disappeared into the crowded street.

Two days later, I met Gilles at the reception desk of a fancy hotel on the other side of the Golden Horn, in Taksim. I gave him my passport. As we rode up together in the lift, he spoke to me. "My friend is going to ask you some questions about how you got into Pakistan, about who you met and what you did while you were in Afghanistan and so on. Please, don't be offended by any of his questions, or the way he asks them. Just answer them clearly and honestly, as I know you will." He smiled weakly.

Gilles then led me into a suite with a large table in the center. A few minutes later a bald, middle-aged man arrived. He carried a leather suitcase and wore a beige trench coat, the kind agents wear in third-rate spy films. He grunted at us both to say hello, and then threw his coat on the bed and sat down.

"Can I have your passport?" These were the first words he spoke. Gilles handed it to him. I was beginning to understand Gilles's warning in the elevator.

"I want you to tell me everything that happened—from the minute you landed in Pakistan until you got off the plane in Istanbul."

I repeated the story I had told Gilles two days earlier, but the man asked me all sorts of questions along the way. Not interesting questions about what I had seen or who I had met or what I had learned in the camps, just questions to confirm my story. How long did the drive to Khaldan take from the border? What did the refugee camp in Peshawar look like? How old was Abu Zubayda?

I could tell from the man's questions that he knew a lot about Pakistan and that he had spent time there. But I could also tell that he was trying to trip me up. Throughout the interview, he scattered all sorts of ridiculous questions. So Abu Zubayda is the emir of Darunta? So you crossed into Afghanistan from Karachi? So Khaldan is near Islamabad?

Finally, I had enough. "What the fuck is this?" I demanded. I was there to talk about incredibly serious things, about poisons and bombs and sleeper cells. But they didn't want to hear about any of it. They thought I had made the whole thing up.

"This is a waste of everybody's time," I barked. "Why are you trying to make me say things that we both know aren't true?"

Gilles quickly stood up.

"I think we've had enough for today," he said.

The bald man looked surprised at first, but then he packed up his things, put on his overcoat, and left. Once the door closed behind him, Gilles turned to me with a sheepish smile. "I warned you that it might be annoying."

The interrogation went better the following day. The bald man was more polite, and didn't ask me any more trick questions. When we were done, Gilles and I went on a walk together through the city. He seemed worried. "How are you going to do it?" he asked at one point.

"Do what?"

"Do what Abu Zubayda and Ibn Sheikh told you to do. Establish yourself. Form a cell."

I was surprised by the question, though I suppose I shouldn't have been.

"With your help, I assume," I said firmly.

"Oh, but that's not what they would expect." Gilles explained that normally a sleeper would have to get a fake passport somehow, or obtain one somewhere like Bulgaria or Romania.

I saw where the conversation was headed and I stopped it in its tracks. "I'm not going to do it that way," I said, staring straight at him. "I risked my life a hundred times over in Afghanistan. Why would I take another risk with you? What if something goes wrong? What if I get arrested? There I am with my Bulgarian passport and you can pretend you've never heard of me."

Gilles said nothing. He could hardly deny it; he had tried to send me to jail once already.

"When I signed on for this," I continued, "you asked me what I wanted in exchange for my work. I told you that I wanted the DGSE to take care of me. I think it's time for you to do that now."

Gilles looked very awkward standing there. Clearly, he hadn't planned for this. It was nearly a minute before he spoke.

"I need to go back to Paris," he said. "I'll be back in two weeks." Then he gave me a new phone number and said I could call it and leave a message if I wanted to speak to him.

When Gilles came back, he told me that I had to go to Dakar to get a French passport. He didn't explain why. He explained apologetically that I couldn't fly to Dakar via Europe, because I didn't have a transit visa. Then he handed me an envelope.

"There are five thousand dollars in here," he said. "Go find a travel agent and find a way to get to Senegal without going through Europe. Call me when you've got it, and we'll meet up again."

I ended up buying a ridiculous ticket; it turned out that it was nearly impossible to get to Dakar without going through Europe. Instead, I had to fly via Dubai, Nairobi, and Abidjan. All told, it would take more than four days.

I met with Gilles again the next day at a café by the Bosphorus. He told me he had arranged for me to meet with a friend of his in Dakar. I would give him my Moroccan passport, and he would give me a new French passport in exchange. Gilles and I would meet again in Paris.

With the arrangements all in place, Gilles and I were both able to relax. We left the camps behind and talked about Istanbul and the tourists and the food and the architecture instead.

But as we finished our lunch, he looked up at me with a serious expression on his face. "You know," he began, "no one believed you would come back. I told them you would. I told them that I would cut off my right hand if you disappeared—I was that sure of you. But for the last few months, every time I walked into the office someone would make fun of me. 'Why do you still have your right hand?' they would ask."

Gilles laughed just slightly as he told the story. Then his expression turned serious again, and he moved his face in closer to mine. "Thank you for coming back."

Paris

I spent a month in Senegal waiting for my passport. Finally, a man showed up at my hotel and introduced himself as a friend of Gilles's. He gave me a stack of dollars and francs and a new passport. When I opened it up to look inside, I saw it was in the name of Abu Imam al-Mughrabi. It was the Moroccan name I had used in the camps. It annoyed me. I knew exactly what the DGSE was up to. They knew very well that it would be nearly impossible for me to fly anywhere on my own with a passport in this name, and that was just what they wanted. They wanted to keep me under their control.

I met Gilles when I landed at Charles de Gaulle. He took me to the same hotel where I had stayed after I left Belgium. We walked up to a room without stopping at reception, and Gilles let us in. As soon as we were inside, I took out the passport and handed it to him. "The name is clever," I said. "But you'll have to get me a new one."

Gilles grimaced slightly and took the passport. "That was a joke," he said.

It was a lame excuse. The DGSE wasn't exactly known for its sense of humor. But I bit my tongue.

Gilles then told me that I would stay in Paris for a few weeks while they fixed the arrangements for my next mission. He told me to relax and enjoy the city.

"You should buy yourself a raincoat," he said to me as he was about to leave.

"Why?" I asked. It was the middle of summer.

"It rains a lot where you're going." And then he was off.

During the weeks that followed, Gilles came by my room at the hotel many times. He asked me lots of questions about Afghanistan. We talked about the training. He was particularly interested in the explosives. I told him how we learned to make many high explosives out of simple items and that we were taught how to blow up cars, trains, buildings, and airplanes. I told him about the experiments with mustard gas and cyanide.

But Gilles focused on the Europeans in the camp. I told him about the Moroccan who lived in London, the one who got to use the GPS instead of me. And of course I told him about Abdul Kerim. Gilles was most interested in him, and asked me all sorts of questions. I told him what Abdul Kerim looked like, and that he had been sent to the camps by the GIA. I told him that he had trained with me in explosives and that he was planning to leave the camps soon.

"Do you think he'll come back to France?" Gilles asked.

"I doubt it," I said. "He told me that the police had been giving him trouble here."

"Is he going to stay in Europe, or go somewhere else?"

"He'll stay in Europe," I told him. "He has a daughter here. He might go to Belgium. I know he has contacts there."

Gilles came back to the subject of Abdul Kerim many times.

I spent most of my time in Paris enjoying the city. I had been in Paris before, but this was the first time I was there with money. I went up the Eiffel Tower and saw all the different museums and spent my evenings eating in expensive restaurants and drinking in chic bars. There were beautiful girls everywhere. After a year spent only with men, I savored each one.

And then one afternoon, I met my wife. Of course she wasn't my wife then, but as soon as I saw her I knew she would be. She was standing in the hotel lobby with four friends. All five of them were beautiful, but my eyes latched on to just one. She was quieter than the others, and smaller. She had long black hair and fair skin. I recognized her immediately: she was the girl I had seen in my vision on the mountain in Khaldan, when I begged God for a wife and a family.

I walked over to the girls and flirted with them. After I told them I was in Paris on my own, it didn't take long for them to ask me to join them for dinner. That night, we all went out to a restaurant on the banks of the Seine. The girls were all witty and charming—or at least I think they were. I can't remember, really. I was completely focused on one, Fatima, all evening. She was so shy; she barely looked at me. But at one point, she offered me a shrimp from her plate and our eyes connected, and I knew she felt the same way I did.

After dinner, I asked her to take a walk with me. We spent hours walking through the city in the warm summer air. She told me about her life as an Arab growing up in Germany, and I told her about mine. At one point, she asked me what I did for a living. I stopped walking and held her wrist to stop her, too.

"I can't tell you everything," I said. "All I can tell you is that there are people in the world who want to do very bad things. I want to stop them."

As she looked up at me, I could tell she was confused. But she didn't ask any more questions, and we continued walking. I wanted desperately to convince Fatima to spend the night with me. I tried to kiss her again and again, but she kept brushing me away. But she didn't go home, either. Finally, as the sun began to rise over the city, she let me kiss her once.

"Marry me," I said as I pulled away.

She smiled. She didn't say yes, but she didn't say no, either.

That afternoon, Fatima came by my room to say goodbye. Her holiday was over and she was going back to Germany. She handed me a piece of paper with a phone number on it and told me that it belonged to one of her friends. She said she didn't know me well enough to give me her own number. We kissed once more, and then she was gone.

I didn't have much time to think about Fatima, because early the next morning Gilles came by the hotel. He gave me a passport and a French identity card under the name Pablo Rodriguez. It would be much easier for me to travel with a Spanish name than an Arab one, he explained. I spoke Spanish well—I had learned it when I was guiding tourists in Morocco. He told me that I would be leaving the next morning for London.

It surprised me. I had always assumed that I would be working somewhere on the continent. England meant nothing to me. When I thought about what lay to the north of France, I pictured only water. And what I did know about London I didn't like. I imagined grime and fog and Jack the Ripper.

"Why London?" I asked.

"There are a lot of interesting people in London," he said. "We'd like to learn more about them." Then I caught his meaning: I had been reading in the papers about the crackdown on the GIA in France in the wake of the Paris bombings. Many of them had moved to England.

"Are you afraid?" Gilles asked.

"Of course not," I said. And yet it did cross my mind to wonder who I might find in London. I knew that Hakim, Amin, and Yasin had all been put in jail. But who had they spoken to? And when would they get out?

London

I left Paris the next day with Gilles. We pretended not to know each other. We took the bus to Calais, where we went through customs. It was the first time I had traveled on a European passport and I was amazed: the official let me pass through with little more than a glance. I thought of the humiliations I had endured crossing borders on my Moroccan passport. How long are you staying? Where? Can I see your return ticket? Your money? It was as if I had become a totally different person just because I carried a European passport.

We traveled by Eurostar to Dover, and then took a bus into London. Gilles sat next to me the whole time. When we got off the bus at Victoria Station, Gilles gave me the room confirmation for a hotel in West Kensington. He told me that I would be staying there for a while. He said that I should call him the following morning to make arrangements for our next meeting. Then he disappeared into the crowd.

I realized then that Gilles had traveled with me the whole way from Paris just to make sure I didn't disappear. I was, after all, a trained terrorist, and he had to keep his eye on me. Now that I was in London, there were surely plenty of eyes in the British secret services to watch every move I made.

I went to the hotel and the woman at reception showed me to my room. I left my things on the bed and went out to explore the city.

London was nothing like what I had imagined. It was far cleaner than Paris—not grimy at all, as I had expected. I took a tour on a double-decker bus and fell in love instantly with the Victorian architecture. There were no skyscrapers in that part of the city, so everything was in the right proportion to everything else.

What amazed me most, though, was the police. When I got off the bus I couldn't figure out where I was. I was studying my map and when I looked up I saw a policeman approaching. My body tensed instinctively, but then the policeman asked if he could help me find my way. After years of trying to escape from the police in Morocco, and then just recently in Pakistan, this kindness stunned me.

Gilles and I met the next day in a very fancy hotel near Green Park. He greeted me at the reception desk. The British services had been following me since I arrived in London—I was sure of that—so there was no point in playing our usual game of cat and mouse.

Gilles guided me into a conference room. He told me not to go to mosques or seek out contacts just yet. I should use the next two weeks to get to know the city. He said that I should start looking for a flat as well. I asked him how to do that and he told me I had to figure it out by myself, the same way any immigrant would. He explained that it was important for me to start building my cover. He told me to call in a week to check in with him.

During that meeting, I asked Gilles for only one thing: audiotapes of the Ku'ran. I could feel myself slipping away from its language and its rhythms already. I was no longer going to mosque or speaking to anyone who knew the language of the Ku'ran the way the brothers at the camps did. But I knew that I would have to have it on the tip of my tongue if I was going to convince the Muslim brothers in London that I was for real.

I took Gilles at his word. I spent the next two weeks getting to know London. During the day I walked around the city or went to the museums, and in the evenings I went out to bars or the cinemas near Leicester Square. I loved the energy of London and the bright lights and the people of so many different colors.

I called Gilles after the first week, and when he called back he told me to go to the station the next day and take a train to Stansted airport. He gave me the name of a hotel nearby and told me to meet him there at the reception desk.

It took about an hour to get to Stansted. As I walked towards our meeting point, I looked up and saw someone standing behind a plate-glass window. He was pointing a camera at me.

I waited for Gilles in the reception area. As I was sitting there, I saw a man with a huge camera around his neck walking just outside the window. I was astounded by the lack of subtlety.

It only got worse when Gilles arrived and took me uptairs. I could barely keep from laughing when I walked into the room: it was covered entirely with mirrors. But I said nothing. Gilles opened his suitcase and took a box out from inside.

"Thank you for coming out here," he said with a smile on his face. "I wanted to bring you these." He handed me the box and I looked inside. It was the tapes of the Ku'ran I had asked for.

Then Gilles furrowed his brow. "I'm so sorry," he said. "I've forgotten something. I'll be back in a minute."

He walked out of the room, and I looked around. The first thing I saw was Gilles's wallet. It was lying open at the top of his suitcase. It was so stuffed with currency that several fifty-pound notes were peeking out from the top.

I was furious. Did the British really believe I was stupid enough to steal from Gilles? I knew Gilles would never have come up with such a ridiculous plan, but I was annoyed with him, too, for going along with it.

I smiled at the mirror on each of the walls and then walked into the bathroom. I sat down on the toilet and took a shit, leaving the door open to make sure they caught it on camera.

When Gilles came back to the room, he didn't even pretend that there was any other purpose to our meeting. It was awkward, so I decided to break the silence.

"Thanks so much for the tapes," I said. "But you know, I'll need a stereo to listen to them."

Then I gave Gilles my biggest grin. "I'm sure you can get me one," I said with honey in my voice. "I mean, it's not like you don't have the money."

Daniel

The following week, I met up with Gilles in another hotel near Green Park. When we got to the room, he told me that a British friend of his would be joining us. A few minutes later, a tall man in his thirties burst into the room. He threw his briefcase on the couch and then stuck his hand out towards me.

"My name is Daniel. I'm with the British intelligence services. I'll be handling you while you're in England." We shook hands, and he sat down at the table.

I immediately disliked Daniel. I disliked the way he threw his briefcase, I disliked the way he spoke, I disliked the way he told me he'd be "handling" me as if I were a circus animal. I looked at Gilles and he gave me a sympathetic smile. Then we both sat down.

"So, you say you were in Afghanistan?" There was no mistaking the sneer on his face. And then it made sense: he had been watching me for two weeks already, or at least he'd been hearing from people who had. He knew I had been out dancing and smoking and drinking. He had imagined someone else when he was told to work with me, and now he was disappointed.

"Why do you think I'm here?" I answered.

"All right," he said, fixing me with his gaze. "Now I'm going to ask you some questions."

I was angry at this point, and I opened my mouth to say something.

"No," Daniel said, interrupting me before I could speak. "I'm going to ask *you* questions. You don't get to ask me any."

I looked over at Gilles. He was staring down at his fingernails. "You know what?" I said to Daniel. "I don't feel well. Actually, I feel quite sick. I need to see a doctor." I wasn't going to let this bastard control the conversation.

He looked surprised, confused. "How do I find a doctor in London?" I asked.

"You can go to any GP, I suppose," he stammered.

"But I'm not a British citizen."

"Well, I think you just have to give your address, you know, prove you're a resident."

"But I don't have an apartment yet." I said. "You'll have to help me. Do you have a doctor? Can you show me where your doctor is?"

Daniel looked completely flustered by now. He tried to give me directions at first: a right, then a left, past a light, and so on. But I pretended to be confused and he gave up and began to draw a map for me. As he focused on the map, I glanced up at Gilles. He was still staring down at his fingernails, but I could see that he was smiling.

I walked out of that meeting as soon as Daniel finished the map. The next meeting, a week later, didn't go much better. Gilles and I met at a new hotel in the same area. When Daniel came in, he put his briefcase on the floor rather than throwing it. But apart from that, his attitude hadn't changed.

He sat down and put on a pair of glasses. "I want you to tell me everywhere you've been and everything you've done since I saw you a week ago."

His arrogance set me off. "What do you mean by 'everything'?" I asked sarcastically. "Do you want me to tell you everything I've eaten? Every restaurant I've been to? Every girl I've kissed? Or if they're boys? How much time I spent in the disco and the cinema and the bar? You want to know *everything*?"

Daniel leaned back and nodded. "Yes, that's exactly what I want to know."

"Well I'm not going to tell you. If these are the terms, then I'm not going to work for you. You don't own me."

There was a long silence after that. Gilles still said nothing; I could tell he felt awkward, too. He wasn't running the show, as he was used to. He was in England now, and he had to put up with this prick just as I did.

Daniel's tone was calmer when he replied. "We need to know these things for the sake of your security."

That did it. "Bullshit!" I exploded. "Were you looking out for my security when I was in Afghanistan defusing detonators and landmines? Were you looking out for my security at every checkpoint in Pakistan, where the police were arresting every goddamned Arab they could find? Where were you then?"

Daniel's eyes were wide open now, and his mouth was closed.

"Don't give me this bullshit about security," I fumed. "I'll take care of my own security. And I'll keep my private life to myself."

Daniel was only slightly less obnoxious the third time we met. I came to the meeting annoyed because I had been looking for a flat for three weeks and still hadn't found anything. I asked Gilles and Daniel to help me but they said they couldn't. It was important for me to find it on my own, just like anyone else would. I had to establish my cover.

Then Daniel reached into his briefcase and pulled out an envelope filled with photographs and dumped them on the table. He spread them out and asked me to show him who I recognized. I looked down, and there they were: my mother, Hakim, Amin, Yasin, Tarek. It had been a year and a half since I left Belgium, and here I was still looking at the same photographs.

As I pointed to the people I recognized, I glanced up at Gilles. He was staring intently at the table. I could tell from the vein throbbing in his forehead that he was angry. I realized that this exercise was frustrating for him, too. The

British services didn't trust the French; they were still testing me to see if I was who I claimed to be. It was insulting to both of us.

After he put the photos away, Daniel began to tell me what the British services wanted from me. "There are some people we want you to learn more about," he said. "Islamic radicals. We want you to find them in the mosques and the prayer rooms here in London."

It was what I expected. "OK," I replied. "Why don't you give me a list of your mosques and I'll start there."

Daniel shook his head. "No, I can't do that. You have to find them for yourself. You can't just show up like a tourist."

"But how am I supposed to know where to look?" I asked. "I've only been here for a month."

"That's just the point. You need to learn for yourself. You need to start spending time with other Arabs." Daniel didn't say it, but his face told me exactly what the next sentence would have been: "And stop spending time with girls in cafés."

Then Daniel gave me a phone number. "You can use this number to reach both me and Gilles. This is the only number you should call while you're here in England."

I looked over at Gilles. "What about your number?"

Gilles was quiet for several seconds. He looked very unhappy. When he finally spoke I could tell he was choosing his words carefully. "You can use my number if you have any personal questions for me," he said. "But for anything related to your job here, you'll need to call Daniel."

Abu Qatada

The next Friday, I went to the mosque in Regent's Park for the al-Jum'a prayers. Inside, there were all sorts of display cases outlining the history of the mosque. Churchill's War Cabinet had purchased the site in 1940 to thank Indian Muslims who had died defending the British Empire. It was quite clear to me that this was not the place to find Muslim extremists.

The mosque was enormous. Inside, the floors were covered with rich-colored carpets, and there was a huge chandelier hanging from the ceiling. I sat down as worshippers streamed into the hall, and then listened to the *imam* speak about the importance of being honest and helpful. It was hardly a radical sermon.

At the end of the lecture, the *imam* reminded us of the third pillar of Islam, the *zakat*. The obligatory alms-giving. He enjoined us to give generously to the poor on the way out. In every mosque in every country of the world, the *imam* will speak about the *zakat*. But a radical *imam* won't talk about giving to the poor. He will tell his audience to give money for the *mujahidin* on the front, and for the widows and orphans they leave behind.

After the lecture was done, I made my *salat* and walked towards the door. There was a *zakat* collector standing there behind a table with all sorts of official newsletters. I walked right by him and out to the front of the mosque. I knew what I was looking for. At every mosque in Europe, after Friday prayers there will be men waiting outside to sell political publications for one group or another. I immediately spotted the man selling *Al Ansar* and put twenty pounds in his donation box. I could tell I had caught his attention, but he didn't say anything.

I read the paper in front of the mosque. The GIA stamp wasn't the one Tarek had used in Brussels, but otherwise *Al Ansar* was more or less the same. There were celebratory accounts of attacks on villages, military convoys, and police stations, along with tallies of the number of soldiers the GIA had killed and the quantity of weapons and munitions they had captured. Towards the back of the paper there were reports on the struggles in Palestine, Chechnya, and Kashmir. But to me, the most interesting part came on the very last page. It was an invitation to attend a conference that coming Sunday. A sheikh named named Abu Qatada would be speaking.

If *Al Ansar* supported this sheikh, I knew he must have connections to the GIA. Abu Qatada would be my point of entry.

I met with Gilles and Daniel later that afternoon; we always met on Friday. When I showed them the copy of *Al Ansar*, they both looked pleased.

"I'm going to go," I told them. "I think it will be a good way for me to start making contacts."

"Yes, you should go," Daniel said. "But keep a low profile. I want people to see you there, but don't talk to anyone yet."

The conference was held in a school gymnasium. When I walked in, there were already about fifty men seated on chairs facing the podium at the front. Almost all of them were cleanly shaven and dressed in Western clothes. The conference had already begun, and there were three men at the front of the room speaking to each other in Arabic.

I had never seen a picture of Abu Qatada before, but I recognized him immediately. He had a kind of aura; it was clear that he was in charge of the conversation. He was in his thirties, but he already had a large belly. He was dressed like an Afghan, although I could tell he wasn't one. The clothes were a political statement—he was demonstrating his allegiance to the land of *jihad*.

As I listened to Abu Qatada speak, it became clear that he was very intelligent, very learned. I couldn't make out everything in Arabic, but he was leading the conversation about the veracity of certain *hadith*. The two other men would contribute now and then, and some members of the audience asked questions as well. I could tell from their accents that they were Moroccan and Algerian mostly, though there were a few Pakistanis also. The discussion was strictly scholarly—the only thing that made the conference subversive was the fact that it had been advertised in *Al Ansar*.

Once the conference ended, Abu Qatada stood up and quoted Hadith Qudsi 11. "'On the authority of Abu Harayrah (may Allah be pleased with him) from the Prophet (peace be upon him), who said: Allah (mighty and sublime be He) said: Spend (on charity), O son of Adam, and I shall spend on you.' 'Please give as much as you can to the *mujahidin*," Abu Qatada then concluded, "and to their families, and to the widows and the orphans they have left behind."

I put fifty pounds in the charity box on my way out, and took a copy of the newsletter from a table by the door. Inside, there was an invitation to a discussion with Abu Qatada and three other clerics on the subject of *jihad*. It would be held that Thursday evening, at a place called the Four Feathers Youth Center.

Four Feathers

A few days later, I finally found a flat. It had taken me weeks. I looked at the listings in the papers every Sunday, but by the time I called they were always gone. Eventually, I found a listing on a bulletin board outside a tube station, which is how I ended up living in a tiny flat in Kensal Green, in a house owned by a Portuguese taxi driver.

That Friday, I took the Bakerloo line from Kensal Green to Marylebone. I followed the directions on the page in the newsletter and walked towards Regent's Park. I spotted a man just ahead of me who was wearing Afghani clothes. I caught up with him and showed him the paper. "*Assalamu'alaykum*, brother," I said. "Can you tell me how to find this address?"

"*Alaykum assalam*, brother. I'm going there, too." He spoke English with a very heavy Afghan accent.

He led me to a large brick building on Rossmore Road and we went inside. There were at least 150 men sitting on prayer mats on the floor of a basketball court. The Afghani pointed me to a staircase and I went downstairs to make my ablutions. When I came back up, I joined the other men the gym .

I studied the faces around me. Most were North African. I saw a few Indians and Pakistanis also, and a handful of blacks. Most of the men wore street clothes, but I also saw a few men in *djellaba* as well as some in the Afghan *shalwar kameez*. But many of the men in the *shalwar kameez* were from the Middle East or North Africa, not from Afghanistan.

There were three men at a podium at the front of the room, and there was a video camera set up in front of them. One of the men was Abu Qatada, and another was one of the clerics who had been with him at the conference earlier in the week. I didn't recognize the third man.

Abu Qatada signaled to the audience and everyone sat quiet and still. "*Salamu'alaykum wa-rahmatu liahi wa-barakatuhu. Bismi'allahi'al-rahmani'l-rahim, wa-sallatu wa-salamu ala rasuli Allahi sayedna Muhammad sala Allahu'alihi wa-salam.*"

Abu Qatada's voice was rich and deep as he uttered the prayer. All praise and thanks are due to Allah and peace and blessings be upon his messenger.

Then Abu Qatada began to speak about the obligations of *jihad*. He said that if even one woman were taken hostage by the infidels, it was the responsibility of every Muslim around the world to bring her back. Then he went on to list the different levels of *jihad*: the *jihad* of the heart, the *jihad* of the tongue, the *jihad* of knowledge, the *jihad* of the hand, the *jihad* of the sword. He made it clear that the armed *jihad* was the most noble form of all.

I was struck by the language Abu Qatada used. It was almost identical to the language I had heard at the camps. For just a moment, my mind flashed back to the mosque at Khaldan. By the time I refocused, Abu Qatada had moved on to the familiar distinction between the defensive or obligatory *jihad* and the offensive *jihad*.

Then Abu Qatada began to talk about Algeria, I noticed that the audience, which had been silent up until this point, began to rustle. Some of the men were whispering to each other. When Abu Qatada opened the discussion for questions, several men raised their hands. They asked very direct questions. Is the *jihad* in Algeria an obligatory *jihad*? Are the Muslims who don't stand with the GIA really Muslims at all?

Abu Qatada answered most of the questions himself, but on occasion he would give the floor to the man next to him, the one who had been at the earlier conference. Abu Qatada referred to him as Abu Walid. Unlike Abu Qatada, Abu Walid was very thin. He was slightly younger than Abu Qatada, and had a strong Arab face.

I listened carefully to his voice when he answered questions. All of a sudden, it hit me: Abu Walid had been in the camps. Even as the audience around him became more agitated, his voice remained quiet, serene. Then I studied Abu Qatada again to see if I had missed this in my first impression of him, but I hadn't. His mannerisms were different. His voice had more inflection, and his face was too soft. Abu Qatada had never been a *mujahid*.

I met with Gilles and Daniel the next day, and told them about the two meetings at which I had seen Abu Qatada. I told them that there were extremists at the Four Feathers Youth Center, and that Abu Walid had been trained in the camps. I told them that most of the conversation the day before had been about the GIA.

Both Daniel and Gilles seemed pleased with my work. Daniel repeated what he had said during our previous meeting, that I should lie low for the time being.

But Daniel asked me only one question about the meeting: "Did he say anything about attacking England?"

Money

I went back to Four Feathers the next day for *al-Jum'a*, and again every Friday after that. There were lectures and debates on other evenings during the week, and often I would attend those as well. Abu Qatada always gave very learned expositions. He talked about theology, and it was clear he knew a great deal about Islam. The lectures weren't easy—he demanded a great deal from his audience.

Abu Walid sat next to Abu Qatada most of the time, and he gave the sermon on Friday if Abu Qatada wasn't there. Sometimes, when I stayed after the prayers were over to help tidy up the prayer rugs, I would see Abu Qatada and Abu Walid counting the money from the donation box. Once they had finished, Abu Walid packed up the money and took it with him.

I studied the men who came to Four Feathers very, very carefully. Some of them were young, but there were also many men in their thirties and forties. They seemed educated; they knew the Ku'ran well and listened intently to the sermons. It was clear that Abu Qatada was speaking a language that they understood.

It was clear to me that there were a number of extremists at Four Feathers. I noticed all the things that Hakim had taught me about in Morocco years earlier: the way these men moved their lips in constant, silent prayer, the way they made their *salat*, the way they kept their eyes trained on the ground in front of them, the way their pants always hung just above the ankles.

With just a very few of them, I noticed something else, too: the way they walked. It was the same light step I had seen and learned in the camps. When I studied these men more carefully, I noticed other things as well—the tranquil voices, the calm, steely eyes, and the dark circles beneath them.

Every Friday, after the services were over, I met with Daniel and Gilles and they would ask me about Four Feathers. Daniel asked the same questions many times over. Is Abu Qatada inciting people to wage *jihad* within England? Does he encourage his followers to attack Americans on British soil?

Daniel and Gilles wanted to know if I had ever heard Abu Qatada's name mentioned in Afghanistan, and I told them I hadn't. They wanted to know if I thought Abu Qatada was recruiting people to go the camps. I told them I didn't know, but that it was clear to me there were men at Four Feathers who had been trained there. And, I reminded them, Abu Qatada said over and over again that the life of a *mujahid* was the highest calling for any Muslim.

One day, Daniel gave me a mobile phone. "Don't lose this," he said as he held it out in front of him.

"Don't worry," I said, "I won't."

Daniel didn't let go of the phone. "I mean it, you really have to be careful with this. Don't leave it anywhere. Make sure you have it with you all the time, OK?"

"OK." I reached out to take the phone, but he still wouldn't let it go.

Daniel went on. "If it breaks, bring it back to me, OK? Don't take it into an electronics shop or anything like that."

By now I was getting annoyed. I got it: the phone was tapped. Daniel really wasn't very sophisticated in the way he presented things.

Daniel always brought photos with him to our meetings. Loads of them each time. He would dump them out on the table and ask me to go through them and point out anyone I recognized.

I recognized a lot of people, because most of the photos that had been taken outside of Four Feathers. So I would point to the men I had seen before and Daniel would ask me what I knew about each one. I knew nothing about any of them; Daniel had told me to lie low, not to make contacts yet. Then he would ask if I had any general impressions. Is this man interesting? Does that one look like a fanatic to you? I knew how to differentiate and so I would tell him who to keep an eye on. He took pages and pages of notes.

One Friday, Daniel and Gilles told me to call Abu Zubayda and give him my mobile phone number. When I called the number Abu Zubayda had given me, a man picked up on the other end of the line. I didn't recognize his voice. I told him I wanted to speak to Abu Zubayda and he asked me my name. "Abu Imam al Mughrabi," I said.

There was a rustling, and then another voice came on the line. "*As-salamu'alaykum*, Abu Imam. This is Abu Said. How are you, brother?" It was Abu Said al-Kurdi, the man I had met in Peshawar and who drove with me up to Darunta. He sounded happy to hear from me.

"*Al-hamdu lil-lah*, Abu Said," I replied. "How are you?"

Abu Said told me that Abu Zubayda wasn't there, but that he could pass a message on to him for me. I said I was in London, and gave him my phone number. I told him I would send Abu Zubayda my address as soon as I was settled in.

Daniel and Gilles looked very excited when I rang off. I think Daniel was finally realizing that I was for real, and that I could be very valuable to him.

"I'm going to get a post box," I told them. "And I'll need some money to wire to Abu Zubayda."

All of a sudden, Daniel and Gilles stopped smiling. They looked shocked. "What do you mean?" Daniel asked.

"I have to send some money to Abu Zubayda. That's why he gave me the number of the bank account." I explained again what Ibn Sheikh had told me that last night at Darunta: I was expected to send money back to support the *jihad*. It was one of the reasons they sent me to Europe.

"We can't send money to these people," Daniel said. He spoke very slowly, and Gilles nodded his head in agreement. "It's not legal."

"Well, how do you expect me to keep my cover then?" I demanded. "I just told them that I'm living in London and that I have a mobile phone. Of course they think I'm going to send them money." I was angry at both of them. They were letting me take all the risks, but they weren't taking any.

Daniel and Gilles looked at me silently, and then at each other. Gilles cleared his throat and spoke quietly. "Why don't we talk about this another time?"

Message

Over the course of my first few visits to Four Feathers, I could tell the level of tension was rising. Members of the audience were pressing harder on the subject of the war in Algeria. The civil war was escalating on the ground; the GIA was becoming ever more aggressive. Now they were killing entire families, even whole villages at a time. Anyone who didn't support the GIA was fair game. At one point, GIA members disguised as policemen set up a road block and stopped two buses filled with civilians. They slit the throat of every last one—more than sixty in all, including many women, children, and elderly people. Another time, they broke into a mosque during prayers. In front of the *imam* and everyone else assembled there, they beheaded four men with daggers and axes.

The GIA had proclaimed itself as the only legitimate opposition to the military regime. Only the GIA could enforce *sharia*, and determine who was and was not a true Muslim. Anyone who didn't pray, anyone who didn't give their *zakat* directly to the GIA, any woman who left the house without a veil—all of these were apostates, deserving of death. The GIA was looking more and more like the Taliban every day.

There were many questions at Four Feathers about the GIA. The Algerians, of course, were particularly agitated. Many didn't believe the reports they read in the newspapers. They believed the Algerian military was committing these atrocities in order to turn people against the GIA.

As always, Abu Qatada was most interested in the theological questions. One Friday, he gave a sermon that was much longer than usual. He began by talking about the *ulama'*, the learned men who possess knowledge of the Ku'ran and the *sunna* and the *hadith*. He said the role of the *ulamā'* was to defend the true Islam against the innovators.

Abu Qatada didn't mention the GIA directly at first, but he talked about the concept of *takfir*, the declaration that a person or a group is no longer truly Muslim. It is, in effect, a sentence of death. Abu Qatada explained that the *fatwa* of *takfir* could only be handed down by learned men. The GIA had over-reached; they were not in a position to decide who the real Muslims were and were not. Abu Qatada made it very clear that he believed it was the responsibility of every Muslim to work for the overthrow of secular regimes everywhere. But he also said that the GIA had no right at all to kill other Muslims.

The audience listened carefully, but I could tell as the sermon went on that some of the Algerians were getting angry. Not all of them, by any means; some of them were nodding their heads in agreement with what they were hearing. At the end of the sermon, Abu Qatada announced that he was cutting off his ties to the GIA. He denounced them as innovators. Then he ended with a prayer.

The tension was thick as we stood up to leave. A group of men clustered around Abu Qatada and Abu Walid, and elsewhere I could see brothers arguing with each other. When I walked out, there was a man handing out copies of a leaflet written in Arabic. In it, Abu Qatada formally announced he was severing his ties with *Al Ansar*.

When I met with Daniel and Gilles that afternoon, I showed them the bulletin. I also told them I had organized a post box, and they were pleased. They told me to call Abu Zubayda to give them the address. I asked them again about the money, and again they deflected my question. They said we would speak about it later.

When I rang Abu Zubayda's number this time, an old man answered. I gave him my name and he told me that Abu Zubayda was not there. He offered to pass him a message and so I gave him the address of the post box.

"You are in London?" he asked.

"Yes," I said. "I live here."

"Do you know someone named Abu Qatada?" he asked. I was surprised by this. I had never heard Abu Qatada's name in Pakistan or Afghanistan.

"Yes," I replied. "I know him. I see him every week."

"Could you pass him a message for me? Please tell him to contact brother Abdullah in Pakistan. Tell him it's important."

I agreed to pass on the message and hung up. When I told Daniel and Gilles what had happened, they were both very pleased.

The following Friday, I approached Abu Qatada after the prayers had ended. I had never spoken to him before, and I waited until he was alone to pass along the message. He looked surprised at first. "Who gave you that message?" he asked.

"A brother in Pakistan," I told him.

We held each other's gaze for a few seconds, but neither one of us said anything more.

A couple of weeks later, when I arrived for my meeting with Gilles and Daniel, there was an envelope lying on the table. It contained one thousand dollars.

"It's the money you asked for," Daniel said.

Later that afternoon, I went to a foreign exchange bureau for tourists near Trafalgar Square. I wired the money to the bank account Abu Zubayda had given me.

The services gave me the same amount of money to send to Pakistan two more times after that. I always had to ask for the money, but I didn't have to pressure them like I did the first time.

Abu Hamza

Abu Qatada's audience on Fridays shrank slightly after he made his announcement about the GIA. I noticed that some of the Algerians weren't coming anymore. Those who stayed were still talking about Algeria, and debating the actions of the GIA. But it was less tense in Four Feathers. Clearly, the angriest members had simply stopped coming.

On my way out one Friday afternoon, I was handed a flier with an invitation to a debate the following week. Abu Qatada and Abu Walid would be there along with two other clerics: Abu Hamza and Sheikh Omar Bakri Mohammad. I had never heard of Abu Hamza, but I knew about Sheikh Omar because he had been in the papers and on television a few months earlier. He had tried to hold a huge rally for Muslims in London, but it had been banned by the British government.

I decided to go to the debate, even though it was in a distant section of London where I had never been. When I emerged from the tube station, I didn't know which way to go. There were two young men coming out of the station at the same time as me, though, and I recognized them from Four Feathers. I showed them the flyer and asked if they could point the way, and one of them told me they were going to the same place and that we could walk together.

Both of the men were Algerian. One was slightly older than the other, and also taller. It was clear to me that they were both GIA. It was just the tiny signs that distinguish extremists from other Muslims: both wore their jeans cuffed so they fell just above the ankles, and they were wearing ski hats even though it was warm outside.

I introduced myself as Imam. The taller one introduced himself as Khaled: and the other was Samir. We began to speak, and I realized both men were Algerian rather than French Algerian. I knew this because they both spoke terrible French, and we ended up talking mostly in Arabic.

"Where are you from?" Khaled asked.

"Morocco."

He smiled. "No, I mean, where have you come from?"

I paused for a moment and then told him. "Belgium."

"Oh, I know a lot of people in Belgium," he said, sounding pleased. "Why did you leave?"

In just a fraction of a second, I calculated my options. I could tell him about Amin and Yasin. Quite possibly, it would give me instant credibility with these men, as it had with Ibn Sheikh in Peshawar. There was a slight chance, of course, that they had spoken to Amin and Yasin, and that they would figure out who I was. It didn't seem likely to me, though, so I jumped in. "I left because I had to," I explained. "Do you know the brothers Amin and Yasin?"

"Yes, of course!" Khaled seemed astonished.

"I was involved with *Al Ansar* along with them. The police were looking for me when the raids came, so I had to leave the country."

Neither Khaled nor Samir blinked at all; they just seemed very happy to meet me. I knew then that we were going to become friends.

That was the day I saw Abu Hamza for the first time. He was a very strange-looking man: he had only one eye, and no hands. Where his right hand should have been, he had a strange prosthesis with a silver hook at the end. He looked like a pirate. After a few moments, it came to me: this was the brother that As-sad Allah had told me about at Darunta, the one who had blown his hands off preparing nitroglycerine. I was amazed.

I was even more amazed when I heard Abu Hamza speak. He knew nothing at all about theology, which seemed odd for someone who had gone through the camps. He was very loud and very passionate, but to me he also seemed very stupid. He was trying to defend the GIA in terms of Islamic law, but it was clear to me that he didn't know what he was talking about. It was clear to Abu Qatada and Abu Walid as well; they demolished every argument he put for-ward. Omar Bakri Mohammed was more articulate, and he helped Abu Hamza make his case.

I came out of that meeting understanding two things very clearly: Abu Qatada was a true scholar, and Abu Hamza was nothing more than a dema-gogue.

When I told Daniel and Gilles about the debate with Abu Hamza, they were very pleased. When I told them what Assad Allah had said about Abu Hamza, they were both surprised and amused. They said Abu Hamza claimed he had lost his hands defusing a land mine on the front lines in Afghanistan.

Daniel and Gilles were very interested in Khaled and Samir, particularly when I told them that they knew Amin and Yasin. Amin and Yasin were code names, of course, and they weren't in any newspapers. So Daniel and Gilles knew as well as I did that Khaled and Samir must be well connected in the GIA. They instructed me to get closer to both men.

One Friday, I went to my normal meeting with Daniel and Gilles, but only Daniel was there. In the elevator on the way up to the room, he told me he had asked Gilles not to come that day. I was surprised; Gilles was always at our meetings.

When we walked into the room, there was a table laid out with an elegant lunch. I turned to Daniel for an explanation.

"We didn't get off to a good start," he said. "I think it's time for a new begin-ning."

We talked that day for several hours. He was interesting; he knew a lot about politics, though not necessarily about Islam. He asked me about my life, also. For the first time, I felt I wasn't just a pawn to him. Our relationship was much easier after that.

Big Fish

I was spending more and more time with Khaled and Samir. Because I had proven my GIA credentials when I mentioned the names Amin and Yasin, they both spoke openly with me. But it was Khaled who did most of the talking. Samir was very quiet and submissive to his more assertive friend.

It didn't take long before Khaled told me the police had been looking for him in France after the bombings in the summer of 1995. He had fled to Germany, where he lived in Wuppertal for a little while. But he said he didn't feel safe there, either, so he had emigrated to England.

One day, Khaled told me that some friends of his from Germany were visiting London and would be coming to Four Feathers for the Friday prayers. By the time the service began, however, they still hadn't arrived, so Khaled, Samir, and I sat down to listen to Abu Walid speak.

After a few minutes, I saw Khaled turn his head towards the door of the gymnasium. I turned to look, too, and saw three men in the doorway. A chill ran down my spine—I recognized one of the men. But even though I knew that I knew him, I couldn't put my finger on who he was.

As Khaled and Samir walked over to their friends, I stared at just this one man. He was sharply dressed—he wore a dark leather jacket with jeans and trainers. But I still couldn't figure it out, but there was no doubt in my mind I had seen him before.

There was something dangerous about the man; I felt it in my blood. For the rest of the lecture, my mind was racing as I tried to figure out who he was. I was so close, but I couldn't quite get it. I knew this man was important somehow, and that I should stay clear of him.

When the service was over, I dashed towards the entrance to the hall. I passed by Khaled and Samir on my way out and hastily said goodbye. I took one last look at the man and then walked out into the street. And then I did something that Daniel had told me never to do: I called him from my mobile phone, right outside of Four Feathers. Daniel had warned me against this because he knew it could raise suspicions, but I knew I couldn't wait until our meeting later in the day to tell him about this man. I left Daniel a message and he called back immediately.

"Daniel, there's someone here at Four Feathers. You need to get your men on him right away." I had seen so many pictures taken outside of Four Feathers that I knew there must be photographers very nearby.

"Who is it?" Daniel asked.

"I can't quite figure it out," I admitted. "I've seen him before, though, and I know he's a very big fish."

I met with Daniel and Gilles two hours later. When I walked in the room I could tell that they were excited. Gilles in particular looked ecstatic. "Do you know who that was?" he asked.

"No," I said. I still hadn't figured it out. "But I think he's important."

Gilles grinned. "Yes, you're absolutely right. That was Ali Touchent—Tarek from Brussels. He was responsible for the bombings in France last year."

I was dumbfounded. I couldn't believe I hadn't recognized him. We had lived under the same roof in Brussels for weeks.

"Are you sure?" I asked.

"We're absolutely sure," Gilles said. "Our photographers caught him on camera."

I thought about it some more. Tarek had been very fit when I knew him, but this man was slightly chubbier. It was possible Tarek had gained weight, and that it showed up in his face. His hair was longer, too, and I wondered if that was why I had been confused. What Daniel and Gilles were telling me began to seem more plausible. If it was true, then I had just given the services a huge break.

"What are you going to do?" I asked.

"We've got our men on him," Daniel said confidently. "We'll get him this time."

The next time we met, I asked Daniel and Gilles if they had caught Ali Touchent. They looked at each other and said nothing.

"Well, what happened?" I pressed.

Finally, Daniel spoke. "We lost him."

"What?" I couldn't believe what I was hearing. I looked over at Gilles and could see that he was seething. "How could you possibly lose him?"

Daniel looked embarrassed. "He was at a café. Our guys were watching him. And then somehow he disappeared."

I looked at Gilles again, but he was staring at the table. I looked back at Daniel, but I realized that there was nothing more to say. I'm wasting my time here, I thought to myself. The Brits have no idea what they're doing.

A few weeks later, another bomb ripped through the Paris metro. The details were all too familiar. Like the bomb that had gone off in the Paris metro when I was in Khaldan, this one was also placed on an RER train at rush hour. According to the news reports, the bomb itself—a gas canister filled with explosives and nails for shrapnel—was also the same.

The explosion killed four people and injured nearly two hundred more. Authorities across Europe began an intensive search for Touchent. He had already evaded arrest many times at that point, after the raids in Brussels and then several more times after the bombings in Paris that summer. And he would escape again this time.

In February 1998, the Algerian authorities reported that Touchent had been killed nine months earlier in Algiers. The French asked for fingerprints, and when they came the police confirmed a match with the prints they had on file for Touchent. But when the French put dozens of suspected GIA members on trial that same month for their alleged roles in the 1995 bombings, the courts convicted Touchent in absentia. They were not convinced he was really dead.

During that trial, several of the defendants claimed Touchent was not a member of the GIA at all. They said they had been manipulated by him, and that he was really an *agent provocateur*, put in place by Algeria's military intelligence services. These rumors continue to circulate to this day.

When it comes to Ali Touchent, it seems that nothing is certain.

Takeover

Khaled was not happy that Abu Qatada had severed his ties with the GIA. He still attended Four Feathers sometimes, but he talked about how Abu Qatada had betrayed the brothers in Algeria. He also talked about Abu Hamza, and told me he had been attending more of his meetings. One Friday, he suggested that I meet him the following week at the Finsbury Park mosque, where Abu Hamza had started preaching regularly.

I hadn't heard about the Finsbury Park mosque before that, but when I told Daniel and Gilles about it they were very excited. So the next Friday I took the tube to meet with Khaled and Samir.

The mosque was a very strange, modern building. I waited for a few minutes until the others arrived and then we went inside. Khaled led the way up two flights of stairs. We walked out onto a balcony above a large hall filled with at least two hundred people.

It wasn't anything like what I had expected. Daniel and Gilles had been so excited that I had assumed I would find a hall filled with extremists. But most of the men I saw were nothing of the sort. They were immigrants from Pakistan and India and North Africa and the Middle East, nothing more. I saw a few people wearing the *shalwar kameez*, but they could have been Afghanis; I wasn't sure. Mostly, though, I saw men who had simply come to mosque for their *al-Jum'a* prayers.

There was an elevated platform at the front of the mosque, and Abu Hamza was sitting there. But a Pakistani *imam* was speaking from the *minbar*. He wasn't speaking in either English or Arabic, so I couldn't understand a word he said.

I met Khaled at Finsbury Park the next Friday. It was even stranger this time. In fact, it was total chaos. People were shouting at each other everywhere. In the auditorium, on the staircases, in the entryway.

The battle lines were clear: Arabs against Pakistanis. They were arguing in English, so I could understand everything they said. They were fighting for control of the mosque. The Pakistanis wanted their *imam*, and the Arabs wanted Abu Hamza.

I knew which side Khaled and Samir came down on, so I just stood back and watched. I saw a number of men I hadn't seen the week before: younger men, mostly from North Africa. They were clustered around Abu Hamza.

It was getting louder and louder inside the mosque. People were yelling at each other so intensely that it would not have surprised me if some of the men started fighting physically. But then suddenly, just as it was time for the prayers to begin, everything went quiet. It was a walkout: scores of Pakistanis and Indians and even some of the North Africans just left. Then Abu Hamza walked over to the *minbar* and began to speak.

I was completely confused by what I had seen that day. But in the weeks that followed, I learned from the newspapers that Abu Hamza had taken over the mosque at Finsbury Park. It was very controversial; the Pakistanis were angry, and they wanted their mosque back.

But Abu Hamza had installed himself, and the mosque changed with him. Different people came to Finsbury Park after the takeover, people who were younger, less settled in their lives.

The new audience was less educated, as well. I knew this because no one truly educated in Islam would have listened to Abu Hamza. He knew nothing at all.

He would just wave his hook wildly and shout. He shouted constantly about *ji-had*. He didn't explain it at all, the way Abu Qatada did; he just yelled about its necessity. *Jihad* against America. *Jihad* against the Jews. *Jihad* against the infidels. *Jihad* against governments of Algeria and Egypt and Yemen. *Jihad, jihad, jihad*.

I found it very hard to listen to Abu Hamza, not just because he was so loud, but because his preaching was so stupid. But I understood that Abu Hamza himself was not stupid. He was playing to his audience. And more and more over the weeks that followed, I recognized his audience, literally. Many men were migrating over from Four Feathers to Finsbury Park, just like Khaled and Samir had. No, Abu Hamza was not stupid at all. He knew that people were angry with Abu Qatada for breaking with the GIA. Abu Hamza had seized the moment.

I went to Finsbury Park regularly after that. When I would report back to Daniel and Gilles about Abu Hamza, Daniel asked the same question over and over again. Was Abu Hamza inciting his followers to attack within England?

In fact, Abu Hamza was not. He was inciting his followers to attack just about everywhere else, but never within England. He came very close to this line many times. He incited his followers to attack anyone who tried to claim Muslim land. He said many times that British soldiers and colonizers on Muslim soil were fair game.

But I could never give Daniel the quotation he was hoping for. For as long as I attended Finsbury Park, Abu Hamza never crossed that line.

The Spiritual Leader

Even though I was going to Finsbury Park regularly with Khaled, I continued to attend prayers and lectures at Four Feathers as well. I preferred being there, because Abu Qatada and Abu Walid were very smart and rigorous in the way they taught. They were no less extreme than Abu Hamza; in fact, quite the opposite. But they went about it differently. They talked about the Ku'ran and the *sunna* and the *hadith*. They talked about the laws of *jihad*. They talked about the process by which a man could become a *mujahid*.

I knew from my own experience in the camps how seductive this language could be. Abu Qatada and Abu Walid could penetrate the minds of their followers more deeply than Abu Hamza ever could; I was sure of that. Abu Hamza only sounded dangerous. Abu Qatada and Abu Walid really were.

Of course, I knew that Abu Qatada and Abu Walid were dangerous for another reason, too. I was passing messages to them directly from Abu Zubayda and the men who surrounded him in Peshawar. One day, I spoke to Abu Zubayda himself, and he asked me to speak to Abu Walid for him. "Tell him the *amana* never arrived," he said. "And ask him to bring the book for the brothers next time he comes."

The messages were always like this: coded, obscure. But it wasn't important whether I understood them or not. The important thing was that messages were going directly to Four Feathers from the men who ran the training camps in Afghanistan.

At least I thought that was the important thing. Daniel and Gilles didn't seem to agree, because not long after Abu Hamza took over the Finsbury Park mosque they told me to stop attending Four Feathers.

I was mystified, and I was angry. I had made progress at Four Feathers. I had passed messages from Peshawar to both Abu Qatada and Abu Walid. There were men from the training camps in Four Feathers. It was where I had spotted Ali Touchent.

Abu Hamza was a demagogue; a barking dog, nothing more. I argued with Daniel and Gilles and tried to explain that Abu Qatada was more dangerous than Abu Hamza, even though he seemed less fiery. But they wouldn't listen to me, and they wouldn't back down.

I had my orders. From then on, I would attend Finsbury Park exclusively.

I'll never know why Daniel and Gilles made me stop going to Four Feathers. Maybe they were running someone else there and didn't need me any longer. Or maybe they were just wrong. I do know now that I was right about Abu Qatada and Abu Walid.

Abu Qatada is now well known. He has been described as the spiritual leader of Islamic militants in Europe. He is currently in prison in England awaiting extradition to Jordan, where he has been convicted in absentia for plotting terrorist attacks.

Many believe that Abu Qatada was a recruiter in London for Al Qaeda. Certainly, many of the most dangerous figures within Al Qaeda were either mentored or influenced by him. His videos were found in the apartment of Muhammad Atta, the leader of the 9/11 attacks.

Djamel Beghal, who later confessed to organizing a plot to blow up the American embassy in Paris, said he had first been drawn to radical Islam because of Abu Qatada. And numerous accounts report that when the perpetrators of the Madrid bombings found themselves surrounded in their apartment by police, they tried to call Abu Qatada in prison just before blowing themselves up.

Abu Walid was also connected to Beghal and to the Madrid bombers. Less is known about him, though, because he disappeared into Afghanistan. No one seems to know where he is now.

We do know where Abu Zubayda is now: he's in Guantanamo Bay. At the time of his arrest in 2002, he was ranked number three on America's list of most-wanted terrorists, right after bin Laden and his deputy, Ayman al-Zawahiri. Abu Zubayda was bin Laden's chief recruiter for Al Qaeda. He oversaw the administration of sleeper cells all over the world, and his name has appeared in connection to any number of terrorist attacks.

Fatima

Daniel and Gilles were very interested in Khaled, and pressed me to get closer to him. And I did. I spoke to him regularly and went to Finsbury Park every week.

Khaled was very well connected in both Afghanistan and Algeria. He often told me about events well before they made it into the papers; the killing of a GIA leader in Peshawar, for instance, or a car bombing in Algeria.

One day, I decided to tell Khaled that I had spent a year in the Afghan training camps. I knew this would lead him to reveal more of himself. And I was right: Khaled told me he was preparing to go to Afghanistan to train in the camps. He needed the proper documents first, he said, and was close to getting them. He had a friend who was forging an Italian passport for him, but he needed to get a photo first. He was trying to find green contact lenses.

Daniel and Gilles were very excited about all this. They were always able to confirm the stories that Khaled reported from his contacts abroad. They wanted to know more about him, and to see how far he would go.

One day, Daniel came to our meeting with a plan. The services would rent a warehouse. I would tell Khaled that I was stockpiling weapons there to ship to Algeria, and ask him if he had any brothers who needed a place to store their munitions. If so, I would be happy to help them. Then, if Khaled or anyone else showed up with weapons, the police could arrest them on the spot.

I nearly burst out laughing. "Don't you think that would look a bit suspicious?" I asked.

"How so?" Daniel looked perplexed.

"Because I think these guys are smart enough not to risk what they have in England," I explained. "It's a safe haven for them."

Daniel nodded, but it was clear that he still didn't get it. I went on. I explained that England would be a stupid place for anyone to keep weapons, anyway. Border controls are the most dangerous part of weapons smuggling. France, Spain, Germany, Italy—they're all part of the Schengen agreement, so there are no border controls between them. But England isn't part of Schengen. Why would the GIA risk storing weapons somewhere with the danger of an extra border?

I shouldn't have had to explain all of this to Daniel. It was becoming more and more clear to me that the British services didn't understand much about how these groups worked.

Daniel had another idea a few weeks later. "Tell Khaled that you have a grenade," he said. "It'll get his attention. Then you can show it to him. I bet he'll ask to keep it, and you can give it to him."

"You want me to give Khaled a live grenade?" I asked.

Daniel shook his head. "No, of course not. Not a live grenade."

I realized what Daniel wanted me to do. He wanted me to give Khaled a grenade with some sort of tracking system inside. Then the services could find out where the GIA kept their weapons. It was completely crazy.

"Are you kidding?" I asked.

"No," Daniel said. "Why?"

"Because it would blow my cover immediately, and I would probably be killed."

"Why? I mean, they probably won't open the grenade."

It was mind-boggling. "Of course they will open the grenade!" I said. "In Afghanistan we learned everything about grenades. How to trick them, how to defuse them. We even learned how to drink out of them! Do you think that anyone who knows anything about explosives wouldn't open it up and look inside?"

It was almost laughable how little these so-called terrorism experts knew about their own enemy. They didn't seem to get that these were serious people with a great deal of knowledge, not children playing games with toy weapons.

Daniel's plans also made me angry, because they showed me how willing the services were to put me in real jeopardy. They didn't seem to be thinking anything through, or trying to learn more about how the enemy operated. They were letting their fantasies run away with them, and putting me in danger as a result.

More and more, I came to realize that I was playing with fire. Of course, neither Daniel nor Gilles knew the extent of the danger I was in, because neither of them knew about that conversation I had the day before the raids. They didn't know that Amin, Yasin, and Hakim all knew that I had flipped to work for the DGSE.

I knew that I was putting myself at risk from the moment I told Khaled about Amin and Yasin. But the names were my calling card. The names had gotten me straight into the camps. Once I got to Khaldan, I had learned that many of the other brothers there had been vetted for months before they were allowed in. It had taken me one day.

Now I was in a terrible position. The thing that was allowing me to do my job as a spy was also making it more and more likely that I would be caught.

One day, it became horribly clear how close I was to the brink. Khaled told me that some friends of his in Belgium had gone to see Amin and Yasin in jail. He didn't say anything more than that, so it was clear that no one had made any sort of connection this time. But what would happen the next time, or the time after that?

My life in London was stressful in ways my life in the camps had never been. Partly, I was frustrated because there seemed to be no purpose to my activities. When I worked with Gilles in Belgium, it had always been clear to me that we were working towards something. The DGSE wanted to make arrests and destroy the GIA network.

But in London, it wasn't so clear. I felt like I was just there to watch. Every week I would go to Finsbury Park, and every week Daniel would ask me the same questions. I looked at photograph after photograph and nothing ever seemed to amount to anything. The one time I gave them something really big—Ali Touchent—they blew it.

More than ever, I needed to blow off steam in London. I spent a lot of time at Covent Garden in the evenings, drinking wine in the restaurant on the bottom floor and listening to the musicians. I knew Daniel didn't want me there; he wanted me to be making friends with Arabs and sniffing out extremists. But I wanted to keep a life for myself, as well.

One day, I decided to call Fatima. I had been busy during my first months in London, and I had put it off. But now I wanted to talk to her, to see her again. And so I called the number she had given me, the number of her friend.

It was a small miracle. When her friend picked up the phone, Fatima was right there in the room. They were packing up the apartment because her friend was moving the next day. If I had waited only twenty-four hours longer, I would never have found her again.

Fatima and I picked up right where we had left off in Paris. And once we started speaking, we never stopped. I called her every day after that, and ran up thousands of pounds in phone bills.

Notebook

One of the things that surprised me about Daniel was that he never asked me anything about the training camps in Afghanistan. Gilles had asked me some questions when I was in Paris, but Daniel showed no interest whatsoever. The only thing I could think of was that the British services must have had spies of their own within Afghanistan. I thought about the guide who had taken me into Khaldan. The cooks. The drivers. It would have been very cheap and very easy for the services to buy one of them off.

Daniel wasn't a bad guy; he just didn't seem to understand what the West was facing. Early on, he and Gilles asked me if I had heard the term *Al Qaeda* in the camps, and if I knew what it meant. I knew what it meant: *Al Qaeda* means "the base" in Arabic. But I had never heard the term used in the camps. Then they asked if I had heard of Osama bin Laden. When they told me a little more about him, I realized they were referring to the same person that the Canadian boys, Hamza and Osama, had talked about at Khaldan. Daniel asked if bin Laden was the leader of the *jihad*, and I had to explain to him that bin Laden himself was irrelevant. *Jihad* is not a political movement, I explained. *Jihad* is not the IRA or the Baader-Meinhof gang. *Jihad* is an order from God. No human intermediary is necessary.

Gilles seemed to understand this better than Daniel. Of course, the French had lived for centuries with the Muslim world at their back door. But Gilles also understood the language of Islam. He asked interesting questions about the speeches of Abu Qatada and Abu Hamza. He would ask me to clarify a point of theology, or explain the meaning of a particular *surah*. Daniel seemed interested only in the immediate danger these men posed to Britons.

Daniel and I got along well after our difficult beginning. Sometimes we would go out for a drink or a meal. He was always very nice to me; once, he even consoled me when I'd had an argument with Fatima. But every time we got together, I would tell him the same thing. "Daniel, I don't feel like I'm doing anything here in England. I don't feel like I'm useful."

"Of course you're useful!" he would tell me. He said the services were gathering all sorts of useful intelligence because of me. But it never seemed that way to me. Neither he nor Gilles ever gave me any sense of how the information I was giving them fit into a bigger picture.

One day, I finally said it. "Daniel, I think that there is a lot more I could be doing. Right now, it's not much of a job."

Daniel looked down at the table and shook his head. "You're right," he said. "You're right."

Of course, there were successes, too. I was checking my post box in Trafalgar Square once a week, and one day it arrived. A package from the university in Peshawar. I opened up the envelope and there it was: my notebook from Darunta, with all the formulas and instructions for building bombs.

As I took the bus home that day, I was elated. This one was big. It wasn't just the information on explosives that made it so important, it was the notes Abdul Kerim had scribbled in the margins. Gilles had been asking me about Abdul Kerim constantly since I returned from Afghanistan, and I knew he was desperate to get his hands on the notebook so he could get a sample of Abdul Kerim's handwriting.

When I met with Daniel and Gilles the next day, they couldn't stop smiling. I had told them several times the notebook would come, but I don't think they completely believed me until it was actually in front of them.

The London mosques were crawling with spies. I knew this because Daniel and Gilles rarely seemed surprised by the information I brought them from Finsbury Park. This only added to my frustration. Why did they need me spying on Abu Hamza if they already had other men on him?

I was always on the outside of things in London, and it was hard for me. In Brussels, I had been right at the center of GIA operations; I could offer Gilles something that no one else could. And of course this was even more true in Afghanistan. But in London I was just one of many watching and waiting for something—anything—to happen.

One day, I lashed out. When Daniel asked me if I had seen anyone suspicious at Finsbury Park that week, I told him I had seen one man who was obviously working for MI5. Daniel looked stunned. "What makes you think that?" he demanded.

I told him the truth. That it was impossible to explain. There were just little signs: the stress in his face, the way his eyes moved, the tiny hesitations in his step.

Daniel fixed his eyes on me intently. "What does this man look like?"

"You don't need me to tell you that," I said with a smile.

Daniel inhaled sharply. I could tell he was angry. He moved his face in towards mine. "Don't play these games with me," he said. "Tell me what he looks like. Right now."

"I can't tell you right now. I'll have to go back and look at him. I see hundreds of faces every week."

I knew Daniel wasn't at all satisfied, but there was nothing he could do. "All right," he said. "I want you to concentrate on this man and come back next week with a detailed description."

The next Friday I picked out the most innocent-looking member of the audience I could find, a Moroccan immigrant who clearly had nothing to do with radical Islam. When I described him to Daniel, he was incredibly relieved.

I didn't know who the spies were at Finsbury Park; I just knew they were there. And I wanted Daniel and Gilles to know that they couldn't bullshit me.

Yemen

After my first few months in London, Daniel, Gilles, and I began to meet in flats rather than hotels. There were several different ones and we alternated between them. One was near Elephant and Castle, another just off Regent's Park, another in central London. All the apartments were nicely furnished but completely anonymous. Only very occasionally I'd see a lipstick or a bottle of aftershave in the bathroom.

One day, I arrived to find a third man at the apartment with Daniel and Gilles. He was young, no more than twenty-five years old. Gilles introduced him as Alexandre. Gilles explained to me that Alexandre would be taking his place in the meetings from there on out. I was surprised; I had been working with Gilles for years and it hadn't occurred to me that someday he would stop handling me. Alexandre seemed shy at first, reserved. I assumed that this was because he was young and new to the job.

A few weeks later, Daniel left as well. His replacement was a middle-aged man named Mark. Mark was quiet, but not in the same way as Alexandre. Mark was older, and he seemed hardened. Daniel and Mark came to the meetings together for a few weeks before Mark took over for good.

After his last meeting with me, Daniel took all of us—me, Mark, Gilles, Alexandre—out for an incredible dinner at the River Café. Mark brought someone else with him that evening, a very young woman named Penny. He introduced us and told me that Penny worked with him and the two of them would share responsibility for me.

In the course of just a few weeks, I had met three new handlers and lost two of the old ones. Later, I think I figured out why: I had been transferred from MI6, which is responsible for British security internationally, to MI5, which handles domestic security issues. I was still a French spy, but the British were taking more control of my case. Presumably, this was why Gilles left as well.

We had a marvelous time that night at the River Café. I was touched that Daniel had chosen such a fine restaurant. It was his way, I think, of showing me respect. As we sat looking out over the Thames talking and laughing, I felt happy for the first time in months. All of the tension—between me and Daniel, between me and Gilles, between Gilles and Daniel—was gone.

Before he left, Daniel took me aside to say goodbye. He thanked me for my work and then put out is hand. "I'm sorry this is ending," he said. "It's been a lot of fun working with you."

Fun. As I shook his hand one last time, I reflected on what he had said. *Fun* seemed like a strange word to use to describe our collaboration. But I knew that in his heart, Daniel had meant to say something kind.

Nothing much changed when Mark, Penny, and Alexandre came on board. I was still doing the same thing: going to Finsbury Park, looking at photos, going to Finsbury Park, looking at photos.

Finsbury Park, however, had changed a lot in the months since I first went there. By now, it was comprised almost entirely of young people and angry people. The old guard was completely gone. And there were many new people coming in. A couple of the rooms on the ground floor of the mosque had been converted into dormitories. Very few people knew this, but sometimes the doors to these rooms were left slightly ajar when I was there in the evenings. When I looked inside, I saw sleeping bags laid out on the floor.

Abu Hamza continued to rant as he always had, but he had shifted his focus slightly. Algeria had become a very tense subject, even at Finsbury Park. The GIA massacres were larger and bloodier with each passing month. Sometimes I could hear people debating about it under their breath.

The GIA and Algeria were not Abu Hamza's main subject, anyway. Abu Hamza was obsessed with Yemen. He believed that the global Islamic revolution would begin there. "It will come out of Aden," he always said. If *sharia* was established in Yemen, other secular regimes would fall like dominoes.

I tried to explain all of this to Mark and Alexandre. They didn't seem to understand why Abu Hamza, an Egyptian, was so fixated on Yemen. I told them about the *al-Mahdi*, the great redeemer of Islam, who would transform the world into a perfect Islamic society before *Yaum al-Qiyamah*, the day of resurrection. There are signs announcing the arrival of the *al-Mahdi*, and one of them is a great fire in Aden. Abu Hamza didn't have just a political ambition, he had an apocalyptic vision.

Alexandre seemed very interested in my explanation, far more so than Mark. Mark was much smarter than Daniel—that was clear from the outset—but like Daniel his knowledge of Islam was very shallow. It was frustrating for me when I tried to explain these important ideas and Mark would come back around to that eternal question: "Yes, but did he say anything about attacks in England?"

I was getting closer to Khaled over the course of these months, and deeper into Abu Hamza's circle. Often I would go to Finsbury Park in the evenings to attend religious discussions with a smaller group. Sometimes Abu Hamza would show us propaganda videos from Algeria.

One day, Khaled introduced us. He told Abu Hamza that I had been in the training camps. "*Masha'allah*, brother," he said, looking at me with his one good eye. "Can you meet with me in the office after the *salat*?"

"Of course," I told him.

When the *salat* was finished, I stood outside of the small office on the first floor. Soon, Abu Hamza approached with a young boy by his side. He gestured with his hook and the boy opened the door for him. We sat down on the floor and Abu Hamza asked the boy to bring us tea.

Abu Hamza asked me which of the camps I had been in, and I told him. He seemed very interested. Then I leaned forward slightly. "I met someone you know," I said in a conspiratorial voice.

Abu Hamza raised his brow just slightly.

"I trained with Assad Allah," I told him. "He told me about the nitroglycerine, and how you lost your hands."

Abu Hamza looked away. "Brother," he whispered, still not meeting my gaze, "please don't share that story with anyone."

I assured him that I would not, and he seemed relieved. Soon after, the young boy returned with tea. We sat for a few moments and then Abu Hamza stood up to signal that the meeting was over.

Just as I was leaving, he spoke to me. "*Al-Hamdu lil-lah* that God sent you to us. One day, we may need your assistance and your knowledge."

Daniel and Gilles hadn't said anything more about the explosives notebook before they left, and I was curious to know what had become of it. So, finally, after a couple of months, I asked Mark.

"You'll have to ask Alexandre," he said. "The French still have it."

I could sense a tiny bit of resentment in his voice. From the outset, I had realized that the relationship between the French and the English services wasn't an entirely comfortable one. Before he left, Daniel told me that the two countries had never run an agent together in this way. There were still some wrinkles in the operation, clearly. It was several more months before the French handed over the notebook to the British.

Later, Mark told me that the British services had gone through all the formulas and tested each one. He said they were struck by how sophisticated some of them were. "You know," he said, "our specialists told me that they learned a few things from that notebook."

Fugue

As the months wore on, there were frustrations as well as successes. With the help of Khaled and Samir, I was getting closer to Abu Hamza. We would hang around in his office after the prayers on Friday, and I would watch while he and his entourage counted the piles of money they had collected from the *zakat*. I doubted very much that it was going to the poor.

Once, Abu Hamza asked me to do a favor for him. He asked me to buy an extra telephone and fax machine for his office. The services were more than happy to oblige.

Everyone—Mark, Alexandre, Penny—was pressing me to get closer to Khaled. He invited me to his home once, and they all thought I should invite him to mine in return. I flatly refused. I didn't want him to know where I lived.

But we were able to get plenty of information out of Khaled anyway. One day, he couldn't find his mobile phone and asked to borrow mine. I loaned him the phone Daniel had given me, and he placed a call to Algeria. He borrowed it again several times after that, and used it to make calls to Algeria and all over Europe. The services were able to record all of them.

There was only so far I could go with Khaled, though. It wasn't just that I was fearful, but also that the services wouldn't let me do the things that would have gotten me real access. Khaled told me one day that Abu Hamza had arranged for combat training for a few of the brothers, and he suggested that I could come along and show them some of the skills I had learned in the camps.

When I told Mark and Alexandre about Khaled's suggestion, they both blanched. Then they forbid me ever to participate in any sort of physical training with the men from Finsbury Park. It was completely illegal for an agent to share skills with terrorists. If Khaled ever asked again, they instructed me, I should tell him I was busy with other things.

One Friday, when I met up with Khaled outside of Finsbury Park, Samir was not with him. When I asked after him, Khaled looked upset. He told me Samir had gotten a job and moved up to Swindon. He was angry that Samir had chosen to pursue a life of comfort, rather than fighting for the Muslim *umma*.

When I told Mark about Samir, he smiled. "Did you know that Samir is a homosexual?" he asked. There was a glint in his eye. "Islam isn't very sympathetic towards homosexuals."

I knew right then and there: the services had blackmailed Samir, and now he was working for them.

One Friday, Mark and Alexandre told me not to go to Finsbury Park. Nothing more; they just told me not to go. Two days later, Khaled said the police had raided some houses around London and arrested some brothers. After that, I didn't hear anything more about it.

Afghanistan

I had been in London for more than a year, and I was bored, and I was fed up. I was doing the same thing week after week—Finsbury Park, photos, Finsbury Park—and it seemed to be going absolutely nowhere. And I was in love with Fatima, but saw her only rarely because she lived in Germany.

I worried that my life could go on like this forever if I didn't put a stop to it, so one day during my meeting with Mark and Alexandre I insisted on discussing my retirement. Both of them told me that they had no say in the matter, and assured me that someone would get in touch with me. I told them that I would stop working until I spoke to whoever was in charge.

Three days later, Gilles called. I hadn't spoken to him since the night we ate at the River Café. He arranged to meet with me and Mark in London a few days later. When we met, Gilles asked me what I wanted, and I told him I still wanted exactly the same things I had asked for during our first meeting in Brussels: a new identity, a passport, and help finding a job. I said I wanted to get married and end my career as a spy.

Gilles and Mark glanced at each other and then Gilles began to speak. "We haven't talked to you about this yet," he said, "but we were thinking of sending you back to Afghanistan."

Afghanistan. I liked the idea. It would be far more interesting than what I was doing now. And maybe this time, they would give me a proper objective. I could really accomplish something.

"When?" I asked.

I saw Gilles and Mark lock eyes very briefly. "Maybe next year?" Gilles said.

I was pretty sure at that moment that the trip to Afghanistan wasn't ever going to happen.

I had another meeting with Gilles three days later, in Paris, to talk more about my retirement.

"I'll stay a year in Afghanistan," I told him. "Not more. When I come back, I want to retire and marry Fatima and live with her in Germany."

Gilles was silent for several seconds, and then he spoke.

"I'm not in control of that," he said. "But tomorrow I would like you discuss all of this with my boss."

Gilles had never mentioned his boss before.

"I don't want to talk to your boss," I said. "I want to talk to you. You're the one who promised to take care of me, back when I first came to you in Brussels."

Gilles wouldn't look at me—he just shook his head. I could tell he wasn't happy, either. So we both stood up and shook hands and said our goodbyes.

At the time, I had no idea that this was the last conversation I would ever have with Gilles.

"There's a brother who would like to meet with you."

The words surprised me. I was with Khaled at Finsbury Park, and the *al-Jum'a* prayers had just ended.

"Who?" I asked. My heart was racing. I was frightened that it might be someone from Brussels, someone who knew what I had done.

"Someone you know," he told me. "Someone from *al-Jibal*." Someone from the mountains. The training camps. My heart slowed down slightly but still I was anxious, as I was each time my two worlds seemed on the brink of colliding. Khaled told me to go to Four Feathers the following Friday. They would be waiting for me there.

When I told my handlers, they were very excited. They told me to make the meeting last as long as possible, and to walk with him outside if possible so they could get good pictures.

When I got to Four Feathers, I couldn't find Khaled. I sat down towards the back of the hall and made my *salat*. When I stood up, I spotted Khaled standing with Abdul Haq, the Moroccan from Khaldan. The one who lived in London with his sister. The one who got to use the GPS first.

It was very strange seeing him there, in a crowded gym in London. I had a brief flashback to my life in the camps: the taste of the food, the constant sound of gunfire, the hard, cold ground I slept on every night. I walked over and saluted Abdul Haq. Khaled wandered off, leaving the two of us alone.

"We shouldn't be seen together here," he said under his breath. Then he told me to meet him the following Friday at the *al-Jum'a* services at Regent's Park. I agreed.

When I met Penny and Alexandre that afternoon, they were very excited. They had taken hundreds of photographs of Abdul Haq as we walked out of Four Feathers, and wanted to take more in Regent's Park.

Abdul Haq and I spent two hours together the following Friday. We sat on a bench in the park and he passed along greetings from Ibn Sheikh and Abu Bakr. He told me that Assad Allah had hurt himself very badly in an explosives experiment, and had lost one of his hands.

Abdul Haq told me that he had been in London for six weeks, and that he was going back to Pakistan in a few days. He asked me if I, too, was planning to return to the camps.

"Yes," I told him. "Probably in a year or so."

Abdul Haq was the only person from the camps I ever saw in London. But I learned more about Abu Bakr from Alexandre. One day, he came to our meeting and slapped a photo of Abu Bakr down on the table in front of me. "Do you know who that is?" he asked. He was clearly excited.

"It's Abu Bakr," I said. I was eager to know more.

"That's right!" Alexandre was grinning from ear to ear. "We just picked him up in Jordan."

That's the last thing I ever heard about Abu Bakr.

GIA

The civil war in Algeria raged through the summer of 1997. There were new reports of massacres in the papers almost every day. The conflict was taking its toll at Finsbury Park. Even some of the men who had migrated over from Four Feathers because of Abu Hamza's support for the GIA were growing alienated. The arguments that had once been conducted in low whispers were now loud and very public.

By August, the massacres had reached a new order of magnitude. Towards the end of the month, the GIA killed hundreds of people in an attack on Sidi Moussa, outside of Algiers. They arrived late at night and butchered into the morning. They burned corpses and left severed heads scattered around the village. When they left, they took several young women with them as trophies.

Even Khaled was beginning to have his doubts. Rumors continued to fly that the massacres had been committed by the Algerian military in order to turn people against the GIA, but Khaled was finding these harder and harder to believe. Eventually, he told me that he had learned that the GIA had been infiltrated by the *mukhabarat*, the secret service. The GIA had been corrupted, he said, and he was withdrawing his support.

Abu Hamza was smart enough to see what was happening. Although he had rallied his followers on behalf of the GIA earlier in the year, he was much more tentative now. He spoke less and less about Algeria in his sermons.

One night, Abu Hamza brought a small group of us into his office to talk about the GIA. He asked everyone to sit down and then he picked up the phone and dialed a number. Eventually, a voice came on the line. Then Abu Hamza put on the speakerphone and then explained to us that the voice belonged to a GIA commander in the field in Algeria.

Abu Hamza was tough on the commander that night, and pressed him to explain the GIA's actions. The commander was speaking on a satellite phone and it was hard to hear everything he said, but I understood enough. The villagers had supported the FIS, he explained. The GIA represented the true Islam. The villagers had therefore ceased to be Muslims.

A few weeks later, Abu Hamza publicly denounced the GIA, just as Abu Qatada had done many months earlier. And like Abu Qatada, he announced that he would no longer support *Al Ansar*.

More than anything else, this episode proved to me that Abu Hamza was a sham. His objectives shifted with the wind. He needed the GIA to seduce followers away from Abu Qatada. Now, he saw that he might lose more than he gained by continuing to support it. For Abu Hamza, it was all about the *zakat*, the money he collected every week after the *al-Jum'a* prayers. The more people attended, the more cash there would be.

I was pretty sure where the money was going. Algeria had never really mattered to Abu Hamza. Only Yemen did.

It would take years for the British to crack down on Abu Hamza. He wasn't arrested until 2004, and then only because the Americans demanded his extradition. Abu Hamza had been trying to set up a training camp in Oregon.

Abu Hamza had already been in trouble in 1998, when he was linked to the kidnapping of sixteen Western tourists in Yemen. In exchange for releasing prisoners, the kidnappers allegedly demanded the release of five British men who had been arrested in Yemen a few weeks earlier on charges of trying to stage terrorist attacks within the country. One of the men was Abu Hamza's son.

Abu Hamza was convicted in Britain early in 2006 of crimes including solicitation to murder and incitement to racial hatred. He was sentenced to seven years in prison. America is still hoping to extradite him so that he can face charges in the United States as well. Among other things, the FBI is investigating Abu Hamza for allegedly transferring funds to his old friend and mentor Abu Khabab al-Masri, his former explosives trainer at Darunta.

Abu Hamza and Abu Qatada were both editors of *Al Ansar* in London. But there was at least one other editor as well. His name was Rachid Ramda. He was arrested in London at the end of 1995. The French accused him of being one of the conspirators in the Paris metro bombings the previous summer. They desperately wanted him extradited to France, but the British took a full decade to do so. The long delay caused tremendous friction between the French and British intelligence services. The French were so frustrated with the British that at one point they considered grabbing Abu Hamza off the street and taking him back to France to stand trial. They knew the British would never do it on their own.

Rachid Ramda was finally extradited to France at the beginning of 2006. In March 2006, he was convicted for criminal conspiracy in the Paris metro bombings. He was sentenced to ten years in prison and may stand on trial on further counts of murder and attempted murder, also for those attacks.

Rachid Ramda operated in Europe under the code "Elias." It was the name I had heard so many times in Brussels, on the lips of Amin and Yasin and Tarek, the man I would later come to know as Ali Touchent.

World Cup

One day, Alexandre brought just a single picture to our meeting. This was unusual; he and Mark generally showed me stacks at a time. He put the photo down on the table and I studied it carefully. The man in the picture looked familiar, but I couldn't say why.

"That's Abdul Kerim," Alexandre said. "From the camps."

"No." I shook my head. I was almost certain it wasn't him. The man in the photo had some of the same features as Abdul Kerim, but it wasn't the same man.

The following week, Alexandre came with a different photo.

"That's Abdul Kerim," I said. This time, I recognized the picture immediately, before Alexandre was even able to put it down on the table.

"That's right," he said. He had a huge smile on his face. "We got him. His name is Farid Melouk."

I was dumbfounded, and I waited for Alexandre to tell me more.

"You were a big help on this one," he said. That was all. We never spoke about Abdul Kerim again.

Farid Melouk was arrested in early March of 1998, during a series of raids around Brussels aimed at dismantling a GIA cell. Since 1995, Melouk had been on France's list of most-wanted criminals. He was convicted in absentia in France in 1997 as an accessory to the Paris metro bombings.

Farid Melouk didn't surrender when his house was raided. Instead, he fired at the police. He held out for more than twelve hours before they were finally able to arrest him. The newspapers reported that when the police searched the house they found forged passports, detonators, and other materials for making explosives. Farid Melouk and the other men who were arrested with him were said to have been plotting an attack on the World Cup soccer tournament in Paris that summer.

Later in the spring, European police forces raided GIA cells across the continent. There were arrests—nearly one hundred in all—in Belgium, France, Germany, Italy, and Switzerland. The raids were said to have prevented a massive attack on the World Cup.

In 1999, Farid Melouk was sentenced in Brussels to nine years in prison. He had been convicted on charges including stockpiling weapons and running a major trafficking ring in forged passports and identity papers for the GIA in Europe.

The World Cup that year came off without at hitch. I watched most of it with the phone to my ear. I had never been any good at soccer, and had never paid much attention to matches when they were on television. But Fatima was a huge soccer fan and we liked to watch the games together, even though we were apart.

Sometimes, Mark and I would talk about politics. Mark was very smart, and I could tell that he was trying to understand what he was up against. But he had huge blind spots as well. I think he understood, for instance, why the Soviet invasion of Afghanistan was such an important watershed for Muslims. He understood that in that case the *mujahidin* were fighting for their land.

But I tried to explain to Mark that it wasn't just foreign armies that were invading Muslim countries. Just as often, it was foreign money or propaganda or weapons. All the Western puppets ruling the Middle East and North Africa, the Russian puppets in central Asia.

"You won't be free of what you call terrorism," I said, "until you get off our land and out of our politics."

Mark still seemed confused, and I tried to explain it to him more clearly.

"Look what you've done in Algeria," I said. "The Algerians had a democratic election for the first time, and when the West realized it wouldn't like the outcome, you shut the whole thing down."

"It wasn't our fault!" Mark protested. "The Algerian military shut those elections down."

"And what did you do about it?" I asked. "Nothing. You did nothing. And now you negotiate with them as if it were a legitimate regime."

"What else can we do?" he asked. "We have to talk to *someone*."

Amin

And then one day it happened. The thing I had been dreading for three years, since I left Brussels. My past finally caught up with me. Or at least I think it did.

I was leaving Finsbury Park one night and walking towards the tube station when I was stopped by three men. They were all young, no older than twenty. They surrounded me and blocked my way forward. I immediately sensed that I was in danger.

"*Assalamu'alaykum*," said one of the men. He wasn't smiling, nor were the others.

"*Alaykum assalam*," I replied, staring him straight in the eye.

The man held out a piece of paper. "Amin would like to see you," he said.

My heart nearly stopped. I took the piece of paper and opened it up. There was a short note scribbled in Arabic: "Follow the brothers. They will bring you to me. Amin."

I stayed calm, and looked the man in the eye. "I don't know anyone named Amin," I said. "You've made a mistake. You must be looking for someone else." I handed the note back to him.

"We're not making a mistake," he said. "Amin was in the mosque tonight, standing just a few feet away from you. He pointed you out to us."

I shook my head. "I'm sorry, but you really are making a mistake. I really don't know who this is."

With that, I pushed my way past them and into the tube station.

All of my senses were on high alert that night. I was aware of every person, every movement around me. I watched in the tube station. I watched on the train. I watched on the street as I walked home. I watched everything and everyone to make sure I wasn't being followed.

When I got home, I locked the doors and lay down in bed, but I couldn't sleep, so I got up and put my clothes back on and went outside. I walked around the block, and then around the next two blocks on every side to make sure there was no one staking me out. I found nothing, so I went back to my flat.

As I lay awake that night, I thought about what it could mean. Of course, my first instinct was to assume that Amin had been released from jail and had come to find me in London. He was going to exact his revenge. He would have me killed for my betrayal.

But there was another possibility as well, one just as frightening. Maybe Amin was someone else. Maybe the men had used the name the way I had used it with Khaled and Ibn Sheikh, as a kind of code for insiders. They knew that it was a name I would respond to.

What, then, did they want? I could think of only one possibility: I was being called up for a mission. I had been in London for nearly two years and maybe my time had come. I hadn't spoken to Abu Zubayda or anyone else in Peshawar for nearly a year, but this meant nothing. My job for them was to watch and wait.

Either way, I was in real trouble. I tossed in bed all night. I would fall asleep and then wake up minutes later in a state of panic. For years, I had successfully maintained two very different roles: spy and *mujahid*. But now everything was caving in on me. I didn't know what to do.

Mark, Alexandre, Penny—they were all angry with me when I told them what had happened. They wanted to know why I hadn't followed the men. Of course,

I couldn't explain it. I just told them that in my gut it didn't feel safe. They wanted me to find the brothers again at Finsbury Park and take them up on their offer.

"We'll provide you with security," Mark said.

Of course, it was obvious to me that none of them cared at all about my security. They never had. But it didn't matter. There was no amount of security that would have made me follow those men.

I knew one thing only: I needed to get away. I needed to leave London and put an end to my life as a spy.

Africa

I was incredibly tense in the weeks after my encounter with the three men outside Finsbury Park. I was wired all the time, aware of everything and everyone around me. I continued to go to Finsbury Park on Fridays but avoided it at all other times; I didn't want to run into those men again. I avoided Khaled, too, as much as I could, and when I saw him I guarded my words.

I had trouble sleeping—it was impossible to relax. Even Fatima couldn't calm me down, because I couldn't tell her what had happened. I didn't want her to worry. And so I went to Covent Garden every night. I knew I was safe in Covent Garden. No one would look for me there, and anyway there were crowds all around. I sat at the café for hours at a time, listening to music and drinking wine. The tightness in my chest would ease slightly, and my mind wouldn't race like it did the rest of the time. It was the best I could do.

And then, in an instant, my life changed completely—again. On August 7, 1998, the American embassies in Dar es Salaam and Nairobi were attacked within minutes of each other. Hundreds were killed; thousands were injured.

I watched the story unfold that morning on CNN. Images of the destruction alternated with so-called experts who tried to explain what had happened and why. They drove me mad. They understood nothing. They used different words and phrases, but every one of them ended up saying the same thing: this happened because the Muslims hate us.

It wasn't the experts who bothered me most, though. It was one of the images of the scene in Nairobi. Huge sections of the embassy had collapsed and the site was chaos. There were American soldiers everywhere, but they weren't dressed like soldiers. No one had expected this to happen, and when it did they must have raced to the scene. The soldiers were carrying rifles, but they were still wearing their street clothes.

I saw something horrible happen then. It took just an instant. There was an African man walking through the rubble. He looked dazed. He was either a victim or he was looking for one. But one of the American soldiers pushed him away. I could see the soldier yelling at the man, and threatening him. Even though the embassy was gone, the American was still guarding it.

The image sickened me. Hundreds of Africans had died that day, not because of anything they had done but because they were in the way when the Americans were attacked. They were collateral damage, nothing more. They died because the Americans were there in the first place. But that American soldier didn't care. All he cared about was the American victims, the American embassy. Nothing else mattered.

That afternoon, I did something I had never done before. I turned off my mobile phone. When Daniel gave it to me, he told me to carry it with me all the time. And I had. It was always on, in case one of my handlers called me or someone from Peshawar or even Khaled, whose phone calls were always recorded. But that day I turned it off and left it on the table by my bed.

I walked for hours through London that afternoon and into the evening. Everything I had tried to keep out of my mind spilled back in all at once. It was like a huge dam had broken. Memories I didn't even realize I had suddenly returned. My father and mother fighting. My brother shot dead in the school yard. Buck Danny and my ear and Édouard and Hakim and Amin and Yasin and Laurent and Tarek and my first meeting with Gilles and the car trip to Morocco and the raids and then Pakistan and Afghanistan and the guns and the bombs and the Chechens and Ibn Sheikh and Abu Bakr and Assad Allah and Abu Khabab and the embassy bombing in Islamabad and my reunion with Gilles in Istanbul. Image after image after image, like the photos that Gilles and Alexandre and Mark and Daniel and Penny always showed me. But unlike the photos, every one of these images meant something to me, even as they shifted in my mind and changed shape. They all seemed sinister now.

When I returned home late that night, the telephone was ringing. I picked it up.

"They called me." It was Fatima's voice.

"Who called you?" I asked.

"Mark and Alexandre," she said. "They couldn't find you. You didn't have your mobile with you. They want you to call right away."

No one from the services had ever called Fatima before. I had given Gilles her contact information early on, but I never thought they would use it. I knew instantly that it must be serious, so I called Mark's number and left a message. He called back almost immediately, and arranged a meeting for the next morning. I could tell from his voice that he was incredibly tense.

When I got to the flat, Mark and Alexandre were already there. We sat down and Alexandre began speaking. "This may come as a surprise," he said, "but because of the bombings yesterday, we've decided to accelerate the schedule for your trip to Afghanistan." Then he pushed an airline ticket across the table towards me. "You'll be leaving for Dakar later today."

I wasn't particularly surprised by any of it. I just felt incredibly relieved. They could have sent me anywhere at that point, so long as I could leave London.

It was Mark's turn to speak. "We need you to go home and pack up just what you'll need at the beginning," he said. "We'll have the rest sent to you." Then he leaned forward slightly. "Leave behind everything that connects you to London—phone numbers, addresses, photographs. Everything."

It became clear at that moment: the British wanted to get rid of me. I had gone missing on the day of the bombings. They must have worried that I was, in fact a sleeper and that I had disappeared to pursue some mission. I couldn't blame them, of course. I was a trained killer. From the very beginning they hadn't trusted me; I knew that. I had pushed them on some things, like the money. Other things I had refused to do. And I suppose my politics put them off as well. It would have been easier if I had seen the world in simple categories of good and evil.

The British must have wondered which side I was really on. Of course, I knew which side I was on; I was no double agent. I had lived in both worlds, and I understood them both. But I was never working for Ibn Sheikh or Abu Zubayda while I was in London. That was always clear to me, even if it wasn't clear to them.

In the end, I think the British had an image in their minds of what a spy should be, and I had never lived up to it. I was no James Bond, fighting for queen and country. I think I had always confused them. But now, the day after two embassies blew up, I probably scared them as well.

Mark told me to leave everything behind that connected me to London, so I handed him back the mobile phone Daniel had given me two years earlier.

"Oh, no, you can keep that," he said, pushing the phone back towards me. "Take it to Dakar with you. You can give it to your handler there."

The Brits tried to be subtle, but they could never quite pull it off. "You really don't trust me, do you?" I asked Mark.

Of course, I already knew the answer and so did he. As long as I had the moble phone with me, the Brits could track my whereabouts. They wanted to get rid of me, but they also wanted to know exactly where I was every minute of the day.

As we stood up to go, Alexandre and I arranged to meet so he could take me to the airport. It was clear I would never see Mark again, so I shook his hand and said goodbye. Then I went home to pack my things.

Later that day, I had drinks at the airport with Alexandre before my departure. Of the three of them, I liked Alexandre the most. He was young but very serious, and I could tell his work was important to him.

"I hope I didn't waste your time," I said at one point.

Alexandre understood what I was saying. He understood that I had been unhappy in London. "You didn't waste our time," he said. "I can assure you of that. You should see the stack of files we have from everything you told us. It's taller than I am."

I was grateful to him for saying that.

GERMANY

Dakar

I met Philippe at the airport in Dakar. Before I left London, Alexandre had told me that Philippe was the *chef*—the boss. Both he and Gilles reported to Philippe. But even if Alexandre hadn't told me so, I would have known that Philippe was someone important. He was middle-aged, and his face was in no way extraordinary. But I could see scars on his hands and arms. Real scars, from real fighting. I was impressed.

On the way to the hotel, I noticed something else—his voice. I knew that I had heard it before, but it took me several minutes to figure out where. Then it dawned on me: Philippe was the man I had talked to the night after the raids, when I was at the commissariat on the French border. He had spoken to me very gently that night, and he had used my first name. I remembered that very clearly because it was the only time anyone in any of the services ever did.

That day, Philippe just smiled when I asked him if he was the man who had called me that night. Several months later, he would admit that he was.

Shortly after I arrived in Dakar, Bill Clinton launched air strikes in Sudan and Afghanistan in retaliation for the embassy attacks. The Americans targeted terrorist bases near Khowst, only a few miles from Khaldan, and Jalalabad, quite near Darunta. I couldn't believe that the DGSE would send me back to Afghanistan after that, but Philippe assured me the mission was still on. He set me up at a gym with a personal trainer so that I could get back in shape, and told me to enjoy myself while the DGSE put their plans in place. He said that he was traveling a lot, but that he would stop off in Dakar several times a month to meet with me.

I stayed at a luxurious hotel in Dakar, and got an outrageous amount of money each week. Thousands of dollars—more than I had ever gotten before. At first, I didn't understand. And I didn't care, really. I was focused on getting back into the field. In many ways, I was looking forward to Afghanistan. After nearly two years of boredom in England, the intense activity of the camps seemed thrilling. And I looked forward to seeing Ibn Sheikh and the others after so much time.

My work as a spy also seemed more urgent now. The world was finally paying attention to Afghanistan. Earlier in the year, bin Laden had issued his *fatwa* against the United States, and the West had learned from the embassy bombings how serious the threat really was. Now, finally, people would be interested in what was happening inside the camps.

But two months after I arrived in Dakar, Philippe told me that the mission had been canceled. I wasn't completely surprised. From the first time Gilles mentioned it to me in London, I doubted it would ever really come off. But still, I wanted to know why.

"They've found out who I am, haven't they?" I could rarely extract information from Philippe, but sometimes if I offered a proposition I could tell from his reaction whether I had nailed it or not. His expression gave nothing away this time.

"There are all sorts of reasons," he told me. "Some of them have to do with you, and some of them have to do with other things out in the world."

That was as close as I would ever get to an explanation.

A few days after that, Philippe gave me my Moroccan passport, and took back the French one that Gilles had given me in Paris. The last stamp in the Moroccan passport was the one I had gotten in Dakar more than two years earlier, before I went to London. There was no way I could use it. I would be arrested on the spot at the Dakar airport when they saw that I had been in the country for so long. But when I protested to Philippe, he told me not to worry. The DGSE would have a new one for me in a couple of weeks.

Of course, the passport didn't appear in a couple of weeks, or a couple of weeks after that. Philippe assured me that these were just minor holdups, that it would be coming any day. He continued to give me absurd amounts of money every week.

Soon I was fed up, and I told Philippe that if I wasn't going to Afghanistan then I wanted to go back to Germany to get married. I had given up on the DGSE. But the DGSE hadn't given up on me, and Philippe tried to convince me to change my mind. Every time we met, he would ask me if I was certain that I wanted to marry Fatima. Every time, I told him I was. Finally, one day, he said it outright.

"I think you're making a mistake."

"What do you mean?" I asked.

"I think you'll get married and retire and then after three months you'll miss the work and you'll want to come back."

"I could do both," I said. "I can work when I'm married."

Philippe shook his head. "No," he said. "A married agent is only half an agent." Then he smiled and looked down at his wedding band. "Trust me, I know."

I waited for months in Dakar. Every time I saw him, Philippe assured me that the DGSE was putting plans in place with the Germans for my new life there. But nothing ever came of it.

After five months, I'd had enough. Philippe had replaced my British moblie phone with one wired by the DGSE (although of course he never admitted that). So I used the phone to call Fatima.

"I'm sick of waiting for them," I told her. "I'm going to find a way to get to Germany on my own." It was the only way to put pressure on the DGSE. I knew they didn't want to let me out of their control; they had no idea what I would do. And they knew that if I set my mind to it, I would be able to slip into Europe on my own. After all, I had infiltrated the Afghan training camps without their help.

And so I wasn't remotely surprised when Philippe showed up the next day.

"Good news!" he said with a wide smile. "We've sorted everything out. You're flying to Germany in two days."

It wasn't until much later that I understood what the DGSE was trying to do in Dakar: they wanted to keep me from getting married. That's what all the money was for. They wanted to show me how glamorous the life of a spy was. Exotic cities, expensive restaurants, fancy hotels.

Of course, spying had never been glamorous for me. I had slept on the bare earth in Afghanistan for a year and eaten nothing but lentils and stale bread. In London, I lived in a flat not much bigger than my own body. But I never really minded any of it.

This was what the DGSE had never understood: it was never about the money for me. Gilles had assumed it was, and that's why at the very beginning he didn't believe that I would give the twenty-five thousand francs back to Tarek. He had made this mistake again in Istanbul, when he thought he could make me disappear for fifteen thousand dollars. And Philippe was making the same mistake now, in Dakar.

Of course I liked the money, and I spent it when I had it. I enjoyed the fancy restaurants, the five-star hotels. But I didn't need them. These were not the things that motivated me.

What did motivate me? Different things at different times, I suppose. At first, when I was in Belgium, I needed the DGSE to protect me and my family. I didn't work for them because I believed in what they were doing, but because I didn't want to get killed. But that changed over time, as I learned more about the group I had fallen in with, about the GIA. Then the DGSE's mission became mine.

At some point during my time in the camps, our missions had diverged again. Of course, we agreed on many things still: we didn't want to see innocent people murdered, whether it was on a metro in Paris or at an embassy in Nairobi. But after I returned from Afghanistan, I knew that there was little I could do to prevent it. Even if I helped stop one attack, like the plot to blow up the World Cup, something else would come soon after. These attacks were inevitable as long as the West refused to try to understand the Muslim mind, the logic of *jihad*. I had tried to explain it to my handlers again and again. I had tried to explain what I had seen and heard and felt in those camps. But they didn't want to hear it.

The day before I left, Philippe explained what would happen in Germany. He told me that a French contact would await me at the airport, and then would help insert me into Germany. I would tell the German authorities I was an Algerian fleeing the war and claim refugee status. I would get my new identity, and the German services would help me begin a new life. I would get married, and I would be safe.

I had grown to like Philippe during the five months I spent in Dakar. I liked him because he had been so kind to me on the phone that night after the raids in Brussels. And I liked him because in Dakar he had also been kind, in his fashion. I could tell he believed in me, that he wanted me to stay on as an agent. I think he really believed it was the life I was cut out for.

On my last night, Philippe took me to an elegant restaurant outside the city. I was in a wonderful mood because I was looking forward to the new life I was about to begin. I felt like celebrating, so I ordered *langoustines*, the most expensive item on the menu.

"Oh, no," Philippe said. "You don't want that. You should try the grouper instead. It's fabulous here."

I immediately understood something about Philippe, and I laughed.

"This is where you take your lovers, isn't it?" As I looked around the room it seemed completely obvious to me. The candles, the soft music.

Philippe looked shocked at first, and then he laughed, too, and I knew I was right.

He shook his head and smiled. "You really are a motherfucker," he said, still laughing.

At that moment, I think we understood each other completely.

Germany

Philippe had given me back my French passport for the trip to Germany, so I breezed through customs when I got to Frankfurt. I met my contact, Olivier, outside the baggage claim. He was in his late twenties, and he was quite extraordinary. He was one of the most fit Europeans I had ever seen. He had a handsome face, and he was very elegant. He wasn't wearing anything special, just jeans and a blazer, but his clothes were very fine and perfectly cut. He was the only intelligence officer I had worked with who actually looked like James Bond.

Olivier gave me careful instructions on what to do next. I was to go to the police station and present myself as a refugee. I would get some papers there, and I would take them to a refugee-processing center nearby. I would stay there overnight, and then they would take me to a holding center for asylum seekers. There I would meet a German agent, who would steer me through the process.

Before he dropped me off, Olivier gave me some notes outlining the story of my trip to Germany. I was to tell the police and anyone else that I had traveled from Algeria to Turkey, and then worked my way across Europe through Bulgaria, Romania, Hungary, Slovakia, and the Czech Republic. He gave me cash in the currency of each of those countries to use as evidence in support of my story, to prove where I had been.

Before he left, Olivier told me not to worry about anything. The German secret service had planned for my arrival. He gave me a phone number I could use to reach him, and took my French passport. Then he drove away.

I went to the police station as Olivier instructed me, and then to the processing center to check in. The official there told me that the next morning a bus would take me to Eisenhüttenstadt, a city on the Polish border.

I had no intention of staying overnight at the processing center, so I got myself a hotel room in downtown Frankfurt instead. I also didn't want to take a bus across the entire country, so the next day I bought myself a train ticket for Eisenhüttenstadt.

Eisenhüttenstadt is an ugly Stalin-era city at the eastern edge of Germany. A few kilometers outside of town, there is a military base once used by the Red Army. Now it's a detention center for asylum seekers.

I checked myself in with the papers I had been given in Frankfurt. I ended up staying for six nights without any contact from the services. It was heartbreaking. The place was crammed full of refugees from some of the most dismal places on earth: Africa, Sri Lanka, Afghanistan. They had been traveling for weeks to get here, and they were filthy.

These were desperate people. They had given up whatever homes they had to make this journey. Many, of course, were not running from war or persecution; they were fleeing from famine or wrenching poverty. Of course, these were the ones that were supposed to be turned back. Terrible suffering was not grounds for asylum.

In the end, it didn't really matter why any of these people were there, because most of them would be sent back. A great many would die as a result. I knew how careless the Europeans were about asylum-seekers, how unwilling they were to allow all these dark-skinned people across their borders.

The sadness was oppressive inside the center, and I needed to get out. I learned I could get a pass that would allow me to check out for a few hours to go into the city. But nobody else ever wanted to come with me. After a few days, I asked an Afghani why everyone was staying inside. He told me people were scared to leave. There were skinheads all over the city who preyed on refugees, insulting them and beating them mercilessly and even killing them sometimes.

On any given day, there are thousands of people from all over the world praying to God for a chance to live in a country such as this.

It was in Eisenhüttenstadt that I first met Klaus. It was a complete disaster. A guard came to collect me in the dormitory and took me into an office. Klaus was waiting for me there.

"*Guten Tag. Mein Name ist Klaus. Wissen Sie wer ich bin?*"

Of course, I knew German—I had learned it from Fatima—but it made me angry anyway. I thought of all of the refugees in the center and I imagined what it must be like for them, to be confronted by these arrogant Europeans in a language that they couldn't understand.

"I'm sorry," I said. "Could you repeat that in English?"

"I'm Klaus," he said impatiently. "Do you know who I am?"

Apparently Klaus was a prick in every language.

"Yes, I know who you are. You're with the German secret service."

"That's right," he said. He had a smug look on his face that I didn't like at all. "Now you're going to answer some questions."

That was enough for me. I had been waiting for nearly a week in this hell-hole. I had no patience for this horrible, condescending German.

"I'm not answering any questions here," I told him. "If you want to ask me questions, then we can do it back in west Germany." I wasn't going to let him have power over me, and as long as we were in the detention center he had it. The air was heavy with an implied threat: he could leave me there if I didn't obey his orders. But I knew better. I got up to go.

"What are you doing?" he asked.

"I'm leaving."

"You can't leave," he said. "Not until you get your papers."

"I don't need any papers," I told him. "I can travel anywhere I like." Then I wrote down my mobile phone number and handed it to Klaus. "Call me in a few days. We'll find another place to talk."

I left the center and took a taxi to the train station. I bought a ticket to Cologne, where Fatima lived. But I had barely settled into my seat on the train when my phone rang.

"You have to come back right now." It was Klaus. "You need to get your papers." He told me that I had to go through these steps just like all the other refugees if I wanted to establish my identity.

I wasn't going to go through any more steps. I remembered what Gilles had told me the first day I met him: *If you want all these things you'll have to do more for us.* I had done more—more than anyone expected. I had spent six years working for these people. I had risked my life again and again. I had gotten into the heart of this global menace they were now calling Al Qaeda. What more was there?

"No," I told Klaus. "No. I won't do it. It's your responsibility to get me the papers. You figure it out." Then I hung up.

I met with Klaus again two weeks later, at an airport hotel in Hannover. He was there with another man named Matthias. There was tension in the room already when I arrived; as soon as Klaus and Matthias began talking it was obvious that they didn't like each other. Because Matthias didn't like Klaus, I immediately liked Matthias.

In that meeting, and in several more that followed, it became very clear that the Germans had no plan for me at all. There was no way for me to get a proper job without the papers. Klaus and Matthias kept promising them, but they never seemed to materialize. There was no way for me to get married, either, which was even more frustrating. We couldn't live together until we got married. In the meantime, I was living in a small apartment Fatima had rented under her name.

I met with Olivier a few more times during my first months in Germany. He told me again and again that there was nothing he could do. I had to rely on Klaus and Matthias as long as I was in Germany. The DGSE had coordinated everything with them. But it didn't seem very coordinated to me. Whenever I mentioned Olivier's name to Klaus and Matthias, they shook their heads and told me not to talk about him. They were never going to acknowledge that there was any sort of agreement in place between the German and French services. They never said it, of course, but it was obvious that they wanted total deniability. They didn't want to take responsibility for me, either.

I needed money. I was living off of Fatima's tiny income and I hated it. I needed money to pay for my apartment and to eat. And I also needed to save money for my wedding. I couldn't earn money on my own, however, without the papers. It would have been very hard even if I had them: I was thirty-two years old and had never held a job. At least not one I could list on my résumé.

There was only one way to make money: I had to work as a spy. At first, it seemed like a good idea. It was certainly what the Germans expected of me. But it didn't take long to figure out that they had no real assignment for me. I was sent to a Muslim community center in Oberhausen, a city with a large North African population about seventy kilometers from Cologne. I went there every Friday.

When I met with Matthias and Klaus after each trip, they didn't even show me photographs. "What are your impressions?" they would ask. My impressions were very simple: it was a group of Moroccan teenagers who played sports together and studied the Kur'an. There was nothing to worry about.

It was much worse, even, than my work in England. The job was incredibly boring and completely useless. But the real problem was that I couldn't afford to do it. I was spending hundreds of Deutschmarks a month just for the gas to drive back and forth, but the Germans were paying me almost nothing. They knew they could get away with it because I was trapped. I didn't have papers, so I couldn't work for anyone else.

After a few months, I was going crazy. I told the Germans I needed more money, but I never got it. I felt like Klaus was still punishing me for our first meeting. He would let me beg for just a few more marks, and then delight in telling me no. I despised him, and we clashed all the time.

Matthias tried to help when he could, but he seemed powerless as well. Once, when we were alone, Matthias explained that he and Klaus worked for different divisions within the service, and that he had no authority to intervene. Sometimes, he even gave me money out of his own pocket. He obviously felt as helpless as I did.

Finally, something good happened. After nine months in Germany, I got my marriage license. It had been almost three years since Fatima and I had met in Paris. Since that day, I had never once thought of her as my girlfriend. She was my future wife. Now the future had finally arrived.

A few days after the papers came through, I met with Olivier. I needed money for the wedding, and I wasn't going to get it from Klaus. I was entitled to the money, I told Olivier. The DGSE had promised to help me get married, and now I needed help.

We met again in a hotel room a few days later. Olivier was already there when I arrived, sitting at a table. He had a thick envelope in front of him, and it was open at the top. Inside, I could see the distinctive green of American dollars. My French passport was on the table as well. And an airline ticket.

I sat down across from Olivier.

"Are you sure this is what you want to do?" he asked.

"What do you mean?"

"Are you sure you want to get married?"

"Of course I am," I replied.

Olivier frowned. "You're a spy," he said. "I don't think you're cut out for married life. You'll be bored."

"I've been thinking about this for three years," I told him. "It wasn't a hasty decision. I know what I want."

Olivier exhaled. "That's a shame," he said. "I think we could do great things together." He seemed genuinely disappointed. There was a long pause between us as he waited for me to change my mind.

I shook my head. "I know what I'm doing."

Olivier smiled weakly. "All right, then," he said. "Then I'd better give you some money for your wedding." But he didn't pass me the envelope on the table. Instead, he reached down into his bag and pulled out a much smaller envelope. I opened it and looked inside. It was a thin stack of Deutschmarks.

Then Olivier stood up to leave, and I stood up as well. He held his hand out to me, but just as I was reaching forward he pulled back. "Wait," he said. "I almost forgot. I have something else for you." He plucked something from his bag and held it out to me.

It was my notebook from Darunta. It was so sick I almost laughed. They were truly ruthless. The DGSE had finally figured out that no amount of money was going to convince me to stay. And so they were going to *make* me stay. There were police outside waiting for me—I was sure of it. If I took that book, they would arrest me the minute I walked out the door. I was a terrorist; the book proved it. They would lock me up for years. Unless, of course, I decided to go back to work for the DGSE.

I looked at the notebook, and then at Olivier. "You've got to be kidding."

And then I walked out.

Soon after, I got married.

A few days after the wedding, I met up with Matthias in a café. We talked for a bit, and he congratulated me. As we were leaving, he handed me an envelope. "Someone asked me to get this to you," he said. He didn't explain himself further.

I opened the envelope. There was a single photograph inside. It was a picture of me and Fatima from the day we became officially engaged. I was wearing a suit and she was wearing a dress, and we were both so happy we were smiling like crazy people. It was my favorite photograph of the two of us, but I had left it behind in London with all my other things when I cleared out right after the embassy bombings. Nothing from that flat had been returned to me, and I had assumed I would never see the picture again.

The photo was my wedding present from Philippe. I was sure of it. It was his way of showing me that, everything else aside, he had delivered on this part of the promise.

Afterlife

They never delivered on any of the other promises.

I continued working for the Germans for a few months after my wedding, but it was going nowhere. I had a wife to support now, but they were still paying me less than a subsistence wage. They did eventually get a passport for me—under my own name. No new identity, no back story that would enable me to create a new life for myself. It was Klaus's doing, of course. He wanted power over me, and he wanted to punish me.

Eventually, Klaus and Matthias turned me over to a new handler, a young man named Georg. But I was too demoralized to start again, and so the first time I met alone with Georg I told him that I wanted to quit. He wasn't at all surprised; he had obviously heard all about my disastrous relationship with Klaus. He didn't even bother trying to convince me to stay on.

Georg sat there for a few minutes shaking his head. "I wish this wasn't happening," he said. "This isn't right." I could tell he felt awful. Then he reached inside his coat pocket. He took out a pack of cigarettes and handed it to me.

I was mystified. "What are these for?" I asked.

Georg gave me a sad, gentle smile. "I feel like we should be giving you something," he said. "But this is all I have." We both laughed.

I met with Matthias a few weeks later. He was more angry than sad. "You should get a lawyer," he said. "What happened to you is wrong."

It struck me as odd that a secret service officer was telling me to sue his own agency. And anyway, what lawsuit could I possibly bring? I had no proof of anything. Spies don't get employment contracts.

"I'm really not sure what that would accomplish," I told him. "I don't even know how to find a lawyer."

"I know one," he said. He jotted down a name and phone number on a piece of paper and handed it to me. "He's very good. You should call him."

I never called the lawyer, but Matthias and I met again a few weeks later. This time he told me to go to the media. He told me who I should go to, and outlined what I should say.

I knew that I was getting sucked into some further intrigue, and I didn't like it. I began asking questions. Slowly, Matthias revealed the truth: everyone hated Klaus. They knew that he was a problem, but there was nothing they could do because he had been forced on the service by a member of the Bundestag. The only way to get rid of him was to expose him publicly. With a lawsuit, for example, or an embarrassing story in the media.

Matthias tried several times to enlist me in his battle, but I wasn't interested.

"Don't you want to tell your story?" he asked. "Don't you want people to know what he did?"

"Don't worry," I said. "I'll tell my story. But not now. Not this way."

Now I have told my story. Why now?

When I started writing, I suppose it was mostly anger that motivated me. I had been living in Germany for five years without any papers, working in the most degrading jobs imaginable. I worked on assembly lines. I worked scrubbing toilets. I worked for bosses who treated me like dirt because I was a foreigner, an Arab. And no matter how much I worked I could never earn enough to support my wife. I still live off of Fatima's income.

Matthias was right: what happened to me was wrong. I gave up everything in the end. For years, I wanted to expose them—the Germans, the DGSE. But I didn't because I was afraid for Fatima. And I'm still afraid. But eventually I realized that I was going to lose her anyway. It has been very, very hard for her. It's not easy to live with a man who has no past. Most of the time I can't even use my name. My wife has never met my family, and she can't tell her family who I am or where I come from. She has to lie about me to her friends. We're hiding all the time.

This life has been too much for us, and it has nearly torn us apart. We both know that I am putting both of our lives at risk by publishing this book. But we don't have much of a life to lose.

There is another reason why I am telling my story now, however. An even more important one: the world has changed dramatically since 2000, when I quit my life as a spy. And I am devastated by what I see.

Like everyone else, I was horrified by the attacks of 9/11. But I wasn't surprised. I had been inside Al Qaeda for years, and to me the attacks seemed the inevitable outcome of all of the forces I had seen developing over the course of the 1990s. 9/11 was nothing more than a spectacular extension of the perverse logic the GIA used to justify the slaughter of so many innocents across Algeria. It was the logic of the Paris bombings, the logic of the embassy bombings in Islamabad and Nairobi and Dar es Salaam. Later, it would be the logic of the Madrid bombings, and the London bombings after that. It is the logic of the supply chain: anyone who supports the enemy is fair game. There are no civilians anymore. Everyone is at war.

This is the logic of the global *jihad*, and I despise it. There are soldiers, and there are civilians. Killing soldiers is war; killing civilians is murder. This is not merely my opinion. It is an article of my faith.

Let me be clear: I am a Muslim. And to this day, I would go to war for my faith. I am no longer a spy, but part of me remains a *mujahid*. I think the United States and all the others should get off our land, and stay off. I think they should stop interfering in the politics of Muslim nations. I think they should leave us alone. And when they don't they should be killed, because that's what happens to invading armies and occupiers.

I was appalled by the way the Americans reacted to 9/11. The endlessly naïve outrage: we've been attacked *on American soil*! Three thousand Americans killed *on American soil*! A tragedy, no doubt. And a crime. But what about the millions of Muslims killed on Muslim soil? In the Middle East, in Africa, in Bosnia, in Chechnya, in Afghanistan. Did time stop for them?

And so, yes, I believe that there are battles worth fighting. I believe that there is land worth dying for. But I also believe in laws. Perhaps more than any other religion, Islam has very clear laws about when and how to go to war. I learned these laws in the Afghan training camps. And I learned there that these laws are what make us different from and better than the Americans and the French and the Germans and the Russians and the English and everyone else. *They* kill however they can. *They* drop nuclear bombs on cities and kill millions in gas chambers and destroy whole populations to steal land and riches. *They* kill women and children, and then they shrug and call it "collateral damage."

These things are true. They've done these things for centuries. But we're Muslims, and the Kur'an tells us not to. That is the true Islam, the Islam I learned in the camps—at least in theory. Too often, what I saw in practice was something quite different.

And that is why I've told my story. I haven't told it because I want to save the West from the terrorists. That was never my goal. What I want more than anything is to save Islam from these terrible excesses and innovations.

From the very beginning, that Uzi bothered me. The fact that the Muslim world has become so degraded that we're forced to fight our wars using our enemies' weapons. But now something much worse is happening: we're fighting our wars using our enemies' tactics. If we, as Muslims, let ourselves become like *them*—which is to say, like *you*—then there will be nothing left to fight for.

This is my *jihad.*

Acknowledgments

I thank God for protecting me throughout all of the experiences I have described in this book.

I thank my wife with all of my heart for her trust in me, and for her support and encouragement during the time I spent writing this book. Most of all, I thank her for the tremendous courage it took for her to marry me, and for the courage she has shown in staying by my side every day since.

I thank Lara Heimert, my editor at Basic Books, for her faith in me, and for her energy in helping me bring this book into the world.

Finally, I thank my readers for letting me share my story.

Glossary

Algerian Civil War   A bloody conflict that consumed Algeria from 1992 until a declared amnesty in 1999. Also known as *le sale guerre* ("the dirty war"), it is believed to have claimed anywhere from 100,000 to 150,000 lives. In 1989, the ruling National Liberation Front (*Front de Libération Nationale*; FLN) revoked the previously existing ban on the creation of new political parties. Parliamentary elections followed in 1991, and the Islamic Salvation Front (*Front Islamique du Salut*; FIS) claimed a majority of seats in the first round. Fearing an Islamist victory in the second round, the government annulled the elections in 1992. It also banned the FIS, and arrested thousands of its members. The FIS continued to press for new elections, while a more radical splinter group—the Armed Islamic Group (*Groupe Islamique Armée*; GIA)—emerged to demand the implementation of an Islamic theocracy. Bolstered by large numbers of Arab *mujahidin* who had previously fought against the Soviet occupation of Afghanistan, the GIA became increasingly violent over the course of the 1990s. Opposed to both the ruling military government and the FIS, the GIA intimidated civilians by slaughtering entire families and even villages if a single member was known to have collaborated with either the government or the FIS. The government and its security forces, however, may have been partly responsible for some of the violence. They were repeatedly accused of infiltrating the GIA and perpetrating attacks in order to weaken popular support for the group. (*See also* Armed Islamic Group.)

Armed Islamic Group (Groupe Islamique Armée; GIA)   A militant Islamist group formed in the wake of cancelled elections in Algeria. The GIA massacred thousands of Algerian civilians during what became known as the Algerian Civil War. During this time, France was believed to be collaborating with Algeria's military regime. Angered by this, and as well as France's earlier colonial occupation of Algeria, the GIA expanded its operations to France in the mid-1990s. It hijacked an Air France flight in 1994 and claimed responsibility for many terrorist acts, most notably a series of bombings in France during the summer of 1995. After a 1999 general peace accord was passed, attacks began to diminish. In 2004, the head of the GIA, Nourredine Boudiafi, was arrested and the group declared to be disbanded. (*See also* Algerian Civil War; Ahmed Zaoui.)

Azzam, Abdullah   Described as "the Godfather of the Jihad," Abdullah Azzam played a vital role in the development of contemporary Islamic radicalism. His vision of a pan-Islamic *jihad* provided an ideological basis for Al Qaeda. Born in West Jordan in 1941, Azzam joined the Palestinian Muslim Brotherhood early in life. He completed a doctorate in Islamic jurisprudence at Al-Azhar University in Egypt. During that time, he befriended the family of Sayyid Qutb, whose work deeply influenced his own. He also grew close to Ayman al-Zawahiri, who would eventually become Osama bin Laden's second in command. Later, as a lecturer at King Abdul Aziz University in Saudi Arabia, he taught bin Laden himself.

Shortly after the Soviet invasion of Afghanistan, Azzam produced his influential *fatwa*, "Defense of the Muslim Lands," in which he developed the idea of a defensive and obligatory pan-Islamic *jihad* against all infidels who occupied lands of the former Islamic caliphate.

In 1984, Azzam established the *Maktab al-Khidmat* (MAK) in collaboration with his former student Osama bin Laden. The *Maktab al-Khidmat* functioned as a receiving station and training center for new *mujahidin* recruits from foreign countries. Azzam traveled all over the world—including more than fifty cities in the United States—to recruit, raise funds, and preach his vision of a global *jihad*. Azzam is thought to have recruited as many as twenty thousand *mujahidin* from twenty countries over the course of the 1980s.

As the Afghan war against Russia drew to a close, Azzam broke with bin Laden. He remained focused on Palestine as the most important *jihad* for Muslims, while bin Laden wanted to wage war against the United States and the various secular Muslim countries from which the *Maktab al-Khidmat* had recruited *mujahidin*. In 1989, Azzam was assassinated in Peshawar, Pakistan, by a car bomb. Bin Laden subsequently took over the *Maktab al-Khidmat*, which became the core of the group that would eventually be known as Al Qaeda.

Basayev, Shamil Salmanovich   Vice president of the separatist government of the Chechen Republic of Ichkeria, Basayev rose to worldwide attention in 1991, when he hijacked a Russian passenger jet in order to raise awareness of the Chechen cause. During the First and Second Chechen Wars (1994–1996 and 1999–present), Basayev claimed responsibility for several terrorist and military operations. One of these included taking hostage twelve hundred people in a hospital in Budyonnovsk, a town in southern Russia, during the summer of 1995. He also claimed responsibility for the Moscow theater siege in 2002, and the Beslan school massacre in of 2004 in which 350 people—most of them children—were killed. Some Russian authorities have argued that Basayev was connected to Al Qaeda, a charge that Basayev denied. Basayev was killed by Russian security forces in July 2006.

Bhutto, Benazir Prime minister of Pakistan for two terms: 1988–1990 and 1993–1996. Her father, Zulfikar Ali Bhutto, was Prime Minister of Pakistan from 1971 to 1977. When he was executed under the military regime of Mohammed Zia-ul-Haq in 1979, Benazir Bhutto became head of his political party, the Pakistan People's Party. Her coalition government was dismissed in 1990 under charges of corruption, but Bhutto returned to power in 1993. During the latter term, she tried unsuccessfully to combat the rise of Islamic extremism within Pakistan. Plagued by charges of corruption and mismanagement, her government was dismissed in November 1996.

DGSE (*Direction Générale de la Sécurité Extérieure*) General Directorate for External Security in France. Subordinate to the Ministry of Defense, the DGSE is responsible for military intelligence as well as for strategic information, electronic intelligence, and counterespionage outside the borders of French territory.

DST (*Direction de la Surveillance du Territoire*) Directorate of Territorial Security in France, the DST was created in 1944 to "struggle against activities of espionage and against the activities of alien powers on territories under French sovereignty."

Hekmatyar, Gulbuddin A Pashtun warlord and founder of the Islamist *Hezb-i-Islami mujahidin* group. His military efforts helped end the Soviet occupation, but he refused to take part in the *mujahidin* government that followed after the ousting of Mohammad Najibullah in 1992, on the grounds that it was un-Islamic. Throughout the period from 1992 to 1996, his forces fought to capture Kabul and establish a fundamentalist Islamic government within

Afghanistan. He accepted the position of prime minister within the Rabbani government twice—once in 1992 and again in 1993—but on both occasions agreements quickly broke down and Hekmatyar resumed hostilities. He accepted the position of prime minister in June 1996, but Hekmatyar's reconciliation with Rabbani's government came to an end only three months later, when the Taliban overran Kabul, (*See also* Northern Alliance; Ahmed Shah Massoud; Burhanuddin Rabbani; *Hezb-i-Islami*.)

Hezb-i-Islami   See Gulbuddin Hekmatyar.

Jama'at al-Tabligh   A grassroots Islamic movement established in India in 1926 by the religious scholar Mawlana Muhammad Ilyas, it has millions of followers in the Muslim world and the West. *Jama'at al-Tabligh* is Arabic for "the group that propagates the faith." Followers are encouraged to spend their time and money on journeys (*khurooj*) to seek religious knowledge and promote the faith, often among lapsed Muslims. Though the group describes itself as nonpolitical and nonviolent, over the last decade it has come under scrutiny for its connections to terrorist activity. In October 1995, a group of Tabligh soldiers from the Pakistani military were connected to a plot to overthrow Prime Minister Benazir Bhutto. More recently, several of the suspects in the plot to blow up multiple airplanes flying from Heathrow Airport in Britain to the United States are known to have had connections to Tabligh. The group has strenuously denied any connection to terrorist activity.

Khadr, Ahmed Said   An Egyptian national, Khadr emigrated to Canada in 1977. In the 1980s, he worked with the Ottawa-based Muslim charity Human Concern International (HCI). As part of his work for HCI, Khadr traveled to Pakistan and Afghanistan to aid refugees displaced by the Soviet invasion. He first met Osama bin Laden in 1985. In 1995, Khadr was arrested in Pakistan for suspicion of financing a car-bomb attack on the Egyptian embassy in Islamabad, Pakistan, that killed eighteen people. He was released in 1996 after Canada's Prime Minister Jean Chrétien intervened on his behalf. In October of 2003, Khadr was killed by a rocket fired from a helicopter during a firefight with Pakistani security forces along the Afghanistan-Pakistan border.

al-Khidmat, Maktab   See Abdullah Azzam.

al-Libi, Ibn al-Sheikh   Ibn al-Sheikh al-Libi ran several training camps in Afghanistan in the 1990s, and went on to become a high-ranking member of Al Qaeda. Captured in Pakistan in November 2001, he was sent by the CIA to Egypt for interrogation in January 2002. There, he gave testimony that Iraq had provided chemical and biological weapons training to members of Al Qaeda. In February 2002, the Defense Intelligence Agency (DIA) circulated his statements to the intelligence community, but declared it "likely that [al-Libi] is intentionally misleading debriefers." Al-Libi's claims were nevertheless used by officials within the Bush administration to make the case for the invasion of Iraq. Most notably, Secretary of State Colin Powell referenced al-Libi's statements in a February 2003 speech to the United Nations Security Council. In January 2004, al-Libi formally recanted his claims, and in February 2004, al-Libi the CIA recalled all claims based on his intelligence. In the spring of 2006, al-Libi was reportedly handed over to Libyan authorities.

Maaroufi, Tarek   Arrested in the March 1995 raids in Belgium, Maaroufi was released after only a year in prison. Maaroufi went on to become a commander (and possible founder) of the Tunisian Combat Group (TCG), an organization linked to Al Qaeda. He allegedly functioned as a recruiter for Al Qaeda in Europe until his arrest in December 2001 in Belgium on charges of procuring false Belgian passports for the men who assassinated Ahmed Shah Massoud. He was sentenced to six years in prison.

Hamza, Abu   An *imam* at the Finsbury Park mosque in London until his arrest in 2004. Abu Hamza emigrated from Egypt to the United Kingdom in 1979. In 1987, he met Abdullah Azzam, who convinced him to travel to Afghanistan to aid the *mujahidin*. In 1995, he went to Bosnia to support Bosnian Muslims. Arriving at Finsbury Park late in 1996, he took over the mosque in March 1997. He was arrested by the British in London in 2004 after the United States, which had charged him with setting up terrorist camps on American soil, demanded his extradition. He was convicted in London in February 2006 on charges including solicitation to murder and incitement of racial hatred. He was sentenced to seven years in prison.

al-Masri, Abu Khabab   The *nom de guerre* of Midhat Mursi al-Sayid Umar, Al Qaeda's chief bomb maker and chemical weapons expert. Al-Masri was killed on January 13, 2006, during a U.S. air strike in Damadola, Pakistan. Little is known about his background or activities prior to May 1999, when Ayman al-Zawahiri reportedly put him in charge of developing an unconventional weapons program for Al Qaeda.

Massoud, Ahmed Shah   An Afghan *mujahidin* commander in the Soviet-Afghan war. Massoud's army captured Kabul in 1992. After Najibullah's government collapsed, Massoud was appointed defense minister by the incoming president, Burhanuddin Rabbani. Between 1992 and 1996, Massoud led his forces in battle against rival groups attempting to overthrow Rabbani's government, including Gulbuddin Hekmatyar's *Hezb-i-Islami* and the *Taliban*. In 1996, the Taliban captured Kabul, and Massoud and Rabbani's retreated to northern Afghanistan where their Northern Alliance operated as a resistance group against the Taliban. Massoud was assassinated on September 9, 2001, by Al Qaeda agents disguised as journalists. (See also: Burhanuddin Rabbani; Northern Alliance; Gulbuddin Hekmatyar, Tarek Maaroufi)

Melouk, Farid   A French national of Algerian descent, Melouk was convicted by a French court in 1997 for supplying material support to the Armed Islamic Group (GIA) in connection to the Paris metro bombings in the summer of 1995, and sentenced in absentia to seven years in prison. In 1998, Belgian police stormed Melouk's house in Brussels and arrested him after a twelve-hour shoot out. In 1999, he was sentenced to nine years in prison for attempted murder, possession of firearms and explosives, armed rebellion, criminal association, and use of false identification papers. (*See also* Armed Islamic Group; Algerian Civil War.)

Najibullah, Mohammad   President of Afghanistan from 1986 to 1992. During the Soviet occupation, Najibullah served as the head of the Afghan secret police, where he gained renown for his brutality in combating *mujahidin* resistance groups. Russia continued to provide his government with economic and intelligence support after Russian forces withdrew in 1989. Najibullah remained president until *mujahidin* resistance forces captured the capital in 1992. He spent the next four years sheltered in a United Nations compound, but was later executed by the Taliban regime in 1996.

Northern Alliance   Originally a *mujahidin* group comprised of three non-Pashtun ethnic groups—Tajiks, Uzbeks, and Hazaras—the Northern Alliance wrested power from Mohammad Najibullah after the collapse of his government in 1992. In June 1992, Burhanuddin Rabbani became president of Afghanistan, but his government and its military forces—led by defense minister Ahmed Shah Massoud—controlled only segments of the country at any given time. As civil war continued to rage, Rabbani's government was forced to do battle with a warlords across the country. The *Hezb-i-Islami*, led by Gulbuddin Hekmatyar, proved particularly formidable.

The Northern Alliance was ousted by the Taliban in 1996, and reassembled as a resistance group. It controlled several provinces in northern Afghanistan between 1996 and 2001. After 9/11, U.S. forces aligned with the Northern Alliance, enabling it to recapture Kabul. Rabbani, who had been recognized by many countries as the legitimate president of Afghanistan throughout the period of Taliban rule, announced himself as head of state in November 2001. In December 2001, he handed power over to the interim government led by Hamid Karzai. (*See also* Ahmad Shah Massoud; Taliban; Mohammad Najibullah.)

Qatada, Abu   Described as the spiritual leader of Al Qaeda in Europe, Abu Qatada was based at the Four Feathers Youth Club in London. In December 2001, he went on the run on the eve of British government moves to introduce new antiterrorist laws. He was found and arrested for his alleged terrorist connections in October 2002. He has been convicted twice in absentia of terrorist crimes in Jordan, his birthplace. He is currently in Belmarsh Prison, London, pending extradition to Jordan.

Qutb, Sayyid   Influential Egyptian scholar whose ideas form the philosophical and theological foundations for many modern jihadist movements. In the early 1950s, Qutb joined the Muslim Brotherhood of Egypt. In January 1955, Egypt's President Gamal Abdel Nasser outlawed the group and jailed many of its members, including Qutb. He wrote his most influential books, including *Milestones* and *In the Shade of the Qu'ran*, while in prison. Qutb was virulent in denouncing secular regimes in Muslim countries, and was a firm advocate of governance through *sharia* (Islamic law). His work had a profound influence on many Islamists, including Abdullah Azzam and Osama bin Laden. He was executed by Nasser in 1966. (*See also* Abdullah Azzam.)

Rabbani, Burhanuddin   President of Afghanistan beginning in 1992, Rabbani was ousted from power when the Taliban took control of Kabul in 1996. He was nonetheless recognized by the United Nations as president through December

2001, when he relinquished his post to Hamid Karzai. (*See also* Ahmad Shah Massoud; Gulbuddin Hekmatyar; Northern Alliance.)

Ramda, Rachid   An editor of the GIA newsletter *Al Ansar* during the mid-1990s, Ramda was arrested in London at the request of the French government in November 1995. He was charged in absentia by a French court with twenty-three criminal counts in connection to the 1995 Paris metro bombings, including providing logistical support to the Algerian Armed Islamic Group (*Groupe Islamique Armée*; GIA) and acting as its financier. Ramda was held at London's Belmarsh Prison for ten years pending extradition to France, which took place in December 2005. He was convicted in March 2006 and sentenced to ten years in prison. He remains in prison in France and is facing a second trial on charges of murder and attempted murder of the victims of the 1995 bombing.

Sûreté de l'État   The Belgian State Security Service, a civilian agency subordinate to the Ministry of Justice.

Taliban   A fundamentalist Islamic movement that emerged in Afghanistan in 1994, and seized Kabul in 1996 from the government of Burhanuddin Rabbani. Promising social order and an end to corruption in a country riven by civil war, the Taliban gained their initial support from ethnic Pashtuns in southern Afghanistan. By 2000, the Taliban controlled all but the far north of the country, which remained under the control of the Northern Alliance. The Taliban regime drew international criticism and United Nations sanctions for its human rights abuses, for its extreme restrictions on women in public life, and for harboring and aiding Islamic terrorists, notably Osama bin Laden. The Taliban was ousted from power in November 2001 by U.S. forces acting in concert with the Northern Alliance, but the group has since reemerged as a potent resistance force within Afghanistan.

Touchent, Ali   Identified by Algerian authorities as the European head of the Armed Islamic Group (*Groupe Islamique Armée*; GIA), Touchent was one of the alleged masterminds of the bombings in France during the summer of 1995. Later that year, French police arrested forty suspected militants, but Touchent himself evaded capture. In 1998, Touchent was tried in absentia for his role in the Paris metro bombings. During the trial, Algerian authorities belatedly reported that Touchent had been killed by police in May 1997. His body was never produced as evidence; the Algerian authorities sent the French a set of fingerprints instead. Although the French police said they matched prints on file for Touchent, the presiding judge in the 1998 trial nonetheless sentenced him in absentia to ten years in prison. (*See also* Algerian Civil War; Armed Islamic Group.)

Zaoui, Ahmed A former professor of theology at the University of Algiers, Zaoui joined the Islamic Salvation Front (*Front Islamique du Salut*; FIS) to participate as a candidate in the 1991 elections. Zaoui won his electorate in the first round, but the country's military-backed regime cancelled the elections and sentenced Zaoui to death. He fled the country, seeking asylum in Belgium and Switzerland in 1992. (Amnesty International declared him a political refugee in 1992.) He was arrested in the March 1995 raids in Belgium, along with twelve other alleged GIA members. He was initially acquitted, but then retried on separate charges and convicted. While under house arrest, Zaoui slipped out of Belgium. He currently resides in New Zealand, where he has been granted refugee status. Zaoui has consistently denied that he was ever a member of the GIA. (*See also* Algerian Civil War)

Zubayda, Abu A top lieutenant and chief recruiter for Al Qaeda until his capture in Faisalabad, Pakistan on March 28, 2002. He managed Al Qaeda's worldwide recruiting system for Osama bin Laden's training camps in Afghanistan, and was sentenced to death in Jordan for having plotted the thwarted "millennium" bombing of the Radisson Hotel in Amman. U.S. officials believe he was also connected to alleged plots to attack the U.S. embassies in Sarajevo and Paris.

Index of Names